To Tim,
I hope your first
work is just as pink!
— Anne Hyde

AN AMERICAN VISION

The American Social Experience Series

GENERAL EDITOR: JAMES KIRBY MARTIN

EDITORS: PAULA S. FASS, STEVEN H. MINTZ,

CARL PRINCE, JAMES W. REED & PETER N. STEARNS

1. *The March to the Sea and Beyond: Sherman's Troops in the Savannah and Carolinas Campaigns*
JOSEPH T. GLATTHAAR

2. *Childbearing in American Society: 1650–1850*
CATHERINE M. SCHOLTEN

3. *The Origins of Behaviorism: American Psychology, 1870–1920*
JOHN M. O'DONNELL

4. *New York City Cartmen, 1667–1850*
GRAHAM RUSSELL HODGES

5. *From Equal Suffrage to Equal Rights: Alice Paul and the National Woman's Party, 1910–1928*
CHRISTINE A. LUNARDINI

6. *Mr. Jefferson's Army: Political and Social Reform of the Military Establishment, 1801–1809*
THEODORE J. CRACKEL

7. *"A Peculiar People": Slave Religion and Community-Culture Among the Gullahs*
MARGARET WASHINGTON CREEL

8. *"A Mixed Multitude": The Struggle for Toleration in Colonial Pennsylvania*
SALLY SCHWARTZ

9. *Women, Work, and Fertility, 1900–1986*
SUSAN HOUSEHOLDER VAN HORN

10. *Liberty, Virtue, and Progress: Northerners and Their War for the Union*
EARL J. HESS

11. *Lewis M. Terman: Pioneer in Psychological Testing*
HENRY L. MINTON

12. *Schools as Sorters: Lewis M. Terman, Applied Psychology, and the Intelligence Testing Movement, 1890–1930*
PAUL DAVIS CHAPMAN

13. *Free Love: Marriage and Middle-Class Radicalism in America, 1825–1860*
JOHN C. SPURLOCK

14. *Jealousy: The Evolution of an Emotion in American History*
PETER N. STEARNS

15. *The Nurturing Neighborhood: The Brownsville Boys Club and Jewish Community in Urban America, 1940–1990*
GERALD SORIN

16. *War in America to 1775: Before Yankee Doodle*
JOHN MORGAN DEDERER

17. *An American Vision: Far Western Landscape and National Culture, 1820–1920*
ANNE FARRAR HYDE

AN AMERICAN VISION

Far Western Landscape and National Culture, 1820–1920

ANNE FARRAR HYDE

NEW YORK UNIVERSITY PRESS
NEW YORK AND LONDON
1990

Manufactured in the United States of America

Library of Congress Cataloging-in-Publication Data
Hyde, Anne Farrar, 1960–
An American vision : Far Western landscape and national culture, 1820–1920 / Anne Farrar Hyde.
p. cm.—(The American social experience series ; 17)
Includes bibliographical references.
ISBN 0-8147-3466-9 (alk. paper)
1. West (U.S.)—Description and travel. 2. Landscape—West (U.S.) 3. Landscape assessment—West (U.S.)—History. 4. Man—Influence of environment—West (U.S.)—History. 5. Tourist trade—West (U.S.)—History. I. Title. II. Series.
F591.H99 1990
917.8—dc20 89-13558
CIP

New York University Press books are printed on acid-free paper, and their binding materials are chosen for strength and durability.

Book design by Ken Venezio

Contents

Illustrations

Acknowledgments

In the years that it has taken to complete this study, my family, friends, teachers, and colleagues have endured my seemingly endless exploration of the far western landscape with tolerance and good humor. I would like to thank all of them.

I have several significant academic debts. John Mack Faragher of Mount Holyoke College nurtured my first efforts at being a historian and has remained interested and helpful ever since. I owe much to the University of California, Berkeley, where Paula Fass, James Kettner, and Margaretta Lovell provided encouragement and assistance when I needed it most. Patricia Limerick of the University of Colorado gave the manuscript a vigorous reading at an important time. At Lousiana State University, I would like to thank Sally Graham, Burl Noggle, Charles Royster, Victor Stater, and Meredith Veldman.

My most important thanks go to Professor Gunther Barth of the University of California, Berkeley. His patience, wise advice, wry humor, and concern for scholarship make him a model advisor. I cannot thank him enough and I only hope my work reflects all of his efforts.

I would also like to acknowledge the financial assistance I received. Without the Herbert Bolton, Max Ferrand, and Otto Schumann scholarships from the University of California this study could not have been undertaken. My undergraduate institution, Mount Holyoke College, provided me with the Mary E. Woolley Fellowship that funded my first year of research. The Mabelle McLeod Lewis Fund from Stanford University gave me the resources for a final year of writing.

I would also like to acknowledge the help I received from libraries all over the American West. The librarians at Glacier, Grand Canyon, and Yellowstone national parks graciously tolerated my rooting through their files and often located material I never could have found on my own. The staff of the Western History Room at the Denver Public Library provided assistance during my stay there. My greatest debt is to the reference staff of the Bancroft Library. They patiently dragged out enormous tomes, maps, and pictures, allowed me to rummage through shelves and boxes of material, and gave me a quiet place to work. I would especially like to thank Irene Moran and Walter Brem.

New York University Press and its director, Colin Jones, deserve notice for their attention to detail, enthusiasm, and patience.

In addition, I owe much to Nancy Bristow, Bill Deverell, Cathy Kudlick, Steve Leikin, Mary Odem, and Lucy Salyer who gave me critical advice as well as some levity about the tasks of research and writing.

My parents, in large part, are responsible for this project. As easterners transplanted to the Great Basin landscape of Nevada, they showed me the beauty of the Far West. My father introduced me to its "big country" and to its small, delicate inhabitants on hundreds of hiking trips. My mother offered her observations through the window of the car as we drove across various terrains. Both perceptions are enormously important to my notions about landscape.

Finally, I would like to dedicate this study to my husband, Jim McCall. He deserves a dedication for never asking why it took so long, for ignoring the piles of paper that gobbled up precious space, and most especially, for supporting me through it all.

INTRODUCTION

John Charles Frémont and the Problem of Description

The world was so recent, that many things lacked names, and in order to indicate them it was necessary to point.
—Gabriel Garcia Marquez
One Hundred Years of Solitude

In the summer of 1842 a young explorer stood on top of a mountain in what is now Wyoming and tried to describe what he saw. His experiences had given him no precedent for the dazzling view that stretched before him. The shifting of the earth's crust and eons of wind and water had shaped the landscape into forms he had never encountered. As the young man gazed over the barren windswept peaks, he recognized their beauty, but he struggled to find words to express the appearance of the scenery.

John Charles Frémont arrived on this mountaintop at a crucial juncture in the American discovery of the Far West. Americans had always been fascinated with the mysteries of the region, and the expansionistic temper of the 1840s created an explosion of interest in the area west of the one hundredth meridian. Once the Mississippi Valley and the fertile midwestern prairies had been settled, only the expanse of the Far West remained to satisfy land-hungry Americans who demanded great annexations of land. In spite of the interest in the region and the number of observers who had surveyed it since Lewis and Clark's pioneering expedition in 1804–6, the public had little idea of what the West looked like.

By 1840 the efforts of explorers, writers, and artists had created a number of images of the West for the American public. The West contained great deserts, huge mountain ranges, gardenlike parks, fascinating Indians, and plants and animals that existed nowhere else. Yet no one had put together a comprehensive view. The western landscape was a set of puzzle pieces without any clear pattern. Not even an accurate map existed to frame the puzzle.[1]

John C. Frémont set out to solve this riddle on three expeditions between 1842 and 1845. He surveyed what would become the Overland Trail, crossed the Sierra Nevada in winter, and skirted the Great Basin region of what is now Nevada and Utah. Most importantly, Frémont and his wife, Jessie Benton Frémont, wrote an immensely popular report of his adventures.[2] For the first time, Americans had a coherent set of descriptions of the Far West accompanied by a reasonably accurate map and a few selected engravings by Charles Preuss, a skilled topographer.

Frémont's *Report of the Exploring Expedition to the Rocky Mountains in the Year 1842, and to Oregon and North California in the Years 1843–1844* read like an adventure story, but it also provided clear descriptions of the landscape. Frémont, whose account attracted a larger audience than was usual for a government report, used language and analogies that made the Far West comprehensible to Americans. In the words of his most recent biographer, he created "word pictures" of the landscape. Because of the publicity surrounding his expedition and because of the astounding popularity of his *Report*, the words Frémont selected to describe the western landscape had great impact on American perceptions of the mysterious region.[3]

The language in Frémont's report reflected his excitement in viewing such a distinctive set of landscapes and his frustration in trying to describe them for an audience eagerly awaiting his judgment on the value of the Far West for American society. His words demonstrated both the insecurities Americans felt about their culture and their dependence on European aesthetic ideals. Some scenic novelties could be seen in familiar scientific or literary terms or by comparison to well-known European sights. Others, however, seemed so strange they simply could not be described. Frémont understood that he was seeing a new world, but he did not have the cultural preparation to express it.

At first, as he traveled across the Great Plains, Frémont's stock of scientific language and romantic terms borrowed from English poets and philosophers served him well. Often using Latin names, he attempted to place the geology and plant and animal life into familiar scientific categories. To give additional flavor to the dry listings of rock, soil, and plant types, he elegantly described the vastness and thrill of the scene. Upon viewing a great herd of buffalo for the first time, Frémont wrote that "in the sight of such a mass of life, the traveller feels a strange emotion of grandeur." Thrilled, he explained that "when we came into view of the dark masses, there was not one among us who did not feel his heart beat quicker." With a romantic flourish he added, "Indians and buffalo make the poetry and life of the plains,"[4] revealing the importance of properly poetic images to the value of a landscape.

The plains offered additional attractions educated Americans would recognize. Many parts of it, according to Frémont, were "picturesque." The broken hills along the Platte River in western Nebraska presented a "picturesque outline."[5] A mountain stream in the Black Hills offered scenery of a "most striking and romantic beauty," which, he explained, "arose from the picturesque disposition of the objects and the vivid contrast of colors."[6] Literate mid-nineteenth-century Americans understood such terms. A romantic view represented something familiar, something that could be compared to views in Europe or the eastern part of the United States.

Frémont often made specific comparisons to European places, knowing that his readers would recognize such references. The raised creek beds striping the expanse of the plains seemed in Frémont's eyes to be "miniature Po Rivers," because "the long yellow and winding line of their beds resembles a causeway from the hills to the river."[7] Other places could be described as having "the deep-blue sky and sunny climate of Smyrna and Palermo."[8] The great rocks along the plains in southern Wyoming had "parapets," "domes and slender minarets," giving them the appearance "of an old fortified town."[9] These descriptive terms, carrying the full weight of European aesthetic traditions, helped to make the far western landscape understandable to discerning American readers.

Frémont, however, soon realized the limits of his language. Expecting to find a glorious version of the European Alps in the Rocky Mountains, his first view of the range stunned him with its stark rock and jagged shapes. "The view dissipated in a moment the pictures which had been created in our minds by many descriptions of travellers who have compared these mountains to the Alps in Switzerland," he wrote, obviously disappointed.[10] Some days later, having recovered from the shock of this unexpected vision, he began to appreciate the beauty of the scene. At the same time, he recognized how deficient his vocabulary was in describing the undeniably spectacular mountains. "Though these snow mountains are not the Alps," he explained, "they have their own character of grandeur and magnificence, and will doubtless find pens and pencils to do them justice."[11] His own pencil, however, seemed inadequate to the task.

In his efforts to express what he saw, Frémont often resorted to a kind of negative description. While surveying the windy expanse of South Pass in the Rockies of Wyoming, Frémont could only explain its appearance by describing what it was not. "It in no manner resembles the places to which the term [pass] is commonly applied—nothing of the gorgelike and winding ascents of the Allegheny passes in America: nothing of the Great St. Bernard and Simplon passes in Europe."[12] Using a similar method to describe the great heights of the Rocky Mountains, Frémont had more success. "It is not by the splendor of far-off views, which have lent such glory to the Alps," he noted rather tentatively, "that these impress the mind; but by a gigantic disorder of enormous masses, and a savage sublimity of naked rock."[13] He had begun to see and to understand the patterns of description that he could apply to the far western landscape. If a view could not be described as beautiful, romantic, or picturesque, perhaps it could be sublime, another popular aesthetic category.

Some parts of the Far West, however, looked so strange and threatening that they could not be contrasted with more familiar sights or be placed in any scenic category. Frémont's *Report* says surprisingly little about most of the territory he explored. The more arid portions of the Far West presented a special descriptive challenge. Because "the land had any color but green,"[14] it seemed worthless and dangerous to observers searching for arable land and travel routes. To Frémont the "parched and sterile" earth looked "as if it had been swept by fires."[15] Searching for some analogy, he noted that the scenery "gave a body to the foetid creations of the internal Regions."[16] Even the geography of the landscape proved difficult to explain. In describing "the detached hills and ridges which rise abruptly, and reach too high to be called hills or ridges, and not high enough to be called mountains," Fremont complained that "no

Charles Preuss, *Central Chain of the Wind River Range*

Preuss's engraving of the peaks of the Wind River Range exaggerates the spiny and rugged character of these mountains. They appear wilder and more frightening, reflecting the awe Frémont felt in seeing them for the first time. (Lithograph in John Charles Frémont's *Report*. Courtesy of the Louisiana State University Library.)

translation, or paraphrasis, would preserve the identity of these landmarks."[17]

His vocabulary met its greatest challenge in the Great Basin. Although the region "possessed a strange and extraordinary interest"[18] for Frémont, he seemed unable to portray it in words. Its deserts, mountains, and rivers remain puzzles in his text. "In America," he explained, "such things are new and strange, unknown and unsuspected."[19]

The heat and aridity of the strange landscape made it especially threatening to Americans unaccustomed to such terrain. Frémont, faced with extreme physical discomfort, seemed to lose his ability to describe. The land nearly disappeared in his discussions of the horrors of a desert crossing. Words and phrases like "dreary," "dismal," "barren expanse," and "revolting" litter Frémont's discussion of the region he and his men traversed. Indians, whom Frémont had described as "poetry" on the more familiar landscape of the prairies, now were "marauding savages" who "infested" their camps and "swarmed on the hills and mountainsides" like the insects that also tormented them.[20]

Completely removed from anything familiar, the sights and experiences of such forbidding terrain seemed impossible to convey. "Travellers through countries affording water and timber can have no conception of our journeying over the hot yellow sands of this elevated country, where the heated air seems to be entirely deprived of moisture," wrote Frémont to sum up the experience.[21] Such unfamiliar and even terrifying landscapes could not be described in romantic terms or given the dignity of European or American comparisons. In depicting "the leading features and general structure of the country we had traversed," Frémont could only remark that "these are peculiar and striking, and differ essentially from the Atlantic side of our country."[22] His training and his cultural preconceptions did not permit him to give a fuller account. The words and imagery did not yet exist to describe large portions of the far western landscape.

Nearly one hundred and fifty years after John C. Frémont's frustrating attempt to describe the Far West, the region is buried in words and imagery. Americans respond to its varied landscape very differently than did the men on Frémont's expedition. After centuries of neglecting or exploiting the region, people now battle to protect its natural wonders and human resources. Environmental vigilantes chain themselves to road and mining equipment to prevent the scarring of the landscape. Conservationists, business interests, and legislators argue about measures to limit the development that threatens the few pristine areas the Far West still offers. Other groups lobby, march, and raise funds to protect native American cultures.

Further demonstrating the West's importance to Americans, each year millions of visitors flood the western national parks, eager to see the spectacular landscapes within their confines, many of which Frémont would have considered repulsive wastes. When asked about the national treasures they value most, Americans invariably include in their answers the scenery of the Grand Canyon, Yellowstone, Yosemite, and other western landmarks. Many of the most original and important American artists and writers have used the western scene as inspiration for their work. Its varied geography offers scenic marvels that have become important national symbols. The vast spaces, untouched wilderness, and unique geological phenomena represent the potential and originality Americans associate with their society. The landscape of the Far West clearly plays an important role in the maintenance of a national culture.

American pride in the western landscape is, however, a twentieth-century phenomenon. Much of the emotion derives from the region's distinct combination of plain, mountain, and desert—landscape unlike any in the world. As Frémont's efforts demonstrate, the exceptional geography of the West makes describing it a difficult task. Analogies to other places often seem inappropriate, and traditional aesthetic standards do not take full measure of the West's beauty and value.

This unprecedented appearance presents observers with a challenge that nineteenth-century visitors were not equipped to meet. Their conceptions of a beautiful landscape had been imported from Europe, which had no scenery that could be compared to the American Far West. During most of the nineteenth century, the singular qualities of the western landscape horrified most observers because, like John C. Frémont, their education and experience had given them no words or images to describe what they saw.

In the hundred years between 1820 and 1920, Americans faced the task of exploring, observing, describing, and interpreting the immense space between the Missouri River and the Pacific Ocean. Their reactions to the landscape of the far western United States tell us a great deal about the formation of a distinctly American culture during the nineteenth century. In 1820, the unfamiliar deserts, plains, and mountains frightened and embarrassed Americans who looked west. To citizens of a young nation that had only begun to develop its own culture along the eastern seaboard, it seemed to be a world of terrifying distance, strange scenery, and useless space. By the beginning of the twentieth century, however, the Far West had become a celebrated and popular part of the American landscape.

This study examines the striking change in attitude toward the far western landscape and probes its significance for the development of an American culture. My definition of the Far West includes the dry rolling grasslands of the Great Plains; the snow-covered peaks, green valleys, and rock walls of the mountain ranges that make up the Rockies and the Sierra; and the deserts that fill the Great Basin and cover much of the Southwest. It roughly corresponds to the area stretching west to the Pacific Ocean from the line of the one hundredth meridian, which runs through the centers of North and South Dakota, Nebraska, Kansas, Oklahoma, and Texas. This part of the American continent encompasses a geographical variety that challenges the senses of every observer.

Map of the Far West

Map of the American Far West, showing the principal railroads, points of interest for nineteenth-century travelers, and the national parks and resorts in this study. (Map by Susan Birnbaum. Courtesy of the Louisiana State University.)

The explorers, writers, artists, and tourists who ventured west during the nineteenth century had to interpret a region that looked like nothing Euro-Americans had seen before. Few people who traveled over the landscape in the first half of the nineteenth century could accurately describe what they saw. To serve them, they had only the aesthetic categories and ideals they had borrowed from Europe and adapted to the scenery of the eastern half of the country. These concepts, of course, failed in the face of the exceptional landscapes of the Far West.

Eventually, the lack of suitable words, analogies, and images forced observers to create new ones. Coining precise geological and geographical terms to identify landforms and terrain made the landscape comprehensible. Recognizing the wealth of color, shape, and human history gave the West new importance. By the end of the century, Americans had learned to describe the varied scenery. Eastern Americans had confronted the Far West and had developed words that gave them the power to appreciate the landscape and to incorporate it into their culture.

The particular language and imagery created in the century-long encounter with the far western landscape forever altered American aesthetic standards. The strange, but undeniably spectacular sights of the Far West forced Americans to come up with new standards and descriptive strategies independent from powerful European ideals. The process of grappling with a language suitable to the realities of the far western landscape helped to forge a particularly American culture. It integrated the ideas about the importance of landscape developed on the East Coast in the first half of the nineteenth century with the new concepts of beauty and value forged in the West in the second half of the century. The task of accounting for the unique shapes, colors, geologies, and indigenous populations of the West generated new possibilities for writers, artists, and architects to break free from tradition. By the end of the nineteenth century, the struggle to interpret the far western landscape had given Americans the seeds of an independent culture, which would flower in the twentieth.

In the following chapters, I examine this process and its effects from 1820 to 1920. I focus primarily on explorers, travelers, and tourists, the first large groups to visit the West predominantly for the sake of knowledge and pleasure, rather than on emigrants who often had different concerns. Throughout the nineteenth century these visitors observed, evaluated, and interpreted the wonders of the Far West. Because of the publicity the tourists received and the reams of material they published, and because of the heightened attention given the West in this period, their impressions profoundly affected national ideas about the region. Their responses to the landscape also reflect the powerful concepts Americans attached to the Far West. Using literary and visual evidence provided by these travelers, I analyze the ways in which most Americans learned about the West before the age of train travel, how they reacted to the landscape upon viewing it for the first time, and how their vocabulary describing the scenery changed in the later decades of the nineteenth century.

Americans learned about the West in the early nineteenth century, a period of exploration when few people had any conception of what the region offered. During the first decades of the nineteenth century, the landscape of the eastern United States had taken on great importance as the young nation struggled to define its culture. The natural landscape had shouldered the burden of providing the history and culture that Americans felt their nation lacked when they compared it to the rich past of the Old World. In this context, the words and pictures brought back from the West by scientific and military explorers, as well as a few intrepid tourists and businessmen, had tremendous impact on how Americans saw this portion of their nation.

In the middle decades of the century, the efforts to build and publicize the transcontinental railroad further fueled interest in the Far West. Writers, artists, railroad builders, and promoters recognized the importance the region would have for the nation and sought ways to make it attractive to Americans. Largely because of the limitations of a rhetoric that prevented them from seeing the unique beauties of the landscape, these observers latched onto the idea that the Far West could become a version of Europe. Small parts of the landscape fit this model, and publicists of all sorts focused their attention there. Using aesthetic standards and imagery borrowed from Europe and imposed on the eastern part of the nation, they attempted to describe the Far West in language familiar to Americans who could afford to travel.

Late in the century, however, the realities of the far western landscape destroyed fragile and inappropriate European and eastern frameworks and compelled Americans to develop new ones. By the 1890s a century of cultural change and of far western exploration permitted Americans to see the value of the unique landscape. Artists, writers, and railroad promoters now celebrated the particularly American qualities of the western scene.

Central to my argument here is an analysis of resort architecture, clientele, and activities. These resorts, largely the creations of the railroad companies that controlled so much of far western development in the second half of the nineteenth century, provide physical evidence of the impact of the far western landscape on the emerging American culture. The change in style and location of the great railroad resorts mirrors the changes I detect in national culture in terms of the development of distinctively American language and imagery.

Although others have noted some of the cultural transformations I have uncovered in my research, this study does not fit neatly into a historiographical niche. Landscape and its contribution to culture has received important attention in recent years. I have benefited from the work of scholars in a number of fields, including cultural geography, art history, and literary criticism, as well as traditional western history.[23]

In spite of my debts to scholars in other disciplines, however, I remain a historian interested in telling a story by explaining change over time. I have made a start, but much work remains to be done in explaining the distinctive qualities of American culture. All of the complexities of cultural formation cannot be examined in a single study, but it seemed important to begin telling the story of the Far West and the integration of its unique landscape into American culture. The significance of this process has been largely ignored. The fusion of eastern visions with western realities during the nineteenth century created a truly national culture in the United States. Recognizing the role far western landscape has played in this century-long process will help us to understand the evolution of an American culture.

CHAPTER 1

Looking Far West: Assessing the Possibilities of the Landscape, 1800–1850

John C. Frémont's perceptions of the Far West and his technique for describing it had a powerful effect on the formation of popular images of the region. His struggle to describe the unfamiliar scenery demonstrated the significance literate Americans saw in locating certain kinds of landscapes, as well as the difficulty of categorizing western scenery. Frémont's investigations suggested that the Far West was as mysterious as the most fantastic fiction had claimed. The landscape offered hideous wastes, bounteous gardens, strange creatures and peoples, ancient ruins, spectacular mountains, yawning gulfs, and unfathomable opportunities for the development of the nation. Here, in spite of the dangers and mysteries, Americans hoped they could find many of the sights, objects, and riches they wanted and needed, including the seeds of an independent national culture.

Frémont's *Report* appealed to many American readers because it provided a way to interpret some of the sights present in the western landscape. Frémont attempted to use the aesthetic framework American observers had borrowed from Europe and adapted for the landscape of the eastern half of the nation. He defined beauty by a scene's resemblance to

Europe and utility by trees and rainfall. His descriptive efforts also confirmed the narrowness of such definitions. In the 1840s, however, no others were available.

Given the nineteenth-century preconceptions about landscape, Frémont's reaction to the Far West was predictable. He found the plains and the Rockies generally attractive places. They offered fertile fields, flowering meadows, and high peaks, as well as the romantic presence of Indian life. Such landscapes even held splendid scenery that could be compared to the most famous European scenes. Other areas, less green and less familiar, however, did not seem as promising. Frémont labeled regions for which he could find no analogies or any possible use as "wastes," not even worth describing. Frémont's categories of beautiful, romantic, and useful versus ugly, barren, and wasted would define American opinions about the far western landscape for the next fifty years.

His reports about the Far West had great impact because of the importance landscape held for wealthy and educated nineteenth-century Americans who had the leisure to worry about cultural development. Landscape seemed to hold the key to American culture, the aspect of national development about which Americans had the least confidence in the first half of the nineteenth century. Americans observed their political, social, and economic development with great pride. In less than fifty years, they had achieved equal standing with nations that had existed for centuries. Americans had defied Great Britain in the War of 1812, built great cities, and begun an ambitious program of internal improvements to foster an already booming economy; and, equally important in terms of national pride, they had created a political democracy for white, adult males. In these realms, Americans had proclaimed and achieved independence from European traditions.

In the cultural sphere, however, many Americans found much less in which to take pride. They had few examples of national literature, art, music, or historic tradition. European peoples, with whom wealthy Americans constantly compared themselves, had rooted their cultures in a rich and ancient tradition. Literature, art, and music all appeared to depend on the human development of centuries past. Such artistic achievements, it seemed, only developed true patina with great age. In this regard, Americans feared they could never compete with nations that counted their history in centuries rather than in decades.

European Aesthetics and American Landscapes

In their search for cultural accomplishments, some Americans turned to nature and landscape, which had received increasing attention from philosophers, artists, and writers in the eighteenth century. A generation of romantic theorists located answers to questions of human dignity and happiness in undeveloped nature rather than in civilized society. These ideas had extended to a new school of aesthetics that took its cues from the natural world. Uncultivated, uneven, and informal—in a word, natural—landscapes took on new importance as people sought regions untouched by humans to discover eternal truths about the world.[1]

The new emphasis on the importance of the natural world showed up in all aspects of European culture. Artists, writers, and philosophers revolted against the artificial and stiff classical style that informed the early part of the eighteenth century. The change is evident in the development of the English landscape, which Americans took as a model for their own. Landscape gardening evolved from highly stylized formal gardens of great palaces like Hampton Court and Versailles to the engineered informality of the great landed estates of the mid-eighteenth century, which carefully mixed pastoral fields, artful clumps of trees, and Gothic ruins. By the close of the eighteenth century, landscape theorists, such as Capability Brown, Sir Uvedale Price, and Humphrey Repton, had rejected all vestiges of the artificial garden and advocated the emphasis of the natural beauty of the English landscape.[2]

Aspects of this new attitude toward nature coalesced in the "picturesque," which became an obsession and quickly a cliché among the English gentry in the late eighteenth and early nineteenth centuries. The writer and aesthete William Gilpin acquainted readers with the concept in a series of travel books that described how and where to find examples of the picturesque in the English countryside. The picturesque did not describe raw nature; it meant nature artfully designed so that it could be read like a picture. A picturesque scene offered the clear compositional elements present in a proper painting: carefully defined near, middle, and far distances and a balance of light and shade to harmonize the scene. The picturesque permitted nothing startling, surprising, or wild; its purpose was to charm the viewer.[3]

The picturesque ideal certainly enchanted wealthy British and Americans who avidly read Gilpin and his followers. The concept popularized the idea of travel for the sake of viewing scenery. It also imbued nature with the ability to arouse pleasant and noble emotions in the viewer, providing he or she had the proper training. This education required understanding the theory of "association." Archibald Alison's influential *Essays on the Nature and Principles of Taste* (1790) clarified the idea. He explained that an object or a scene had no intrinsic attraction, but that it pleased a viewer with the trains of thought or "associations" that it set off in the viewer's mind. A scene could remind one of great historical events, noble deeds in literature, or of great works of art. Such a theory invested great moral power in artistically arranged landscape because its "associations" could inspire the viewer to have ennobling or enlightening ideas.[4]

The popularity of the theory stimulated a boom in travel and travel literature among prosperous Americans in the early nineteenth century. As the steamship made the trip to Europe more comfortable and less expensive, impressive numbers of Americans rushed to England and the Continent. They wanted to experience European landscape and culture, and the important associations they engendered, which they believed their nation could not yet provide.

No matter how grand their landscape, the institutions and culture Americans had built did not have the dignity of age. This fact became especially clear as more and more Americans traveled abroad and published travel accounts. More than Europeans, literate Americans cherished the relics of the distant past; and they approached European settings with great nostalgia, hoping to find roots and traditions that they could borrow to give the United States a proper national past.[5]

In their eagerness to find and to adore remnants of European history, these Americans idealized Europe and collapsed it into a single glorious, and old, entity. They tended to ignore differences between European nations, as well as any unpleasant aspects of European society that might interfere with their enjoyment of its great age. American travelers, from sophisticated "literary pilgrims" like Washington Irving and Nathaniel Hawthorne to the average tourist, found everything old to be enchanting. A contributor to *Putnam's Magazine* noted that the passion for antiquity often made American travel accounts boring. He complained that "the dullest American, who has never seen a house more than a hundred years old, stands silent with awe before a temple of which history gives no account." Consequently, the writer noted, "there is a great deal of monotony of enthusiasm in our books of travel."[6] Each visitor's detailed responses to various ancient monuments may have been monotonous, but they conveyed a genuine hunger for a glorious past.

What captivated Americans about the European nations was the sense of a human past. Because they measured their cultural progress in European terms and because white Americans denied that Indians could have an appropriate past, their history seemed woefully short. The American poet James Russell Lowell explained his attraction to Italy in these terms: "To the American, Italy gives cheaply what gold cannot buy for him at home, a Past at once legendary and authentic."[7] No American traveler could visit Europe without being impressed by the splendor and age of its antiquities, especially when reminded of the dearth of such monuments in his or her own country.

This emotion spread to the landscape of Europe and especially to England, which mid-nineteenth-century travelers described as "our Old Home." In a book by that title, Nathaniel Hawthorne described the American tourist's response to the English landscape. "To an American," he wrote, "there is a kind of sanctity even in an English turnip field, when he thinks how long that small square of ground has been known and recognized as a possession."[8] Long before he achieved fame writing about American natural history, a young John Burroughs wrote fervently about the English countryside. "Here, something almost human looks out at you from the landscape," he explained. "Nature here has been so long under the dominion of man, has been taken up and laid down by him so many times . . . that she has taken on something of his image and seems to radiate his presence."[9] The influential essayist and travel writer Bayard Taylor found the same kind of attraction in the forests of Bavaria, where "the entire mountain region, fifty miles in extent, resembles a private park." He added for the benefit of his less-traveled American readers, "Fancy the White Mountain group *civilized* in a similar manner! This is nature stripped of her paint and feathers, washed, and her nakedness decently covered."[10] The American continent, though undeniably spectacular, seemed entirely naked and savage in contrast to the gentle, parklike forests of Bavaria.

In the 1840s, the New York lawyer George Templeton Strong noted similar difficulties in appreciating American landscape. "There was neither a legendary past nor a poetic present," he complained. Instead the United States offered only "large mountains, extensive prairies, tall cataracts, long rivers, millions of dirty acres of every cosmographical character which do not provide a basis for poetry."[11] Even those who found mountains, cataracts, and rivers attractive found many parts of the landscape problematic. "Virgin nature has a complete charm of its own; so has nature under subjection, cultivated, enriched, *finished*, as a dwelling place for man; but that transition state, which is neither one nor the other, gives an unsatisfactory impression," wrote Bayard Taylor explaining the obstacles he faced in appreciating American scenery.[12] A large portion of the settled area of the United States took on the character of that transitional state; it was occupied but not mellowed with age.

The wealthy and educated Americans concerned with issues of cultural development sought ways to attain such mellowness in their own nation. They attempted to imitate continental culture, especially that of England, where they had distinct historical roots. They adopted English styles in clothing, painting, architecture, and literature. Many of the important nineteenth-century American periodicals, published in the decades before the Civil War, were founded as vehicles to serialize English novels. American painters could only find success if people could see European precedents in their art. Successful American novelists were those who could be compared to the likes of Sir Walter Scott and Charles Dickens. A beautiful view was one that reminded its observer of a European scene.

In the long run, such slavish imitation could only frustrate Americans. They had learned early on that to search for the picturesque in the United States could only have limited success. This fashionable ideal had not been designed with a true wilderness in mind. Very little of the American continent had been touched by Europeans, much less artistically developed. Few parts of the landscape could be described as rich in the kind of associations advocated by William Gilpin. The American continent presented a vast, untamed, and largely unknown wilderness, which was alien and threatening to Americans and Europeans alike. Searching for the picturesque amidst such a display of raw natural power could only highlight the inadequacies of the American landscape.[13]

Fortunately, the romantic movement had popularized another aesthetic category that seemed perfectly designed for the American wilderness. In 1757, Edmund Burke published an influential treatise defining the beautiful and the sublime in nature. A natural object or scene that inspired awe and a thrilling sensation of fear could be described as sublime. The conditions required for achieving a sublime experience were quite specific. Burke explained that people felt pleasure when "we have an idea of pain and danger, without being actually in such circumstances. . . . Whatever excites this delight, I call sublime." Great size, power, solitude, noise, or silence could evoke the sublime.[14] Parts of Europe and Britain that most people had considered terrifying wastes, such as the peaks of the Alps and the moors of England, now became popular among romantic travelers. Wild, barren, harsh, jagged, and strange landscapes suddenly had aesthetic value.[15]

Here was a realm in which Americans could compete. The United States had more wild scenery than its people knew what to do with. The American wilderness boasted huge mountains, tremendous rocks and trees, and vast rivers and waterfalls entombed in sublime solitude—all of the elements that thrilled romantic writers and travelers.

Once Americans felt confident enough in their wilderness so that its dangers were only possibilities, rather than probabilities, they extolled the virtues of the sublime. Although a certain religious element had always been inherent in European definitions of the sublime, Americans tended to emphasize this quality. The sublime in nature became evidence of God's power and allowed humanity to stand in awe of His work. The powerful influences of transcendentalism, especially prevalent in American thought in the first half of the nineteenth century, soon made the untouched wilderness the equivalent of God. Objects such as waterfalls, great mountains, and deep forests could now be revered as expressions of God's will.[16] The sublime provided a new prestige for the wild state of the American landscape. Only true wilderness, which few European nations now possessed, could show the intentions and power of God.

The interest in the wilderness also developed out of a renewed taste for exploration and discovery in European culture. In the late eighteenth and early nineteenth centuries upper-class Europeans developed an insatiable appetite for the unknown and the exotic that resulted in a new kind of vision of the world. This vision required an innovative method of observing the natural world that gave homage to realistic depiction, rather than to emotional "effects." Careful scientific observation made the sublime more important because human associations were no longer required to appreciate an object. The most stunning wonder of all was one created by the earth itself, or by God.[17]

The proponents of European "scientific vision" created a fascination with natural objects that demonstrated the earth's power, such as rock formations and crags, mountains, deserts, and forests. These interests also brought new popularity for sciences like geology that exposed the history of the earth. This vision, combined with the powerful religious connotations of the sublime, gave great importance to the American landscape. Here, observers could find untouched nature, which provided connections with God and with the history of the earth. Measured this way, Americans had as much history as Europeans, and, in fact, in Barbara Novak's words, "the nature of the New World was superior to the culture of the Old."[18]

By the mid-nineteenth century, Americans had discovered that some of the answers to their cultural concerns lay in nature. Earlier, nature and culture had been antithetical. Now, given the changed attitudes toward the natural world, literate Americans discovered that nature could replace culture. It now mattered less that the United States had no ancient ruins and picturesque human artifice in the landscape. The new celebration of the wild and the sublime in nature carried with it the full weight of nineteenth-century philosophy and aesthetics.

These powerful new patterns of thought, developed in Europe, allowed for an apotheosis of the American landscape. Artists and writers found a new and culturally acceptable subject that would help them to create a national literature and art. In depicting the glories of the natural world, they were delineating national history and national ideologies.

The power of the new attitude toward the landscape cannot be overestimated. In the first half of the nineteenth century, landscape provided an "iconography of nationalism."[19] National destiny became tied to the natural world. Religion, science, history, and national identity would all come out of the American landscape. Intellects as diverse as James Fenimore Cooper, Ralph Waldo Emerson, and Thomas Cole all noted the primacy of nature in American culture. In the early nineteenth century, artists, philosophers, and writers transformed the wilderness of the eastern half of the nation from a terrifying, dangerous, and culturally embarrassing locale to a grand national temple in which the unique destiny of America could be celebrated.

The natural object that received the most attention on both sides of the Atlantic was Niagara Falls. It symbolized all of the grandeur and sublimity of the American landscape. Early in the nineteenth century, the falls became objects of great veneration among wealthy travelers. Rapidly, artists and writers developed conventions to describe America's most sublime and historical scene. Niagara became a symbol of the power of the wilderness and of God's grand intentions for the United States.[20]

The number of tourists who visited Niagara and the profusion of popular prints and literary descriptions of Niagara demonstrated the fascination the falls held for Americans. Its image became an industry. Niagara appeared in newspaper advertisements, political propaganda, and even on wallpaper, always signifying the power of nature and by extension, the power of the American nation. It also revealed the popularity of the sublime, which had suffused American culture in this period. To call something sublime became the highest accolade one could bestow. Niagara's importance to Americans illustrated the vital role the landscape would have in the development of a national culture.[21]

The new perspective toward nature became evident in the attention given to landscape painting. Beginning in the first decades of the nineteenth century, American painters turned to nature for inspiration. The painters who developed a style and subject matter that would eventually be called the Hudson River School depicted an American wilderness that glowed with sublimity in size, power, grandeur, and isolation. Artists such as Thomas Cole, Thomas Doughty, Asher B. Durand, Worthington Whittredge, and Frederic Church celebrated the wild landscape of western New England and the Hudson River valley with their paintings. These works received critical acclaim in the United States and in Europe. Although the artists of the Hudson River School certainly borrowed ideas from European traditions, the style and subject was undeniably American. For the first time Americans had a national art acceptable to European critics, and it came out of the wilderness of the eastern half of the continent.

In spite of the nationalistic trumpeting of the wonders of the American landscape, not everyone seemed convinced. The very intensity of the paeans to the wilderness and the fact that Americans felt compelled to proclaim its superiority so often indicated a certain lack of confidence. In an often quoted essay published in 1836, Thomas Cole, the leader of the Hudson River School, complained that "there are those who through ignorance or prejudice strive to maintain that American scenery possesses little that is interesting or truly beautiful—that it is rude without picturesquesness, and monotonous without sublimity—that being destitute of those vestiges of antiquity, whose associations so strongly affect the mind, it may not be compared with European scenery."[22] Cole dutifully pointed out the value of wilderness as a text for God's wishes and the advantages of American wilderness over the civilized landscape of Europe. However, after proclaiming that "the most impressive characteristic of American scenery is its wildness," he concluded the essay with a discussion of the Hudson River, happily predicting that "we may anticipate the time when the ample waters shall reflect temple, tower, and dome."[23] Clearly, even such a devotee of nature as Thomas Cole felt some ambivalence about the value of empty wilderness, reflecting the tension between pride in American progress and a love for untouched nature.

Because the development of this scenic nationalism occurred when the United States was being closely scrutinized by curious and critical Europeans, defensiveness and ambivalence are understandable. From the moment of the American declaration of independence, educated Europeans had been interested in the "Great Experiment" of the United States, and many came to examine its results. Although representatives from many nations arrived, including such important observers as François René de Chateaubriand and Alexis de Tocqueville, the opinions of British visitors had the greatest effect on Americans.

Beginning in the 1820s, just as some Americans began to develop a sense of their identity through the glorification of the landscape, the tone of British commentary changed significantly. The historian Allan Nevins has noted that British visitors of this era were especially critical, partly because of their fears about the potentially anarchic results of democracy and partly because they were genuinely disappointed in America.[24] The works of Frances Trollope, Charles Dickens, Frederick Marryat, and a whole host of other British dignitaries spewed forth vitriolic criticism of the society and culture of the United States.

An American art critic, Henry Tuckerman, writing from the vantage point of the 1860s, still reeled from the force of these attacks. He described an "inundation of English books of travel," in which the United States and its citizens "were discussed with a monotonous recapitulation of objections, a superficial knowledge, and a predetermined deprecation which render the task of analyzing their contents and estimating their comparative merit in the highest degree wearisome."[25] Even though

Tuckerman pointed out the poor quality of much of this literature, its volume and its popularity made it especially effective. Frances Trollope's *Domestic Manners of the Americans* went through at least ten editions, and Charles Dickens's *American Notes* was a best seller on both sides of the Atlantic. This helps to account for the shrill quality of American nationalism in the first half of the nineteenth century. The critics attacked the newness of American institutions and the lack of patina of American culture, forcing insecure Americans into a defensive posture.

Most Americans who concerned themselves about their lack of culture found the wilderness a source of inspiration in stemming the attack. It provided a history and could be infused with aesthetic values that even the most critical European observers could appreciate. However, this method often created disappointments when the wilderness did not measure up to European standards of beauty.

The Catskills and the Adirondacks of New York State, favorite haunts of American nature enthusiasts, simply could not be compared to the Alps in height, ruggedness, or sublimity. Even the undeniably spectacular trip up the Hudson River disappointed those who sought Europe in the American landscape. Bayard Taylor described a source of his own frustration. "The air was so very clear and keen that the scenery was too *distinct*—a common fault of our American sky—destroying the charm of perspective and color."[26]

Even an eloquent defender of the glories of the American landscape like Thomas Cole experienced a certain amount of insecurity. His paintings exaggerate scenic effects, making them closer to European views. His mountains reach higher, his sky glows more colorfully, and his fields appear more pastoral than anything that existed in the known portions of the continent. Americans could find similarities to Europe in the landscape of the eastern half of the nation, but they also found differences. Because Europe provided the definitions and the standards, most observers considered such differences to be faults.

Many people did recognize the limitations of this cultural dependency and called out for a uniquely American literature, art, and cultural identity. Only by accepting their differences could Americans begin to take pride in them. The author and reformer Thomas Wentworth Higginson expressed the need for national identity when he wrote, "we need to become national, not by any conscious effort, . . . but by simply accepting our own life."[27] Americans had made a start in this direction by recognizing the wilderness as a source of cultural opportunity. But they could not reap its full advantages until they had developed a less provincial way of interpreting that wilderness.

First Reports: Early Exploration and Information

The tension between the search for Europe in America and the desire for cultural independence provided the context for the earliest explorations of the American Far West. Profit-minded Americans had always looked to the West as a source of potential economic development, but in the early nineteenth century as the first reports about the region trickled east, Americans were alerted to the region's scenic value. Widely read explorers like John C. Frémont claimed the West held beauties that would equal those of Europe, even surpass them. The western landscape contained objects and scenes of such sublimity they would silence even the harshest critic. The early investigators of the region also uncovered geological wonders heralding the ancient natural history of America. The lands of the West seemed to hold the beauty and history that culturally insecure Americans desired.

However, the far western landscape also offered strange wonders that left their earliest observers speechless. Such sights would require an entirely new aesthetic language to describe them. Explorers left no doubt that the region contained some horrors. Its vast deserts, dry plains, and solitary mountains presented the kind of wilderness that both Europeans and Americans had long feared. This wilderness could not be domesticated into friendly fields and gentle pastures, nor could its scenery send delightful shivers up the viewer's spine. Visions like these were not sublime. Because the dangers such landscapes held were real, the terror they evoked created no pleasure.

In the midst of the great expansion that characterized the middle decades of the nineteenth century, the possibilities of the West took on singular importance. Its lands could hold the key to a grand national future or they could present a vast wasteland that would limit the spread of the American nation. The West offered both a truly American version of Europe and a challenge to the cultural framework Americans had painstakingly developed to describe their landscape. Here, many people hoped, they could find solutions to the problems of American culture.

Before Americans could decide how to use the opportunities offered by the Far West, they needed solid information about what lay west of the Mississippi. The earliest government explorers of the nineteenth century made this their task. When Lewis and Clark returned from their expedition in 1806, they brought back the first highly publicized news about the American West. Although they explored only a fraction of the area included in the Louisiana Purchase, the details they gathered served as a beginning for scientific investigation and created a hunger for public information about the lands of the West.

The next widely known venture into the reaches of the West, led by Stephen Harriman Long of the Topographical Engineers in 1819 and 1820, brought back rather dismal news. Even though Zebulon Pike had investigated parts of the area between the Missouri River and the Rocky Mountains in 1806–7, Secretary of War John C. Calhoun ordered Long and his men to explore the same region aboard a steamboat. The expedition was a disaster. The steamboat broke down constantly and foundered in the shallow waters of the Missouri and Platte rivers. Because Long's party had little conception of the terrain of the Great Plains, they did not take enough supplies; and the heat, dust, and insect life of the dry prairies nearly killed them.[28]

In spite of such difficulties, Long's adventure made important contributions to the general knowledge and mythology about the West. The American government published a large popular edition of the expedition's report, largely written by botanist Edwin James, in 1823. The report included several illustrations made by the artists who accompanied the expedition, Samuel Seymour and Titian Peale, giving the public their first views of the Great Plains and the Rocky Mountains.[29]

The members of the expedition realized the importance of their journey and self-consciously pointed out the novelty of their experience. From a camp on the Platte River where the group could see the bold outlines of the Rocky Mountains, Captain William Bell wrote in his journal on July 4, 1820, "We are where the imagination only has traveled before us—where civilization never existed—yet we are within the limits of our own country."[30] Americans had long imagined the western portion of their continent, and Long's expedition would test the accuracy of their dreams.

What the expedition found resembled a nightmare more than a dream. No one knew exactly what to make of the dry, treeless, and vast landscape. It did not resemble anything they had been taught to regard as beautiful or useful. Edwin James, the author of the report, described it as having the "dreary solitude of the ocean," and he complained that "the intense reflection of light and heat from the surface of many tracts of naked sand, which we crossed, added much to the fatigue and suffering of our journey."[31] Others were even less charitable. Long himself made the infamous statement that the region was "almost wholly unfit for cultivation, and of course uninhabitable by a people depending upon agriculture for their subsistence."[32]

Long did not, however, describe the plains as a kind of sandy Sahara, suitable only for nomads and camels. He simply believed that it did not have enough water, trees, or fertile soil to support American farmers. Given the agricultural technology of his period, his judgment does not seem so extreme. Nevertheless, the imagery used by the members of Long's expedition did not make the Great Plains particularly inviting.

Washington Irving, the popular American writer, described the plains in more complimentary terms. In 1832, Irving, having lived abroad for most of his literary career, took a trip to the Oklahoma back country. As he traveled west from the Mississippi River with a group of soldiers and Indiana guides, Irving sensed the importance of this new landscape to the society and culture of his own nation; but like most early visitors, he had trouble describing what he saw. The boundless stretch of the plains seemed the strangest of all. He wrote that "to one unaccustomed to it, there is something inexpressibly lonely in the solitude of the prairie." "The loneliness of the forest is nothing to it. There the view is shut in by trees, and the imagination is left free to picture some livelier scene beyond," he explained, trying to find an appropriate analogy. The prairie, however, was different, it was "an immense extent of landscape without a sign of human existence."[33] Like John C. Frémont, Irving could only describe the scenery before him as inexpressible. Even the pencil of this talented writer proved unequal to the strange vista of the Great Plains.

Yet Irving's fascination with the new landscape led him to use the Far West for two more works, *Astoria* and *The Rocky Mountains*. The most interesting of these in terms of Irving's efforts to describe the Far West is *The Rocky Mountains*, published in 1837. The book chronicled the attempt of a rather inept soldier, Captain L. E. Bonneville, to corner the fur trade and gave the reading public its first descriptions of the central portion of the Far West. Bonneville had long wanted to explore the mysteries of the Great Basin, hoping that the untouched region could extend American profits in the fur trade. Bonneville did not find much fur in the Great Basin, nor was he particularly successful in setting up trade routes. He did, however, travel through territory entirely unfamiliar to white Americans, providing Irving with a way to imagine and describe the Far West.

Washington Irving made Bonneville's journals into an exciting adventure that offered a dramatic, if not entirely complimentary, description of the far western landscape. The vast scale and the emptiness of the Far West impressed Bonneville (and Irving) the most. From a ridge along the Continental Divide, "a scene burst upon the view of Captain Bonneville that for a time astonished and overwhelmed him with its immensity." According to Irving, the view included beauty and terror. "Beneath him, the Rocky mountains seemed to open all of their secret recesses: deep solemn valleys; treasured lakes; dreary passes; rugged defiles; and foaming torrents; while beyond their savage precincts, the eye was lost in an almost immeasurable landscape."[34] Such language could have been lifted out of any romantic description of the Alps. Irving, however, seemed unsure whether the view was delightfully sublime or simply terrifying.

Other regions struck Irving as less fruitful in terms of romantic vistas. The Sierra Nevada, which took Bonneville's men twenty-three days to cross, offered little beauty. "Their passes and defiles present the wildest scenery, partaking of the sublime, rather than the beautiful, and abounding with frightful precipices."[35] The landscape surrounding the Great Salt Lake horrified Irving's Bonneville. It seemed to be a true desert, "rivaling the deserts of Asia and Africa, in sterility. There was neither tree, nor herbage, nor spring, nor pool, nor running stream, nothing but parched wastes of sand, where horse and rider were in danger of perishing."[36] Such terrain seemed useless and dangerous, unappealing to either the pragmatic or the romantic.

Irving's descriptions of the Far West did little to make it attractive to American readers. In general, his rendering of Bonneville's travels confirmed and extended Stephen Long's view of the West as a Great American Desert. Irving concluded that "an immense belt of rocky mountains and volcanic plains, several hundred miles in width, must ever remain an irreclaimable wilderness."[37] Irving used words like "desolate," "savage," "barren," and "wild" to describe the appearance of the Far West. The landscape consisted of "dreary and desolate mountains, and barren and trackless wastes . . . occasionally infested with predatory and cruel savages."[38] The threatening language made the region attractive as a setting for adventure stories, but hardly a place for settlement or sightseeing tours. In Irving's view, most of the Far West would remain a howling, uncultivable wilderness.

Another group of chroniclers, while not making the West seem any less wild, found its landscapes and its inhabitants quite attractive. A growing fascination with the rapidly disappearing American Indian drew a number of artists west in the 1830s and 1840s. A large proportion of Indians who had lived in the eastern United States had by this time died of epidemic disease or starvation, been killed, put on reservations, or driven west. Their fate, combined with the romantic view of the Noble Savage created by writers like Jean-Jacques Rousseau, François René de Chateaubriand, and, most importantly, James Fenimore Cooper, created friendlier images of Indians and the regions they inhabited. Now that the Indians seemed to be either fictional children of the forest or dead savages, Americans could safely take an interest in them.

The first flurry of interest in western Indians arose out of an 1821 visit made by a delegation of seven Plains Indian chiefs to Washington, D.C., and Philadelphia. Charles Bird King, an artist trained by Benjamin West, painted their portraits. They became the core of a National Indian Portrait Gallery of 150 portraits of Indians who visited Washington in the years 1821 to 1837. The chiefs also toured Charles Wilson Peale's museum in Philadelphia, where hundreds of curious visitors came to see them. Here, indeed, were the noble "red men" of novels, garbed in exotic feather headdresses, looking as dignified and stoic as white Americans expected them to be.[39]

Just such a vision of heroic figures from the West may have inspired the Philadelphia artist George Catlin to take on the portrayal of the American Indian as his life's work. Convinced of their imminent demise, Catlin hoped to preserve Indians on canvas. Primarily interested in western Indians who had never been painted by white artists, Catlin traveled west in 1832. He visited many tribes in subsequent years until he had made nearly five hundred paintings and collected thousands of Indian costumes, weapons, artwork, and tools.[40]

In both portraits and genre paintings of Indian life, Catlin created a

George Catlin, *Big Bend on the Upper Missouri* (1832)

The brilliant color and the strange landforms that make up this painting introduced Americans to the exotic landscape of the Far West. (Courtesy of the National Museum of American Art, Smithsonian Institution. Gift of Mrs. Joseph Harrison, Jr.)

stunning image of the vibrancy, dignity, and color of these people and their environment. Although Catlin painted few landscapes, his Indian figures hunted, danced, sang, and waited in an environment that offered beauty and variety. In an impressionistic way, Catlin created a vision of a world that was startling and unique. The boldness and originality of Catlin's Indians gave Americans something entirely new to ponder.

Perhaps even more important than the accuracy and the sheer number of Catlin's paintings was the missionary zeal he had for showing them. Catlin began exhibiting his Indian paintings as early as 1833 on a tour of midwestern river towns. He opened his first New York show in September 1837. Initially, he received ambivalent responses from eastern audiences who did not know what to make of the brilliant face paint and the strange customs of the Plains Indians that Catlin depicted in his paintings. Catlin, a born showman, persevered, lecturing to audiences nightly and dreaming up new publicity stunts. He invited a group of prominent New Yorkers, including the mayor, all of the important newspaper editors, Daniel Webster, and Philip Hone, who recorded the event in his diary, to a special showing. According to Hone, the highlight of the evening occurred when they all "smoked the calumet of peace under an Indian tent formed of buffalo skins."[41]

Such publicity efforts made Catlin a popular success. He showed his Indian Gallery all over the eastern seaboard to critical acclaim and huge crowds. In 1839, Catlin offered to sell his collection to the United States government. When government officials balked at his asking price, he took the Indian Gallery on a European tour. Enormous throngs visited his gallery in London and Paris, and Catlin was commanded to give private showings to both Queen Victoria and King Louis Philippe, the ultimate sign of success.

His work reached an even wider audience when he published *Letters and Notes on the Manners, Customs, and Condition of the North American Indians* in 1841. The book contained 312 small engravings of Indians and their environment. In 1844, Catlin issued a more expensive collection of twenty-five colored lithographs called *Catlin's North American Indian Portfolio.*[42] These books and Catlin's exhibitions gave thousands of Americans their first visual information about the West and its people. With brilliant color and intricate detail, Catlin's paintings offered a vision of the West that was exotic and inviting, not at all like the barren desert described by Stephen Long and Washington Irving.

Other artists depicted the Far West with the same wonder and enthusiasm, though they did not receive the same attention as Catlin. Karl Bodmer, a Swiss artist, accompanied Prince Maximilian of Wied-Neuwied on a tour of the upper Missouri River in 1833 and 1834 to record the adventures of the expedition and to keep a visual record of the Indian tribes they visited.

Only twenty-three when he began his American adventure, Bodmer knew little about Indians and less about the far western landscape. Even so, he completed hundreds of pictures of the people and landscape of the upper Missouri and the northern Rocky Mountains. Because, like Catlin,

Bodmer saw preserving the dwindling Indian in paint as his life's duty, he painted with great accuracy. His depictions of the Indians and their landscape included painstaking ethnographic and topographic detail. With images of colorful Indians dancing beneath vast skies and striking red, yellow, and blue landforms, he succeeded in capturing the suitability of the exotic people to the strange landscape.[43]

Bodmer first exhibited his work in Paris in 1836, giving Europeans an early taste of the rich world of the Plains Indians. His paintings received wider attention when eighty-two of them were reproduced as aquatints in Prince Maximilian's account of his trips, *Travels in the Interior of North America in the Years 1832–1834*. Many of these engravings later appeared in popular magazines and as Currier and Ives prints under the names of different artists.[44]

Like Bodmer, Alfred Jacob Miller made his visit to the West to record the exploits of a nobleman. In 1837 he accompanied Sir William Drummond Stewart on a hunting trip to the Rockies, following the route later taken by Frémont. Miller was the traditional romantic among these early artists, and he created a compelling image of the mysterious life of the mountain men and fur trappers at their annual rendezvous deep in the recesses of the Rocky Mountains. He also included in his landscapes many of the landmarks along what would become the Oregon Trail.

Unlike Catlin and Bodmer, Miller did not seek his task as re-creating reality. He wanted to capture fleeting images and impressions of a landscape that intrigued him for its romantic possibilities. Miller found the variety and the originality of the landscape frustrating, and he confided to his journal his fears of not doing it justice. Rather than bathing his images in the clear, bold light that characterized Catlin's and Bodmer's works, Miller's paintings are clouded with mist and haze, making them more reminiscent of European scenes. In these early views of the Rocky Mountains, Miller created what he and his audience wanted to see. The Far West appeared to be a land of romantic imagination, with lakes, mountains, and rivers that resembled Europe. Only the Indians, trappers, and animals in the scenes made them undeniably American.

Miller's work did not receive wide attention even though he gave several shows on the East Coast that received favorable reviews. Critics approved of his style, which presented new objects painted with a familiar vocabulary. "The Alps are nothing to these cold, blue, Mountains of the Wind," remarked a reviewer, even as he claimed "the principal merit of these works is their originality."[45] After this limited success, most of Miller's paintings went to adorn the walls of his patron's castle and hunting lodge in Scotland.[46]

Differing Visions: The Debate over Expansion

By the time of Frémont's expedition, the work of these artists, writers, and explorers had more than piqued the curiosity of the American public. The images they created and the words they used alerted Americans to the variety of attractions offered by the far western landscape. The West could provide novelty, as the Indian paintings of George Catlin and Karl Bodmer made clear, as well as reassuringly familiar scenes. The terrain also included areas so different and so fearsome that they could not yet be described.

John C. Frémont stepped into this whirl of fascinating and contradictory imagery. His four expeditions in the 1840s and early 1850s, the first governmentally sanctioned investigations in nearly twenty years, took place during a peak of American interest in the region. His mapping of what would become the Oregon Trail and his efforts to describe the landscape in comprehensible terms made him a cultural hero. He did not answer all questions about the Far West, but his work made the landscape easier for Americans to imagine. It also helped to ignite a raging debate over the advantages and dangers of territorial expansion as well as the merits of the far western landscape. Propagandists on both sides of the issue used facts, myths, and prevailing attitudes toward landscape as ammunition.

The proponents of western expansion found powerful representatives in Senator Thomas Hart Benton of Missouri, who sent Frémont west to further the cause of territorial annexation, and the promoter and entrepreneur William Gilpin, Henry Nash Smith's "mystic bard of Manifest Destiny."[47] Born to a wealthy Pennsylvania Quaker family, Gilpin was educated in the United States and in England and had traveled extensively before he began his western career. In 1843 he accompanied Frémont's expedition to the Columbia River and rapidly became a passionate advocate of acquiring the Oregon territory. By the 1850s, he had traveled over a large portion of the West and had developed elaborate theories of geopolitics that placed the Far West at the center of world development. By his own account, all sections of the Far West held great riches.[48]

To describe the West, Gilpin used language that he knew Americans would find attractive. For those looking for a farm, he suggested the Great Plains, a term Gilpin probably coined. These plains, he promised, were gardens in disguise. "They are the *Pastoral Garden* of the world," he stated optimistically, claiming further that "the climate of the Great Plains is favorable to health, longevity, intellectual and physical development, and stimulative of an exalted tone of social cultivation and refinement."[49]

Gilpin also saw great promise for farmers in the dry valleys of the Great Basin. He believed that with proper irrigation, the valleys could become an agricultural mecca. "The laborious extermination of the primeval forest; fuel and refuge from inclement seasons of heat and cold; periodical and uncertain inflictions of drought and saturation . . . none of these vicissitudes are seen and known upon the Plateau," promised Gilpin.[50] He did concede that the high mountain peaks of the Rockies offered little of interest to farmers, but he thought herders could prosper even in the highest passes, where "indigenous grasses, fruits, and vegetables abound; it swarms with animal life and aboriginal cattle; food of grazing and carnivorous animals, fowls and fish, is everywhere found."[51]

The wonderland described by Gilipin also offered plenty for devotees of nature and the sublime. Of the scenery of the Rockies, he claimed, "Nature here, more perfectly than at any other point on the globe, unites into one grand *coup d'oeil* all her grandest features." He promised that the stupendous mountains "present to the mind a combination of superlative sublimity, the graphic conviction ever present to the mind of the immediate presence and presiding omnipotence of the Creator!"[52]

Gilpin even managed to find historical associations and antiquities in the western landscape. "We want the prestige of antiquity, but we have it! See the Indian mounds in our West," he wrote, demonstrating his understanding of the grand associations Americans wanted to find in their landscape.[53] Even if few nineteenth-century Americans recognized the historical value of Indian artifacts, they did appreciate the romantic notions of evidence of the Noble Savage. For his eager readers, Gilpin pictured a West that provided everything Americans desired. This new landscape would not threaten their livelihood or their conceptions of beautiful scenery.

Gilpin did not originate the idea that the Far West contained a garden of the world. It had much older roots, growing out of the idea voiced by Thomas Jefferson and Hector St. John de Crevecoeur that the vast lands of the West would always provide an Edenic region for the virtuous and independent yeoman farmer who made up the backbone of American society. It also played on the conceptions of a beautiful, pastoral landscape that Americans adopted from Europeans—ideals that clever promoters quickly recognized as important.[54]

Promotional tracts designed to attract people to the Mississippi River regions, the West of the 1830s and 1840s, reflected the hopes Americans had for their western landscape. They promised gentle meadows and rich soil. Promotional material aimed directly at women played on their desire to live in fecund gardens and green pastures. Upon arriving in the barely settled region, women expected to find flowered prairies in a gentle climate with fertile soil where they could build "domestic Edens." What they did not expect or want was an untamed wilderness.[55]

Some actually discovered the kind of Eden they expected. Margaret Fuller visited the Illinois frontier in 1843 and found something even better, a landscaped park. "Illinois bears the character of a country which has been inhabited by a nation skilled like the English in all the ornamental arts of life, especially in landscape gardening. The villas and castles seem to have burnt, but the velvet lawns, the flower gardens, the stately parks . . . all remain."[56]

Others found the region to be a true wilderness. Shocked by the vast treeless spaces of the prairies, many observers called them desolate deserts, despite the nutritious grasses and blooming flowers. One of the first people to express this opinion was Caroline Kirkland in her widely read novel, *A New Home*, published in 1839. She wrote the book to counter the unrealistic impressions created by promoters and romantic novelists about the ease of life on the prairies. She portrayed the loneliness, the brutal work of breaking land, and the harsh climate that swept these prairies. A good life could be eked out of this landscape, but not with the ease that the images of a new Garden of Eden conveyed.[57]

The debates grew more heated in the 1840s as settlement moved beyond the fertile region of the Mississippi Valley. The reports of explorers like Long and Frémont had created apprehension about the Great Plains, which was given additional weight in fictional treatments like James Fenimore Cooper's *The Prairie* (1827). Even though Cooper had never ventured west of the Mississippi, his widely read adventure tale described the center of the continent as being filled with "deep morasses and arid wastes," and as being a "bleak and solitary place."[58] Though Frémont's account was a bit more optimistic, many people viewed the Great Plains as the limit of the United States's arable land. Standard maps in textbooks and government documents labeled the area the "Great American Desert." Newspapers in the Mississippi Valley warned of moving too far into this inhospitable region, claiming it was impossible to farm and perilous to cross.[59]

The warnings and praise given to the new West took on special import once Oregon fever broke out. Few people actually settled on the Great Plains in the 1840s, but an increasing number of people moved across the far western landscape on their way to Oregon and California. Americans found themselves swamped with contradictory information about the West. Newspaper editorials, guidebooks, political speeches, and travel accounts all recounted the horrors or wonders of the trip west and the lands that awaited those who made the crossing.

During the early years of his long career, the influential editor of the *New York Tribune*, Horace Greeley, made a personal crusade out of discouraging people from going to Oregon. He accused Oregon boosters of deliberately endangering thousands of American lives by encouraging emigration to Oregon. Gleefully, he printed horrible stories about the dangers of life on the trail from Indians, deserts, and wild animals. The news of the suffering of the Donner party while crossing the Sierra Nevada validated all of his claims. Other newspapers and influential politicians followed suit, advising restless Americans to stay in the East where plenty of good land still awaited them.[60]

Naturally, much of this debate revolved around political decisions about annexing new territories. Daniel Webster, who was a foe of expansion because he believed it would tear apart the delicate fabric of the nation, called Oregon "a region of savages and wild beasts, of deserts, of shifting sands and whirlwinds of dust, of cactus and prairie dogs." He wondered, "what use have we for such a country?"[61] British newspapers, quite understandably, also took a negative view of American settlement in Oregon and described the hazards of the trail and the inhospitable nature of the land in graphic terms, hoping to discourage American emigration that threatened British claims on Oregon.

In the Southwest, military conflict replaced the war of rhetoric. As tensions grew between the United States and Mexico, the Southwest became the subject of more intensive investigation. The outbreak of armed conflict in May of 1846 created a demand for new information. The army needed information about possible routes for moving supplies and troops, and the public had an almost insatiable appetite for news about this first war of empire. Reporters and artists brought back news and imagery to be displayed prominently in American newspapers, while topographers and artists accompanied army engineers who sought out precise information for military maneuvers.[62]

John Mix Stanley was one of the first artists to attempt an interpretation of the strange landscape of the Southwest. The army hired Stanley to make scientifically accurate depictions of the territory as he accompanied Colonel Stephen Watts Kearney to New Mexico and California in 1846. The novelty and beauty of the scenery drove him to create idealized rather than realistic masterpieces. *Chain of Spires along the Gila River* (1855) reflected Stanley's delight in the colors and shapes of the geology and plant and animal life of the desert. He could not resist combining them in impossible ways. Cacti, ferns, spires of rock, horned toads, and deer all crowded the same painting. Stanley's perception of the Southwest seemed to be a bizarre cornucopia—desert forms in lush profusion.[63]

Other artists made important attempts to capture the scenery of the Southwest on canvas. In 1848 Richard and Edward Kern accompanied John C. Frémont on a disastrous winter crossing of the southern Rockies in an effort to find a railroad route across the mountains. Despite the failure of the expedition, the Kerns produced a number of stunning sketches of the New Mexico mountains. Though more concerned with accuracy than Stanley, the Kerns' sketches also showed romantic flourishes. Their work, however, especially that of Richard Kern, emphasized the sharp lines and emptiness of the landscape. Kern's gorges are deeper, his mountains more pointed, and the land more barren than in reality, but wonderfully sublime. This vision of the Southwest, however, grasped the stark beauty of the land that would not attract most Americans until the twentieth century.[64]

John Mix Stanley, *Chain of Spires along the Gila River* (1855)

The distinctive shapes of the plants and the geographic features of the landscape appear in great profusion, making the stark desert seem lush and hospitable. (Courtesy of the Phoenix Museum of Art.)

The Kerns found themselves intrigued with the Southwest and traveled with several other army reconnaissance expeditions. They painted the cliff dwellings of ancient Indians at Chaco Canyon and Canyon de Chelly. Richard Kern began to master the brilliant colors and clear atmosphere of the region. His work offered clues to a whole new genre of American art based on the clean lines and stark forms of the desert. In his own lifetime, however, little of his art reached public view. Lithographs appeared in government reports and several were pirated by other artists, but his new vision of the far western landscape informed few people.

The work of such artists reflected the fact that by 1848, Americans had accomplished a part of their manifest destiny, and the nation now stretched from the Atlantic to the Pacific. Through war and diplomacy, Americans had great tracts of land to explore, interpret, and settle. Thousands of

Richard H. Kern, *Robidoux's Pass, White Mountains, New Mexico* (1848)

The height and narrowness of the mountain pass are exaggerated in this watercolor, while the dead trees in the foreground emphasize the forbidding aspects of the landscape. (Courtesy of the Amon Carter Museum, Fort Worth.)

Richard H. Kern, *Rock and Pueblo of Acoma, New Mexico* (1851)

Kern's watercolor captures the vast space of the southwestern landscape and the forms the humans adapted to live in it. Both the rock and the pueblo seemed alien to nineteenth-century Americans. (Courtesy of the Amon Carter Museum, Fort Worth.)

people, encouraged by news of fertile territory in Oregon and gold in California, set off to inspect this new region for themselves. Millions of others waited to hear their reports. What these travelers discovered were opportunities for profit, glory, and cultural development that seemed beyond description.

Presenting the West: Literary Travelers and Artists

The vast majority of Americans, who themselves had no desire to go to Oregon or California, still found such reports fascinating. They eagerly read the works of literary travelers who journeyed west in the tradition of Washington Irving, simply to see the sights. Two of the most popular of these literary travel accounts were Edwin Bryant's *What I Saw In California* and Francis Parkman's *The Oregon Trail.* Both authors traveled west in 1846 and published descriptions of their trips soon afterward, enjoying rave reviews and enormous sales.

Edwin Bryant's account of his trip through the Far West demonstrates the power of the images of the region that had been created long before. Bryant expected to find the prairies to be gardens and the central portion of the Far West to be a great desert. Naturally, he found gardens and deserts. What surprised him were the sights he could not fit into these neat frameworks, such as the great rock formations of the Wyoming plains, the massive peaks of the Rocky Mountains, and the Great Basin of Utah and Nevada.

Bryant's reaction to his first view of the plains west of the Missouri River showed his familiarity with standard aesthetic categories and with the travel literature of the day. "The view of the illimitable succession of green undulations and flowery slopes, of every gentle and graceful configuration," he declared, "creates a wild and scarcely controllable ecstasy of admiration."[65] He managed to control his ecstasy enough to express the proper reverence for the sublime in the scene: "The power and taste of Omnipotence had here been manifested, preparing for His children a garden as illimitable in extent as it is perfect, grand, and picturesque in appearance."[66]

The drier portion of the plains in western Nebraska and eastern Wyoming did not receive such an enthusiastic response. Here was the great American desert that Bryant expected. "It is scarcely possible to conceive a scene of more forbidding dreariness and desolation that was presented to our view on all sides," he wrote using the standard terms adopted by earlier visitors. "A few straggling and stunted sage-shrubs struggling for an existence in the sandy and gravelly soil were the only objects that saluted our vision."[67] Clearly, a generation of observation had already created a pattern of description for the Far West.

Bryant understood which parts of the barren landscape would please Americans in search of scenic wonders. His descriptions of the great rock formations of Chimney Rock and Scott's Bluff gave them cultural value in terms of the sublime. "No language," Bryant claimed of Scott's Bluff, "can portray even a faint outline of its almost terrific sublimity."[68] Even more inspiring, he used grand language to point out the historical associations available to the educated viewer. "While surveying this scenery," Bryant wrote, "the traveler involuntarily imagines himself in the midst of the desolate and deserted ruins of vast cities, to which Nineveh, Thebes, and Babylon were pygmies in grandeur and magnificence."[69] Such a description would certainly thrill any armchair traveler who hoped to find a version of the Old World in the New.

Other aspects of western scenery did not suit themselves as agreeably to magnificent analogies. When Bryant saw the Rocky Mountains, their bleak heights surprised him. His description of them seemed rather lukewarm. "The view from this ridge, to one unaccustomed to mountain scenery is strikingly picturesque, although the extensive landscape presents a wild, desolate, and inhospitable aspect," he noted with evident disappointment.[70] He never compared these mountains to the European Alps, as had most earlier observers, including Frémont and Washington Irving's Captain Bonneville. Perhaps the shock of their size, isolation, and barrenness prevented him from making the usual romantic connection.

The landscape surrounding the Great Salt Lake, the real deserts of the American West, also astounded Bryant. He could find no European analogies to describe "this scene of dismal and oppressive solitude." Attempting to express the shock he felt at the size and silence of the desert he explained, "there was no voice of animal, no hum of insect, disturbing the tomblike solemnity. All was silence and death." Even the wind, he noted, "seemed stagnant and paralyzed by the universal dearth around."[71] He could not describe what the desert looked like, he could only convey the impression of its silence. He had no words to attach to its curious landforms, plants, and animals.

Like Bryant, Francis Parkman traveled the Overland Trail not as a participant in the great migration, but rather as an observer of the migration and of the interior of the continent. Parkman described his trip as "a tour of curiosity and amusement to the Rocky Mountains," but he also had more serious motives.[72] Plagued by poor health that forced him to interrupt his studies at Harvard Law School, he hoped that a summer of outdoor adventure would prevent him from becoming an invalid. Parkman also believed this would be his last chance to see the Plains Indians, long one of his passionate interests, before American movement through the region wiped them out entirely.[73]

From the very start of his trip, Parkman sensed that he would be moving into a new world. "I was half inclined," he wrote on his first day out, "to regret leaving behind the land of gardens, for the rude and stern scenes of prairies and mountains."[74] Although he had been prepared for the sight of the plains by "picturesque tourists, painters, poets and novelists," he found their descriptions inadequate.[75] Because he had expected scenery that he could place in standard aesthetic categories, Parkman could not find the proper terms to define the famed prairies. Puzzled, he described the scene as "strange" and "striking to the imagination" even though it "had not one picturesque or beautiful feature, nor had it any of the features of grandeur, other than it vast extent, its solitude, and its wildness."[76]

When he reached the Rocky Mountains, Parkman found the scenery equally wild, but more aesthetically satisfying. Reverently, he described a moment "when the sun was just resting above the broken peaks and the purple mountains threw their prolonged shadows for miles." The mountains offered sublime visions that could be depicted in familiar terms. Of this striking sunset, Parkman noted, "Could Salvator Rosa have transferred it to his canvas, it would have added new reknown to his pencil."[77] Finding a scene that seemed worthy of the finest European artists validated the landscape in his eyes. Like Edwin Bryant, Parkman saw little beauty in many parts of the Far West. Although he did not cross the Rocky Mountains, Parkman also found some horrifying deserts. The high plains of Wyoming stunned Parkman with their unfamiliar expanses of rock, sand, and sage. "If a curse had been placed upon the land, it could not have worn a more dreary and forlorn barrenness," he wrote with complete disgust.[78] Parkman saw nothing that he could describe in European terms. These great spaces did not fit into traditional aesthetic categories and certainly did not offer scenery to inspire the likes of Salvator Rosa.

With the discovery of gold in California in 1848, large numbers of people traveled to California over the same territory and reached similar conclusions. The steady stream of information about the Far West that flowed east in the 1840s became a torrent in the 1850s, reflecting the growing intensity of interest Americans had in the region. During the height of the Gold Rush, newspapers printed hundreds of letters about the trip to California, offering practical advice concerning the difficulties and delights of the trip west, as well as contradictory reports about the riches of the Mother Lode. All of the major American and British periodicals also described the wonders and horrors of overland travel and California. The dazed reader of such fabulous and often conflicting information could only conclude that the Far West contained sights that could not be easily interpreted.[79]

The popular essayist Bayard Taylor, who already had made a name for himself with descriptions of his European travels, claimed to settle some of these issues in a book about California called *Eldorado*, published in 1850. Although Taylor did not travel overland, choosing the more common route of ship travel, he and his fellow passengers were well acquainted with the literature describing the trip across the continent. He wrote that on board ship "nothing was talked of but the land to which we were bound, nothing read but Frémont's Expedition, Emory's Report, or some work of Rocky Mountain travel."[80] He also listened carefully to the stories of those who traveled overland, summing them up dramatically for his readers: "The amount of suffering which must have been endured in the savage mountain passes and the herbless deserts of the interior cannot be told in words."[81] By now, the inexpressible qualities of the far western landscape had become standard rhetorical devices.

Taylor did manage to describe much of the California landscape. Though his most vivid memory seems to have been the armies of fleas that tortured him every night, he did depict the scenery in ways that surely pleased his audience of prosperous armchair readers. He explained that the "charming" mountain landscape of the Sierra Nevada was "equal to any in Tyrol."[82] He also approved of the Sacramento valley, which "seemed to be some deserted location of ancient civilization and culture." Happily, he noted that "the wooded slopes of the mountains are lawns, planted by Nature with a taste to which Art could add no charm" and that "the trees have nothing of the wild growth of our forests; they are compact, picturesque, and grouped in every variety of graceful outline."[83] Like many observers before him, Taylor promised that this part of the Far West held an American version of Europe. He also found rocky defiles and deserts too hideous to describe.

The observations of Bryant, Parkman, and Taylor echoed those of explorers of earlier decades. These widely read descriptions of plains, mountains, and deserts along the Oregon and California trails in the 1840s and 1850s developed a standard for describing the far western landscape that stood for nearly half a century. Based on European precepts of beauty and sublimity, the interpretation of the narrow strip of territory around the forty-first parallel came to represent the entire Far West. The mountains and the greenest parts of the prairies provided views in which Americans could take pride. They offered the sublime and the picturesque that Americans had long sought in their scenery. The dry plains and the deserts, however, were too novel to be easily interpreted. Wordlessness became a ritual response for such unfamiliar scenes. Few Americans had developed the analytical tools necessary to celebrate the originality of their far western landscape.

Even though wildness and strangeness made people uncomfortable, the West still fascinated them. Entrepreneurs quickly realized the potential profitability of graphic representations of the Far West to supplement written description. One of the most popular forms of graphic information in the middle decades of the nineteenth century was the moving panorama. This early version of "moving pictures" had been imported from Europe in the form of elaborately painted newsreels. American audiences flocked to see the exploits of Napoleon (his funeral cortege proved to be the most popular of all), the explosions of volcanoes, and the beauties of Versailles. Artists painted these events on tremendous canvases mounted on rollers that moved the scenes past the audience. The effect of the moving canvas and the painted scene created the closest illusion of reality that audiences had yet seen.[84]

Quickly, American artists introduced their own version of the panorama focusing on the most saleable aspect of American culture, the landscape. River journeys proved to be the easiest to create and the most popular. The stage became a river vessel, and painted scenery moved along the back wall, so that those in the audience felt as if they were sitting aboard a ship. Because of the great fame and size of the Mississippi and Missouri rivers, panoramas depicting these rivers, and the sights along their banks flourished in the late 1840s.[85]

John Banvard claimed his *Panorama of the Mississippi River* to be the first and largest of these stupendous canvases, painted on "three miles of Canvas; Exhibiting a View of Country 1200 Miles in Length, extending from the Mouth of the Missouri River to the City of New Orleans."[86] Banvard asserted that his vast canvas would introduce audiences "to every detail of life on these river banks." After two years of touring, Banvard boasted that 400,000 Americans had viewed his extravaganza. Other enterprising artists quickly capitalized on Banvard's success, and at least five of them toured the country with great success.[87]

None of these panoramas still exists. Because the canvases were constantly moved on rollers and transported from city to city, many simply wore out. Others passed from owner to owner until they no longer made a profit and then were discarded or placed in attics or warehouses and lost to public knowledge. Only a few lithographs made to advertise the panoramas and a few oils made by the artists remain to tell us what Americans saw in the darkened theaters. Advertising pamphlets and the texts of some of the lectures that accompanied the shows help to explain how these landscapes were presented.

The most successful panoramas, like Banvard's, used both genre and landscape scenes, capitalizing on the American penchant for the sublime and the picturesque. The most unknown portions of the landscape, like the region of the Upper Missouri, received the most dramatic treatment. "At first," Banvard's pamphlet explained, "the river is a furious mountain torrent, leaping in wildness from rock to rock through deep gorges. The scenery in these remote regions has an aspect of majestic grandeur rarely witnessed upon the globe." The pamphlet then provided metaphors to make the scenery culturally important, noting that the bluffs along the river often resembled "the ruins of ancient cities, with their domes, towers, and castellated walls."[88] These landscape scenes alternated with views of Indian encampments, hunts, and dances. Such depictions of the West helped convince Americans of the value of their wild and beautiful landscape. Here, in the Far West, they could find the romantic peoples and ancient ruins that they could incorporate into their culture and make it equal to that of Europe.

In the early 1850s, panoramas about the California gold rush and the Overland Trail replaced river trips in American theaters. The shows gave a huge number of Americans their first look at the landscape of the Far West. One of the earliest of these extravaganzas, James F. Wilkins's "Moving Mirror of the Overland Trail," attracted audiences with its claims of vicarious experience and glamorous scenery.

Like Banvard, Wilkins clearly understood what Americans expected of their landscape. As he traveled west with a slow-moving wagon train in the summer of 1849, he sketched scenes he knew would attract a paying audience. Exciting Indian dances, buffalo hunts, and, most importantly, stupendous mountains, great rock formations, and vast prairies littered the "Moving Mirror." Washington Irving could have written his script. It used all of the standard phrases that signaled viewers that they were observing a properly romantic landscape. A review of Wilkins's work exulted, "One moment the beautiful passes before the eye, the next the grand, then the terrific mingled with the sublime and awful." The reviewer grew even more enthusiastic about specific scenes. "Mountains with their snowy tops and ragged sides, seen in the distance, gilded by the last rays of the setting sun, remind us of all that Byron or Coleridge have written or sung of the far-famed Alpine scenery."[89] Although the exact appearance of Wilkins's panorama remains a mystery, we do know that it satisfied American demands for sublimity and splendor, and that this approach proved profitable.

The contents of another enormously popular panorama, "Jones' Pantoscope of California," are more accessible. J. Wesley Jones, an artist and daguerreotypist, traveled over the Overland Trail in 1851 with a team of several artists. Jones daguerreotyped much of the landscape, and he and his artists filled in the gaps with sketches. Using the sketches and daguerreotypes, Jones painted a spectacular panorama. The text from the accompanying lecture, a scattering of field sketches, and a promotional book written by one of Jones's artists, John Dix, detailing their harrowing adventures, make the "Pantoscope" easier to re-create.

Jones depicted all of the usual sights with more honesty than many boosters would have liked. Although he masked the monotony of the Great Plains with exciting views of buffalo, antelope, and Indian encampments, he did not make them into fertile gardens. "Every day's journey marks a gradual assimilation to the desert wastes which skirt the base of the distant Mountains," he explained in his lecture. "The grasses upon the hills become thin, short, and finally almost disappear. . . . Such is Nebraska and Kansas, fit only for the wandering tribes to whom it has hitherto been devoted by nature." John Dix wrote about the same region that "at one place, not a tree or a shrub is found along the valley of the Platte for upwards of two hundred miles. The scenery is monotonous in the extreme."[90] Because artists relying on visual excitement to sell their work could not use the crutch of wordlessness, such scenes must have frustrated them.

Like Francis Parkman and Edwin Bryant, the artists found Chimney Rock, Scott's Bluff, and Courthouse Rock a great relief. They had something worthy of artistic notice. These wonders resembling huge architectural ruins provided a satisfying sublime and historical vista. The formations along the Green River received the most attention because they could be depicted in the most familiar terms. "As far as the eye can reach are seen huge masses resembling the ruins of ancient palaces and temples," noted Jones with obvious pleasure.[91]

The deserts of Utah and Nevada could not be described in such complimentary language. Jones devoted only one scene of his panorama and one paragraph of his lecture to this portion of the trip. He described the desert crossing economically. "We strike the Humboldt River, down which we follow, as it meanders through a region of dreariness and desolation, to the great American desert where it is lost among the parched sands. Thence crossing the desert we strike the Carson river at its sink, seen in the remote corner of the Picture."[92] John Dix, in an effort to dramatize the desert and to drum up interest in even the dullest portions of the "Pantoscope," described the Humboldt as "a crooked stream, worse than a serpent's path zig-zaged through a desert of ashes and lime." He continued dramatically, "All of the horrors of the desert follow. Broken wagons, dying animals, and men feeding on their carcasses, groaning in the agonies of despair and death."[93] If the desert had no scenic value, at least it had theatrical potential.

The Sierra Nevada presented an easier task for the artists. Their peaks offered views that could be painted in the grandest European tradition. Jones described the reaction of one of his artists for his lecture audiences. "As we climbed the highest crags our German Artist threw down his book in excessive delight and admiration of the scenery before him. 'Never have I seen such magnificence,' he exclaimed, 'As a student and an artist I treaded the mazes and mountain paths of the Alps and Jura, sketch book in hand, but never have I beheld such vastness and sublimity.' "[94] Such a reaction spoke well of the possibilities of the far western landscape. The sublime views reminding people of Europe would, promoters hoped, make up for the less familiar scenes present in the desert and plains.

Because of the curiosity Americans had about the far western landscape, Jones's "Pantoscope" met with great success when it opened on the

East Coast. The Boston *Bee* reported that the show played to "overflowing houses, where it met with the most triumphant success. Extra railway trains brought in large parties on excursions from neighboring towns. In the city of Lowell, the Pantoscope was crowded for many weeks by the thousands."[95] Shows like the "Pantoscope" gave many people their first look at this new and strange region. The promoter, John Dix, quoted the minister Henry Ward Beecher as saying, "It communicates important knowledge about a large tract of our own territory, the like of which for its peculiar, wild, and original features, is nowhere else to be seen on earth."[96]

Not only did successful panoramas introduce people to this "peculiar," "wild," and "original" scenery, but they also gave them important clues about how to interpret it. The vocabulary and style of the artists suggested which parts of the landscape were worthy of appreciation and which parts were not. The high mountain passes and rock formations emphasized by the artists of the "Pantoscope" and other panoramas demonstrated that the United States had scenery comparable to Europe. The truly "original" parts of the West, the high plains and the deserts, seemed too risky to interpret for artists dependent on audiences who craved European scenes.

The Challenge of Distinctive Landscapes

From the very beginnings of the American discovery of the Far West, however, many observers recognized that the equation with Europe would never be exact. Even the narrow strip of land surrounding the Overland Trail that had so often been described presented scenery that challenged these European definitions. Some aspects of the West, however, were too wondrous and accessible to ignore even though they did not always fit the aesthetic categories Americans had developed. Objects and places like the Big Trees of California and Yosemite Valley had to be reckoned with in the American interpretation of the Far West.

In the 1850s, the Yosemite Valley offered new challenges for the American interpretation of the Far West. The stunning glacier-carved valley, officially "discovered" in 1851, resembled nothing on earth. The first tourist group made its way into the valley in 1855, led by entrepreneur James Mason Hutchings and accompanied by artist Thomas A. Ayres. Quickly, Yosemite became a great hit with American readers and travelers. Reproductions of Ayres's drawings appeared in prominent eastern magazines. One of the earliest appeared in the Boston weekly *Ballou's Pictorial* in 1859. Recognizing the difficulty of describing such scenery to a public unfamiliar with such landscapes, the accompanying text was brief. "The engraving on this page will serve to give the untravelled reader some idea of the scenery in the wildest and most romantic part of the land of gold."[97]

The first visitors to the valley struggled to portray it in words. Thomas Starr King, the popular Universalist minister, nearly found the task beyond him. In 1860 he wrote one of the first widely read descriptions of Yosemite in a series of letters to the Boston *Evening Transcript*. He asked, "How can I express the awe and joy that were blended and continually struggling with each other, during the half hour in the hot noon that we remained on the edge of the abyss where the grandeurs of the Yo-Semite were first revealed to us?"[98] King, who had written a book about the White Mountains in New Hampshire, understood the language of the sublime and the techniques of European comparison familiar to American readers. Looking at the wonder of Yosemite, however, he quickly realized the inadequacy of his vocabulary. Yosemite was different. Like Fremont, he often resorted to telling his readers what the scene did *not* look like. "Is there such a ride possible in any other part of the planet?" King wondered. "Nowhere among the Alps, in no pass of the Andes, . . . is there such stupendous rock scenery as the traveller now lifts his eyes to."[99] In spite of its distinctive appearance, Yosemite offered so much of what seekers of the sublime wanted that, like Niagara, it became a tourist mecca.

Like Yosemite, the giant sequoias of the western Sierra became objects of veneration. The first news of the Big Trees appeared in the East in

Big Tree, Pride of the Forest

The giant sequoia thrilled western observers because of its size and its antiquity. Such trees demonstrated that America had a natural history that could be compared to the human history of the Old World. (In Thomas Nelson, *Nelson's Pictorial Guide-books: Scenery of California*, 1874. Courtesy of the Bancroft Library.)

PRIDE of the FOREST

1851, when two enterprising Californians stripped one of the great trees of its bark and sent it east for a tour and then on to the Crystal Palace exhibition in London. The tremendous size of the bark ignited a scientific dispute in both scientific and popular journals about the age, height, and very existence of the trees. Once reliable sources had confirmed the veracity of the first reports about the "vegetable wonders of the world," the sequoia became a source of great American pride.[100]

Both the age and size of the trees impressed visitors to the famous Calaveras and Mariposa groves. Thomas Starr King, viewing the sequoias for the first time in 1860, asked one particularly hoary-looking tree, "Are you as old as Noah? Do you span the centuries as far as Moses? Were you planted before the seed of Rome took root in Italy?"[101] These natural wonders had outlived the oldest civilizations in Europe. Americans could look upon them as living relics that predated almost every ancient ruin in Europe. The magnificent trees demonstrated that the far western landscape could provide Americans with a natural history, which though different from the human history of Europe, was just as ancient.

Yosemite and the Big Trees showed Americans that their landscape did not have to be an exact replica of Europe's to be worth looking at. Such sights, however, were not so different that they could not be described in familiar aesthetic terms. Yosemite's rock walls could be compared to cathedrals and other man-made monuments. The awesome scenery of Yosemite provided an American example of the sublime, more spectacular than even Niagara. The ancient sequoia could compete in age and size with the antiquities of Greece and Rome. Though distinctively American, these aspects of the western scene still fit the framework Americans had borrowed from Europe to interpret their landscapes.

Other parts of the Far West, beyond the pale of the Overland Trail and the known parts of Colorado and California, presented visions so unique that no borrowed framework could incorporate them. The arid lands of the Southwest shocked most visitors with their strange colors and landforms. An army officer, George Brewerton, described the deserts of Arizona in 1853 for the readers of *Harper's Monthly*. "The whole country looks more like the crater of an immense volcano than anything else I can compare it to, or, to use the words of one of our men, he believed 'that darn place had been afire, and hadn't quite got cool yet.' "[102] The unfamiliar desert rock formations, plants, and colors, though appreciated by a few observers, varied so greatly from the usual conception of beautiful scenery that most visitors despised them.

As late as 1860, the entire Southwest continued to be hated and feared. The famed British explorer, Sir Richard Burton, who had a deep interest in the American West, refused an opportunity to take the southern route to California, which, he explained, traversed "the vilest and most desolate portion of the West." He had heard that the hideousness of the region and the rigors of wagon travel often drove passengers crazy and that they "are often obliged to be strapped to their seats."[103] Observers could find nothing in the landscape to describe as sublime, romantic, picturesque, or beautiful, at least as mid-nineteenth-century Americans understood these terms. Such scenery did not remind Americans of Europe, nor did it provide them with objects and sights that offered familiar and grand associations. Quite simply, they did not know what to make of it.

Even though the desert still mystified Americans, the five decades between Lewis and Clark and J. Wesley Jones and his "Pantoscope" left a number of ideas about the significance of the western landscape in people's minds. The steady flow of information about the West in the form of government reports, magazine and newspaper articles, travel literature, and paintings and lithographs indicated the stunning variety of scenery and the ways in which it could be interpreted.

Despite the plethora of information, the Far West remained mysterious. Even though explorers had now established its basic geography, they had solved few of its most interesting puzzles. Places like the Grand Canyon, Yellowstone, and the heights of the Rockies and the Sierra Nevada remained unexplored and unmapped by white Americans. After fifty years of intensive investigation, Americans had still not seen much of the West, nor had they decided how to use it. They did, however, sense the cultural, as well as the economic, opportunities present in the far western landscape.

The West included great tracts of potential farmland, glorious prairies, hideous deserts, immense mountains, mysterious Indians, and fabulous riches in precious metals. Not only did this wealth promise a glowing economic future, but it suggested solutions for the cultural inadequacies many Americans detected in their developing nation. By ignoring large portions of the landscape, observers could describe the Far West as an American version of Europe—complete with sublime views, ancient ruins,

Alpine peaks, picturesque scenes, and Mediterranean shores. However, if even a casual observer looked carefully, he or she recognized that the western half of the nation contained a different brand of scenery.

Only a few of those who witnessed the Far West in the first half of the nineteenth century could look beyond its unfamiliarity. The work of artists like George Catlin, Karl Bodmer, Richard Kern, and John Mix Stanley acknowledged the distinctive qualities of the region. The buffalo, cacti, glowing red canyons, Indian tepees, and great mesa formations in their paintings showed Americans that the West could never be entirely equated with European scenery.

Learning to appreciate the real variety offered by far western scenery, however, would take several more decades. The western landscape's challenge to the fragile cultural definitions Americans had formed to explain the eastern part of the nation could not yet be met. For most observers, it seemed easiest to describe sights that could be explained in familiar aesthetic terms. Educated Americans had been conditioned to look for landscapes that resembled Europe. They wanted to find English parks, Swiss Alps, and Italian vistas; and in parts of the Far West, they found them. Thrilled with the possibility of discovering American scenery that equaled Europe's, most visitors did not immediately recognize that their landscape could far surpass it.

Before Americans could recognize the cultural possibilities of the landscape, much less utilize them to create an independent national culture, the new realm had to be made accessible. From the moment John C. Frémont returned from his adventures and reported on the wonders of the Far West, Americans dreamed of a railroad to take them there.

Debates about the feasibility, location, and construction of a railroad to the Pacific made the Far West a focal point of national attention in the 1850s and 1860s. As the railroad promised to link East and West physically, Americans sought ways to connect them culturally, and thousands of interested people traveled west to observe the process. The observations, judgments, and interpretations of this rapidly increasing group of visitors solidified American ideas about the West.

CHAPTER 2

Tunnel Vision: The Spectacle of the Transcontinental Railroad, 1850–1869

I hear the locomotives rushing and roaring, and
the shrill steaming whistle.
I hear the echoes reverberate through the grandest
scenery in the world.

—Walt Whitman
"Passage to India"

In April 1869, as the long-awaited transcontinental railroad neared completion, the inveterate western booster Samuel Bowles heralded its glories in the *Atlantic Monthly*. "I often think," he wrote, "of the many delightful surprises in store for those of us who go out over it into our new and unknown West, before the tribe of guidebook makers, newspaper letter writers, and photographers have 'done it to death' with pen and collodion."[1]

Although Bowles seemed unaware of it, by 1869 parts of the Far West had already suffered this fate and Bowles had contributed his share. A generation of explorers, artists, and writers had created a panoramic vision of what the Far West held. The fascination with the building of the transcontinental railroad had steadily narrowed this vision from the infinite possibilities it once offered. Journalists, artists, and photographers who invaded the region in the 1860s concentrated on the thin ribbon of land stretching from Omaha to Sacramento along the forty-first parallel. They ignored most of the tremendous swath that spread north to Canada and south to Mexico. The narrow focus created a kind of tunnel vision that prevented most people from looking beyond the railroad tracks.

The tunnel vision developed out of a need to "sell" the landscape surrounding the railroad to the American people. Railroad interests, along with writers and artists, sought images to make this portion of the far western landscape comprehensible and attractive to eastern Americans. They created a balanced package from bits of the Old World interspersed with American novelties, wrapped in promises of safety and comfort. By 1869, the Far West had become a cleverly packaged commodity, ready to be consumed by wealthy train travelers.

The importance of the railroad to American perceptions of the Far West cannot be overestimated. The wonders and riches announced to the world by a generation of exploration and description could not be reaped until the Far West became accessible. For most travelers and entrepreneurs, the tremendous space between the Pacific Ocean and the Mississippi seemed insurmountable. In an age of steamship and locomotive travel, few people had the time or energy to inspect the possibilities of the new landscape from a stagecoach. Most waited for the old dream of a Passage to India to become a reality.

Railroad Surveys: Discovering a New World

Almost as soon as railroad technology appeared in the United States in the 1820s, people discussed the potential of a transcontinental railroad. The annexation of Oregon, the conquest of the Southwest, and the discovery of gold in California convinced many of the need for a railroad to link east and west. By the early 1850s, sectional tensions between the North and the South made the selection of a route a delicate political problem. In 1853, Secretary of War Jefferson Davis tried to defuse the issue by convincing Congress to charter four official surveys so that the railroad route could be chosen on scientific, rather than political, grounds.

These railroad surveys brought the American vision of the Far West to its broadest point in the nineteenth century. Four separate teams of scientists, artists, and cartographers, accompanied by military escorts, set off in the spring of 1853, spreading out like a fan over the Far West. The northernmost survey covered the expanse of land between the forty-seventh and the forty-ninth parallels, near the Canadian border. The others examined the possible routes along the thirty-eighth, in the southern Rocky Mountains; the thirty-fifth, in what is now northern New Mexico and Arizona; and the thirty-second, near the southern border of the United States. The route along the Oregon Trail, also a contender, was deemed too well known to warrant another extensive reconnaissance.[2]

Because of the sectional rivalry involved in the surveys, the unknown territory they covered, and the promise of adventure that accompanied them, the expeditions fascinated the nation. The debate over what the explorers would find raged in newspapers, popular periodicals, and scientific journals. "How it will be when all the vast extent of our continent which stretches between us and the great Pacific is traveled over, we cannot now conjecture," mused the editor of *Harper's Monthly*. "We shall doubtless know more when the several surveying parties have returned home."[3] The scope of the investigation and the scale of the expeditions assured that the reports brought back to an eagerly waiting public would have great impact.

Once the members of the surveys returned, the public had to wait quite a while for more news. Preliminary reports of their findings were occasionally published, but the final report did not appear until 1860. The government spent at least one million dollars on printing the thirteen-volume, lavishly illustrated report, twice what the surveys themselves had cost.[4] This unprecedented expenditure demonstrated the importance attached to the information collected and the conclusions made by the surveys.

The *Reports of Explorations and Surveys to Ascertain the Most Practicable and Economic Route for a Railroad from the Mississippi River to the Pacific Ocean* included detailed botanical, zoological, geological, and geographical analyses. The artists accompanying each expedition contributed sketches and lithographs that complemented both the scientific discussions and the descriptions of the landscape. The *Reports* made public a great storehouse of information, introducing Americans to a spectacular new West.

Like earlier explorers, the scientists and artists of the Pacific Railroad surveys shared the attitudes toward landscape developed by Americans in the early nineteenth century. Their standards of beauty and usefulness deviated little from those used to interpret the Far West in decades before. They hoped to find green pastures, graceful trees, stupendous mountains, and sublime views that could be described in romantic terms, as well as harsh deserts, and barren plains. Prepared by explorers like John C. Frémont, they also expected to find something new.

The *Reports* of the Pacific Railway surveys demonstrated that the Far West met many of these expectations. Lieutenant Henry Abbott of the Forty-seventh Parallel Survey wrote that "the five grand snow peaks" of the Cascade Range delighted him with their sublimity. "On every side," he exulted, "terrific convulsions of nature had recorded their fury."[5] From the summit of the Rockies, an artist surveying the thirty-eighth parallel "beheld a panorama of unspeakable sublimity . . . continuous chains of mountains reared their snowy peaks far away in the distance, while the Grand River, plunging along in awful sublimity through its rocky bed, was seen for the first time."[6] Many earlier observers had described such mountainous regions, indicating the European-based language suitable to convey the meaning of the landscape's appearance.

In other places, the stark scenery and the lack of greenery shocked the survey members. However, the rock formations created by great rivers often pleased them, just as they had earlier travelers. Lieutenant E. G. Beckwith of the Thirty-eighth Parallel Survey found the scenery around the Green River spectacular. "Where no sign of vegetation exists," he wrote, "is the appearance of an unfinished fortification, on a scale which is pleasing to the imagination." As if surprised by his appreciation of the scene, Beckwith added, "desolate as is the country through which we have just passed, the view is still one of the most beautiful and pleasing I remember to have seen."[7]

Descriptions of rocks that resembled "stately facades, august cathedrals, amphitheaters, rotundas, castellated walls, and rows of time-stained ruins" provided a way to describe the far western landscape for a culture that could only envision scenery in European terms. Given such preconceptions, the members of the surveys found Europe in the most unlikely places. "As we approached the town," reported Amiel Whipple of the Thirty-second Parallel Survey as his party approached an Indian village, "the Germans of the party almost imagined themselves in the 'Father-

Lithograph from Beckwith's Report on the Thirty-eighth Parallel

This lithograph represents a first attempt to depict the torturous course of the Colorado River and the violent geography created by its waters. The carved canyons and the great walls of rock stunned early observers. (*Pacific Railroad Reports*, vol. 2. Courtesy of the Bancroft Library.)

land.' " He explained how the hazy mist filtered the sun, making the scene "strikingly similar to pictures of Dutch cities."[8]

Other, stranger kinds of scenery proved more difficult to describe. As with earlier explorers, the deserts and mountain formations of the Southwest and the high plateaus of Wyoming and Montana often stunned the survey parties into descriptive silence. Their experience with eastern scenery and European aesthetic ideals offered no words to attach to the landscape. Most of these explorers, however, were scientists; and, when more conventional language failed them, they turned to the language of science. Once members of the surveys reached areas that could not be discussed in familiar European-inspired terms, their prose dwindled to dry listings of plant and animal life and geology.[9]

Even this meager discussion proved difficult at times. Lieutenant Joseph Christmas Ives, who explored southern Arizona in an 1857 survey, constantly noted the sheer emptiness of the landscape in his journal, complaining that "every form of vitality is rare. The scarcity of vegetation has been alluded to; of fish, but a single one."[10] Heinrich Baldwin Möllhausen, the zoologist and artist for the Thirty-second Parallel Survey, expressed his own disappointment at the clash between expectation and reality in the landscape when he looked at the Rio Grande for the first time. "We had been dreaming, perhaps, of luxuriant vegetation—of lofty palms and giant ferns," he wrote unhappily. Instead, "there stretched before us a treeless, clay-coloured flat, and a shallow muddy river."[11] E. G. Beckwith found northern Utah equally disappointing. He described it as "desolate and disheartening in the extreme." He added as proof that "except for three or four small cottonwood trees in the ravine near us, there is not a tree to be seen by the unassisted eye on any part of the horizon."[12]

In the midst of such unfamiliar territory, however, many of the surveyors found portions of the landscape strangely appealing. Amiel Whipple seemed unable to explain his attraction to the saguaro cactus because "an idea of barrenness is associated with the whole cactus tribe, detracting from the delight with which we witness the rare and beautiful forms here developed."[13] Struggling to explain how something barren could be attractive, Whipple could only say that the cacti were "singular" and "strange," and hint that they might be considered beautiful, if only they were not connected to the idea of barrenness. He recognized that he was appreciating a unique kind of beauty, but he did not understand why.

Joseph Christmas Ives dealt with the same rhetorical problem in the canyon lands of Arizona. He characterized the region as "in a scientific point of view, of the highest interest, and presenting natural features whose strange sublimity is perhaps unparalleled in any part of the world."[14] He found the scenery "strange" and full of "interest," but he could not describe it as beautiful in the way he understood the word. In only one aspect did he find the landscape beautiful. He could not resist the "new and surprising effects of coloring" in the landforms and the sky of the Southwest. "In the foreground," he explained of a particular vista, "light and delicate tints predominated and broad surfaces of lilac, pearl color, pink, and white, contrasted strongly with the sombre masses piled up behind. In their very midst, a single pile of vivid blood red rose in isolated

Desert View, From A. W. Whipple's Report on the Thirty-second Parallel

The great size and the unfamiliar shape of the cactus overwhelms the man mounted on a horse in this exaggerated drawing of a cactus in the Arizona desert. (*Pacific Railroad Reports*, vol. 3. Courtesy of the Bancroft Library.)

prominence."[15] Here, indeed, was a new sight, strange perhaps, but beautiful nonetheless.

The news of such peculiar beauties, however, was not what Americans wanted to hear. Even though earlier explorers and travelers had noted the great deserts and the treeless plains, many people still dreamed of green gardens and unlimited fertility. Throughout the 1840s and 1850s, the supporters of expansion had promised a west of green pastures, gold fields, and snow-covered mountain ranges, skipping over the inhospitable and unfamiliar aspects of the Far West. Such expectations were evident in discussions of the findings of the Pacific Railroad Survey.

A discussion of a preliminary report in the *North American Review* reflected the hopes riding on the official explorations, as well as the disappointment many Americans felt when deserts and dry plains dashed these hopes. "The recent exploring expeditions, sent out under the auspices of the government, have enriched us with a more accurate knowledge of this country," began the author, "and unfortunately, perhaps, have dispelled many illusions hitherto entertained respecting it."[16] He explained that vast plains did exist, but they were far from fertile; and that gorgeous mountains did pierce the sky, but they were more dangerous than grand. Occasional fertile spots hid in secluded valleys, but "these form too inconsiderable a portion to enter into an estimate of the general character of the country."[17] Clearly disappointed, he summarized the results of the extensive surveys. "Our rich possessions west of the 99th meridian have turned out to be worthless. . . . Whatever route is selected for a railroad to the Pacific, it must wind the greater portion of its length through a . . . dreary waste."[18]

The Pacific Railroad surveys did not discover the kind of landscape most Americans wanted. Certainly, the Far West offered bits of splendid scenery and richly forested, well-watered land. The surveys' reports presented a landscape of weird rock formations, oddly colored plants and

Southwestern Canyonlands

Egloffstein dramatizes the southwestern canyonlands in this lithograph. He makes the walls higher and the canyons narrower, reflecting the nineteenth-century appetite for the sublime. (From Joseph Christmas Ives, *Report upon the Colorado River of the West*, 1861. Courtesy of the Bancroft Library.)

sand, rivers that ran through seemingly barren deserts, and tremendous snow-covered defiles. For the first time, Americans had a comprehensive and realistic description of what lay in the Far West. For the moment, much of this new landscape was a disappointment. Only the perceptive few who actually visited such regions and who could look beyond the unfamiliarity and dryness of the landscape saw something new and uniquely attractive. It would take another thirty years before many others would come to recognize this different beauty.

If the highly publicized and expensive search for a railroad route had failed to discover a new Eden, it also failed to settle the question of where to build the railroad. Because of the intensity of sectional rivalries, most politicians wisely shelved the issue, probably recognizing that war would soon solve the problem.

The outbreak of the Civil War made the question of building a transcontinental railroad central once again, especially in the North where the bulk of the nation's railroad track as well as the raw material necessary to undertake such a project lay. After the southern routes had been ruled out because of war, only the forty-first- and forty-ninth-parallel routes remained possibilities. Because the forty-ninth-parallel route went through almost unknown territory and because it did not end in San Francisco, politicians and engineers rallied around the familiar route of the Oregon, California, and Mormon trails—the forty-first parallel—even though this route had not been included in the Pacific Railroad surveys.

Although well-known because of John C. Frémont's expeditions, Oregon travel, and the gold rush, the newly chosen transcontinental route had never been systematically examined. No one really knew if a railroad could be built over the Rockies and the Sierra Nevada, much less over a thousand miles of barren plain and desert. Nevertheless, Abraham Lincoln signed the Pacific Railroad Act into law on July 1, 1862, creating the occasion for an intensive investigation of a narrow strip of land from the Missouri River to Sacramento, California.

Narrowing the Vision: Journalists and the Forty-first Parallel

The initial debate over the necessity for a railroad and the search for a practical route widened American knowledge about the Far West considerably. However, after the Pacific Railroad surveys introduced Americans to the almost inconceivable variety of the far western landscape, the Pacific Railroad Act limited the focus of their examination. New interest in the railroad and the specific terrain it would traverse riveted attention on a thin strip of land. Despite the beauties and strange sights present in other areas of the Far West, for the next thirty years few Americans would look beyond the path of the old Overland Trail.

The building of the railroad became an object of national fascination. Even in the early stages of construction, when little track was being laid and when most Americans were preoccupied with the Civil War, the railroad and the land it would open up received great publicity. The significance of the railroad in the development of American society combined with the untold possibilities offered by the Far West made the transcontinental railroad a great news story.

Once the government indicated the importance of such a railroad by spending vast sums on the Pacific Railroad surveys and by initiating construction, Americans wanted to know how the new railroad would affect them. Even before Lincoln signed the railroad bill, journalists and editors recognized this new demand for information and rushed west to investigate the lands the railroad would cross. Although explorers, traders, farmers, miners, travel writers, and artists had crossed it before, people now looked at it with different eyes. The railroad made it a region to be interpreted, developed, and settled, rather than just "passed through." The far western landscape had become a commodity, and journalists wanted to observe how it could best be used and sold.

One of the earliest of these observers was Horace Greeley, the outspoken editor of the *New York Tribune*. Greeley began his career as a staunch opponent of expansion, but by the 1850s he had become an enthusiastic supporter of western development. He built the *Tribune* into the most influential newspaper in the United States. Its daily and weekly editions went out to every section of the country, except the increasingly alienated South. By the late 1850s Greeley's paper reached a circulation of over 300,000, far above the totals for any other publication.[19]

Realizing that it was only a matter of time until the railroad opened, Greeley kept his readers informed about opportunities in the Far West and carefully followed the controversy over the railroad's location. In the spring of 1859, with the excitement surrounding the gold discoveries near what is now Denver and the constant news about riches in California, Greeley decided to see for himself just what the West offered and what opportunities a railroad would create.

Greeley wrote of his adventures and observations in a series of letters, printed in the *Tribune* throughout the summer and fall of 1859 and later published in an extremely popular book, entitled *An Overland Journey from New York to San Francisco in the Summer of 1859*. Greeley intended to be a dispassionate observer, critically examining the landscape to see what it offered the American people. His excitement at viewing the region he had so long imagined and his expectations for the region, however, were evident from the start.

Greeley had little interest in the physical beauty of the landscape; he wanted to know how it could best be used. Because he believed that agricultural development was most important for the nation, he hoped to find fertile soil that resembled the rich farmland of the eastern half of the nation. He found Kansas to be the land of his dreams. He had noted Margaret Fuller's observation that Illinois resembled an English park, and he applied it to the buffalo-covered high plains of Kansas, which seemed covered with pastoral vistas of fields and grazing animals. "It is hard to realize that this is the center of a region of wilderness and solitude," he wrote with wonder.[20]

With his interest in timber and fertile soil, Greeley had little concern for the scenic qualities of the landscape. In Greeley's view, land had no value if it could not be used for farming or for growing trees to form stout farmhouses or railroad ties. Even the Rocky Mountains, usually the objects of great admiration and flowing rhetoric, scarcely appear in Greeley's narrative. He found them too harsh, too remote, and too jagged to be of use. Upon hearing claims of the healthful climate in the mountains, he remarked dryly, "It is likely to be some time yet before our fashionable American spas, and summer resorts for idlers will be located among the Rocky Mountains."[21]

He found other areas even less hospitable. Because Greeley measured the value of the land by the number of trees it produced, he found most of the land west of the one hundredth meridian unattractive. Of the high plains of western Kansas he wrote, "we came in sight of the Republican [river], which has a little—a very little—scrubby cottonwood nestled in and about its bluffs. . . . This is a region of sterility and thirst."[22] The absence of trees in northern Utah upset him as well. "I have not seen the raw material of a decent axe-helve growing in all my last thousand miles of travel," he estimated peevishly.[23] He saved his most violent excoriation for the lands surrounding the Humboldt River in Nevada. "I only wish to record my opinion," he stated, "that the Humboldt, all things considered, is the meanest river of its length on earth." To justify his dislike for the region he explained, "I believe no tree of any size grows on this forlorn river. . . . Half a dozen specimens of a large worthless shrub, known as buffalo brush or bull-berry, with a prevalent fringe of willows about the proper size for a schoolmarm's use, comprise the entire timber of this delectable region."[24]

Although much of the landscape seemed barren and useless to Greeley, he also found much to celebrate. "The soil of the adjacent prairie seems light and sandy, but well-grassed and capable of yielding oats, potatoes, etc.," he noted happily in the high plateau west of the Rockies. Best of all, trees "lent a grace and hospitality to the landscape."[25] Even the Nevada desert had its points of oasis in the Carson and Truckee river valleys. "Large cottonwoods dot its banks," wrote Greeley of the Carson River, "and its valley, wherever moist, is easily rendered productive." With obvious relief, he added, "You feel that you are once more in a land where the arm of industry need not be paralyzed by sterility, obstruction, and despair."[26] Because of his obsession with trees, the Sierra Nevada received his most fervent compliments. "Almost every road is covered by giant, glorious pines!" Greeley exulted. "In short, I never saw anything like so much good timber in the course of any 75 miles travel as I saw crossing the Sierra Nevada."[27]

Despite his utilitarian bent, Greeley used some of the same conventions more romantic writers employed when describing the far western landscape. Like many others before him, he attempted to compare the Sierra Nevada range with the Alps. In some ways, the Sierra came up short as they lacked "the glorious glaciers, the frequent rains, the rich verdure, the abundant cataracts of the Alps," but they far surpassed them "in the wealth and grace of their trees."[28] Not unexpectedly, given his predilection for trees, Greeley came closest to waxing truly romantic in his description of the giant sequoias. The great size and extraordinary color of the trees impressed him, as did their incredible age. Obviously awed, he estimated "they were of very substantial size when David danced before the ark, when Solomon laid the foundations of the temple."[29]

Greeley rarely made such poetic digressions. He saw his task as in-

Laying Track on the Pacific Railroad

Here, railroad workers lay track in the midst of the plains, while a locomotive waits impatiently for its completion. The covered wagons in the distance and the Indians in the foreground demonstrate the soon to be obsolete frontier stage of development. (From Samuel Bowles, *Our New West*, 1870. Courtesy of the Bancroft Library.)

forming the American people of the West's agricultural possibilities. He believed the railroad would open the region for rapid settlement, and he wanted to assess its potential affect on the nation. Since he never strayed far from what would be the line of the transcontinental railroad, much of what he saw must have disappointed him. Great tracts of land from Kansas to California seemed to have no practical value. Aside from occasional mining rushes, which Greeley believed to be highly disruptive to the progress of the nation, much of the Far West offered nothing.

Greeley's disappointment in the natural landscape of the Far West only strengthened his resolve about the necessity for a railroad. What nature had left out of the West, industrious Americans could provide. Even if the land could not be farmed, a Pacific railroad would provide immense profits in passenger and freight traffic between California and the rest of the nation, stimulate important trade with the Orient, and, most importantly, help to unify the rapidly dissolving Union. Greeley concluded his book by stating, "My long fatiguing journey was undertaken in the hope that I might do something toward the early construction of the Pacific Railroad; and I trust that it has not been made wholly in vain."[30]

Much to Greeley's delight, Lincoln authorized the building of the Pacific Railroad only three years later. Greeley also set a pattern for journalistic travel in the West of the 1860s. The combination of utilitarian interest and poetic rhetoric characterized American responses to the landscape. As the transcontinental line became a reality later in the decade, other journalists followed Greeley, until the steady stream of visitors resembled a veritable invasion. Almost moments after reporting on the surrender at Appomattox, journalists came to cover the next news story of the era, the construction of the Pacific Railroad.

One of the earliest and most publicized visits of the railroad-building era included Schuyler Colfax, then speaker of the House of Representatives, Samuel Bowles, editor of the important Springfield *Republican*, and Horace Greeley's crack western correspondent, Albert Dean Richardson. The purpose of the trip was clear: they wanted to drum up enthusiasm for the coming railroad, to survey what the far western landscape could contribute to the developing nation, and, perhaps, to give Americans something optimistic to read about after the carnage of civil war.

Even though their interest in promoting the railroad resembled Horace Greeley's, this group of newspapermen saw a very different West. Less concerned about the actual fertility of the land, Bowles and Richardson could hardly contain their enthusiasm for the potential of a landscape that only needed the magic of the railroad to convert it into tangible wealth. "You will see half a Continent waiting for its vivifying influences," Bowles promised. "You will witness a boundless agriculture, fickle and hesitating for lack of the regular markets the railroad would give."[31] Equally effusive, Richardson believed the Pacific Railroad to be "the grandest material enterprise of all time. The very thought of it is inspiring."[32]

Like Greeley, they thought of themselves as pioneers, even though hundreds of thousands had traveled this path before them. Samuel Bowles wrote in the introduction to his book, "I could hardly realize, until I had examined the subject, that there was in our literature no connected and complete account of this great Western Half of our Continent." He admitted that others had seen the West before, but he believed "that they have gone with other objects than to see, to study, and to describe . . . and have taken little time to look about them and observe the fantastic fashions of Nature, or worship the majestic beauty."[33]

However incorrect his conceit may have been, it did reflect the new importance the impending construction of the railroad gave to the Far

West, and especially to the line of the forty-first parallel. More than ever the facts of the landscape would affect Americans. Observers wanted to examine all of its possibilities, yet the knowledge of the path the iron horse would take across the continent limited the scope of their investigations. Instead of looking at the broad panorama proffered by the West, they inspected only the slender strip of the transcontinental line. Paradoxically, the new vision made possible by the railroad also blinded many of these observers to the variety in the western landscape.

With irrepressible enthusiasm, Bowles and Richardson set off to describe what the railroad would bring to the American people. Predictably, they both found Kansas to be a dream come true. "No land could be richer," wrote Bowles in his best booster style, "no sight could more deeply impress you with the measureless extent of our country, and its unimproved capacities."[34] The usually utilitarian Richardson believed that a magician must have touched uninhabited Kansas, for "it appears the perfect counterfeit of cultivated field and orchard."[35]

However, as they left the green prairies, differences in the outlooks of the two journalists quickly appeared. Richardson, clearly a protégé of Horace Greeley, hated the brown and treeless landscape. Because he could not envision it supporting farmers, it had no beauty. The most memorable portion of his ride across the plains was a pool of stagnant water "covered with green scum, " from which he was forced to drink. "As I lay down to drink," he remembered with obvious disgust, "a sluggish lizard crawled in from the bank."[36] Bowles, on the other hand, attempted to find something attractive in every kind of landscape. Nothing could be entirely useless. Of the drier portion of the Great Plains, Bowles believed that it was "not a desert, as such is commonly interpreted —not worthless by any means. . . . It is, indeed, the great Pasture of the Nation."[37]

The word *pasture* gentled the landscape and made it into something Americans could understand. His use of such language demonstrated that Bowles recognized the importance of making the Far West familiar. He became a master at finding analogies, however inappropriate. Richardson, perhaps a less flexible observer or perhaps simply more honest, looked for places where American families could settle and raise a crop.

As they continued west, the differences in their observations increased. In Denver, Richardson complained about unkempt mining towns and the rockiness of the soil. In the tradition of Horace Greeley, he wanted to find stable agricultural communities with green pastures and trees. Bowles, however, found something of great value as he looked out of his window in Denver: an American Switzerland. Thrilled, he wrote that "all my many and various wanderings in the European Switzerland, three summers ago, spread before my eye no panorama of mountain beauty, nay none equaling, that which burst upon my sight."[38]

Such a description merely repeated what John C. Frémont and a host of other observers had said about the Rockies. The railroad, however, made the American Switzerland accessible. Even more than fertile farmland or great pastures, European scenery transfixed eastern newspaper readers. Bowles understood this and made the dry plains between Laramie and Salt Lake City attractive to his readers by finding bits of Europe in them. He considered the ride through Echo Canyon "most picturesque." It was "a very miniature Rhine Valley in all but vines and storied ruin."[39] The sight of Echo Canyon after the monotony of the dry plains moved even Richardson to use romantic analogies about "mountains that rival Switzerland" and "skies of Italian beauty," a very unusual slip for him.[40]

Bowles, now dependent on European comparisons, found himself in a difficult position when he reached the great deserts of Nevada and Utah. They resembled nothing he had seen before, leaving him no language for an optimistic description. He saw the region as a place "whose uses are unimaginable, unless to hold the rest of the globe together, or to teach patience to travelers."[41] Richardson had better luck. His interest in agriculture alerted him to the possibilities of irrigation. He believed that irrigation would make the desert a "thing of the past." Happily, he imagined that "the thousands upon thousands of miles of sage-brush and grease-wood, sand and alkali . . . will yield barley oats and fruit as profusely as the Mississippi Valley."[42]

Both writers found much to compliment in California. It offered the rich farmland Richardson dreamed of as well as the spectacular scenery preferred by Bowles. While Bowles ranted about the Italian and Swiss beauties of Lake Tahoe and the Sierra, Richardson ogled the great ranches of the Sacramento Valley and the green hills north of San Francisco. The trip to Yosemite struck both of them dumb—momentarily—until they could grip their pens more tightly and spew out twenty pages of description. Here, where even Horace Greeley had penned romantic phrases, Richardson and Bowles let loose with European analogies.

The accounts of Greeley, Richardson, and Bowles represented the kinds of description possible in the 1860s when the railroad inched across the continent. Their styles ranged from the entirely utilitarian to the unabashedly romantic. Greeley, interested only in finding landscapes that would suit the small farmer, used almost no European analogies, while Bowles found bits of Europe in nearly every part of the Far West. Greeley measured worth by the number and size of trees, and Bowles by how much a particular region resembled Europe. Richardson, though clearly Greeley's disciple, found European analogies soothing in places that seemed impossible for agriculture.

Interestingly, rather than choosing the compromise between the two modes of description that Richardson represented, writers, tourists, and artists chose Bowles's methods for the next two decades. Because most tourists had little interest in farming and because many people in this privileged group craved an American Europe, they found Bowles's words most appealing. Bowles's *Across the Continent* reads like a blueprint for every guidebook, travel account, and tourist reminiscence to appear in the first decades of transcontinental train travel.

Bowles examined the scenery offered by the Pacific Railroad route carefully and immediately recognized which parts American travelers would find acceptable and which parts they would despise. He did not look for unique landscape nor for ways to create new farmland. He understood that the people who would become American tourists wanted to find Europe in America, and he gave them ways of seeing it.

Once leading newspapermen like Greeley, Richardson, and Bowles deemed the Far West suitable for journalism, thousands of writers, artists, photographers, and tourists poured west to investigate the railroad route. They sought a combination of an American Europe and American novelty, hoping to thrill armchair readers and to please their editors.

The presence of such reporters reflected the popularity of travel literature and western themes in this era. *Harper's Monthly*, the most widely read American journal, had a circulation of over 200,000 throughout most of the 1860s. *Harper's Weekly*, a less expensive publication, probably reached even more readers.[43] Descriptions of the West and tales of western adventure remained popular throughout the 1860s, but after the end of the Civil War, hardly an issue of these publications went by without an article on the West of the transcontinental railroad. The *Atlantic Monthly*, a prestigious literary journal of the late nineteenth century, also showed considerable interest in the Far West. Equally influential were the books published by famous travelers such as Bayard Taylor and Fitzhugh Ludlow, who had long pleased Americans with their descriptions of European jaunts.

Most journalists stayed in the path of the new railroad and described it with methods developed over the last thirty years. The Far West offered exciting adventure. Because it had not been entirely settled, a few dangers still existed. Travel involved uncertainties about food, weather, and hostile natives. At the same time, the region also provided some wonderful and safe novelties in the buffalo, prairie dogs, mines, and Mormons. Ideally, then, this landscape could be represented as having the beautiful scenery of Europe with the added spice of American dangers and eccentricities.

Upon seeing the far western landscape for the first time, however, most writers forgot about possible dangers and concentrated on the wonders. Their words showed the frustrating split between the unique scenery they saw and their ability to describe it for their readers. These journalists recognized that the Far West did not replicate Europe. In fact, they insisted that it presented something entirely new. In 1867, Bayard Taylor wrote in the *Atlantic Monthly* that the western territories "are not mere repetitions of the old lands, suggesting to us the magic of a past which our people can never really possess." He added that the landscape was "unlike any other scenery in the world."[44] Similarly, Fitzhugh Ludlow, the author of the popular *Heart of the Continent*, explained that the front range of the Rockies could not "be described by any Eastern analogy; no other far mountain view I ever saw is at all like it."[45]

Despite the claims about the originality of the far western landscape, these writers used European analogies to describe every possible aspect of the scenery. While crossing the prairies, Fitzhugh Ludlow recorded that he found it "impossible to convey the strange impression of this lovely region of lawns without mansions."[46] As he neared South Pass in Wyoming, Ludlow claimed "in all the wonderful suggestions of Dore's 'Wandering Jew' there is nothing to compare with the frightful stone shapes and faces which occur on this plateau."[47] His reaction to Church Butte in the Green River demonstrated the same inability to find appropriate language. Ludlow saw "the suggestions for an order as fresh and original as . . . the life and energy, spirit and material of the New World," but he struggled to find words for this new order. In desperation he wrote that the butte resembled "the pure Greek of the Parthenon or the Gothic of Salisbury Cathedral."[48]

Describing the Rocky Mountains presented similar problems. Bayard Taylor warned "who-ever comes to the Rocky Mountains with pictures of the Alps in his memory, expecting to find them repeated on a grander and wilder scale, will certainly be disappointed."[49] However, Taylor claimed, Colorado was "destined to become for us what Switzerland is to Europe." He could only explain the attraction of the terrain by demonstrating how it resembled the Alps. "If you could take away the valley of the Rhone," he calculated, "and unite the Alps of Savoy with the Bernese Overland, you might obtain a tolerable idea of the view of the Rocky Mountains."[50] Other observers agreed. "This is a true Swiss scene," exulted William Dixon, "a scene as striking in its natural features as the more famous view of the Oberland Alps from Berne."[51]

Even if parts of the landscape did resemble Europe, writers also found entirely unfamiliar areas. Many ignored these regions, especially if they involved looking beyond the line of the railroad. J. Ross Browne, a frequent contributor to *Harper's Monthly*, took a trip across southern California and Arizona in 1864. His efforts to find suitable analogies for the sights in that region revealed the difficulty of such an endeavor. The opening of Browne's article showed the negative impressions Americans had already received about this region. "I have now to offer a new programme of exploration and adventure," he promised his readers. It would present "extraordinary advantages in the way of burning deserts, dried rivers, rattlesnakes, scorpions, Greasers, and Apaches; besides unlimited fascinations in the line of robbery, starvation, and the chances of sudden death by accident."[52]

In spite of this grim and melodramatic beginning, Browne found much to offer his readers in the desert. Mono Lake, the mysterious alkaline water body in California's Owens Valley, could be compared to the Dead Sea. "Not even that wondrous sea, whose bitter waters wash the ruined sites of Sodom and Gomorrah, presents a scene of greater desolation." Even so, Browne noted, "for grandeur of scenery and for interesting geological phenomena, this lake of the Western Sierras is far superior to the Oriental Sea."[53] In the Mojave desert, despised by most visitors, Browne found "a perfect model of architectural beauty," complete with "ramparts and embattlements melted into a dreamy haze, out of which gradually emerges a magnificent palace, with pillars, cornices, and archways, and a great dome."[54]

Other writers rarely ventured into such odd territory, finding the railroad route perplexing enough. When Fitzhugh Ludlow tried to describe the vegetation of the high plains of Wyoming to his eastern readers, he stooped to less glamorous comparisons. He explained that eight hundred miles of plains were covered with "a stunted piece of herbage, growing in ash-tinted spirals, . . . giving the Plains an appearance of being matted with curled hair."[55] As the land grew drier farther west, his description grew even less complimentary. Simply, it became "a landscape which Genius itself could not beautify."[56]

Though many writers seemed reluctant to describe landscapes that they could not immediately classify as European, they enjoyed writing about a few anomalies that made the landscape especially picturesque. Observers understood that many of the creatures that bounded, slunk, and flew across the lands of the West had no European counterparts. Because they recognized from the start that comparisons to European fauna would be inappropriate, the journalists found new ways to describe buffalo, prairie dogs, and antelope.

Much of the material concerning the fauna of the Far West focused on the joys of hunting, especially the buffalo. By the 1860s large numbers of wealthy sportsmen came west to hunt buffaloes before the railroads drove the shy animals away. Americans took great pride in the lumbering beasts that roamed the plains, but they also loved to shoot them, most not realizing this would eventually destroy the animals and, eventually, their sport.

Like many observers in the years immediately before the advent of train travel, Fitzhugh Ludlow found the sheer multitude of buffaloes most impressive. As he watched a herd numbering in the hundreds of thousands, he remarked with awe, "never did I see such an incarnation of vast multitude, or resistless force, which impressed me like the main herd of buffalo."[57] Bayard Taylor also saw the great herds, but he worried about their wanton slaughter. As stagecoach travel became common in the 1860s, so did the practice of shooting the animals from the coach for amusement. Each passenger could kill dozens. Taylor also noted the effect "this wanton killing of their game" had on the Plains Indians, who depended on the buffalo herds for survival.[58]

Many visitors in the 1860s expected Indians, like the buffalo, to add a charming, American dimension to the landscape. However, the railroad and the white people it carried west changed the lives of many tribes irrevocably. The powerful tribes on the Plains recognized the threat represented by the railroad. It would bring white people to stay. White settlers would break up their hunting grounds; white travelers would kill off their source of meat; and white businessmen would introduce cattle to graze on their lands. These justifiable fears convinced some tribes to take a stand and battle the intruders.

Warfare broke out on the Great Plains by the mid-1860s. United States troops covered the region and met the Indians in a series of bloody encounters. For the Indians who chose to fight, this was a battle to the death. Nearly thirty years of war destroyed much of Plains Indian culture, either by disease, starvation, or outright butchery. The few who survived the decades of battle and who managed to stay off of the reservations either fled to distant reaches of the Plains in small bands of outlaws, or were reduced to begging for survival in the new towns that sprang up along the railroad line.[59]

Now that the railroad would bring new groups of white Americans into contact with native Americans, writers faced the problem of describing these people to a generation of Americans who had never seen an Indian. Because tribes in the eastern United States had been wiped out or driven onto distant reservations, most white ideas about Indians came from the novels of James Fenimore Cooper and the paintings of George Catlin, which presented images of noble children of the forest or Plains warriors. At the same time, correspondents reporting on the Indian Wars described bloodthirsty savages.

This split in American attitudes toward native Americans complicated the expectations of visitors to the West. Fitzhugh Ludlow, like many observers of the 1860s, waited anxiously for his first view of the Indians of his dreams. "I was particularly anxious to see the noble Indian," he wrote, for he regarded the Indian "as a sort of every-day Alexander the Great, slightly tinctured with Damon and Pythias."[60] Bayard Taylor could hardly restrain his joy upon his first sighting of Indians. "Indians, with vermillion faces and streaming black hair," he exulted. "Beautiful beings, all of them with paint smeared faces and hideously suggestive hair and blankets. Uncas and Cora—heroes and heroines of romance!"[61]

Because visitors expected to find Cooper's Uncas and Cora residing along the train tracks, they were almost inevitably disappointed. The U.S. government had forced most Indians onto reservations far from the railroad line, and the few that remained in sight of tourists did not have the nobility that white Americans expected. As Samuel Bowles stated matter-of-factly, "the red man of reality is not the red man of poetry, romance or philanthropy." Instead, Bowles judged, "he is false and barbaric, cunning and cowardly, attacking only when all advantage is with him, horrible in cruelty."[62] A reporter from *Harper's Monthly* described some Kiowa Indians in a similar way. "A wilder-looking crew could scarcely be imagined; cunning, duplicity, treachery, were stamped upon every lineament."[63] Clearly, many white observers believed Indians should be romantic additions to the landscape, shadowy figures that added charm to the passing scene, not cunning savages who had the power to frighten white Americans.

Even worse, from the perspective of romantic observers, were the degraded Indians present at stage stops and railroad towns. Robbed of their ability to hunt and forced to live at the fringes of white society, these people appeared to be drunken beggars, even farther from Cooper's heroic figures. In 1867 Albert Dean Richardson looked sadly at an Indian man dressed in tattered clothes and drinking from a whiskey bottle. "Mr. Cooper died too early," he noted. "I think one glance of this aboriginal would have saved his pen much labor, and early American literature many Indian heroes."[64] Another visitor described these Indians in blunter terms. "Filthy, stolid, degraded wretches . . . They infest every station." He concluded, "They are not human."[65] Because the Indians did not turn out to be picturesque additions to the landscape, many visitors reacted angrily. The "false and barbaric" savages or the "degraded wretches" did not add the delightful native charm nineteenth-century travelers expected.

These real Indians, complete with human defects, threatened the package promoters had created to sell the far western landscape. Writers sought out comparisons to Europe even as they realized the West also

The Journalist's View of the Indian

The journalists who came west to observe the building of the Pacific Railroad in the 1860s were disappointed by the Indians they saw along the tracks. The Indians did not live up to the images created in fiction, and journalists created a vicious new stereotype. (From Albert Dean Richardson, *Beyond the Mississippi*, 1867. Courtesy of the Bancroft Library.)

contained some strange anomalies that would have to be included in a full description of the scenery. They hoped such oddities as buffalo, antelope, and Indians could add a picturesque quality to the often monotonous terrain. Many parts of the region, however, could not be described in any reassuring romantic, picturesque, or even sublime language. Few writers had the rhetorical tools to make the scenes attractive or comprehensible.

Capturing the View: Artists and Photographers in the 1860s

Most of the artists and photographers lured to the Far West by the railroad had a similar lack of vocabulary. Like other western observers of the 1860s, artists had strong preconceptions about the landscape. Now, few accompanied explorers, and they did not have the same topographic or ethnographic purposes as the artists who ventured forth in earlier years. Trained in Europe or in European ideals of beauty, they hoped to capture the sublime and beautiful scenes that would please Europeans and Americans alike. The West, they believed, could make American landscape painting significant.

The first artist to make the far western landscape famous and familiar was Albert Bierstadt. An ambitious young man from New Bedford, Massachusetts, Bierstadt studied in Europe for several years. He made little impression on the painters studying in Düsseldorf, but he did learn a lot about mountain scenery in his travels around the European countryside. He returned to New Bedford in 1857 and began to develop a modest reputation as a painter. In 1859 Bayard Taylor came to New Bedford to lecture on the Far West. As he listened to Taylor describe the fabulous scenery and the interesting personalities, Bierstadt decided to travel west. The unpainted void of plains and mountains would give him fresh material and a chance to make a name for himself.[66]

A few months later, Bierstadt joined Colonel Frederick Lander's expedition to map a new route for the Overland Trail. The young artist recorded his adventure in letters to the prestigious art journal the *Crayon*. The scenery did not stir Bierstadt until he reached the Rocky Mountains. Here he discovered massive peaks that "resemble very much the Bernese Alps." Happily, he reported that "their jagged summits, covered with snow and mingling with clouds, present a scene which every lover of landscape would gaze upon with unqualified delight."[67]

Albert Bierstadt, *The Rocky Mountains, Lander's Peak* (1863)

Bierstadt's popular and tremendous painting gave many Americans their first view of the mountains of the Far West. It presented the European landscape Americans hoped the West would contain. (Courtesy of the Metropolitan Museum of Art. The Rogers Fund, 1907.)

Like many observers, Bierstadt loved the Rockies because they could be compared to the Alps and because they also had unique characteristics. After commenting on the resemblance to European scenes, Bierstadt noted, "We are among a different class of mountains; and especially when we see the antelope stop to look at us, and still more the Indian, his pursuer, who often stands dismayed to see a white man sketching along in the midst of his hunting grounds."[68] Such scenes inspired Bierstadt to create an American version of the picturesque landscape.

When Bierstadt returned to his studio, he painted just that: towering Alps with American flourishes. His first famous painting, *The Rocky Mountains* (1864, Metropolitan Museum of Art, New York), featured massive granite peaks, partly obscured by snow and hazy cloud formations in a brilliantly lit background. The foreground depicts an Indian camp, complete with tepees, braves, horses, dogs, and sagebrush. The two parts of the painting are sharply divided, with the sublimity and power of the European Alps floating above a tranquil American genre scene.

This combination met with the wild approval of critics and the public. *The Rocky Mountains* brought Bierstadt instant fame. In 1864 he entered the colossal painting (nearly 6 feet by 12 feet) in the painting competition at the New York Sanitary Fair and hung it in a hall directly across from Frederick Church's already famous *The Heart of the Andes* (1859, Metropolitan Museum of Art, New York). In a competition for audiences, Bierstadt hired some Indians to camp in a wigwam in front of his painting while Church arranged exotic tropical plants in front of his. Such stunts encouraged thousands of people to view the two paintings. Bierstadt cashed in on this popularity by arranging for a salesman to stand by and take orders for chromolithographs of his painting.[69]

Not only did Bierstadt impress the public at the fair, he also received accolades from important critics. The art critic Henry Tuckerman raved about *The Rocky Mountains*. He called it "a grand and gracious epitome and reflection of nature on this continent—of that majestic barrier of the West, where the heavens and the earth meet in barren proximity, where snow and verdure . . . primeval solitudes, the loftiest summits and the boundless plains, combine all that is most vast, characteristic, and beautiful in North American scenery."[70] He meant, of course, all that was most European.

The results of an 1863 trip to the Sierra Nevada and to Yosemite increased Bierstadt's popularity and the fame of the far western scenery. Engravings and chromolithographs of his paintings sold in editions numbering in the thousands, and many prints of his work appeared in popular journals. The paintings themselves often brought in $5,000 to $35,000 each and graced the walls of the most prestigious homes and museums in the nation.[71]

Bierstadt's vision of the Far West presented exactly what educated Americans hoped to find in their landscape. It combined aspects of the sublime and the picturesque by contrasting towering peaks and boiling clouds with peaceful gatherings of people and animals below. Bierstadt's paintings made the West seem safe by creating scenes that enclosed the viewer and denied the vast empty space of the Far West that made Americans so uncomfortable. He offered a West that tamed its sublimity to meet the standards of European beauty, and combined it with identifiably American picturesque elements.

His work attracted Americans because its style drew on several European traditions. Bierstadt's training on the fringes of the Düsseldorf School appears in the clean lines, sharp crags, and precise details of his landscapes. The traditions of the pastoral scenes of Claude Lorrain are evident in the leafy trees that frame the scenes and in the water and mountains that fade into the background. The turmoil of his clouds and the color of his sunsets make clear Bierstadt's debt to the more dramatic works of Salvator Rosa and other romantics. Although this may have been a deceptive view of the Far West, such a recognizable artistic lineage made both the paintings and the landscape understandable for their viewers.

The paintings had an unmistakable impact on American expectations about the landscape in the 1860s. Many travelers went west looking for the scenes Bierstadt depicted on canvas. "Bierstadt," explained Samuel Bowles in the preface of his book, "has caught the glow and the inspiration and the majesty of some chief natural wonders in these distant regions, and spread them on immortal canvas to excite a world's wonder."[72] Albert D. Richardson noted that many people had written about the scenic wonders of the Far West, but such sights "did not attain wide celebrity until lately," when "the bold pencil" and "warm coloring of Albert Bierstadt" found them.[73] An English tourist wrote that "the very mention of the California landscape draws English thoughts toward Bierstadt, and the great painter has honor in his own country, no less than in ours."[74] On canvas, Albert Bierstadt captured what many tourists dreamed of finding in the Far West: sublime American visions that could be described in European terms.

The same vision appeared in other media. Just as the tracks of the transcontinental railroad began inching over the Far West, the technology of photography provided new ways to see the landscape. Photography, first introduced in the United States in the form of daguerreotypes in 1839, had a special attraction because it promised to capture reality. Using a variety of chemical processes, the daguerreotypist seemed to snatch the true appearance of objects, people, and places out of the air and to re-create them magically on glass or, later, on paper.

Such a re-creation of reality suited the landscape of the American West perfectly. Photographs promised the accuracy Americans had sought in written descriptions, paintings, lithographs, and panoramas. Finally, they hoped, they could truly discover the Far West that the railroad would

bring them. Explorers, writers, artists, and railroad promoters could now prove the existence of the natural wonders they had struggled to describe.

Landscape photography developed rather late in the history of western exploration and of photography. The complex methods and the bulky equipment required for daguerreotypes made field work nearly impossible. These methods seemed suitable only for portraiture in which the subject could sit in a carefully controlled environment. Despite such limitations, western explorers saw the importance of photographic images for mapping and topographic work, as well as for publicizing the region. Several of the Pacific Railroad surveys had photographers along to supplement and verify the work of artists, but these pioneers had little success with landscape photography in less than ideal conditions.[75]

The first successful daguerreotypist of the far western landscape, Robert H. Vance, capitalized on the hunger for reliable information about California in 1851. He planned to offer eastern audiences a complete view of life in California, and he made three hundred images for a New York exhibition. Large crowds rushed to see the prints because as the catalogue assured customers, "these views are no exaggerated and high-colored sketches, got up to produce effect, but are as every daguerreotype must be, the stereotyped impression of the real thing itself."[76]

Audiences responded to Vance's exhibit because it claimed to tell the truth. It appeared at the same time as many of the popular panoramas depicting the Far West, but it provided realism beyond the dreams of any panorama artist. Photographs seemed to offer vicarious experience. A review of Vance's show demonstrated the attraction of this idea. "On looking upon these pictures, one can imagine himself among the hills and mines of California, grasping at the glittering gold that lies before him; wandering over the plains, along the beautiful rivers."[77] Even more than painting, photographic images promised to tell people what was really there. Although Vance enjoyed some success, the complexity of the daguerreotype method and its inability to make more than a single image prevented his work from becoming well known.

Steady advances in the technology of photography soon made it possible for photographers to work outside and to make multiple prints for widespread distribution. One of Vance's apprentices, Carleton E. Watkins, was the first landscape photographer to take full advantage of these improvements.[78] Watkins developed a style that combined painterly aesthetics and photographic reality to make the western landscape appealing to American audiences. His success inspired a host of photographers to fan out over the railroad line in the 1860s and to take photographs using many of his techniques.

Watkins achieved fame with his photographs of Yosemite Valley, which he first showed in New York City in 1862. Oliver Wendell Holmes reported in the *Atlantic Monthly* that Watkins's photographs were "a perfection of art which compares with the finest European work."[79] Large numbers of influential New Yorkers saw the show, bringing national attention to Yosemite Valley and to Carleton Watkins.

American viewers liked these early photographic masterpieces because they resembled paintings. The scenery captured by Watkins combined many of the same elements that made Bierstadt's work appealing. Like Bierstadt, Watkins did not present a complete picture of the Far West or even of Yosemite Valley. He photographed objects and scenes that he knew would please his audience. Tree-covered mountains, rushing streams, fabulous waterfalls, and great rock formations fill the images he made of the California mountains. To create such visions, Watkins relied on the same aesthetic sense that guided painters of the time.

Watkins's use of painterly aesthetics and his conception of proper material for images are evident in a collection of photographs in *The Yosemite Book*, issued by the Geological Survey of California in 1868. California officials recognized the important publicity good photographs could produce, especially since the railroad would soon bring curious tourists west. They asked Josiah Dwight Whitney, the head of the survey, to write a popular book in addition to the official report "to call the attention of the public to the scenery of California."[80] Watkins's images illustrated both the official report and the book intended for the public.

The twenty-eight photographs Watkins used in *The Yosemite Book* demonstrate the style that made his photographs so appealing. His composition included careful framing and a sharp contrast between light and dark. Most of the photographs have tall trees in the corners of the foreground, not unlike the framing used by Claude Lorrain and his American followers in the Hudson River School. Watkins also combined a sharply focused dark foreground with a hazy, but brightly lit, background. Each photograph centers on a single object, such as a rock monolith or a waterfall.

Carleton Watkins, *The Three Brothers* (1868)

The dramatic rock walls of Yosemite soar above the quiet forest in this image. The careful composition of the photograph demonstrates the influence of painting in Watkins's work. (In Joseph Dwight Whitney, *The Yosemite Book*, 1868. Courtesy of the Bancroft Library.)

A plate entitled *The Three Brothers* centers on a massive three-tiered rock formation that fades into the background. Sharply defined trees fill the foreground, while light sparkles off the river running through the lower right corner of the image. The picturesque and quiet river scene softens the towering sublimity above. Another image, *The Yosemite Falls*, features the hazy plumes of the falls fanning out over a sheer rock wall. Dark oak trees and carefully focused plant life dominate the foreground.[81]

Like Bierstadt's paintings, these images present an ideal version of the landscape—carefully balanced, silent, and grand. Watkins presented a view of Yosemite that people wanted to see: a pristine wilderness containing sublime objects and pastoral moments. Bierstadt's paintings of Yosemite and the Rocky Mountains demonstrate analogous interests and compositions. Watkins and Bierstadt made these mountain regions into

Carleton Watkins, *The Yosemite Falls* (1867)

The trees in the foreground form a perfect frame for the splendor of Yosemite Falls in this classically composed image. (In Joseph Dwight Whitney, *The Yosemite Book*, 1868. Courtesy of the Bancroft Library.)

places Americans could instantly understand and appreciate. They provided American scenery with an acceptable vocabulary.

Carleton Watkins's work had special impact because it used the medium of photography, which gave the illusion of creating exact replicas of the objects photographed. Watkins, however, clearly recognized the art involved in photography. He learned how much he could manipulate conditions and compositions. His sharp focus and light contrast made Yosemite and its surroundings into a region of fantastic sculptures in granite and water. The stupendous scenery, elegantly composed and deceptively framed in Watkins's photographs, reassured Americans of the scenic value of the Far West.

Most people saw the work of Carleton Watkins and the photographers that followed him through the lenses of a stereoscope. First invented and marketed in England, the stereograph brought photography into the daily lives of millions. A double image, mounted on glass or paper and viewed through a lens that brought the two images together, created a three-dimensional effect. A Philadelphia firm introduced the stereograph into the United States in 1854. It became available to large numbers of Americans in 1859 when Oliver Wendell Holmes, a dedicated photographer as well as medical scholar, invented the handheld stereoscope, which made viewing easy and inexpensive.[82]

Stereographs quickly became a nationwide rage. Large American firms developed mass-marketing techniques and sold vast numbers of views. From the start, landscape views were the most popular because they produced the most dramatic illusions of depth. Such views, seen through Holmes's stereoscope, became fixtures in American parlors. *Frank Leslie's Illustrated Weekly* deemed the stereograph "the poor man's picture gallery."[83]

Holmes himself explained the attraction of the stereograph in a series of articles in the *Atlantic Monthly*. "The first effect of looking at a good photograph through the stereoscope is a surprise such as no painting ever produced," he claimed. "The mind feels its way into the very depth of the picture. The scraggy branches of a tree in the foreground run out at us as if they would scratch our very eyes out."[84] The combination of three-dimensional effect created by the double images and the fact that the stereoscope allowed a photograph to fill the viewer's entire field of vision created a startling illusion of reality. In fact, Holmes predicted, stereographs would make travel unnecessary. "The sights which men risk their lives and spend their money and endure sea-sickness to behold," he wrote enthusiastically, "these sights are offered to you for a trifle, to carry home with you, that you may look at them at your leisure, by your fireside."[85]

Many of the places Americans wanted to see without leaving their firesides were located in the Far West. Among the most popular series published by E. and H. T. Anthony, one of the largest stereograph producers in the 1860s, were "Yosemite Valley, California" and "Glimpses of the Great West." Other companies specialized in images of the new transcontinental railroad. Carleton Watkins's Yosemite stereographs received the dubious honor of being immediately and widely pirated by other photographers.[86]

When Americans looked at these images, many of them had a specific idea of what they wanted to see. They hoped to be reassured by familiar European beauties in the Far West, not shocked by a strange landscape. Because stereographs were a consumer item, photographers created what they believed people desired. Photography had not yet developed into a muckraking or even an investigative medium. Its consumers expected images to reflect and to illustrate what they already knew, not necessarily to present things in a new light. Essayist Susan Sontag notes that "the characteristic visual taste of those at the first stage of camera culture" is to believe that "photographs are supposed to display what has already been described."[87] Mid-nineteenth-century Americans exhibited exactly this "visual taste" by purchasing views that were reassuringly familiar.

In photographs of cities, perhaps the most popular subject for early photographers, Americans sought immaculately crisp images that demonstrated the dignity, beauty, and grandeur that politicians promised progress would bring. People who bought photographs wanted to see stately facades, wide clean streets, and splendid gardens and fountains adorning their cities. Historian Peter B. Hales has done an extensive analysis of urban images from mid-nineteenth-century America. He concludes that photographs produced for popular consumption created just such an image of dignified grandeur, despite the unfinished state of many nineteenth-century cities.[88]

This same tendency to create fantasies rather than to present reality appears in photographs of the Far West. Carleton Watkins and a few other photographers developed a set of suitable conventions for presenting western scenery, and others copied it faithfully. Carleton Watkins's Yosemite pictures had created a great stir, alerting photographers to the possibilities of American landscape. It could offer a profitable combination of European sights and more exotic visions.

Explorers, journalists, and artists had told Americans over and over again that the Far West contained rich farmland, great cities, spectacular scenery that resembled Europe, and picturesque additions such as buffaloes and Indians. Therefore, the public expected photographs to show them these things. They wanted images to reassure them that the Far West could be made comfortable, familiar, and civilized. The views Americans chose portrayed either the evidence of progress or familiar kinds of scenery.

The producers of stereographs obliged. The San Francisco firm of Lawrence and Houseworth, one of the largest retailers of western stereographs, began publishing views in 1862. Quickly, they discovered that scenes of the most familiar areas sold best. San Francisco, Yosemite, the Big Trees, and certain landmarks along the new transcontinental railroad seemed most popular. Their catalogues offered views of mines, railroads, and cities, demonstrating the American fascination with technological development. Landscape scenes included objects like the Big Trees, high peaks, and mountain lakes. These images produced a superlative image of the Far West that included "the most gigantic of these forest growths" and "the most sublime portions of this scenery."[89]

Lawrence and Houseworth sold almost no images of deserts, Indians, or strange wilderness. In 1870, they advertised a series on the Central Pacific Railroad. It contained 135 stereographs, all of railroad tracks, tunnels, cars, or mountain scenery. No views of the Nevada deserts or mountain ranges, Indian tribes, or even California farmland appeared in the collection. The firm did issue a small series on Nevada, but it included only the Comstock mines and street scenes of Virginia City.[90] Apparently, Americans would pay for familiar kinds of scenery or evidence of progress. Images of unfruitful deserts and unsettled plains seemed to be a marketing risk.

From almost the moment they began laying track, railroad companies recognized the importance of photography for publicizing their endeavor. At the same time, aspiring photographers sensed the public demand for pictures of the region covered by the railroad and of the building of the line. People wanted to know what the railroad would bring and where it could take them. Photographs, they believed, could provide this information. Photographers and railroad publicists hoped that such images could provide fame and profit, and the efforts of Carleton Watkins showed them a way to do this.

Many photographers traveled west, including those hired by the railroads and independent operators who searched for objects and landscapes that would sell well in the East. Both groups faced the task of creating a vision that Americans would pay to see. The location of the railroad line and prejudices about what made a beautiful view limited the scope of the photographic vision of the West in the 1860s. This vision complemented what had been described before, but occasionally, it provided tantalizing glimpses of the novelty the Far West could offer.

Scores of photographers spread out over the lengthening railroad line, but I have chosen the work of three to discuss here. Because each of these photographers worked in a different geographic region and each found different solutions to the "problem" of the far western landscape, they represent a wide range of approach. Alfred A. Hart operated independently out of Sacramento, taking pictures of the Central Pacific Railroad as it climbed out of the Central Valley, over the Sierra Nevada, and into the Great Basin. Hart reasoned that the railroad would bring a stream of travelers through Sacramento who would want photographs as mementos. For similar reasons, Charles R. Savage set up shop in Salt Lake City, hoping to capitalize on the new tourist trade. The Union Pacific Railroad hired Andrew Joseph Russell as its official photographer in 1868 to help attract customers.[91] Taken together, Hart, Savage, and Russell demonstrate how photographers dealt with the geographic diversity and the often unfamiliar appearance of the Far West.

Alfred A. Hart seemed to have the easiest task. He chose to photograph objects and places that could be portrayed in the aesthetic styles demonstrated by Carleton Watkins. Hart made several series of stereographs covering the entire line from Sacramento to Promontory Point, Utah. These series, however, did not represent a complete view of the area. Hart concentrated on the scenery of the Sierra Nevada and the heroic efforts of the Central Pacific to cross them. Nearly all the images are scenes between Sacramento and the onset of the Nevada desert. He

A. A. Hart, *From Tunnel Number Ten, Looking West*

This image is part of a stereograph series on the Sierra Nevada mountains. The ragged tunnel opening dwarfs the human figures, making the scene ominous rather than triumphant. (From Stereograph Series, 1867–69. Courtesy of the Bancroft Library.)

emphasized familiar mountain scenery and the bold forms of bridges, snowsheds, road cuts, retaining walls, and tunnels.

Hart chronicled the presence of man in a difficult environment, and in most of the photographs nature dominates. The trees, mountains, and boulders dwarf the most impressive bridges and tunnels. A stereograph entitled *From Tunnel Number Ten, Looking West* positions the viewer inside

A. A. Hart, *Rounding Cape Horn*

Hart creates a dramatic moment in this image, which would be deepened by the three-dimensional effect of the stereograph. The train appears to be heading for a cliff as it rounds the track that clings to the mountainside. (From Stereograph Series, 1867–69. Courtesy of the Bancroft Library.)

the tunnel, looking at a group of men building a retaining wall. The hillside looms over them, and the dark, ragged tunnel opening threatens to swallow the tiny railroad track. A stereoview of a locomotive engine rounding Cape Horn on the steepest western slope of the Sierra has a similar motif. The locomotive, though it fills a large part of the image, clings precariously to the edge of a cliff as the track disappears around a corner, seemingly into space. The three-dimensional effect of the stereograph increases the illusion of a mighty engine teetering on the edge of oblivion.[92]

Hart's pure landscape views are gentler. He composed views covering great panoramas, rather than focusing on single objects as Carleton Watkins did. *Summit Valley from Lava Bluff* includes snow-covered hills, quiet streams meandering through grassy meadows, and the distinctive peaks surrounding Donner Summit. Such an image contained everything Americans enjoyed in landscape: sublime peaks, thick forests, and pastoral meadows.[93] Only when the railroad had to conquer such terrain did the landscape seem hostile. Left alone, it presented a strong but quiet beauty.

A. A. Hart, *Summit Valley from Lava Bluff*

Hart's stereograph presents the kind of mountain scenery tourists craved. He managed to find a scene that combined mountain peaks, meandering brooks, and lush forests. (From Stereograph Series, 1867–69. Courtesy of the Bancroft Library.)

Hart seemed unable to grapple with the desert landscape of the Great Basin, which offered none of the familiar scenery favored by tourists. He solved most of the problem by ignoring the region. In a guidebook he advised tourists to settle comfortably for the ride across Nevada, for "we pass over a vast expanse of uninteresting desert."[94] The few images Hart did include of the six-hundred-mile section emphasized the barrenness of

C. R. Savage, *Temple Block, Salt Lake City* (1867)

Savage's photograph focuses on the huge forms of the Mormon Tabernacle and the Mormon Temple, still under construction. These architectural wonders seem monumental in the Great Basin landscape. (Courtesy of the Bancroft Library.)

the scenery and the task of laying track across it. Railroad ties, locomotives, and workers serve as focal points in these pictures, demonstrating the human domination of the landscape.[95] In his guidebook, Hart included only pictures of mountain scenery. Deserts and railway building did not seem as important in attracting tourists.

Because C. R. Savage chose the center of the Great Basin as his territory, he could not simply ignore desert landscape as Hart had. He did dismiss a large portion west of the Great Salt Lake. "I do not think it possible," he stated in a letter to a Philadelphia photographic journal, "to secure more than five or six good views in the distance of four hundred miles west from Salt Lake City."[96] Instead, he focused on the small portions of it that could be made comprehensible to eastern viewers. In the region including Salt Lake City, the Wasatch Mountains, Echo Canyon, and the Great Salt Lake, Savage found a more congenial landscape, filled with natural and man-made architecture.

He discovered the sculptural qualities of the strange forms that dotted the landscape. His photographs emphasized single objects, such as *Temples of the Rio Virgin*, or various forms in Echo Canyon. These objects could be described in architectural language and became landmarks for tourists. Savage also learned to describe the scenery in biblical terms. Rocks became temples; and salt deserts became Sinais, giving the scenery added historical weight.

Savage also civilized the strange landscape by depicting urban development. Much of his inventory consisted of images of Salt Lake City, especially buildings that could be identified as "Mormon," which made them especially attractive to eastern buyers, fascinated by the imagined evils of Mormonism. The city, combined with mountains, deserts, and lakes, made Utah into a conglomeration of natural and man-made temples, sculptures, and gardens. Forms that could not be described in architectural or sculptural terms rarely appeared in Savage's images.

The Union Pacific photographer A. J. Russell, deprived of alpine vistas or urban scenes, dealt with the starkness and strangeness of the far western landscape in a powerful way. He did not deny its presence or search for references to other places. Trained as a photographer during the Civil War, Russell learned to take pictures of military bridges, buildings, and fortifications.[97] Union Pacific officials clearly hoped he would glorify their construction in the same way, showing the domination of technology over nature. They also wanted him to portray the scenery so that it would lure tourists west on the new Pacific Railway.

Russell succeeded at both of these tasks. Like Savage's work, Russell's photographs often centered on a distinct object though he also captured the magnificent spread of the landscape. In *Castle Rocks*, the stunning butte that rises up from the Green River looms over the left rear quadrant of the image. The river and the bluffs on its bank disappear into another corner, showing the awesome sweep of the view.[98] Russell evoked even more drama in his railroad views, which depict a battle between human effort and the power of nature.

His best-known work focused on the building of the Union Pacific Railroad. Like Alfred A. Hart, Russell saw great tension in the relationship between the natural environment and the structures created by the

A. J. Russell, *Castle Rocks* (1868)

Russell chose natural architectural monuments as the focal points of his landscape. The stately butte looms over the tiny figure fishing in the river. (In Ferdinand V. Hayden, *Sun Pictures of Rocky Mountain Scenery*, 1870. Courtesy of the Bancroft Library.)

railroad. Russell, however, found a bigger challenge in uncovering the drama and beauty of the high plains regions of Wyoming and Utah. Hart gave up when confronted with the Nevada and Utah deserts; Savage turned them into architectural displays; but Russell found power in such landscapes. His most successful photographs balance the stark grandeur of the landscape against the heroic task of building the railroad.

In *Citadel Rock* a great, dark butte rises up out of the snow-dusted plain. A set of sturdy railroad tracks looms up in the right corner of the foreground. Both the tracks and the butte seem powerful, ordered, and permanent, but the humans and other structures look oddly puny and disorganized.[99] Russell often utilized this theme of human insignificance, which fit well with the taste for the sublime in the nineteenth century, though it might have disturbed railroad promoters. In many images,

A. J. Russell, *Citadel Rock*, (1868)

The tremendous bulk of Citadel Rock trivializes even the heroic task of railroad building. All of the human additions to the landscape appear puny and temporary in comparison to the natural landform that provides the focus in this photograph. (From Ferdinand V. Hayden, *Sun Pictures of Rocky Mountain Scenery*, 1870. Courtesy of the Bancroft Library.)

tremendous rock formations as well as man-made structures dominate human figures. Humanity appears unable to control nature or its own creations.

The Union Pacific Railroad issued Russell's dramatic work in a series of stereographs and in a lavishly illustrated book called *The Great West Illustrated*. Both of these appeared in 1869, just as the railroad prepared its opening festivities. Ferdinand V. Hayden, head of the United States Geological Survey, who burst into public view as the official discoverer of Yellowstone, wrote a book accompanied by many of Russell's photographs. Hayden modeled *Sun Pictures of Rocky Mountain Scenery* after Josiah D. Whitney's successful *Yosemite Book*. He explained that he intended "to present to the world some of the remarkable scenery of the Rocky Mountain region, through the medium of photography, as the nearest approach to a truthful delineation of nature."[100] Photographs, in Hayden's view, would tell people the truth about the landscape.

Hayden designed the book as a vicarious trip across the Union Pacific. Its thirty photographs appeared in geographical order from Cheyenne to Salt Lake City so that they worked as a kind of panorama of the landscape. They presented the windswept plains as a stupendous collection of awe-inspiring rock formations, cliffs, jagged mountains, railroad cuts and bridges. This heroic landscape met American expectations about the Far West. It offered sublime landforms, and also paid tribute to American determination and skill in the silhouettes of water towers and bridges.

The photographers of the 1860s did not necessarily widen knowledge about the Far West. For the most part, despite their claims about the truthfulness of photography, their images echoed the tradition developed by explorers, writers, and artists in earlier decades. As artists, they immediately attached themselves to prevailing ideals of scenery, which included sharply delineated definitions of the romantic, beautiful, or sublime. As businessmen, they photographed objects and scenes that would appeal to Americans concerned with the lack of ideal scenery in their landscape. Once again, the concept of the Far West as a haven of European beauties and sublimities stood out in images presented to eastern viewers.

These photographers developed acceptable ways to read the landscape. With careful composition and judicious choice of subject, they made the deserts, high plains, and mountains into a vision Americans could understand. They presented dramatic Alpine landscapes, architectural wonders, and powerful railroads. They did not always deny the existence of deserts, they just filled them with great sculptures and castles. Americans who saw the work of such photographers believed that it represented a total view of the Far West. Even more eagerly than ever, they awaited the opening of the transcontinental railroad.

Building a Vision: Promoters and the Pacific Railroad

Railroad officials encouraged interest in western landscape. From the very moment of ground-breaking in Omaha and Sacramento, they sought ways to publicize railroad construction and the scenery through which it traveled. Both the Union and Central Pacific railroads hired publicity agents and offered travel passes and other perquisites to writers, artists, and photographers. Promoters developed two general themes to keep the railroad on display. The first emphasized the heroic qualities of the task of construction. The second adapted the concept of an American Europe to include some of the unique traits of the far western landscape.

In the earliest phases of construction, as ground was broken and as engineers and workers battled to cross mountain passes, the drama of railroad building made exciting reading. Again, in the final years of construction, 1868 and 1869, when the two railroad companies raced to reach Promontory Point, the feverish pace of building riveted national attention. Almost daily, newspapers reported on the miles of track laid and on the valiant efforts of workers and management.

The middle years of the railroad project, immediately following the Civil War, however, presented a publicity problem. Not only had construction slowed to a crawl, but the line had also reached the singularly un-European landscapes of the high plains and deserts. The escalation of Indian warfare only compounded the problem. Plains Indians on the warpath did not convey the romantic and safe images railroad officials had hoped to create. To combat the image problem, promoters came up with elaborate publicity stunts to showcase the favorable aspects of both the railroad and the far western landscape.

In October of 1866, when the Union Pacific line reached the one hundredth meridian on the Nebraska-Wyoming border, only several hours by rail from Omaha, the railroad staged a grand celebration. Actually, railroad officials had little to celebrate. In four years they had laid only a few hundred miles of track across a flat plain. People everywhere grumbled about the expense, slowness, and obvious corruption of the project. In order to combat such public-relations setbacks, Thomas Durant and Silas Seymour, the most active officials of the Union Pacific, organized a train excursion for two hundred politicians, financiers, and journalists.[101]

Hoping to prove the safety of the railroad and the beauty and economic potential of the West, Durant and Seymour extended invitations to "the President of the United States, and members of his cabinet; also to all the members of Congress, Foreign ministers, military and naval commanders, and the principal railroad men and leading capitalists throughout the country." Not everyone accepted the invitation, but nearly two hundred people agreed "to join in a grand excursion from New York City to the 100th meridian in the Great Platte Valley."[102]

Railroad officials orchestrated every aspect of the trip in keeping with the images they wanted to portray. After spending nearly a week on a train from New York City, with festivities in many of the towns they passed, the invited guests gathered in Omaha for a "gala ball." From there they took a flag-festooned excursion train to Fort Kearney, right near the one hundredth meridian line. The two-hundred-mile trip took more than two days, and the railroad hosted a luxurious camp-out for the dignitaries.

To demonstrate its control over the Indian population and to suggest the romantic, rather than the dangerous, possibilities of traveling across the plains, the railroad staged an elaborate Indian battle. They hired a group of Pawnees to pose as a Sioux tribe and to attack another Pawnee group in a sham battle. Apparently, the battle thrilled every spectator. "All was confusion and intense excitement," reported Silas Seymour, "until at length the victorious Pawnees brought their vanquished enemies into camp, amid the most tempestuous shouts of triumph and exultation."[103] Such a domesticated Indian battle pleased American travelers. This was the sort of Indian they hoped to find in the Far West—brave, strong, romantic, primitive, but entirely safe—and the railroad made sure to provide this version of the Indian.

After demonstrating control over the Indian population, the railroad emphasized the power of technology at elaborate festivities at the one hundredth meridian line, marked by a huge white banner that stretched across the empty plain. Here, the guests took part in a grand celebration that included marching bands and a magnificent fireworks display.[104] The railroad had brought the wonders of civilization to what most Americans considered the middle of nowhere. The photographer of the event, John Carbutt, stressed the human presence in his pictures of the extravaganza. Elegantly dressed dignitaries, a flag-covered train, workers swinging heavy hammers to lay track, and blanket- and feather-covered Indians peopled a blank landscape stretching into an enormous sky.[105] Silas Seymour, the Union Pacific official who planned the extravaganza, noted proudly that this display of modern civilization must have amazed the "distant savages and wild beasts, who might happen to be the witnesses of this first exhibition of the kind in the great Platte Valley."[106]

Railroad officials tried to be equally obliging about far western scenery. The one-hundredth-meridian celebration put them in a difficult situation because the short distance the railroad could take visitors contained none of the kind of scenery Americans hoped to see. Cleverly, they planned the most important parts of the excursion for night when much of the landscape was invisible. They provided a war dance and a sham battle by firelight; and on the return from Fort Kearney, officials arranged to set a distant tract of prairie on fire. Seymour explained the purpose of the destructive act: "The train was immediately halted and time given for all to drink their fill of the sublime spectacle."[107] Such sublimity, they hoped, would make up for the lack of mountains, forests, and waterfalls in the Nebraska prairie. The additional excitement of a buffalo hunt and a visit to a prairie-dog village helped to make the landscape novel, rather than ugly.

The Union Pacific excursion demonstrated the concern promoters felt about making the Far West attractive, exciting, and safe. Clearly, railroad officials believed that the Far West needed selling, especially the regions crossed by their railroad. They planned the excursion to convince Americans that the railroad would carry them to a fascinating place in absolute safety. In publicizing the excursion, they emphasized the glamour of Indians, buffalo, and prairie fires, but they also pointed out the power of the railroad in taming the landscape and its inhabitants. The formula developed for this grand event was apparently a success. Like a panorama, it paraded the most acceptable parts of the Far West past an audience eager for entertainment. The authors of travel accounts, guidebooks, and railroad publicity material used the Union Pacific excursion as a blueprint for what they offered American readers and tourists in the next fifteen years.

A year later, in 1867, the Central Pacific Railroad planned a similar celebration when the track reached the summit of the Sierra Nevada, 105 miles from Sacramento. Though less grand than the Union Pacific excursion, the event planned in December of 1867 by Central Pacific officials involved more people. Clearly, the Central Pacific wanted to demonstrate their successes and to show the nation the wondrous possibilities of the railroad.

Although the event received wide press coverage, it could hardly be claimed as a public-relations victory. From the start a series of embarrassing incidents plagued the excursion.[108] On the morning of December 7, more than seven hundred invited guests, including every important official in California and every available reporter, climbed aboard ten bright yellow railroad cars. The trip began well. The train moved up through the heavily forested foothills, which presented "scenery and atmospheric coloring worthy of the brush of the Heart of the Andes" artist [Frederic Church] himself," according to a reporter.[109] The excursionists gazed happily at mountain scenery that could satisfy such an esteemed artist as Church.

At Emigrant Gap, about halfway to the summit, the trouble began. A jerky start from the station pulled a bumper off of a passenger car, hurling a passenger from the train. Fortunately, he sustained only minor injuries and the trip continued. Upon reaching the summit, some seven thousand feet above Sacramento, the train stopped again, allowing the passengers to enjoy the scenery and to examine the handiwork of the railroad. Some of the excursionists listened to the inevitable speech given by a railroad official, but as one observer reported, "a more numerous body engaged in snowballing with great zest."[110]

At this point the train engineers pulled the train into the uncompleted main summit tunnel to give observers more opportunity to appreciate the grand feat of railroad building. However, as the locomotive moved out it left most of the passenger cars in the smoke-filled tunnel, and "great consternation prevailed." After about fifteen minutes, the engineers realized their mistake and reattached the cars. Almost immediately one passenger discovered that his pockets had been picked, leading to "the impression that the difficulty in the tunnel was caused by pickpockets who wished to practice their art during the opportunity thus afforded."[111]

This episode, plus the increasingly cold temperatures, sobered the excursionists considerably. The fact that another car broke off on the trip down did little to improve their perceptions of railroad travel. Like the Union Pacific, the Central Pacific had tried to advertise the beauties of the far western landscape and the way in which the presence of the railroad made this scenery safe and accessible. The trip up to the summit did convince the guests of the Central Pacific that the Sierra Nevada offered lovely scenery, but it did not impart much confidence in the railroad. A newspaper reporter gave the excursion a lukewarm review. "Notwithstanding all of the drawbacks," he concluded, "everyone was pleased with the trip."[112]

A. J. Russell, *Promontory Point, May 10, 1869*

This photograph by A. J. Russell appeared all over the nation after May 10, 1869. The two locomotives and the men shaking hands represent the literal joining of east and west that signified the completion of the transcontinental railroad. (Courtesy of the Bancroft Library.)

Such publicity stunts, even unsuccessful ones, kept the railroad and its limited portion of the Far West in full public view. However, from the moment trains moved on newly laid tracks, so did great numbers of correspondents from eastern papers and magazines. These writers competed to present the most exciting stories and the most current information about the progress of the railroad, further intensifying national interest in the thin line of the railroad. Most correspondents emphasized the themes already developed by the railroad: the European beauties of the landscape, the power of the railroad, the distinctive flora and fauna, and the exciting but safe presence of Indians.

By the mid-1860s, American readers had been bombarded by information about the landscape traversed by the railroad. The riches it would bring them and the new experiences it would make possible had all been discussed in rather astounding detail. By 1866, *Harper's* J. Ross Browne could promise at the beginning of an article describing his adventures in the Far West, "I will not subject the reader to the perils of another trip across the mountains. The road is familiar to him by this time. He has seen it in winter, spring, and summer—by daylight and by moonlight."[113] Another correspondent noted the ubiquity of travel writing when he commented, "I do not know of any traveler who has visited San Francisco without writing a book."[114] His observation may not have been wildly exaggerated. Most issues of popular journals of the period included some mention of the far western scene; and hundreds of books described the trip west, reflecting the curiosity Americans had about the area.

If the building of the railroad created a burst of interest in the region surrounding the forty-first parallel, the actual opening of the line encouraged a literal frenzy. Hundreds of reporters from east and west, and equal numbers of eager spectators, raced to the windy spot in the middle of the desert to witness the historic joining of the Central and Union Pacific railroads on May 10, 1869. The long-awaited passage to India was now a reality.

Journalists rushed to ticket offices hoping to arrange passage on the first transcontinental trains. The lucky few who managed to be included could be sure that their stories would receive wide attention. Less than ten days after the completion of the track, the first trains rolled out of Omaha and Sacramento filled with important railroad officials and established journalists like Horace Greeley, Samuel Bowles, and Albert D. Richardson. Even though these early trips could not be described as complete successes because of the discomforts of hastily laid track, poor and exorbitantly priced food, and scheduling difficulties between the two railroads, most of the reports from these first trips were positive.

Throughout 1869 as the Union and Central Pacific worked the many kinks out of the poorly constructed track, hundreds of writers described the heady experience of transcontinental travel. Optimistically, the editor of *Harper's Monthly* wrote, "The Pacific Railroad has opened not only a new country for travelers, but a new vein of literature for readers."[115] A journalist who regarded the Far West as his territory could not summon up the same enthusiasm about the swarms of writers. "Every man who could command the time and money was eager to make the trip, and all who could sling ink became correspondents. . . . My local occupation was spoiled."[116]

Most writers reported just what railroad promoters hoped they would, repeating what had been said earlier, only with new enthusiasm. According to the first eagerly read accounts of the trip over the newly opened line, passengers could see sublimity that would instantly transport them to parts of the Old World. Many claimed the scenery far surpassed anything one might find in any other part of the world. One observer noted a spectacular prairie sunset that "in Italy, would have been gorgeous, unrivaled, and worthy of any amount of florid description, but on our western prairie was simply beautiful," indicating the superlative and European appearance of the landscape.[117] Samuel Bowles, whose book *Our New West* appeared almost immediately after the opening of the Pacific Railroad, made extravagant claims about the West's European beauties. In describing Gray's Peak in the central Rockies, he exulted "in impressiveness, in overcomingness, it takes rank with the three or four natural wonders of the world. . . . No Swiss mountain view carries such majestic sweep of distance, such sublime combination of height and breadth and depth."[118] such effusive reports seemed to promise the Europe Americans had always wanted.

Even better, western scenery offered more than a re-creation of Europe. Many writers noted the presence of Indians, prairie dogs, and buffalo, which gave the passing vista an American version of the picturesque without robbing it of its European grandeur. Journalists also underscored the safety and civility of the railroad experience, hoping to play down the violent images that had come out of the Plains Indians Wars and the struggle against the Mormons. No lesser expert on life on the plains than Margaret Carrington, who had written a book about her experiences as an army officer's wife on the Great Plains, made promises about the safety of the railroad. "In fact, the course of the road does not lie through the regions where the Indians dwell or make any abiding halts." She assured anxious readers that "a *railroad* is not easily injured by the Red Man, and he has too much to risk with too little to gain by such enterprises."[119]

As with the Indians, promoters often felt obligated to assure potential passengers that they would not be physically or morally endangered by the Mormons who were thriving in the Great Basin desert. Most writers noted the beauty and economic success of Salt Lake City. "I thought it the most beautiful place I had ever seen," explained one journalist, "and failing to note that nearly all this beauty was of nature's making, it appeared to me that they could not be a bad people who occupied such a place."[120] Samuel Bowles, long suspicious of the Mormons, did think of them as a bad people. He told potential visitors that the steadily rising Great Salt Lake would soon take care of the difficulty. He mused hopefully, "Does Providence propose to drown the Mormons out, and with water solve the problem that is puzzling our moral philosophers and statesmen?"[121]

Despite the exciting scenery and inhabitants of the Far West, many writers found parts of the trip a disappointment, mostly because of the unfortunate location of the new track. Naturally, it avoided the highest peaks of the Rockies and the Sierra and made its way across the flattest and driest sections of the Far West. As one person noted, "the summit of the Rocky Mountains is gained by a scarcely perceptible ascent. They are physically more difficult to comprehend than when you see them traced by a decided line on a map, or when you look at Bierstadt's picture."[122] Bierstadt had obviously created expectations that the railroad route was unable to fulfill. Samuel Bowles, the eternal booster, managed to find the material advantages of this scenic deficiency. "Nature graded a grand pathway for the locomotive across our Continent; the mountains fall so far away that we catch only the dim outline of their greatness."[123]

The huge expanse of the Great Basin frustrated the most sanguine observers. At best they found ways to describe it as sublime in its dreariness. "Not a green tree, shrub, or spear of grass was to be seen," exclaimed one shocked traveler who found the entire region to be "scorched and bare as if blasted by the lightnings of an angry God. All seemed sacred to the genius of drought and desolation."[124] Most writers, however, simply pretended the region did not exist, and their descriptions jumped from Echo Canyon or perhaps Salt Lake City to the familiar glories of the Sierra Nevada.

In addition to their efforts to portray the landscape in time-honored aesthetic terms, early advertisers for the Pacific Railroad also noted the presence of something new in the Far West. A contributor to the *Overland Monthly* noted the unique appearance of the landscape with some surprise. "Strange as it may seem," she admitted, "I was not prepared for the absolutely new appearance of the country."[125] Samuel Bowles, who had dedicated a great deal of effort into describing the Switzerland and the Italy of America, admitted that he could not categorize all of the Far West in this way. In one of the first guidebooks describing the transcontinental route he stated, "The field is too broad, also the variety of experiences to be had too great, and the forms and freaks of nature too strange and too numerous,—the whole revelation too unique and too astonishing—to be readily catalogued."[126] Sounding rather like John C. Frémont, Bowles recognized the problem of describing a distinctive place.

Even while commenting on the originality of the far western landscape, most writers used descriptions they knew would please the reading public and powerful railroad promoters. By 1869, a decade of intensive investigation by artists, photographers, and journalists had built upon preconceived ideas about far western travel. The popular reception of books by Horace Greeley, Samuel Bowles, and Albert Dean Richardson and of grand paintings by Albert Bierstadt and photographs by Carleton Watkins solidified these preconceptions. Guided by these precedents and by those laid out by the railroad in publicity excursions and pamphlets, the flood of literature in 1869 refined the safely mixed version of a Europe in America. Most writers provided a litany of awesome plains, picturesque prairie dogs, romantic Indians, sublime prairie fire, stupendous mountains, and pastoral fields. They rarely described anything outside of these categories.

From the wondrous, expansive landscape of the Pacific Railroad surveys of the 1850s, the landscape of the Far West had evolved by 1869 into a series of predigested vistas, spread out along the narrow line of the railroad. The Pacific Railroad surveys alerted Americans to the variety and novelty of the region, but the subsequent building and publicity surrounding the railroad narrowed this broad vision. Ironically, even though the presence of the railroad opened the West for settlement and faster economic development, it slowed recognition of the region's distinctive attributes. Railroad promoters had detected the hot-selling ticket of an American Europe, and they imposed this view on the parts of the far western landscape passengers could see from train windows.

This European-inspired framework hardly encouraged the "original discovery" heralded by Samuel Bowles, but it did lure thousands of pleasure travelers west in the 1870s. Early in 1869 the *Atlantic Monthly* advised potential passengers to "make a ninety-day note for your expenses, —well, say five hundred dollars a month,—the average Atlantic reader will hardly get off with less,—and leave a good endorser for any little contingency or delay, such as a pressing invitation to visit a 'friendly' Indian village."[127] Many privileged Americans took this advice and set off for the Far West, expecting to see what a generation of publicists had promised them: European scenery dotted with American novelties.

CHAPTER 3

Passage to an American Europe: The Tourist Experience on the Transcontinental Railroad, 1869–1880

When the transcontinental railroad opened in May of 1869, the Far West became accessible to Americans. For the first time, travel across the great distances of the West could be made quickly, comfortably, and safely—at least for those wealthy enough to purchase a ticket. The West became a tourist destination. Finally, Americans could see for themselves the wonders that had been so widely portrayed in newspapers, magazines, paintings, and photographs. As tourists, they hoped to find a landscape that would resemble Europe in beauty and in cultural value. They also hoped for an introduction to the eccentricities that gave the Far West an American flavor.

In turn, railroad promoters intended to do everything in their power to make sure eager tourists found just what they looked for in the scenery. Using imagery and rhetoric imported from Europe to describe the West, railroad publicists carefully created a program for seeing it. Because the railroad route limited the tourists' vision to a narrow and often drab path, writers and agents had to work hard to make the trip exciting. They stretched European analogies beyond credibility and attempted to deny the existence of some areas, testing the gullibility of the most eager tourist. Even so, the experience of transcontinental railroad travel convinced most travelers that the Far West did indeed hold some stunning sights, even if they did not always resemble European scenes.

Not everyone could afford to have this experience. For the first several decades of transcontinental service, the cost of traveling by train to the Pacific remained prohibitive to most Americans. Only the wealthiest and most leisured tourists could spend the time and money necessary for a trip across the continent. A round-trip ticket from Boston or New York City cost at least $300 and more if passengers chose to purchase a sleeping berth. One-dollar meals taken in haste at railroad stations had to be added in to the total cost. Side trips to see the Rockies or Yosemite ran $150 to $200 each. A guidebook published in 1873 estimated that a trip to California and back, with a few side trips to "the chief points of interest in California and Colorado," would cost at least $1,200, a price far beyond the means of most Americans.[1]

This kind of travel appealed to wealthy and educated Americans who could travel to Europe and who spent long vacations at elegant resorts on the East Coast. Many tourists and guidebook authors noted that a summer trip across the Far West cost the same or perhaps more than a summer in Europe. One traveler noted that it cost a New Yorker as much to see the Big Trees in California as it did to see Mont Blanc in Switzerland or St. Peter's in Rome.[2] For this kind of investment, American tourists expected a lot from far western scenery. They wanted to see the same kinds of natural and cultural wonders that enriched the Old World and that their own country lacked. For years, the Far West had been held out as the region that would fill the cultural gap with scenery that could be compared to the most famous sights in Europe. Certainly, a place that cost as much as Europe to visit should pack an equivalent cultural wallop.

Apparently, American tourists found something worth their time and money in the far western landscape. During the first decade of transcontinental travel, the numbers of travelers aboard first-class passenger cars increased steadily. In 1871 nearly thirty thousand boarded the Union Pacific cars in Omaha, headed for San Francisco. By 1875, this number had more than doubled to seventy-five thousand. By the end of the decade, one hundred thousand people traveled along the Union and Central Pacific lines every year.[3]

These numbers represented only part of a boom in tourist travel that began after the Civil War. Increasing national wealth, new attitudes toward leisure, and steadily lessening travel costs made vacation travel possible for much larger groups of Americans. Swarms of tourists poured into the traditional East Coast resorts and even to Europe.

The new, less wealthy and less "cultured" traveler upset the traditional leisured classes. They complained about the "horde of cheap tourists" who could now afford pleasure travel in the Old World. "An ignorant, pretentious, gregarious mob, they roam about aimlessly, talking loudly, putting on swaggering airs," noted one disgusted observer.[4] This sort of tourist, brilliantly satirized in Mark Twain's popular novel *The Innocents Abroad* (1869), became a stock complaint in travel literature of the period. The same "cheap tourists" now journeyed to the once-exclusive seaside resorts of Cape May and Long Branch, New Jersey.

The fact that American and European watering places could now be easily reached by large, new groups of travelers made them less attractive to their older, more traditional patrons. The expense and difficulty of travel to the Far West made this region especially interesting to the wealthiest Americans. In addition, the outbreak of the Franco-Prussian War in 1870 (soon after the opening of the transcontinental railroad), which made European travel more problematic, also helped convince many people to consider far western travel. They viewed the West as an exclusive region, free from the new groups of tourists who had invaded the eastern seaboard and Europe. They also hoped that it would satisfy their long-held desire to find an American version of Europe.

Creating Expectations

American tourists had very clear expectations about far western landscape. Years of travel in Europe and effective publicity about the West had provided them with an aesthetic language and a set of images concerning proper landscape and its far western version. An early guidebook to the transcontinental route defined the qualities Americans expected from the landscape. "The country visited must possess objects and scenery that will afford all of these three sources of pleasurable emotions: beautiful and charming vistas, grand and magnificent views, and grand, stupendous, magnificent, and sublime sights."[5] Terms like *beautiful*, *magnificent*, and *sublime* had specific meanings that referred to European scenery. Fifty years of exploration and description of the Far West had isolated and celebrated the bits of landscape that fit these definitions. Americans tourists wanted to see picturesque prairies, magnificent rock formations, and sublime mountains.

By the 1870s, however, most observers recognized that the Far West could offer more than a series of European vistas. Tourists wanted to see evidence of a West that seemed uniquely American. From the safety of the train, they wanted to view strange animals, as well as miners, desperadoes, Indians, and Mormons. At the same time, they wanted to be reminded of the power of civilization with huge and luxurious trains, telegraph wires, developing cities, good food, and pleasant hotels. The wildness of the landscape could only be comfortably accepted when it had been reduced to a few romantic details.

These desires and expectations about the Far West had been fueled by the publicity of the railroad-building years. Americans read accounts of the transcontinental trip, looked at photographs, paintings, and prints of the new region, and flocked to illustrated travel talks. Such information created a prefabricated West for future travelers who would know just what to expect. Technological developments in photography made vicarious "tours" even more lifelike and further imbedded the expectations developed in earlier years.

Just as the new railroad opened a device called the magic lantern was invented, which projected photographic images onto a large screen. A practiced lecturer, Stephen James Sedgwick, immediately recognized the importance of the device for travel talks, and he rushed west with the Photographic Corps of the Union Pacific Railroad to develop a series of illustrated lectures. He made some of his own views, and he also bought up a large number of A. J. Russell's glass negatives. Sedgwick understood what elite Americans wanted to see in the Far West. The images he projected and the commentary he provided created a vision of the far western landscape from Omaha to San Francisco that thrilled his audiences. He showed them only views that they expected and nothing that would surprise or shock them.[6]

A review from a Long Island newspaper explained the attraction of Sedgwick's lectures. "His audiences were transported to distant wilds, to terrific heights, translucent lakes, and natural scenes of . . . peerless sublimity. . . . We were made to feel eager to journey over the route to witness the scenes so charmingly presented."[7] Sedgwick's lectures appealed to audiences because they provided future travelers with a set of objects to look for, which reduced the huge expanse of the Far West into a series of familiar sights. Sedgwick himself explained that he hoped his show would "be of service to the travellers making the 'Transcontinental Journey,' inasmuch it indicated the principle objects they may desire to see."[8]

Sedgwick offered his audiences views of the West using imagery and rhetoric already familiar to them. They expected to see sublime mountain scenery in the Rocky Mountains. Obligingly, Sedgwick provided stunning views of the central range of the Rockies, even though none of these peaks could be seen from the train. Tourists also hoped to find picturesque prairies as they crossed Nebraska and Wyoming. However, much of the region crossed by the railroad was bone dry and anything but picturesque. Sedgwick solved this problem by showing a few views of the green area along the Missouri River just outside of Omaha and describing it as typical of the plains. "Here we enter upon that region where one beholds mile after mile of meadow, now level, now undulating," he wrote in the text for this part of the lecture. "Formerly, a stray gray wolf, an antelope, or a buffalo would break the monotony," he continued, but now "every few miles a thriving village, and fields of grain, orchards and large plantings of trees are seen."[9] The images from the magic lantern suggested to Sedgwick's audiences that the Garden of the World did truly exist and that the desert had been conquered.

If sublime mountains and picturesque prairies did not provide enough scenic delights, Sedgwick found rock formations that could replace the famed cathedrals and ruined castles of Europe. His show included a long series on the formations in Echo Canyon and another on the fantastic rocks in the Garden of the Gods, just south of Denver. Sedgwick likened these to "labyrinths, or ruins of medieval cities . . . or the ruins of the palaces of a race of unseen beings."[10] Such impressive rock formations helped convince American tourists of the value of a trip to the Far West. Their own country could provide them with a natural version of the cultural heritage they had found in Europe.

Sedgwick also emphasized the splendor of train travel. The images he chose made it quite clear that the Far West had all the trappings of civilization so important to the traveler. To assure tourists of the comfort and safety of travel, he included photographs of train tracks, immense bridges, and, especially, opulent train interiors. Such surroundings made the sublime and magnificent wilderness pleasant to look at but never threatening.

Oddly, Sedgwick never played up the image of the romantic Wild West. He chose to emphasize the European aspects of the far western landscape, rather than anything particularly American. He included no pictures of Indians, gun-toting desperadoes, or miners that Americans had read about so eagerly. Rarely, he showed a lone buffalo or antelope, but never the great herds that pleased so many observers.

Here, Sedgwick misjudged his audience. Most tourists, though they did not like the idea of venturing into an entirely alien wilderness, clamored for romantic bits of savagery. They did not seem to want a replication of Europe but rather an American version of it, which included standard sublime and picturesque vistas dotted with buffaloes, Indians, Mormons, and frontier gunmen. One tourist noted that when the train arrived at a western Nebraska train station, "the female members of our party brave the savages on the platform and stare wildly about in search of desperadoes." Much to their disappointment, all they found were "sober, quiet-looking citizens."[11] Another visitor noted his excitement at leaving the settled regions for more exotic sights. "Here we take leave of schools and churches and keep our eyes peeled for buffalo."[12] Most tourists expected to be thrilled but not ever frightened by reminders of the Wild West.

Even though Sedgwick's show ignored some of the distinctive elements of the far western landscape, it reflected the expectations of the first generation of railroad tourists. He provided them with the scenery, history, and associations lacking in most regions of the United States. Sedgwick did not create the concept of an American Europe, but his use of photographs and his compelling commentary convinced his viewers that it existed. Playing on the descriptions provided by several decades of travelers and explorers, performers like Sedgwick located the pieces of scenery that could be compared directly and effectively to European views. He found and described a tiny portion of the Far West, hoping to convince his audiences that a version of Europe existed in the Far West. The West, however, also contained many things that could not be compared to Europe.

Occasionally, these differences attracted visitors. Mark Twain's 1872 book, *Roughing It*, describes a trip he took in 1861 and illustrates the appeal of selected American novelties. Even though Twain's book describes a period before railroad travel, the parody of the foolish tourist encountering the Far West demonstrates American expectations about the region. To write the autobiographical account, Twain adopted the persona of an untraveled innocent who, like many early train passengers, viewed the Far West as a national depository of wonder and mystery. He could hardly contain his delight at the prospect of traveling "on the great plains and deserts, and among the mountains of the Far West," where he would see "buffaloes and Indians, and prairie dogs, and antelopes."[13]

Twain expected great things from his western adventure; and, at first, it met all of his expectations. He and his brother set out from Omaha in an express mail coach, hoping to reach Carson City, Nevada, in about three weeks. Spreading out the mailbags into comfortable couches, they prepared for a constant parade of wonderful sights. The prairie did not disappoint them. Its "impressive solitude" and "atmosphere of such amazing properties that trees that seemed close at hand were more than three miles away" more than lived up to their billing.[14] They soon saw their first prairie-dog villages, antelopes, coyotes, and genuine alkali water. This last item seemed to thrill Twain more than any of the others. "I know we felt very complacent and conceited, and better satisfied with life after we had added it to our list of things which we had seen and other people had not," he explained smugly.[15] So far, the West had provided a satisfying combination of familiar scenery and unique wonders.

Several days later, the stage reached South Pass and the Rocky Mountains. Here, Twain noted his first inkling of disappointment. Although he raved about the "convention of Nature's kings" and the "majestic purple domes," he admitted that the pass itself did not entirely meet his expectations. "As a general thing," he explained, "the pass was more suggestive of a valley than a suspension bridge in the clouds."[16] Twain also noted the barrenness of the land surrounding the pass, "a land given over to the coyote and the raven—which is but another name for desolation and utter solitude."[17] This mountainous region hardly resembled the green and merry Alps Twain had imagined and that travel literature had told him to expect.

If the Rockies did not meet all of the qualifications for beautiful and exciting scenery, the wonders of Salt Lake City more than made up for them. Twain found the Mormon city absolutely fascinating. Having read the usual biased accounts of Mormon life, he imagined dark secrets and hideous unknown practices behind every door. "This was fairyland to us, to all intents and purposes—a land of enchantment, and goblins, and awful mystery," he wrote with great delight. "We felt a curiosity to ask every child how many mothers it had and if it could tell them apart."[18] The Mormons represented a distinctly American aspect of the far western scene, and Twain enjoyed them thoroughly.

After spending a day prowling about Salt Lake City attempting to uncover all of its secrets, Twain and his brother reboarded the mail coach intending to enjoy the most exciting and romantic portion of their trip: the journey across the desert. Twain noted that they had crossed deserts before, but always at night so that they had missed what they assumed to be a grand spectacle. "Now we were to cross a desert in *daylight*," wrote Twain with great anticipation. "This was fine—novel—romantic—dramatically adventurous—this, indeed was worth living for, worth traveling for! We would write home all about it."[19]

Such anticipation only set Twain up for disappointment. The dry, sandy, tedious reality of the desert clashed with every idea he held about deserts. Historian Patricia Limerick has described the way in which the desert made a fool out of Twain. Instead of making him feel like a romantic and brave adventurer, it "left the human dwarfed beyond vision, passengers in a coach itself on the scale of a bug."[20] The dust stung his eyes, the heat wilted his clothing and his spirits, and the dryness parched his mouth. The desert offered nothing familiar, comfortable, or exciting. Twain commented rather darkly about his first true encounter with a desert, "The poetry was all in the imagination—there is none in the reality."[21]

Twain once again noted the difference between poetry and reality when he encountered his first "real" Indians, members of the Goshute tribe of the Great Basin. These Indians repelled Twain, who described himself as "a disciple of Cooper and a worshiper of the red man," with "disgust." Crushed with disappointment at the appearance of these real Indians, Twain noted that "it was curious to see how quickly the paint and tinsel fell away from him and left him treacherous, filthy, and repulsive."[22] The Indians of fact, struggling to survive in the desert, did not meet the expectations of the innocent Twain, schooled on the improbable figures created in Cooper's fiction.

Much of the Far West disappointed Twain as he played the role of the gullible tourist in *Roughing It*. The region rarely lived up to the reputation decades of publicity efforts had created. It never seemed as beautiful, romantic, dangerous, wealthy, or as familiar as earlier observers had promised. Even though Twain found the prairies to be glorious, the Rockies to be magnificent, Salt Lake City to be deliciously evil, and Lake Tahoe to be sublimely beautiful, large parts of the Far West seemed completely incomprehensible, alien to everything Twain knew.

The clash between expectation and reality Twain experienced and recorded in *Roughing It* would frustrate generations of tourists. Twain's 1861 experience seemed especially intense, however, because of his method of travel. The slow, jolting, uncomfortable mail coach made the more unpleasant parts of the journey seem eternal. Twain and his companions did not have to toil physically or worry about their survival, but they did suffer hunger, thirst, stiffness, and, especially, boredom. Ten years later, the splendor and comfort of transcontinental train travel altered conditions considerably.

The Experience of Transcontinental Train Travel

Travel by train changed the experience of traveling across the continent. Safety, comfort, and speed made the trip more pleasant and faster but also circumscribed the portions of the landscape that tourists actually saw. The far western landscape looked different from a train than it had from a horse, a wagon, or a stagecoach. Gazing out at scenery while seated in the plush luxury of a Pullman palace car hurtling along the track at twenty-five miles per hour affected the way people perceived the Far West. Mark Twain explained the significance of comfort while traveling when he observed that "nothing helps scenery like ham and eggs."[23] Scenery looks far better when viewed from the window of a coach and when the viewer has a full stomach. Such luxuries took the threat out of the wilderness and made it something to enjoy.

Train travelers in the 1870s enjoyed considerably more than the simple pleasures of ham and eggs. Almost as soon as the transcontinental line opened, George Pullman introduced an especially luxurious railroad car designed for long distance travel. The Pullman palace car oozed opulence, setting the standard for glamorous travel. As the Union Pacific claimed in 1870, "no royal personage can be more comfortably housed than the

Palace-Car Life on the Pacific Railroad

This lithograph illustrates the plush interior and the inward focus of the passengers on the transcontinental trip. They sleep, read, and sing songs, rather than looking out at the scenery passing by the train window. (Frontispiece to Henry T. Williams, *The Pacific Tourist*, 1876. Courtesy of the Bancroft Library.)

occupant of a Pullman car."[24] Passengers lolled in cars "fitted up with oiled walnut, carved, gilded, etched, and stained plate glass, metal trappings heavily silver plated, seats cushioned with thick plushes, washstands of marble and walnut," and ate in dining cars appointed with snowy linen, fine china, and silver flatware.[25] An enthusiastic tourist correctly described the Pullman cars in 1877 as "moving palaces, in which by day or by night the traveler may be surrounded with all the luxurious appointments of a first class hotel."[26]

Encased in a steel train and swaddled in Victorian luxury, wealthy American tourists could now look out at the far western landscape with no thought of danger. The comfort of the train reminded them of the progress of their nation as they gazed at the wilderness outside. A Union Pacific guidebook made the contrast specific. "On either side of the train are the prairies, where the eye sees but wildness and even desolation, then looking back on this long aisle, he sees civilization and comfort and luxury."[27]

Luxurious accommodations had important advantages for the tourist who did not choose to look at the scenery. If he found it too odd or too desolate for his taste, he could find a multitude of other things to occupy his time. Ideally, the quiet, smooth ride allowed travelers to "pursue all the sedentary avocations of a parlor at home."[28] Passengers wrote letters, read books, and gazed at photographs. The comforts of the parlor car made the overland tour "an intense delight," for "here you sit and read, play your games, indulge in social conversation and glee."[29]

People chose to write, read, and play games because the speed and luxury of railroad travel made the scenery tedious. Perceptive travelers had long noted this problem. The swiftness of the train made the scenery a rapidly moving blur. Ralph Waldo Emerson had noted the effect of this as early as 1843. "Dreamlike travelling on the railroad," he noted in his journal. "The towns which I pass between Philadelphia and New York made no distinct impression."[30] Speed had dissolved the landscape into an indistinguishable stream of sights.

A German historian, Wolfgang Schivelbusch, has explained that railroad travel required a new kind of perception. The blurred foreground isolates the traveler from the landscape close to the train and only allows him to see the general outline of the far distance. All detail near the train disappears. Schivelbusch calls this "panoramic perception."[31] The scen-

Northern Pacific Dining Car

Dining in this Northern Pacific Railroad car certainly distracted tourists from the tedium of the landscape and protected them from the uncivilized potential of the world outside of the train. (In Olin D. Wheeler, *Six Thousand Miles through Wonderland*, 1893. (Courtesy of the Bancroft Library.)

ery, which from a slow and bumpy coach had provided the only entertainment available, becomes a boring blur from the window of a train. The artist and critic John Ruskin noted that "travelling becomes dull in exact proportion to its rapidity," so that the train actually prevented sightseeing.[32]

Not only did the speed of train travel affect what people saw from the window, but it also changed their perceptions of the space covered by the train. Many nineteenth-century observers noted the phenomenon of the annihilation of space. The railroad linked places together as its speed destroyed the distance between them.[33] In the American West, however, the new experience of train travel did not conquer space. In a sense, the railroad created new spaces. It initiated large numbers of people to the reality of vast tracts of empty land. Because few towns interrupted the expanse and because travelers now spent days in what seemed like a gigantic void with very little to look at, space seemed to expand.

This sense of expanding space made the Far West seem desolate to many travelers. Its lack of recognizable landmarks often disoriented passengers who could find no way to tell how far they had traveled. Subtle geographical changes in the landscape, noted by early overland travelers, disappeared with the train's rapid movement. "We wake up and find ourselves along the great American desert, a wide expanse of desolation covered with tiny gray-green buffalo grass," remembered one tourist. Shocked by the barren landscape, she could only note that "all is bland and bare."[34]

Even in regions of the Far West that did have widely recognized scenery, many people wondered about the effect of the train's speed. One of the earliest guidebooks to the Union Pacific line told its readers that "the beauties of Echo Canyon are so many, so majestic, so awe-inspiring . . . we can only note some of the most promising features." The author warned, however, that "the only difficulty will be that one will hardly see them at all, as the cars thunder along."[35] Another writer feared that train travel would destroy the beauty of the Far West. "Ah! no one will be impressed by the sublimity of this scenery, when whirled through it at twenty miles per hour." He continued rather bitterly, "In fact, if the comments of the majority of recent passengers are any criterion by which the masses are to be judged, the only points of interest on the entire route are the meal stations."[36]

Much of this criticism was true. Great stretches of the Pacific Railroad route did bore tourists. The speed of the train and the "panoramic perception" it created did make the scenery seem tedious. The unfocused view encouraged travelers to talk, play games, and read rather than gaze out at the landscape. Train stations became memorable as moments when the train stopped, allowing people to get out, look around, and reestablish contact with the landscape—as well as to have a meal. Such artificial landmarks, rather than natural scenes, became highlights of the trip.

The Guidebook Vision: Panorama of Wonders

As the landscape disintegrated into a great blur, except for the punctuation of meal stations, tourists relied on guidebooks to tell them what was passing by their windows. Guides had been around since the late seventeenth century, when travel for pleasure had first come into vogue. With the advent of commercialized tourism in the early nineteenth century, guidebooks had become big business in Europe and in the South and East of the United States. Wealthy American tourists had learned to rely on their trusty *Baedecker's* or *Appleton's* for travel, whether by coach or by train, and a host of writers sought to cover the guidebook market for the American Far West.

Even before the first transcontinental train rolled across the Far West, entrepreneurs began selling guidebooks that purported to prepare visitors for the scenery they would see in the West. A clever entrepreneur, George A. Crofutt, claimed to issue the first one and sold nearly 350,000 copies of his *Transcontinental Tourist Guide* in the 1870s. At least twenty-five other writers published guidebooks in the same period.[37] Such guidebooks could be bought in every railroad station and major hotel in the East or the West, and salesmen roamed the aisles of the train hawking various editions.

These handy books had a very clear purpose. Each author claimed that his guide was the one from which "the tourist can most easily learn what he wants to see and how to see it."[38] George Crofutt made the most extravagant claims. His guide promised to tell the reader "where to look for and hunt the Buffalo, Antelope, Deer, and other game, etc., etc, In fact, to tell you what is worth seeing—where to see it—where to go—

Cover of *Crofutt's Guide*

This cover introduced tourists to the variety of wonders they would see on their trip across the West: Indians, buffalo, antelope, mountain, snowy peaks, and miracles of engineering. (*Crofutt's Transcontinental Tourist's Guide*, 2d ed., 1871. Courtesy of the Bancroft Library.)

how to go—and whom to stop with while passing over the Union Pacific Railroad."[39] A properly written guidebook allowed the tourist to see "the greatest possible variety of interesting places within a limited period."[40] Such claims reassured tourists that the Far West had scenic value and that reading a guidebook would prevent them from missing any important sights.

Some authors made more specific promises. One assured journalists that his descriptions contained such correct and minute detail that they would be able to "describe the wonders of the trip passed in the night, while sleeping soundly in a palace car, equally as well as though they were awake and in perpetual daylight."[41] This freed tired journalists or tourists from the responsibility of actually observing things for themselves. Another guidebook explained that it supplied the historical and statistical information to make the scenery meaningful. Knowing the reason for a name or the height of a landform gave importance to the landscape. Guidebooks provided a way for tourists to make sense of the landscape by describing sights in familiar terms and by making familiar, European comparisons.

Guidebook authors and other publicists recognized that they had to compete with the known attractions of Europe. "A trip to California is far more pleasing than one to Europe," stated one writer, obviously hoping to lure tourists away from the standard European trip. "You are all the while in your own country and the places visited are of far more beauty and interest."[42] Another author attempted to make far western travel a patriotic duty. "Of course no American will think of going abroad until he has seen something of his own country. . . . For really there is no excuse now for one who wants to travel and can afford it, and does not see some of the wonders of the West."[43] Given a proper context and some historic associations, the Far West would become a delightful place for tourists.

To assuage any doubts visitors might have about the dangers involved in western travel, early guidebooks often stressed the safety of the trip. One claimed that the Pacific Railroad will "surely afford as safe a travel as the midland counties of England and the Scottish highlands."[44] Others pointed out the rapid advance of white civilization in the Far West. "Once the home of the savage and wild beast," an 1869 guidebook noted, "the deep gulches and gloomy canyons are alive with the sounds of labor, the ring of pick, shovel, and drill."[45] Evidence of such material progress helped to convince Americans of both the economic potential of the region and the safety of travel.

In addition to being assured of the safety and the cultural importance of seeing the Far West, Americans also hoped to see something unique. Most publicity agents and guidebook writers recognized that large parts of the West could not be made into European vistas or booming towns. Promising tourists a series of novelties seemed to be an attractive way to describe these strange and unclassifiable sights. Charles Nordhoff, a well-known California booster, promised his readers that from the moment they left Omaha, they would "find everything new, curious, and wonderful."[46]

Nordhoff and most other boosters understood, however, that the Far West could not be portrayed as too new or curious. This sort of portrayal might threaten the European analogy writers had worked so long to create. By the end of the 1870s, they had developed a program for viewing the far western landscape that offered a careful balance of European wonders, economic progress, and American curiosities. Tourists expected the Far West to resemble a panorama, providing constant entertainment. Guidebooks attempted to create just such a spectacle. Much like the first publicity venture of the Union Pacific Railroad in the fall of 1866, guidebook writers manufactured an acceptable landscape when one did not appear naturally.

The process began as the train left Omaha and crossed the Great Plains. An 1870 guidebook promised "leagues upon leagues of undulating meadow land, sometimes as level as a verdant pasture, sometimes broken up by considerable ridges or valleys—nearly always boundless as the sea."[47] Rich greenery, rushing streams, and delicate flowers covered the expanse of this "inland sea." However, if the tourist delayed his trip "until the plains have been scorched and the grasses and flowers have withered," warned the guidebook, "he will wonder at the enthusiastic accounts of more fortunate tourists."[48]

Whether green or brown, however, the prairie landscape soon grew monotonous, and guidebook writers searched to discover ways to make it interesting. They pointed out the beauty of the sky. "There is no monotony in the glorious dawns or beautiful sunsets which are the rule on these elevated plains and which go far to relieve the tameness of the landscape,"

Banks of the Platte River

This engraving from an 1870s guidebook presented a vision of the plains that included large trees, flowing water, and snow-covered peaks—hardly what one would see from the train along the Platte River. (In W. H. Rideing, *Scenery of the Pacific Railways and Colorado*, 1878. (Courtesy of the Bancroft Library.)

claimed one writer.[49] Another guidebook hoped to satisfy its readers by explaining that the scene "would be monotonous but for its frequent atmospheric changes and for the occasional appearance of animals."[50]

Several hundred miles out, as the plains grew drier and browner, writers seemed more desperate to make the landscape attractive. One writer pointed out hidden economic boons in the "famous buffalo grass." "Though it gives to the country a dried look, as if the very appearance of desolation and sterility," he noted, "it is the richest grass ever known in the world."[51] Much better than grass, however, were the buffaloes themselves. Many of the guidebooks began advising tourists to "keep their eyes peeled" for buffaloes, which they promised roamed the railroad route in huge numbers.

If buffaloes did not thrill tourists, then the presence of Indians surely would. To describe one of the last stations in Nebraska, the author of an 1871 guidebook wrote, "Here many passengers see Indians for the first time; that is, genuine Indians, who live by hunting and take a pride in getting scalps."[52] Another guidebook made the negative stereotype of Indians less immediate by using the past tense. "Here the emigrant passed through deep ravines, once the dreadful lurking place of the Indians, who waited to surprise unprotected trains."[53]

Still shivering from this distant danger, the tourist now moved onto the high plains of Wyoming, where, the guidebooks claimed, he should begin looking for the Rocky Mountains. According to many guidebooks, observant travelers could see Pikes Peak and Longs Peak at a distance of nearly two hundred miles. Here, most writers delighted in describing the European glories of the Rockies. "The Alps, storied monuments of poetical, legendary fame, cannot compare with these mountains in scenes of sublime beauty and awful grandeur," crowed an 1869 guide.[54] While describing the scenery in Cheyenne, Wyoming, another writer exulted, "I now realize the truthfulness of Bierstadt's paintings of these hills." He claimed tourists would recognize "the dark, deep shadow, the glistening sides, and the snow-capped peaks."[55]

Despite some enthusiastic efforts to create towering Rockies in places that had none, most guidebooks admitted that the Union Pacific route through Wyoming did not provide optimum views of the Rocky Mountains. one of the bluntest stated, "You will not be pleased with the Rocky Mountains and their approaches; they are too crumbly; they look too

After Thomas Moran, *The Cliffs of Echo Canyon, Utah.*

The huge rock walls of Echo Canyon, the high point of the tourists' trip across the plains, lean ominously over the track in this exaggerated view taken from a Thomas Moran painting. (In Henry T. Williams, *The Pacific Tourist*, 1876. Courtesy of the Bancroft Library.)

Salt Lake City

Salt Lake City, with its neat Mormon homes and its tree-lined streets in the midst of the desert, surprised tourists who expected the city to reflect the perceived sinfulness of Mormondom. (In Thomas Nelson, *Great Salt Lake City and Views of Utah*, 1871. Courtesy of the Bancroft Library.)

much like tumbling to pieces while one is looking at them—the very antipodes of the solidly grand and awful."[56] Most writers of guidebooks, however, chose to describe the Colorado Rockies in glowing detail because they assumed that tourists would not want to leave the West "without visiting some of the most remarkable points of interest of the American Alps.[57]

After crossing the bleak and potentially disappointing region of the crest of the Wyoming Rockies, the railroad passed through some of the most spectacular scenery on the route, at least in terms of comparison to Europe. Writers did not have to resort to devious methods to make the region around the Green River and Salt Lake City interesting. They ranted about the fantastic rock formations of Echo Canyon that could be described as castles, fortresses, temples, cathedrals, and monuments. The scenery offered classic examples of sublimity among "the castellated monuments of red rock, whose towering domes and frowning buttresses gave the name to this remarkable opening in the Wasatch Mountains."[58] Salt Lake City, of course, offered so many exciting sights that guidebooks hardly had to invent them. The spectacular though strange scenery of the Wasatch Mountains and the Great Salt Lake combined with fascinating evidence of Mormon success and eccentricity often required a separate guidebook.

The greatest challenge for guidebook writers came when the train passed onto the Central Pacific route and began the trip across the Great Basin. Train schedules often made their task easier by crossing the forbidding terrain at night. Most guidebooks described the desolation quite frankly. "All is desolate in the extreme; the bare beds of alkali or wastes of gray sand alone meet the vision, if we except, now and then a rocky hill."[59] Usually, the guidebook degenerated into a dry listing of stations and mileages, with a few wry comments about the wishfully inappropriate names given to many places. "Why this stream is called Raspberry Creek and the one we last passed Rose Creek we never understood," remarked *Crofutt's Guide*. "We saw no indications of roses or raspberries at either place."[60] Only a few spots seemed to merit any mention at all.

Most writers found that the landscape provided them with nothing to describe. All of the guidebooks agreed that the Great Basin offered "little of interest to note." It had "no game to hunt, no streams to fish in nearby —there is nothing along or near the line of this division to tempt the tourist or the prospector to pause and examine the country."[61] The desert presented no bits of European scenery, no economic prospects, and no charming American eccentricities. Often the handbooks advised tourists to amuse themselves in other ways and to look forward to the pleasures of the Sierra Nevada and California that lay only hours ahead.

Perhaps the dry and uninteresting desert gave writers a chance to sharpen their pencils and refresh their vocabularies, because the last stretch of the transcontinental trip received the most attention and the grandest rhetoric. All of the guidebooks promised their readers feelings of instant delight the moment the train began winding up the wooded canyons of the Sierra Nevada. They often told stories of dour and dignified eastern tourists who exclaimed, "Thank God, I smell pitch once more," and who burst into tears of joy at the sight of trees.[62] The names of stations and the distances between them suddenly became unimportant as descriptions of the grand and familiar landscape filled space in the guidebooks.

The mountains of California would meet the expectations of educated tourists with their giddy heights, majestic forests, and sublime mountain scenery. "As we sweep past each rugged height and grisly precipice it is

impossible not to be stirred in one's innermost soul by the grandeur of the moving spectacle," emoted the writer of *Nelson's Central Pacific Railroad.*[63] Such a "moving spectacle" provided more entertainment than the best panorama. The guidebooks no longer had the responsibility for creating objects of interest out of a monotonous and strange landscape.

The beauties of the California landscape also provided guidebook authors with an easy task. They made much of the contrast between the bleakness of the Great Basin and the warmth and lushness of California. "We have been passing through a region of misery and desolation, whose chief features were alkali-dust and sage brush," Nelson's *Central Pacific* reminded its readers. "Then came a sudden magical change! Warm and genial airs breathed sweetly round us; the sun went down towards the Pacific with a radiant pomp."[64] Charles Nordhoff claimed that "the entrance to California is to the tourist as wonderful and charming as though it were the gate to a veritable fairy-land."[65] Even better than fairyland, California could be compared to Italy. Every guidebook announced California as the "Italy of America" and raved about its gentle climate in which "no Italian air was ever balmier," its clear air, and the blue, green, and golden palette of the landscape that seemed so "Mediterranean."[66]

From the green prairies of Omaha to the Mediterranean shores of California, the guidebooks assembled a view of the Far West that combined everything American tourists hoped to see. Designed for the tourist who saw the far western landscape through the window of a train, the guidebook told the tourist when to look out of the window and how he should interpret what he saw. Guidebook authors worked to make every aspect of the landscape appealing, making analogies to familiar European sights and exaggerating when necessary.

To fill up portions of the landscape that might bore tourists, such as the Great Plains or the deserts of the Great Basin, writers adopted different strategies. Animal life, strange plants, and formerly dangerous Indians and Mormons formed a kind of menagerie to be viewed safely from the passing train. If such living exhibits could not be conveniently marshalled, then guidebooks turned to economic development. They described the great potential of station towns and the spaces between towns in terms of possible urban development, agriculture, or mining. Only in desperation would they ever admit that a landscape had nothing to offer. At such uncomfortable moments, many guidebook advised tourists to sleep or play cards until something worth seeing passed into view.

Writers made such efforts to make the West attractive because of the important role the region already played in the American imagination. The trip from Omaha to San Francisco was more than a way to move between two points. The West's reputation required guidebooks to do much more than simply list stations and mileage between them. Tourists expected to be awed, thrilled, excited, and, most of all, entertained. Promoters had to find ways to enable tourists to meet their expectations about the Far West. Guidebooks made the far western landscape resemble a well-crafted panorama that passed beautiful scenery and exciting tableaux constantly before the audience. According to most guidebooks, a transcontinental railroad trip would introduce passengers to vistas that would remind them of Europe, to regions bursting with economic possibilities, and to charming American oddities like Indians and buffaloes. What American tourists actually found in these early years of western railroad travel, however, was quite different.

View from the Train: The Tourist Vision

The trip started off just as it had been advertised. The tourists adored the lush green prairies of eastern Nebraska. "The bright, fresh billowy pasture-lands . . . so like the English downs," trilled the writer Grace Greenwood, "were very beautiful, and the greater part of that afternoon's journey through Nebraska along the Platte River, I remember as a series of charming pictures."[67] American scenery seemed to resemble a delightful panorama. The "undulating, fertile plains, stretching far away on every side into space uncultivated and untouched" impressed nearly every tourist who wrote about the experience.[68]

The great sweep of space, however, soon lost its visual charm. One tourist grumbled that " the verdant farmlands are soon succeeded by the plains, the monotony of which is excessive."[69] To the relief of many, animal life did prevent boredom, just as the guidebooks had promised. Prairie dogs, "somewhat like large rats," did stick their heads out of their holes to inspect passing trains.[70] Most tourists wrote enthusiastically on the subject of prairie dogs. One man called the small animal "a welcome

Prairie-Dog Village

Although no tourist ever saw a prairie dog in such detail, the sight of their villages did break up the monotony of the trip across the plains. (In Henry T. Williams, *The Pacific Tourist*, 1876. Courtesy of the Bancroft Library.)

friend" because "he relieves us of ennui, and breaks up the wearisome sameness and dull monotony of these wide, expansive, and treeless Plains."[71]

Graceful herds of antelope also appeared on cue, bounding away from the noise of the train. One tourist commented on the eagerness of the passengers to see such prairie inhabitants. "Our palace car resembled rather a district school at a menagerie than anything else."[72] Another tourist attempted to explain the joy of seeing "the graceful fellows, showing the white feather behind," admitting that "to the tame passenger . . . there was a wilderness flavor about it quite strange and wonderful."[73] Some passengers experienced the flavor of the West much more directly. "After watching the graceful movements of the Antelope for several hours, and passing several large cities of the Gopher, or Prairie Dog," reported one satisfied traveler, "we arrived at Sidney, where we found

Shooting Buffalo from the Train

In the earliest years of railroad travel, tourists blasted away at the herds of buffalo that populated the plains. However, by the time large numbers of visitors came west, such activities had largely depleted the herds. (In *Harper's Weekly* 11 [December 1867]. Courtesy of the Bancroft Library.)

awaiting us an excellent and substantial breakfast of Antelope, Elk, and all other delicacies that there abound."[74]

Even though most tourists did get to see prairie dogs and antelope, very few actually saw the great herds of buffaloes promised by the guidebooks. Soon after the completion of the transcontinental railroad, the population of the buffalo dwindled. Not only did the presence of railroad tracks split herds and disrupt migration patterns; the train also created a new version of hunting that slaughtered hundreds of thousands of animals. "The train is slowed to a rate of speed about equal to that of the herd," wrote a *Harper's* journalist to describe the sport. "The passengers get out firearms . . . and open from the windows and the platforms of the cars a fire that resembles a brief skirmish."[75] This kind of massacre, leaving tons of meat rotting along the tracks, killed an estimated six million buffaloes by 1875.[76]

The guidebook had promised that the thrill of seeing buffaloes would make up for the increasingly monotonous landscape that covered western

Nebraska and eastern Wyoming, but disappointed tourists soon noted the effects of the wanton slaughter. "The buffalo have entirely disappeared from the belt of land traversed by the Union Pacific, and only their bones lie bleaching where trails used to run due north and south," observed one traveler.[77] As early as 1873 another visitor complained about the eyestrain he had incurred looking for buffaloes that only existed "in your mind's eye."[78]

The lack of buffaloes made the dry and brown-colored high plains intolerably dull. Almost every tourist complained about the desolate landscape that seemed to extend forever. These "arid and desolate tracts"[79] were not the beautiful prairies they had expected. Many of them referred to the "Great American Desert" that guidebooks never mentioned. Even the romantic concept of a desert did not seem to fit the land that appeared so vacant from the train. One tourist wrote that he expected "that a sphynx and a half a score of pyramids were located upon it," but he found nothing there.[80]

The sheer emptiness of the land shocked most passengers. "Your eye sweeps in vain around the horizon for an object to rest upon," noted an 1871 traveler, "nor shrub, nor tree nor rock is visible at any point or in any direction."[81] The popular poet, essayist, and philanthropist Helen Hunt Jackson found the emptiness to have dire effects. "It would be easy to fancy that journeying day after day across the sage-brush plains might make a man mad."[82] Another tourist explained with relief that he had managed to sleep through most of this territory, which, he advised, "the traveler can well afford to miss, as they are reported to be deserts devoid of interest."[83]

Bored by the terrain of the high plains, most tourists began looking for the splendors of the Rocky Mountains early on. Even though the train route passed well north of the spectacular Front Range and many descriptions of South Pass had been published, most tourists still expected sublime mountain scenery. The guidebooks, of course, did little to discourage such expectations. "There is an eager, expectant look on every face," wrote one tourist describing the activity in the cars when the train reached a point at which the Rockies were supposed to be visible. "Guidebooks are consulted. Hasty questions are asked and answered. The porter is interrogated. Heads are thrust out of windows," he continued, demonstrating the eagerness of tourists to see the legendary peaks.[84]

Despite such preparations, tourists on the Union Pacific line saw little that resembled splendid mountains. "It is possible that these mountain tops may have been discerned in a vision by the compilers of guide books," wrote a frustrated peak seeker. "To the eye of the ordinary and unimaginative traveller, they are invisible."[85] When the train actually crossed the "backbone of the continent" at Sherman, Wyoming, the view hardly lived up to its billing. "You gaze out upon a wide expanse, now arched and broken into ugly hollows and repulsive knobs, devoid of any sign of rich vegetation," explained a rather disgusted visitor.[86] Another unhappy passenger penned a warning for those who followed him: "Those who expect to find high peaks and snow-capped summits towering above them as they proceed along the railroad across the mountains will be disappointed."[87]

Even if crossing the Rockies disappointed most tourists, they only had to wait a few hours for the biggest thrill they had yet encountered. The rock formations along the Green River and Echo and Weber canyons provided tourists with the kind of scenery they had expected. Here were wonders to compare to the Old World. Just where the guidebooks had promised they would be, tourists found "the American Parthenon," "grander than any Grecian ruin that ever crumbled," "Solomon's Temple petrified," along with assorted "amphitheatres, colosseums, and temples that appeal to our eyes with the grandeur of an ancient Rome or an Athens."[88]

Echo Canyon, reputed to be the most glorious vision of the trip, caused "a flutter of anticipation among the passengers," who waited "with full breath, anxious heart, and keen zest" for the sights ahead.[89] For once, the guidebooks had not exaggerated. Tourists searched eagerly for the proper words and analogies to describe the scenery that passed by the train window. Some described the view as alpine, similar to "the magnificent sight to be witnessed between Botzen and Verona when the railway passes near to the gigantic piles of rock which have been fitly entitled the Gateways of the Alps."[90] Others discerned medieval castles in the rock forms, which appeared so lifelike that "feudal labor, and not the patient toil of raindrops, must, we are half disposed to think, have shaped the pinnacles which taper with such fineness, and the towers which are so perfectly round."[91] American tourists worked hard at convincing themselves that these natural rock formations were indeed equivalent to the ancient buildings of Europe. Some created a montage of architectural marvels. "Now I could fancy that I saw a beautiful cathedral, with spires and windows; then a castle, battlements and bastions all complete," an early visitor remembered rather breathlessly, "and more than one amphitheatre fit for a Caesar to have held his sports in."[92]

This landscape pleased American tourists because they could pretend they were touring Europe in their own country. The scenery resembled vistas they had seen in Europe or in books, and they immediately recognized the proper way to describe them. The guidebooks had suggested that the far western landscape would remind well-traveled and cultured tourists of Europe and the Old World. In the rock formations and mountain scenery of western Wyoming and northeastern Utah, they found such scenery. Most tourists devoted more space to describing this region than they had given to the thousand miles that had come before.

Train passengers received the same kind of pleasure and gave the same attention in description to the Sierra Nevada and to California. Once more, the landscape of the Far West provided them with vistas and scenes they could describe in familiar European terms. They could see for themselves that the United States and the New World had spectacular scenery that equaled or even surpassed that of the Old World. Many tourists first rejoiced at the sight of trees and only then began to make the inevitable European comparisons. Grace Greenwood said simply that "it was comforting to see wooded hillsides again."[93] Forested landscapes provided comfortable turf for tourists in search of familiar analogies. A rather dramatic tourist explained that the only way he could describe his feeling upon seeing the wooded slopes of the Sierra would be to quote Dante's *Inferno* at the moment the protagonist left Hell for the "bright world."[94]

Their delight in cool greenery and mountain snow was evident in the enthusiastic praise that appeared in tourists' accounts. Having traveled across the mountains, one optimistic visitor predicted that "the day is not far when the fame and influence of the Sierra Nevada Mountains . . . will not only rank with but eclipse even that of the Alps, the Appenines *[sic]*, the Jura, the Cevennes, the Vosges, and the Côte d'Or."[95] Another tourist confirmed this opinion with the evidence that "European tourists that we conversed with say that the Alps do not produce anything so grand, or so much of it, as do these Nevada ranges."[96] The only com-

Donner Lake

This romantic view of Donner Lake in the High Sierra reinforced the tourists' notion that the West would offer them a Switzerland in America. The sharp, snow-covered peaks and the dramatic clouds, however, were hidden from view by the miles of snowsheds. (In W. H. Rideing, *Scenery of the Pacific Railways and Colorado*, 1878. Courtesy of the Bancroft Library.)

plaints anyone could make about the Sierra and the train ride across them concerned the snowsheds built to protect the tracks from heavy snowfall, which prevented tourists from seeing the full complement of mountain views. "There is scarcely a break in the monotonous succession of sheds," complained Miriam Leslie, "and it so happens that some of the finest points of scenery are congregated along this section of the route."[97]

In describing this region, the tourists echoed the shrill and bombastic tone of the guidebooks. The description of the scenery took on a nationalistic cant. The Sierra became objects of American pride. One tourist explained that "patriotic ardor" induced him "to conclude that [the Sierra Nevada] is an American Switzerland."[98] Oddly enough, national pride drove him to describe American scenery in European terms. In this way, descriptive language became a kind of weapon to fend off criticism. The United States must be as cultured and historic as Europe if it contained scenery that could be so easily compared to European landscapes. The almost frenzied European comparisons reached a crescendo in California, which, every tourist knew from the immense publicity, was Europe newly incarnated.

The tourists adored the scenery that greeted them as they came out of the mountains and entered the great Central Valley of California. They found the "veritable fairy-land" and the "Italy of America" that the guidebooks had described. Grace Greenwood believed "it was almost like witnessing creation" to emerge from the wintry mountains "into lovely fruitful valleys, into soft, balmy, golden airs, past vineyards and orchards and flowery gardens."[99] Another tourist made the Italian connection immediately. "Indeed," he exclaimed, "the feeling of the air reminded me strongly of the sensation one experiences in descending the southern slopes of the Alps and entering Italian territory."[100] Italy, with its wealth of historical associations and its gentle climate, represented everything that Americans looked for in a landscape.

Though the Italian analogy was most popular, other Old World comparisons made their way into travel accounts. Many visitors found a resemblance to the English landscape. The widely spaced live oak trees and the peaceful pastures complete with lowing cattle seemed "to counterfeit the royal Parks of Old England."[101] An especially worldly tourist described California as "a country which might sometimes be Switzerland, sometimes Gascony with its vine-clad hills, sometimes bonny Scotland and sometimes more pleasant and more beautiful Devonshire."[102] No American tourist, worried that Europe had all of the spectacular scenery and the important cultural heritage, could resist such language. With places like Echo Canyon, the Sierra Nevada, and California, Americans could compete with Europeans—at least in terms of the landscape.

The desirability of European analogy is especially evident in tourists' reactions to places bearing no resemblance to Europe. When the train carried its passengers into desert regions, it brought them into an unfamiliar landscape. No slide show or panorama had prepared them for the Great Basin. Even the guidebooks had found no plausible way to make it familiar, European, or even romantic. Tourists hated it. They reacted just as Mark Twain had in *Roughing It*, feeling disoriented and powerless. Every bit of the veneer of civilization that tourists of this era cherished seemed absent from the Great Basin landscape. For the tourist in search of culturally uplifting or at least exciting scenery, the desert offered nothing. It seemed only to be an eternity of dust, sagebrush, brown hills, and especially, monotony.

Tourists complained bitterly about this portion of the trip. Words like "waste," "barrenness," "nothing," "forlorn," and "sterile" characterize most of the descriptions of the journey across Utah and Nevada. One disgruntled tourist explained quite simply, "On the route I found nothing to note . . . until we arrive at a station called Reno."[103] "Weary are the hours as we pass over an arid waste of sand and dust," commented another frustrated observer.[104] Others noted the ubiquitous presence of the sagebrush, a plant they found particularly unattractive. "I became deeply imbued," wrote one man of his desert crossing, "with an undying hatred for the everlasting sagebrush."[105] This scenery challenged the notions of many Americans that they could control the landscape, that they could make deserts bloom.

Some tourists attempted to explain the source of their discomfort in the desert. It seemed to be stripped of everything they associated with comfort and civilization. It had "no smooth, level lawn, no pleasant field or rolling meadow-land, no friendly habitation, no house of any kind, not a tree or a shrub,—in a word, NO GREEN THING WHATEVER."[106] In a similar vein, another visitor noted, "There is space and no atmosphere, soil and no verdure, mountains and no inspiration; the sky has no fleck in its glassy blue."[107] Clearly, the desert had none of the attributes tourists had learned to expect in beautiful scenery. It met none of the requirements American tourists had set for an enjoyable landscape: it did not resemble Europe, and it seemed to offer no immediate economic advantages.

The writer Grace Greenwood found a landscape without atmosphere, verdure, or inspiration quite threatening. "The great brown hills seemed to me," she wrote, "not only utterly denuded, but flayed, stripped of all covering of nature, and gashed and scarred and marred and maltreated in every way."[108] Using only slightly less cataclysmic language, another person described the scenery as a "wilderness" that seemed "to have been desolated by a fire." Frustrated by the strange scene, he concluded that "the blight which oppressed it is indescribable."[109] Like John C. Frémont thirty years earlier, this observer had no words to describe the landscape.

A few observers did attempt to describe the desert in familiar terms, often using various Middle Eastern regions as points of comparison. Such analogies rarely complimented the region. One tourist wrote, "The deserts of Africa or Asia present no more forbidding aspect."[110] "In barrenness it rivals the Desert of Sahara," commented another train passenger.[111] Miriam Leslie used biblical imagery to describe her reaction to the barren desert. "Such a picture must have been in John Bunyan's mind when he described Christian's journey through the Valley of the Shadow of Death."[112]

Some tourists made an effort at accurate description. An observer with an especially active imagination used a series of domestic images. He described the landscape as "an immense batch of wheaten dough hundreds of miles across" that had been "strewn with careless handfuls of salt and sprinkles of mustard and garnished, like the mouth of a roasted pig, with parsley-looking sage brush and tufts of withered grass."[113] Rarely, however, did someone struggle to come up with appropriate descriptive terms. If Old World analogies did not fit a scene, most visitors either condemned the sight or did not describe it.

No matter what terms they used to describe it, few tourists saw anything of value in the Great Basin landscape. It lacked both pleasing vistas and any obvious economic potential. Like the guidebooks, tourists advised future travelers to find something other than observing the scenery to occupy their time. Many advised sleep as the best remedy. One man characterized the region as "a country that tempts the traveller to take his uttermost pennyworth out of the sleeping cars."[114] Another commented wryly that it was "a fortunate thing that the length of the journey admits of a degree of intimacy between the passengers, and the outward ugliness may be forgotten in social intercourse."[115] Disappointed tourists did get some pleasure out of denouncing the Great Basin region; and this soon became a tradition on the transcontinental trip, just as it had for earlier travelers. Despising the desert seemed to be part of the package for tourists. Much as Twain had, they could boast about having "survived" a desert crossing.

Other aspects of the West also disappointed train travelers. One of the most exciting aspects of western travel was seeing live Indians. The guidebooks made little of this, save for promising that tourists would indeed see some at certain points. Perhaps the authors of these guides recognized the high expectations tourists already had about the "noble savage" and wisely decided to skirt the issue. Like Mark Twain in *Roughing It*, most visitors had a romantic view of Indians, nourished by bloodcurdling newspaper and dime novel stories, as well as by Cooper's Leatherstocking tales and Longfellow's Hiawatha. The Indians they saw along the transcontinental train route did not resemble any of these fictional characters.

After the bloody wars of the mid-nineteenth century, the remaining plains tribes lived far from the train's path, attempting to find a region where they could live and hunt in traditional ways. The Indians who gathered at railroad stations had become dependent on handouts from tourists and from the government. They horrified most tourists. Greatly disappointed, tourists reacted with disgust, rather than with any shame or pity at the state to which these people had been reduced. Helen Hunt Jackson, who would later write *Century of Dishonor* (1881) to describe the American government's treatment of the Indians, was stunned by her first view of an Indian. In 1872, this future Indian advocate could not even bring herself to use human terms in her description. "We were told it was a woman," she told her readers. "It was thatched at the top with a heavy roof of black hair. . . . It moved about on bony, brown, stalking members, for which no experience furnishes name. . . . It was the most abject, loathly living thing I ever saw."[116]

Most tourists had a similar reaction. They expected an Indian of mythic proportions, but the faulty mortals they met at railroad stations did not

The Tourist and the Indian

Indians fascinated the tourists who came west, even though real Indians rarely resembled the images created in fiction. This clash between image and reality inevitably disappointed many visitors. (In Henry T. Williams, *The Pacific Tourist*, 1876. Courtesy of the Bancroft Library.)

measure up. Many people blamed James Fenimore Cooper and other writers for their dashed expectations. "Those who expect to see the heroes, or their descendants of Fenimore Cooper's novels," warned a wise visitor, "will be woefully disappointed."[117] Another tourist lamented, "Could these blear-eyed bedlams, crooning a low dischordant plaint, and stretching forth skinny claws for alms, be the sisters of 'Little Fawn' or 'Laughing Water'?"[118]

Tourists had counted on the Indians to provide a certain exotic flavor to western travel. Indians, according to the standards of white tourists, were present only to create romantic associations. The realities of native Indian life were not supposed to intrude on the romantic vision. The remarks of a frustrated visitor at a Shoshone village demonstrated the resentment many people felt when their romantic impressions were destroyed. "A dozen or so tents, discolored with smoke and besmeared with dirt and grease, revealing from six to ten squalid beings covered with vermin, filth and rags," he noted, "is not calculated to create a pleasing impression, or awaken imaginary flights to any great extent."[119]

The sight of Indians gathered around the railroad depots begging seemed to destroy the "imaginary flights" of most tourists quite effectively. The reality of noble braves begging for money or for alcohol horrified most observers. Instead of bringing enormous benefit, white civilization had apparently destroyed the pure Indian of myth. A disappointed tourist remembered that the only Indian braves he came across were at "the depots from the Platte to the Nevada, generally shoeless, covered in red blankets, in an idle sort of way begging quarters from passengers which is immediately exchanged for whiskey."[120]

Disgusted by such behavior, many white visitors concluded that Indians could neither fit into white society nor provide romantic images for it. Therefore, according to nineteenth-century logic, Indians had no right to exist. If the Indian could not accept the blessings of civilization in a more graceful manner, all Americans could do, as Samuel Bowles suggested, "is to smooth and make decent the pathway to his grave."[121] Other observers listed the traits that made Indians deserving of extermination. "The savage, like Falstaff, is by nature a coward; also treacherous, cruel and filthy," commented one visitor.[122] Another remarked, "Industry and frugal habits are foreign to his nature. He hates subjection to law; he despises thrift and order."[123] Apparently, the problem of the romantic Indian gone sour could be solved by "nothing short of extermination."[124] No wonder guidebooks had avoided any discussion of the Indian presence in the far western landscape.

Another group alien to most white Americans, and generally left out of guidebook descriptions, were the Mormons. Salt Lake City received much attention for its green and lush fields and its stunning backdrop of mountains, but the well-publicized marital habits of its Mormon inhabitants rarely appeared in the guidebook descriptions. Nonetheless, tourists arrived in Salt Lake city with very clear expectations. Like Mark Twain, they hoped to find evidence of the evil influence of Mormonism on every corner. As with Indians, decades of publicity about Mormons and their unconventional practices had created strong stereotypes in tourists' minds. They hoped to be disgusted, shocked, and filled with moral indignation at the horrors supposedly inflicted by polygamy.

Much to their disappointment, train passengers saw an attractive and prosperous community. Assuming that the landscape would reflect the immorality and dark practices of its inhabitants, most visitors found the green and fertile Salt Lake valley to be a refreshing surprise. "It would be difficult to exaggerate the glory and beauty of the scenery," wrote one amazed tourist. "We passed smiling homesteads, surrounded by orchards and gardens, meadows as green as those of the Emerald Isle."[125] The neat houses and bright gardens allowed "a vague doubt and certain bewilderment to steal over our prejudices," explained another visitor. The prosperous appearance of the region forced her to admit that "certainly polygamy is very wrong, but roses are better than sagebrush."[126] Grace Greenwood found herself admiring the Mormons. "Let us confess," she wrote, "that this strange people, under their remarkable leader have done a great work in rescuing this region from the desolation and sterility of uncounted ages."[127]

Despite the undeniable beauty of the landscape, visitors looked hard to find unattractive aspects of the city. They delighted in finding signs of "the perpetration of the Mormon deeds of darkness."[128] One man claimed that tourists were too easily blinded by the outward pleasantness of Salt Lake City because they looked at it with "eyes weary of barrenness or sated with monotony." He hinted darkly that "it needs a strong afflatus of the Mormon spirit to gush over the Mormon City."[129]

Most critics, however, chose to focus on the appearance of the Mormons themselves. Typically, they described the children as sickly looking, the women as ugly and worn, and the men as sensual beasts, reflecting stereotypes about Mormonism. Helen Hunt Jackson described her first view of a man she believed to be a Mormon. "His eyes were small, light, and watery, but sharp and cruel. His face was bloated, coarse, sensual: I have never seen a more repulsive man."[130] Charles Nordhoff attributed such physical characteristics to the hard life in the desert and the mental strain of polygamy on normal social relationships.[131] The encounter with the Mormons, for most tourists, was a slight disappointment. Even though the guidebooks had not promised much, the evil of Mormonism was not as obvious as visitors hoped it would be. Salt Lake City was beautiful, but its inhabitants did not live up to their lurid billing.

In all, the railroad tour had not delivered exactly what the guidebooks had promised. The Great Plains turned out to be dull after the first prairie dogs and antelope had been sighted. The Noble Savages and the lordly buffaloes had disappeared from part of the plains visible from the railroad, leaving only an excruciatingly monotonous gray blur of sand, low hills, and sagebrush. The desert, far from being a romantic Sahara, turned out to be dry, dusty, and dull with no pleasing animal life or rock formations to make it interesting. Contrary to the view of the Far West as a panorama of spectacular vistas and romantic tableaux presented in the guidebooks, the landscape the tourists found was often a disappointment.

Only a few parts of the railroad tour actually displayed the kind of scenery tourists expected and the guidebooks promised. The mountain landscapes along the Green River and in the Sierra Nevada and the lush valleys and remarkable coastline of California pleased everyone. These regions could easily be described in familiar aesthetic terms, and they provided the proper "grand, stupendous, magnificent, and sublime sights" that American tourists craved.[132]

The Far West did have mountains that, like the Alps, "elicit and exercise the morale of the soul" and "fire the soul with a spirit of veneration—the palaces of infinite power and majesty."[133] It also had the equally magnificent but gentler landscape of California that boasted scenes reminiscent of Italy, where "rows of Italian cypresses, straight and spiry as those which look on Florence from San Miniato" made the scenery especially appealing.[134]

Along with such European attributes, the landscape of the Far West also boasted characteristics different and in some ways better than those of Old World landscapes. The Far West presented an unusual blend of adventure, magnificent scenery, and economic potential. The efforts of explorers, observers, and promoters had isolated the portions of the landscape that would appeal to the traveling public. Guidebooks exaggerated this allure, making the far western landscape into a kind of three-ring circus, with European scenery, economic enterprise, and eccentric American flourishes as the top-billed performers. Tourists, having read such descriptions, found the realities of the landscape to be a disappointment. Most of the scenic wonders presented in the guidebooks did exist, but only in between long stretches of odd and desolate wastes. Tourists certainly appreciated the dramatic scenery of the Far West, but they did not hesitate to point out its grave deficiencies in comparison to Europe.

Once again, when Americans measured their landscape directly against the Old World, it came up short.

Even though the rocks surrounding the Green River might resemble ancient temples and the Big Trees lived before the time of Christ, these works of nature did not have the same status as the works of man. Western scenery had moments of great sublimity, but it could not claim the historical patina of Europe. In 1871 a promoter tried to make the best of this major difference between the landscape of the Far West and that of Europe. "Of Man's works we have less in this country than there is elsewhere, but of Nature's more. Not only more, but of a higher order, and of a unique type. They have only to be known to be appreciated."[135] Western scenery might be of a higher order, but the cleverest guidebook could not gloss over the fact that in terms of Old World civilization so valued by Americans, the Far West was brand new.

The travel writer Bayard Taylor, while ranting about the Italian beauty of California, also noted its unfortunate lack of history, at least in terms of Euro-American culture. California offered all that a tourist could want, he explained, but for one thing. "It is too new—too recently fallen into the possession of man—too far away from the great centers of the world's life—too little touched, as yet, with the genial influences of Art and Taste."[136] Many tourists agreed with this criticism. "Everything is spic and span new," mourned a typical observer, "no halo of romance, no glamour of ancient legend, invests the landscape with a mysterious charm."[137]

Because white Americans had not yet recognized that the native peoples of North America could offer them a history, it seemed as though the Far West had no human history—at least not one that produced recognizable works of art and historical traditions. Most visitors to the Far West still took pride in the fact that portions of the landscape resembled scenes from the Old World and that the region's natural history provided evidence of great age. They resented, however, the claim made by many of the guidebooks that the Far West could serve as a replica of Europe.

Even the most gullible tourist recognized that the West of the guidebooks was a bit of a hoax. Not only did the railroad route include large portions of indescribable and monotonous scenery, it also bypassed many of the regions that could actually be understood in European terms. The

American curiosities of the trip seemed to have either disappeared in the case of the buffalo or to have become decidedly unromantic in the case of the Indians.

Railroad promoters, guidebook authors, and speculators of all sorts had done their best to describe the far western landscape in a way that would attract Americans with money to spend on travel. Using an aesthetic vocabulary borrowed from the Old World, they had attempted to create an American version of Europe that could be viewed by passengers on the new transcontinental route. Certain aspects of the program worked. Tourists responded with enormous enthusiasm to the mountain scenery of the Rockies and the Sierra and to the coastal valleys of California. In these regions, the equation with the Old World seemed warranted. Vast portions of the landscape, however, simply did not fit the images that promoters had used to describe them. Tourists recognized the exaggerated and inaccurate guidebook descriptions of these unfamiliar areas. Disappointed visitors dismissed these regions as "monotonous," "desolate," and "hideous."

Publicity agents and railroad management, always eager to please their clientele and to attract new business, took the reactions of the tourists seriously. It seemed as if Americans wanted more Europe and less America—more art and less nature. Smart entrepreneurs, led by the railroads, looked to the parts of the landscape that most resembled Europe to meet these desires. Nature, though splendid, could certainly be improved by art. In the next two decades, railroad companies built small bastions of Europe in the heart of the far western landscape.

CHAPTER 4

European Citadels: The Early Far Western Resorts, 1870–1900

In 1869, just as the transcontinental railroad opened up the Far West to tourist travel, General William J. Palmer surveyed the land along the eastern edge of the Colorado Rockies. As director of construction for the Kansas Pacific Railroad, he knew the landscape well. Because he saw the potential for development along the eastern side of the Rockies where mining towns had sprung up in the last decade, he hoped to convince the directors of the Kansas Pacific to build a railroad line in this direction. When they refused, he decided to construct his own line from Denver to Texas and on into Mexico. A clever and enthusiastic promoter, Palmer managed to convince William Gilpin, the first governor of the Colorado Territory, and several English investors to back his scheme. These men owned huge tracts of land in southern Colorado, and a railroad would increase the value of their investments.[1]

General Palmer also had his eye on some land of his own. He bought a large parcel of property in a spot about sixty miles south of Denver at the foot of Pikes Peak, the landmark of the Front Range of the Rocky Mountains. The area offered a healthy climate, a series of natural springs, and stunning mountain scenery. Palmer recognized its attractions for the wealthy visitors streaming west on the new transcontinental railroad.

Satisfying the Craving for Europe: Colorado Springs

Railroad developers like Palmer recognized that American tourists desperately hoped to find a version of Europe in the Far West. The scenery visible from the transcontinental line had not always measured up to this standard. Colorado and California, however, with their more obvious similarities to European scenery, became hotbeds of interest on the part of railroad promoters. By the 1880s, the efforts of railroads and private developers made parts of the two states into tourist meccas, where visitors could find the European scenery they sought so eagerly.

William Palmer, one of the first to build such a version of Europe, recognized that scenery alone could not attract affluent visitors. Prosperous Americans traveled to find education, recreation, and health. In the tradition of the European Grand Tour, they wanted to see recognizable reminders of historical tradition and to enjoy the benefits of a change in climate, all in elegant surroundings. Any region hoping to attract tourists had to provide facilities to meet these needs and the standards set by established European resorts. Places like Saratoga Springs, New York, and Long Branch or Cape May, New Jersey, provided American models. These traditionally upper-class resorts had never lived up to the example of the European resorts. American watering places lacked the scenery and historical associations sought by their privileged American clientele. In addition, the East Coast resorts no longer met the needs of upper-class Americans who were increasingly obsessed with climate and health.

General Palmer recognized that a resort in the midst of the "Switzerland of America" would meet these requirements. Its luxuries would include splendid homes, grand hotels, socially select inhabitants, and a glittering social life. When he dreamed up the concept of the neighboring resorts of Colorado Springs and Manitou, he intended to create a European spa in an American setting, with the addition of proper scenery to make it authentic.

In the spring of 1871, Palmer formed the Colorado Springs Company with himself as president. Along with William A. Bell, another enthusiastic Colorado promoter, Palmer planned a town called the Fountain Colony, which would have expensive town sites and strict regulation of drinking and social behavior. Bell, an English physician, took charge of the area where the springs were located, just to the west of Palmer's site. This later became Manitou Springs. Palmer and Bell designed the project to attract an exclusive clientele. They called the plots of land "villa sites" and hired an architect to advise property owners about housing styles suitable for the location and its inhabitants. The company planted trees and grass to create a landscape they hoped would remind potential investors of an English country estate.[2]

Palmer began an intensive promotional campaign as soon as his railroad, the Denver and Rio Grande, reached Colorado Springs in October of 1871. He based his advertising on three issues: the healthful climate, the exclusive clientele, and the European flavor of the fledgling resort and its surroundings.[3] To attract the kind of wealthy clientele he wanted for his resort, he had to convince people that Colorado Springs could cure their diseases, maintain suitably high social standards, and provide aesthetically pleasing scenery.

Health played a major role in the promotion of Palmer's Colorado Springs. In the late nineteenth century, moneyed Americans as well as upper-class Europeans became increasingly concerned with health. In spite of great strides in medical knowledge, epidemics continued to wipe out huge numbers of people, consumption slowly dragged them to their graves, and nervous ailments made them miserable and unable to function in modern society. Even though consumption and nervousness were common in Britain and Europe, such diseases seemed almost endemic among wealthy Americans.[4]

A magazine journalist reported in 1880 that 91,500 Americans died of consumption or "pulmonary phthisis," which accounted for twelve of every one hundred deaths. Another contemporary writer called consumption "the ravaging of the human race and the accompaniment of its higher grades of civilization."[5] Another ailment causing great concern was nervous exhaustion, or neurasthenia, first "diagnosed" by Dr. George Miller Beard in the 1870s. He transformed the various symptoms generally known as nervousness into a legitimate disease that bestowed status upon its sufferers.

According to Beard, neurasthenia could only strike the highest orders of society in the most progressive society on earth—the United States. Modern civilization with its speed, pressure, and necessity for brain power caused the disease. Using metaphors of electricity, Beard explained that "brain workers" in a highly competitive society drained their nervous energy in the struggle to get ahead, until, like light bulbs, they burned out and began to suffer from dyspepsia, exhaustion, inability to concentrate, or any number of symptoms characterizing the disease. Both men and women could suffer form this loss of nerve power that seemed to strike only the upper orders of society.[6]

Whatever the cause of diseases like consumption or neurasthenia, finding cures challenged patients and doctors. Because doctors could not control the hostile microbes that attacked the body from the outside, the only line of defense seemed to be strengthening the inside of the body with rest and exercise. A long stay in a healthy climate became the standard cure for many of the illnesses plaguing Americans. "After all the years of research devoted to the subject," noted a journalist, "and out of all the methods of cure and prevention, the one that has given the best results and is now being universally adopted is change of climate."[7] Debates raged about which climate, which elevation, and which waters would cure which diseases, creating a whole new medical practice of climatology.

European spas had offered a variety of climates, baths, and springs for many years, and sickly Americans flocked to resorts in the Alps or along the Mediterranean. American springs and spas developed their own devotees, but never attained the status of European resorts because they could not provide the scenery or glamorous atmosphere. An American expert on resorts explained the problem: "A place of resort should not only possess a climate suitable to the physical needs of the patient, but such conditions in the way of scenery, amusements, diversions, and congenial surroundings, as will act favorably upon his mind."[8] Few resorts in the eastern United States met these standards. By the 1870s, wealthy Americans believed that their resorts had too many people, too little to do, and no proper scenery.

In Colorado Springs and Manitou, William Palmer thought he had found the answers to these criticisms. One of the first advertising pamphlets for the Fountain Colony announced that its location "embraces the healthiest part of the healthful climate of Colorado." It went on to claim cures for asthma, consumption, rheumatism, dyspepsia, and diseases of the kidneys. The pamphlet gave weight to these claims by quoting a famous geologist who promised, "These Springs must at some period become a celebrated and popular resort for invalids and tourists from all parts of the world."[9]

To assure people of the validity of his claims, Palmer hired well-respected doctors to supervise the promotion of the healthful aspects of the area. Palmer found a gem in Dr. Samuel Edwin Solly, who arrived in Colorado Springs in 1874. Solly, an English medical expert on tuberculosis, was an invalid himself and had spent much of his life in search of the perfect climate. He found renewed health in Colorado and built a career as a propagandist for the area's climatic charms.[10]

Solly wrote reams of medical literature in praise of Colorado, which he published in scholarly journals, railroad literature, popular magazines, and newspapers. His articles promised relief from scores of ailments, especially those caused by overwork and overexcitement. He advised sufferers to come to Colorado Springs early and to remain there for extended periods of time. He included complex charts and graphs comparing the temperature, humidity, and sunniness of Colorado Springs to the attributes of European spas, with predictably favorable results.[11] Railroad officials, real-estate developers, and chambers of commerce repeated these claims enthusiastically.

By the 1880s, the cant of healthfulness had reached a fevered pitch. Colorado Springs and Manitou were "ideal resorts, having been favored by nature with healing springs equal, if not superior to those of Ems or Spa or Saratoga."[12] Not only were the springs ideal, but "Colorado Springs stands at the head of the list of health resorts for the number of clear days, and in this respect is markedly the superior of even the far-famed Davos, the most frequented of Alpine mountain sanataria."[13] Such claims, combined with the support of the medical profession and with testimonials from thousands of satisfied patients, gave Colorado Springs a solid reputation.[14]

Palmer made sure that his resort was healthy, but he also worked hard at building its social qualifications. Through his machinations, the region attained a social cachet second only to European resorts. Many of the first investors in Colorado Springs and in Manitou were English or Scottish, giving the region a decidedly British flavor. An early visitor to the area was Rose Georgina Kingsley, daughter of the revered canon of Westminster Abbey, Charles Kingsley. She wrote an enthusiastic book about her stays in the Springs and noted in 1873 that "indeed, the English and Canadian incomers are now making a marked portion of the population."[15]

This kind of publicity thrilled General Palmer. When Canon Kingsley himself arrived in Colorado Springs in 1874 to rid himself of a lingering cold, Palmer made the most of the opportunity. He recognized the American penchant for things English and the financial significance of an English stamp of approval on his fledgling resort. He publicized the visit heavily and had Kingsley haunted by reporters who promptly published any vaguely complimentary statement the canon made.

After Kingsley's visit, Palmer began to advertise Colorado Springs as Little London. He hired an Englishman, J. E. Liller, to edit the local paper. Under Liller's influence the paper emphasized foreign, especially British news, relegating events in the United States to the back pages. The front page generally offered detailed accounts of the daily activities of the royal families of various European countries. The paper noted the momentous occasions when the residents of the Springs took up polo and when they tried to organize a hunt club, even though the lowly coyote replaced the usual fox.[16] Such activities verified the aristocratic stance Palmer hoped his town would take.

General Palmer engineered the English atmosphere quite carefully, using architectural styles that reflected British influence. When investors bought their villa lots, the Colorado Springs Company offered them the services of a company architect, George Summers. The homes he designed featured Tudor towers and cupolas and gables with exposed beams, giving the town an early uniformity. Many of the directors of the Colorado Springs Company used Summers's plans, building large stone mansions with carefully landscaped grounds.[17]

Palmer was no exception. His residence, Glen Eyrie, locate in a canyon just northwest of town, demonstrated Palmer's hopes for Colorado Springs. A visiting journalist described it as a "delicious anachronism of a Queen Anne house, in sage green and deep dull red, with arched balconies under pointed gables, and carved projections over mullioned windows, and trellised porches, with stained glass loopholes and an avalanche of roofs."[18] A carefully landscaped park surrounded the house, complete with miles of curved pathways, beautifully carved bridges, and acres of green lawn. When the writer Hamlin Garland visited the estate he reacted in the way

Palmer intended, writing that Glen Eyrie was "a castle" that "made one think of Old England."[19]

Visitors loved the English flavor of Colorado Springs and Manitou, and they recognized its difference from most towns in the American West. Its reputation as a haven for wealthy easterners and foreign noblemen insulated it from the usual stereotypes about shoddy and wild western towns. As one English visitor explained, at least in Colorado Springs "the 'far West,' so often represented as a wilderness given over to the reign of the wild riotous ranchman . . . is in reality peopled by the adventurous sons of Britain and collegians from the more crowded eastern states of America."[20]

The refined population became a boon for promoters and tourists alike. Not only could one find "the cream of eastern society" but also many "wealthy and titled English families."[21] Always alert to what attracted American tourists, a typical railroad advertisement noted, "Among the objects of interest to the American tourist . . . are great stone and brick residences, which are the homes of Englishmen who own immense tracts of land."[22] The presence of these Englishmen signaled Americans that Colorado Springs was indeed a place to see and be seen.

The success of the Colorado Springs area depended on more than the social qualifications of its residents and the general unhealthiness of the late-nineteenth-century population. The physical appearance of the region made it especially attractive to culturally anxious Americans who sought a physical resemblance to Europe, the romance of human history, and evidence of the sublime in their own landscape. Decades of publicity had convinced people that the Colorado Rockies with their perpetually white peaks certainly equaled the mountain ranges in Europe in physical beauty, if not in historical reference. Americans could, and did, point proudly at the Colorado mountains and compare them to the Alps.

In the 1860s, Samuel Bowles, editor of the *Springfield* [Mass.] *Republican* and a staunch western booster, set the tone for claims about the wonders of the Rockies. In *The Switzerland of America: A Summer Vacation in the Parks and Mountains of Colorado*, Bowles described a view from the top of Gray's Peak. "In impressiveness, in overcomingness, it takes rank with the three or four great natural wonders of the world." He boasted that "no Swiss mountain view carries such majestic sweep of distance, such sublime combination of height and breadth and depth: such uplifting into the presence of God, such dwarfing of the mortal sense."[23] Such superlative rhetoric gave Colorado a scenic pedigree.

Each visitor to the Rockies sought an Alpine analogy in every view. Pikes Peak seemed to resemble Mont Blanc, "the great Monarch of the Alps," while the "Via Mala is dwarfed into insignificance when compared with the Royal Gorge."[24] Recognizing the importance such claims held for tourists, some promoters went even further. "All the sublimest glories of the Swiss and Italian Alps, all the picturesque savagery of the Tyrol, and all the softer beauty of Killarny and Como and Naples dwindle to insignificance by comparison with the stupendous scenes that meet the gaze at every turn in Colorado," a Denver and Rio Grande pamphlet claimed extravagantly.[25]

Although alpine comparisons were by far the most popular, Colorado visitors also found analogies to other European regions. "If the highlands of Scotland can furnish such scenes as their own native poets have described, what may not be said and written of the scenery of the Rockies," gushed a guidebook author.[26] Another enthusiastic tourist claimed that the Colorado sky resembled the one over Italy. "Only once before have I seen such color; it was early one morning, going into Naples, on one of the broad-decked Mediterranean boats."[27] From the proper perspective, Colorado could be transformed into almost any European scene.

Other observers accepted the fact that the Rockies did, indeed, possess great physical beauty but worried that the American range did not have the human history that gave the European mountains their special aura. Ernest Ingersoll, a popular naturalist whose books about western travel often went through thirty and forty editions, described Cheyenne Canyon near Colorado Springs. He admitted the canyon had spectacular aspects, but he felt something was missing. "Had legend and history followed it for centuries, South Cheyenne Canyon would have its great features acknowledged. Let a ruined tower stand at its entrance . . . let a nation fight for its liberty through its chasm; and then let my Lord Byron turn loose the flood of his imagery upon it."[28] Apparently, a landscape without crumbling castles could not inspire poetry.

Some observers worried that even the geography of Colorado had too many differences from the Alps to make comparisons possible. Many noted the absence of the vast glaciers and huge fields of snow that characterized the Alps. Some felt the Rockies were not sufficiently craggy.

Others believed that the Colorado atmosphere with its brilliant clarity did not provide the romantic haze so crucial to alpine views. Such differences, inevitably seen as faults by American tourists, made the scenery inferior.[29]

Health promoters, however, often used scenic deficiencies to Colorado's advantage. Some claimed that the picturesque cragginess of the Swiss resorts provided too much shade, and that the glaciers and the long-lasting snow fields made the air dangerously damp. Even the quaint and historic villages, with their ancient plumbing systems and damp walls, created dangers for the invalid. Colorado, of course, was "the paradise of invalids," with its "life giving springs of mineral water, superior in their curative properties to those of Pau; a climate which Mentone or Nice cannot rival."[30] Boosters provided complicated charts in their literature, comparing the temperature, the humidity, the amount of sunshine, and even the number of deaths per season. Inevitably, they concluded that "Ems of the Rhine, Spa in Belgium, Baden-Baden, Karlsbad, and Teplitz in Bohemia, Homburg in Hesse, are not to be spoken in the same day with those of Colorado."[31]

A few observers preferred to describe Colorado as incomparable. Ernest Ingersoll, astonished by his first view of the Rockies, believed it could not be "described by any Eastern analogy; no other far mountain view that I ever saw is at all like it."[32] His response, however, was not typical. Most visitors searched for suitable European comparisons. Scenes that did not look like Europe made them uncomfortable, because European views provided the standard to measure scenic worth and beauty. Faced with distinctive landscape, observers found themselves without the words and images they needed to assure themselves of its value.

This problem was especially clear in descriptions of places in the Rockies that have no European counterparts. Royal Gorge and the Garden of the Gods are unique. They could not be readily compared to familiar European sights. Nineteenth-century tourists recognized the spectacular nature of the landscape in these popular tourist spots, but the unfamiliarity of the terrain challenged their conceptions of proper scenery. Europe no longer provided an adequate vocabulary, and visitors searched the entire world for suitable analogies.

The Garden of the Gods, an enormous collection of red sandstone rock formations just outside of Colorado Springs, stumped the most prosaic of

Pikes Peak and the Garden of the Gods

This engraving shows the snow-covered mass of Pikes Peak, which was far easier to describe than was the Garden of the Gods. Tourists struggled to describe the Garden of the Gods, eventually falling back on hackneyed European analogies that had little place among the eerie rock formations. (In W. H. Rideing, *Scenery of the Pacific Railways and Colorado*, 1878. Courtesy of the Bancroft Library.)

tourists. Ancient or medieval architecture seemed to offer the most promising comparisons. In a single sentence, one observer managed to compare the area to the Great Wall of China, the Egyptian Sphinx, the temples of Greece, and the castles of England.[33] "Here we have hints of Athens and the Parthenon, Palmyra and the Pyramids, Karnac and her crumbling columns," claimed a Colorado promotional pamphlet. Another promoter used a startling mix of architectural, domestic, and technological analogies in his struggle to categorize the sight. "Here are cathedral spires to furnish a very Milan; there a patch of giant mushrooms; on this side, solid rock shafts against which all the forces of modern enginery might beat in vain."[34] Finding suitable words to describe such a strange sight clearly presented difficulties for observers.

Royal Gorge, a huge cleft in the earth along the Arkansas River in southern Colorado, offered a similar challenge. It could be made palatable by using the concept of the sublime, which nineteenth-century Americans had adopted to make their landscape fit European definitions. Most descriptions of Royal Gorge emphasized its age and size, which were well suited to meet the requirements for a sublime view. One dramatic observer saw it as "tons and tons, masses and masses, miles and miles of solid rock, cleft by some Titanic upheaval of the Old Earth's crust, ages and ages gone by."[35] Ernest Ingersoll found himself unable to comprehend the vast scale of the gorge. He wrote that the traveler "strives for language large enough to picture the heights that with ceaselessly growing altitude hasten to meet him. He searches his fancy after images and similitudes that shall help him comprehend."[36] Just as had many of the first observers of the Far West's distinctive scenery, Colorado tourists developed a set of tools to describe what they considered inexpressible.

In addition to indescribability, sublimity, and resemblance to Europe, Colorado also offered another advantage for Americans concerned about the cultural qualifications of their landscape. History-hungry visitors recognized that the geological age of their "natural ruins" made them far older than the man-made ones of Europe. Natural history came to have great importance for American tourists. When a Union Pacific pamphlet promised that a Colorado visitor would be highly satisfied, "for he has seen nature face to face; he has learned more of . . . the world's ancient history, and the lives of ancient peoples than a whole library of books could ever teach him," the author of those words understood the power of such language.[37] The "world's ancient history" as observed in Colorado relieved Americans of some of their insecurities about the cultural worth of their scenery.

Gradually, Americans found other ways to install history into their landscape. Even the despised Indian could provide a certain historical flavor. The discovery of the first cliff houses in southern Colorado and northern New Mexico offered proof of the presence of ancient cultures in North America. A popular guidebook told tourists that "these ruins consist, in part, of cities, temples, walled enclosures and causeways, great castles, and fortresses, enormous burial mounds, cliff dwellings, scattering hamlets, canals of great extent and capacity." Because the author of this guidebook knew that the impoverished Indians most tourists saw at railroad stations did not provide the proper image of great ancient architects, he added that "beyond a doubt the people who possessed the country and built the improvements were of a much more civilized race than those found inhabiting it when visited by our earliest explorers."[38]

Others chose to be vague about who provided the history. One writer admonished his readers not to "forget how populous was this dry and garish valley during those bygone days, when the Crusaders were waking up Europe, and all that was known of America was that the Basque fishermen went to the fogbanks of an icy western coast to catch codfish."[39] It did not matter who made up this population as long as they existed in the distant past. Some promoters romanticized the Indians to fit the images created by Rousseau, Cooper, Longfellow, and other romantics. The Denver and Rio Grande spiced up a scenic description by noting "long ago the Indians of the region built their council fires here. The firelight danced across their swarthy faces." To give the scene an appealing European flavor, the pamphlet added that the fires had "Rembrandt tints" that lit up the "massive walls with a red glow."[40]

The romantic history, the indisputable evidence of geological age, the sublime vistas, the Alpine scenery, and the healthy climate gave Colorado Springs a world-wide reputation as a health spa and a fashionable gathering spot. P. T. Barnum noted its fame when he said of its visitors, "Two thirds of them come here to die and they can't do it."[41] More importantly, Colorado Springs managed to divest itself of the stigma of being "western" as opposed to being European. Its climate, scenery, and society provided a bulwark against the more unfamiliar aspects of the far western landscape, making it equal and even superior to both eastern and European resorts.

Given this reputation, people arrived in Colorado Springs expecting to find European scenery, perfect health, an Old World spa, and foreign royalty parading in the streets. Inevitably, some visitors were disappointed, especially those who arrived in the early years when much of the town was "a bleak, bare, unrelieved, desolate plain," according to poet and journalist Helen Hunt Jackson. Her first look at the Rockies did not remind her of the Alps. They seemed only a "dark range of mountains, snowtopped, rock walled, stern, cruel, relentless." The town did not have the ambience of a European resort. Colorado Springs appeared to be "small, straight, new, treeless," rather than the glamorous spa she had expected.[42]

Isabella Bird, an Englishwoman who came to Colorado Springs on the enthusiastic recommendation of friends, reacted similarly when she first looked at the town. "From the top of one of the Foot Hill ridges, I saw the bleak-looking scattered houses of the ambitious watering-place of Colorado Springs, the goal of my journey of 150 miles," she remembered. "A queer embryo-looking place it is, out on the bare Plains, yet it is rising and likely to rise. . . . To me no place could be more unattractive than Colorado Springs from its utter treelessness."[43]

Despite the unflattering early impressions, the embryos of Colorado Springs and Manitou did indeed develop into popular American versions of European watering places. As early as 1874, Rose Kingsley observed that "thousands of tourists from the Eastern States and Europe have visited these mineral springs in the last two years; while all around, the villa lots worth $500 and $1,000 are being rapidly bought up by people who wish to make their homes in this lovely spot."[44]

The more the Springs came to resemble a European resort, the more the area attracted Americans. Its mountain scenery required a superstructure of resort activity to make it equal to Europe's. Palmer worked hard to produce such an atmosphere. As early as 1873, he helped residents and visitors to organize the Colorado Springs Jockey Club, which sponsored horse races, shooting matches, and hunts. Shops, orchestras, croquet grounds, tableaux, tennis courts, promenades, and carriage rides kept people constantly amused. One observer found the scene too frenetic for his taste. "Hundreds and hundreds of our countrymen, and each with his five hundred friends . . . packed three and four deep in the upper rooms of summer hotels; living all season in valises and trunks; . . . climbing mountains and buying views for friends who had the sense to stay home . . . over-eating, over-sleeping, over-doing, and calling it all enjoyment."[45] This visitor clearly found the array of amusements rather startling.

Despite the wide range of social activities, many visitors spent most of the time attending to their health. Hordes of people frequented the medicinal springs, enclosed "in tasteful pavilions and surrounded by pretty cottages."[46] In 1883 a splendid new bathhouse replaced the rather ramshackle one built in the resort's early days. It offered hot and cold soda baths, Russian vapor, and electric baths in twenty different rooms. A thirty-foot-square plunge tank hosted well-attended "plunge parties." A Denver and Rio Grande guidebook described the exterior of the new baths. "Four tall towers guard the several corners of it and the facade is ornamented with a wide balcony. . . . The architecture is of no particular order, though rather inclined to that of Queen Anne."[47] The water inside the baths, combined with the dry atmosphere of the Colorado Rockies, made the Springs attractive to health seekers. A contented visitor explained his satisfaction by writing that "balmy, healthful Manitou . . . offers more pleasure, distraction and recreative opportunity than any [other resort.]" He concluded, "There is no other region that so nearly approaches the ideal, both in its conduciveness to health and its ecstatic delightfulness."[48]

Perfectly healthy people also found the area of delightful spot to spend a season. "More people, in fact," commented Ernest Ingersoll, "now go for the social life than for the sake of the waters."[49] Colorado Springs's distance from centers of population and its expensive housing made the region exclusive, and its residents and visitors hoped to keep it that way. In 1877, Dr. Samuel E. Solly and a group of wealthy residents founded the El Paso Club. An advertising pamphlet explained the purpose of such a club. "In a city like Colorado Springs, where so considerable a portion of the population belongs to the leisure and transient classes, a Club becomes an institution of peculiar value, giving to the visitor a pleasant introduction into the social life of the place." The pamphlet went on to describe the splendors of the club's building, adding that the visitor could not "fail to be impressed with the extraordinary social conditions whose demands have called into existence so elegant an institution"[50]

These extraordinary social conditions also helped to create the Cheyenne Mountain Country Club, one of the oldest in the nation, which had an exclusive clientele and an elegant clubhouse. It soon became "the most fashionable and exclusive club of Colorado Springs, devoted to out-of-door sports and amusements."[51] Here the residents of the Springs played polo, tennis, and golf and watched weekly horse races. The even grander Colorado Springs Opera House, brilliantly lit with 261 gas jets and graced with a glamorous drop curtain imported from Venice, opened in April of 1881.[52]

General Palmer and the members of the Colorado Springs Company must have been pleased with the success of their plans. In fact, the whole endeavor had been too successful, and the region could not house the flood of aristocrats, dignitaries, and wealthy parvenus arriving each season. As one shocked tourist discovered in 1881, "what I never should have dreamed, that Colorado Springs, known all over the country as a most desirable resort for invalids, has not a single comfortable hotel."[53] Colorado Springs was still a city of homes; and while Manitou did have some small guest houses, these did not meet the increasingly high standards of tourists. Wealthy visitors wanted luxurious facilities, not simply comfort. Residents and promoters alike realized that their city needed a grant hotel to maintain its status as a superlative resort.

The Hotel Del Monte: Europe on the Coast of California

As Colorado Springs's citizens worried about their lack of a proper hostelry, other far western regions with similar climatic and scenic attractions began to court American tourists. The second important resort development in the Far West created its reputation with a great hotel, rather than with a colony of homes as in Colorado Springs. Built by Charles Crocker and the Southern Pacific Railroad on the California coast in Monterey, the Hotel Del Monte soon became, in the words of its most enthusiastic promoter, "the Queen of American Watering Places."

Like Colorado, coastal California, especially the area south of San Francisco, met the requirements of wealthy Americans for a resort area. Though its climate differed from the mountain air of Colorado, California had an environment equally suitable for invalids and pleasure seekers.

California scenery boasted a great resemblance to parts of Europe, Italy, and Spain, rather than to Switzerland as did Colorado.

If possible, the concern about a healthful climate in California reached an even higher pitch than in Colorado. Certainly the coast of California could not advertise the advantages of dry air and high altitude, but it did offer warm weather and sea breezes. As early as 1857, an expert on climate, Lorin Blodget, had given this part of California favorable attention. In *Climatology of the United States*, he compared California's climate to that of Italy, Spain, and Portugal, where the invalids of the world had long flocked. Such claims had little impact until the 1870s, when the railroads made this region accessible. Sensing the possibilities for enormous profit, a group of medical "experts," encouraged by the railroads, embellished the science of climatology.[54]

This group published reports in medical journals, popular magazines, railroad guidebooks, and advertising pamphlets, announcing that coastal California had the most health-inducing climate in the world. Its claim to superiority rested on its year-round pleasant weather. California offered "a dry, equable climate, cool, rather than hot, having the least daily, as well as annual range of temperature, the most sunshine, the greatest exemption from storms."[55] Promoters claimed that this combination of factors made California a better place for the invalid than the resorts of Europe and the eastern United States.

By the late 1870s and the early 1880s, when the railroads took a serious interest in developing southern California, the issue of climate became paramount in their promotional schemes. California would become the new Mediterranean. Climatological experts made grandiose claims. "We find nowhere another all-the-year-round climate; none where the delicate invalid can find a winter mild enough for his strength, combined with a summer suitable to a northern constitution; none where endemic or local diseases do not threaten him."[56]

Undoubtably, the southern California coast offered a healthful climate; but perhaps more important to late nineteenth-century Americans, it offered scenery that could be compared to Europe's. The writer Charles Dudley Warner made the classic claims about California's resemblance to Italy that were quoted in thousands of advertisements, guidebooks, and promotional material. To the delight of American tourists, Warner proclaimed it "our Mediterranean region, on a blue ocean protected by barriers of granite from northern influences . . . Our New Italy."[57] Although most of the analogies involved southern Europe, California's variety of landscape provided fruitful ground for comparisons to all parts of Europe.

Others preferred to range farther in their search for analogy. "Southern California is very like Palestine in natural features, resembling that country far more than it does Italy, to which it is so often compared," explained one observer.[58] Some writers used even more worldly comparisons. "Imagine a land girdled by the blue waters of the Mediterranean, kissed by the soft winds of Greece, overarched by the ever sunny skies of Italy; give it the green meadows and branching oaks of Old England . . . paint upon it the valleys of France and Spain, the towering crags of the Rhine, and the snow capped mountains of Switzerland and Asia . . . and you have Southern California."[59]

Often, these descriptions referred to the issue of health, stating that the climate was "superior in many respects to the celebrated resorts in the Old World." One promoter announced that "compared to sunny Italy, its beautiful lakes, the enchanting banks of the Rhine, the renowned Adriatic and the shores of the Mediterranean, the climate of Southern California is unequalled."[60] Another writer, hoping to attract an international group of health seekers, explained "the invalids and wealthy idlers of Europe spend their summers in Switzerland, and their winters in Spain, Southern France, Italy, Greece, and Palestine." California, however, offered superior attractions because one could stay in one place year-round as "the natural features of all these countries are approximately represented in California."[61]

In terms of natural features, California did resemble parts of Europe; but, like Colorado, it lacked the historical features to make the analogies complete. John Hittell, a much-quoted publicist as well as an early historian of California, put it quite bluntly. "California has few ruins, and those few are not grand in size, nor beautiful in design, nor rich in historic associations."[62] This disturbed both promoters and tourists. The historical traditions of the Indians and the Spanish missions seemed crude and uninteresting compared to the buried cities of Greece, the Renaissance heritage of Italy, and the ruined castles and cathedrals of France, Germany and England. Most people simply chose to ignore this grave flaw and concentrated on the appearance of the landscape.

As in Colorado, however, landscape alone could not attract wealthy visitors. Even with its spectacular climate and its stunning scenery, few investors had dared to build the kind of resorts wealthy visitors demanded. "In accommodations and attractions we are still behind the hotels of Europe, with their bands of music, promenades, operas, libraries, and casinos," admitted one promoter.[63] Practical reasons lay behind this lag in development. Until 1881, southern California could not be reached by railroad from the east. Even when the transcontinental railroad made San Francisco and northern California accessible, the only way to reach southern California was by boat or stagecoach. Finally recognizing the region's potential, the Southern Pacific Railroad began building a line down through the Central Valley in the mid-1870s.

The project created great possibilities for real-estate developers and resort builders. The Southern Pacific took advantage of the opportunity and, in the guise of the Pacific Improvement Company, bought up seven thousand acres on the Monterey Peninsula—about one hundred miles south of San Francisco. Hoping to increase ridership on the railroad, which ran almost empty cars south of San Jose, and hoping to encourage development of Southern Pacific land along the coast, the company built a spur to Monterey and planned a glamorous resort hotel.

The project became the special pet of Charles Crocker, one of the four founders of the Central and Southern Pacific railroads. He intended the resort to outshine anything built in California, and for that matter in the United States. He boasted it would be the largest resort hotel in the world, and he personally supervised every aspect of its construction. To design the building, Crocker chose architect Arthur Brown, who had worked his way up through the Southern Pacific organization. Brown had designed bridges and snowsheds for the railroad, along with station hotels along the Central Pacific. Finally, Brown demonstrated his skill at designing opulence in the building of the splendid homes of Charles Crocker and Leland Stanford.[64]

Brown and Crocker chose the site for the hotel carefully. They located it in a spot just north of Monterey in great grove of trees, slightly removed from the ocean to protect the building and its guests from wind and spray. Because of the hotel's location, Crocker chose the name Del Monte, which he translated as "of the woods." During the winter and spring of 1880, when the tremendous structure went up, Crocker spent most of his time in Monterey watching his European fantasy take form.[65]

The Hotel Del Monte opened to great fanfare on June 5, 1880. A large group of "the flower of San Francisco's aristocracy" crowded aboard six elegant drawing-room cars to attend the opening ceremonies in Monterey. What met their eyes upon reaching Del Monte was indeed "the latest monument to Pacific Coast enterprise and prosperity."[66] California now had a resort that could rival any in the nation, perhaps in the world.

The Southern Pacific wasted no time in spreading the news about its glamorous new resort. By 1880, the railroad had devised a publicity system that included agents all over Europe and the United States. They paid writers like Charles Nordhoff and John Hittell to include Southern Pacific holdings prominently in their descriptive works on California. In 1879, the directors of the railroad hired Major Benjamin C. Truman to be the first professional public-relations agent on the West Coast. The opening of the Del Monte gave Truman his first nationwide exposure. In the fall and winter of 1880 he made a grand whistle-stop tour, distributing 25,000 pamphlets and displaying one thousand photographs of the hotel.[67]

Truman coined the phrase the "Queen of American Watering Places" to describe the Del Monte, a phrase quoted in nearly every discussion of the hotel. He emphasized its continental qualities as part of his effort to make the Del Monte the premier resort in the West. Recognizing that American visitors wanted to find health and pleasure in surroundings that reminded them of Europe, he quickly developed a vocabulary of European analogies, which were rapidly snapped up by other writers. Depending on the image he wanted to convey, Monterey could be Mediterranean, "Semi-Tropical," balmy, Greek, invigorating, or British, but never western, Californian, or American.[68] Truman clearly understood the economic advantages of creating familiar and comforting European images rather than unfamiliar and strange American ones.

Health remained a critical concern in promoting Monterey and the Del Monte. Promotional material attempted to prove Monterey to be "the healthiest and most delightful spot in the state and . . . the most perfect place for the invalid and valetudinarian to winter on the Pacific Coast, and perhaps in the world."[69] Publicists quoted climatologists and used elaborate statistics to demonstrate the superiority of Monterey. Ben Truman, along with many other writers, claimed, "A comparison of the meteorological tables show that the Pacific Coast from Monterey to Santa Monica has a better climate for consumptives than the famous Riviera of the Mediterranean Coast."[70] Other pamphlets used tables showing deaths per thousand people from pulmonary diseases, consumption, and malarial fevers. Not surprisingly, Monterey had a vastly lower rate than any place in the United States or Europe.[71]

Promoters with interests in all parts of southern California made similar claims, and Monterey's publicists had to find a way to make its climate seem extraordinary. Many praised the area for its even temperatures, using the ubiquitous charts to demonstrate that Monterey's temperatures varied less each day and between seasons than other places. Some claimed that the atmosphere created by the combination of ocean, pine trees, and mountains provided an extra boost for invalids, "for the pure oxyde contained in every atom of air, and snuffed in at every breath, has a most efficacious effect upon the system."[72]

However, what really made Monterey different or better than the rest of southern California was the presence of the Hotel Del Monte. As one guidebook noted, "while Monterey has always had the reputation of being the healthiest and most delightful spot in the state, it is only since the completion of the Hotel Del Monte that invalids and tourists have the comforts, enjoyments and surroundings which refined and cultivated people desire."[73] Because of its carefully crafted continental aura, the spectacular structure in the beautiful surroundings of the Monterey Peninsula attracted wealthy Americans and Europeans as no other spot in California could.

Charles Crocker and the Southern Pacific intended their resort to be for the rich and fashionable, and the place soon acquired a suitable reputation. An early description of the hotel noted that the Del Monte was "the fashionable and favorite watering place of California . . . a sanitarium of the prosperous kind that has received the imprimatur of fashion."[74] A weekend or season at the Del Monte soon became a requirement for wealthy San Franciscans or those who wanted to court favor with the powerful Southern Pacific. Society editors from the important San Francisco newspapers established correspondents at the hotel during the winter social season and printed daily columns about the activities of the guests. This reputation spread beyond California, and the Del Monte became a required stop for fashionable tourists. In a phrase first used by Ben Truman, but quoted by innumerable others, the Del Monte became "the court in which Queen Fashion holds her levees."[75]

Hotel Del Monte Exterior (1890)

The gray bulk of the Hotel Del Monte, lightened with turrets, towers, and gingerbread, represented the ideal for American tourists. Its carefully landscaped grounds surrounded guests with the luxurious feeling of an "English country manor." (Photo by C. W. Johnson; Courtesy of the Bancroft Library.)

The builders and promoters of the Del Monte created a resort cherished by late nineteenth-century tourists. However, climate and status made up only a part of the attraction of the Del Monte. Most importantly, it seemed comparable to European resorts. The railroad magnates who built the Del Monte recognized the American desire to find Europe in their own resorts, and acted upon it consciously. A description used in nearly every account of the Del Monte explained, "In its external and internal appearance, and in the social atmosphere and tone which pervade the entire establishment, the Hotel Del Monte reminds one more of a modern English country mansion than of an American watering place hotel."[76] No higher compliment could be paid.

The exterior of the hotel employed an amalgam of architectural styles, a polyglot of Europe that appealed to wealthy Americans. Architectural historian Harold Kirker called the hotel the largest Eastlake conception of the century, referring to Charles Eastlake's description of overblown

Victorian style. Contemporary observers, however, could not decide how to define the vast structure.[77] It combined Swiss stick style and Queen Anne, with a confusion of turrets, towers, gingerbread woodwork, and half timbering—all painted a pale dove gray. Some observers loved the hotel for "its airy modern Gothic facades, its incisive angles, its many sharp gables, minarets, and towers." One visitor had a harder time describing its style, noting "the hotel itself is, I suppose, Gothic—but I should say it is a mixture of splendid styles, making one of its own."[78]

If both tourists and promoters searched for words to describe the hotel, they agreed that it was the most splendid resort to appear on the West Coast. Ben Truman claimed it was "the handsomest watering place hotel in America. No seaside hotel open on the Atlantic coast can approach its plan of exterior."[79] A satisfied guest agreed that "it certainly is the hotel I like best of all I've seen, and you may be sure we haven't traversed this continent without taking in a goodly share of those public buildings."[80]

The interior of the hotel met with equal acclaim. At the opening ceremony, a San Francisco paper reported that "even the most sanguine of the visitors were delighted at the mighty and magnificent scale of everything about them."[81] The public rooms included billiards parlors, numerous sitting and writing rooms, glassed-in verandas, a ballroom, separate dining rooms for children and servants, and a tremendous lobby. The guest rooms provided lavish accommodations with chandeliers, plush carpeting, elegant tapestries, and telephones and running water (quite rare in this period).[82]

The carefully chosen décor created the impression of a European resort. Nothing reminded the visitor that he or she was in California rather than in England, Italy, or the south of France. English tile facings decorated all of the fireplaces with scenes out of Shakespeare, Walter Scott, or Greek mythology. The dining room, painted a brilliant white, seated eight hundred people in chairs copied from the Bank of London. Table linens imported from Italy, French tapestries, and English bone china completed the cosmopolitan scene.[83]

The building certainly had a European flavor in architectural design and interior décor, but the extensive grounds gave the resort an extraordinary atmosphere. A work force of forty full-time gardeners cultivated several hundred acres. The grounds included croquet plats, an archery ground, swings, lawn-tennis grounds, vast flower beds, carefully sculpted shrubs, and winding walkways—"in short, everything which an experienced landscape gardener's artistic eye can suggest." Many compared the grounds favorably to the famous English gardens of Kensington and Kew.[84]

Such a comparison was not accidental. The head gardener had been imported from England, where, according to the publicists of the Del Monte, he had trained in the gardens of English noblemen. He carved vast lawns out of the old forest in a "style after the manner of English landscape—gentle undulations of the surface." To complete the effect, he ripped out the natural cypresses, live oaks, and pines and replaced them with twelve hundred English walnut trees. An impressive evergreen-hedge maze, modeled after the one at Hampton Court, stood at the very center of the gardens.[85]

Even the few trees left in their natural state evoked memories of the Old World. George Wharton James, an influential California journalist, pointed out literary characters in every tree. "Here is a perfect Quilp, bringing *The Old Curiosity Shop* to remembrance. Yonder is Shakespeare's Richard the Third, humpbacked, but masterful . . . and if you stand here at a certain angle, yonder live oak projected against the tower brings vividly to mind Victor Hugo's Hunchback of Notre Dame."[86] Such literary associations were exactly what Americans had always hoped their landscape would evoke.

Although England garnered most of the honors in scenic comparisons, other Old World regions received attention as well. One advertisement claimed that the light streaming through the trees in the Del Monte forest was "such as is met with in the ancient minsters and Moorish alcazars of Europe."[87] Along the spectacular Seventeen Mile Drive that wound through the cliffs surrounding Monterey Bay, many people noted a resemblance to Italy, calling Monterey Bay the "Naples of the New World." They often found similarities in the vegetation of California and Italy. "Here and there one of the Monterey cypresses stamps the scenery with an astonishing likeness to points of view common in Italy, so strong is the resemblance between this tree and the stone pine, dear to the recollection of all travelers," commented an observant promoter.[88]

The famous cypress trees aroused a variety of European visions for visitors. They reminded a Boston journalist "of the weird cedars of the Roman Campagna which Inness is so fond of introducing in his Italian pictures."[89] A correspondent for *Harper's* believed the trees resembled "all the fantastic shapes imagined in Doré's illustrations to the 'Inferno.'" [90] Others preferred to point out the great age of the trees, comparing them to the cedars of Lebanon but insisting they were even older. "Some of these moss grown monsters, still living, still clinging to the rocks, give evidence that they were old when Christianity was still young," pointed out a guide to the resort grounds.[91]

As in Colorado, American tourists sought evidence of antiquity in their scenery. "There is antiquity for you here!" wrote George Wharton James obligingly. "The waves are composed of the same elements that dashed upon the shores of the primeval ocean, the granite is of the very foundations of the earth, and the cypresses and pines are hoary with age and the storms of unknown centuries."[92] For tourists determined to have human rather than natural history, the old settlement of Monterey could be made properly hoary. Guidebooks, exaggerating its age, claimed inaccurately that it was "founded by the Spaniards 174 years before the signing of the Declaration of Independence, and long before Shakespeare wrote his plays."[93]

For most visitors, however, the actual history of the area held little romance. The primitive adobe huts and mission churches seemed embarrassingly crude when compared to the cathedrals, temples, and castles of Europe. One early tourist stated bluntly that she found "nothing at all remarkable about Monterey, except that it is very dirty."[94] The Spanish and Mexican heritage of California, just like that of the Indians in other regions, had not yet had a glorious historical past attached to it. In the 1870s and 1880s, most tourists still found these people a shameful reminder of their nation's rawness. For now, natural history would have to satisfy their desire for antiquity. Most tourists seemed to accept the claim that "besides being climactic and scenic, Monterey is likewise historical," even if its ruins were "not the ruins of the splendor of Greece and Rome."[95]

The thousands who visited the Hotel Del Monte generally ignored this historical flaw and reveled in its climate and scenery. They could imagine themselves in a variety of Old World settings while basking in the equable temperatures of California. A souvenir pamphlet distributed by the hotel boasted that "one can rest in the shade of the pines and . . . catch a view of a French chateau, with oak studded glades, English park lands and manor house, and castles, in Spain or elsewhere, in the chimneys and

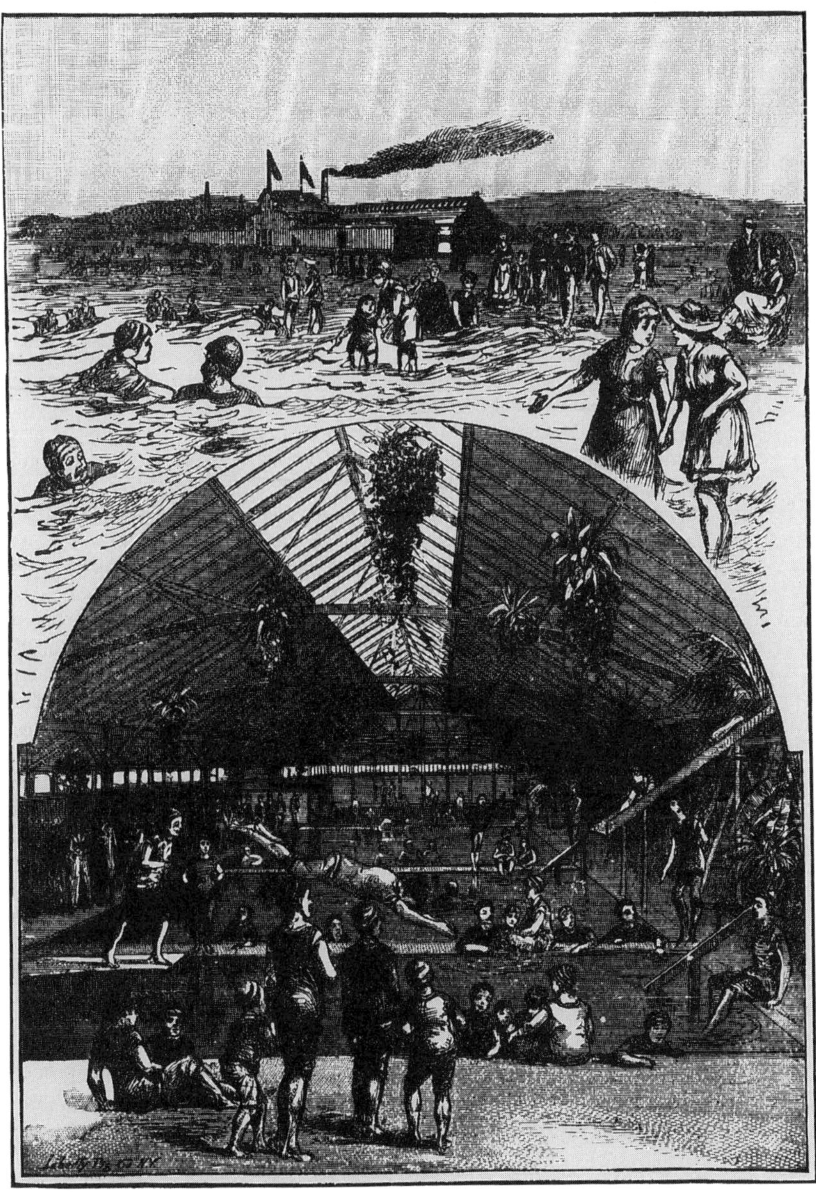

Swimming at the Hotel Del Monte

Guests at the Del Monte had their choice of water activities in the heated indoor pavilion or in the frigid waters of Monterey Bay. The sight of large crowds enjoying the surf, as in this advertisement, were undoubtably rare occurrences. (In Stanley Wood, *Over the Range to the Golden Gate: A Complete Tourist's Guide*, 1889. Courtesy of the Bancroft Library.)

angles of forest-hidden Del Monte."[96] If the Del Monte indeed held the title of "Queen of American Watering Places," it had attained this royal standing by emulating Europe better than any other resort in America.

Guests at the Del Monte did more than take the waters and gaze at the scenery. The hotel provided a full range of resort activities. People could play croquet, swing, walk in the garden, find shady benches or romantic places in the forest, or take a coaching trip along the Seventeen Mile Drive. For more excitement, guests could wander over to the race track and polo grounds where, during the season, races and matches were frequently held.[97]

In addition to the splendors of the hotel and its gardens, the beach and bathing pavilions attracted hotel guests. Because the surf rarely reached a comfortable swimming temperature in Monterey, the hotel built four large heated swimming tanks enclosed in a great hall. Hotel employees filled the tanks daily and heated each to a different temperature, hoping to please the most fastidious bathers. In 210 dressing rooms, both male and female bathers donned swimming apparel "to attend the natatorial matinees and to enjoy the exhilarating pastime of plunging, and screeching, and pulling, and swimming, and floating."[98]

Because of such activities, tourists from all parts of the globe enjoyed a stay in Monterey. Even the most practiced complainers could detect little to criticize at the Del Monte. Carolyn Dall, a well known suffragist sent west for her health, found western hotels disappointing. A chronic complainer, she saw nothing that met her standards until she settled at the Del Monte. The California climate seemed unreliable, hotel facilities fell far below her standards, people treated her disrespectfully, and even the Pacific Ocean disappointed her because it was "deficient in salt." The only person, place, or thing she liked during the entire seven months of her trip was the Hotel Del Monte. She raved about the scenery and the hotel itself, although she wondered if the raw society of California appreciated such splendor, for "it [the Del Monte] is furnished and finished in a manner that would not suit the Pacific shore for half a century."[99]

Everyone who visited the hotel and wrote about it could only praise the place. "Well we have spent a night and a day at this rarest of watering places, and I wish you were here to enjoy it with us," wrote one man to his children. "Your mother has just reveled in the garden today, and says this spot alone is worth the journey from New York."[100] An English tourist who spent most of his tour of the United States complaining about Pullman cars and American restaurants found no fault with the Del Monte. In fact, he suggested that "anyone who could contrive to get up a real *bona fide* grumble at the accommodation offered here, ought to be rewarded with a gold medal, and to be stuffed and placed in the British museum after death, as a curiosity."[101] James Muirhead, author of the enormously popular *Baedeker's Guide to the United States*, sealed the reputation of the Del Monte when he pronounced it the best hotel in the United States. Because he could make no criticisms of the hotel, Muirhead wondered if "the absolute perfection of the bright and soft Californian spring when I visited Monterey, and the exquisite beauty of its environment, may have dulled my critical facilities to a state of unusual somnolence."[102]

The Del Monte's European-inspired combination of architecture, landscape, and climate made the hotel a success. When the main hotel building burned to the ground on April 1, 1887, the Pacific Improvement Company recognized its value and rebuilt it almost immediately. They hired San Francisco architect A. Page Brown to design the new hotel. Brown, known for his eclectic style, had shown his talents in several major buildings that varied from Romanesque to Queen Anne.[103] By the beginning of the season in 1888, a new Hotel Del Monte greeted enthusiastic visitors.

Brown generally preserved the style of the first structure, though he enlarged it with two large wings connected to the main building by great sweeping verandas. New promotional literature described the hotel as having "Swiss architecture with a turreted and pinnacled skyline and broad comfortable verandas."[104] Quite understandably, descriptions boasted about the new fire-safety features of the buildings and emphasized the hotel's new size.

The hotel now accommodated more than one thousand guests in the same atmosphere of serene European elegance and comfort that impressed so many earlier visitors. Carpets from France and Belgium, wood paneling with English oak and San Domingo mahogany, daintily painted English tiles, and Flemish and Italian tapestries covered the interior of the building. The promoter George Wharton James described the new exterior as "a modern adaptation on a large scale of the old Flemish structures, just as one sees in Belgium, and occasionally in Switzerland."[105] In the eyes of its boosters, the new building perfected the European resort built by the Southern Pacific on the coast of the "American Italy."

In the last decades of the nineteenth century, the Hotel Del Monte reigned as the largest, most elegant, and most successful resort in the West. Its delights as a watering place received international attention. A tourist guide to the state of California boasted that "Del Monte has proved to be one of the rarest hotel successes on record." The writer explained that "instead of being a resort principally for the pleasure loving Californian," the Del Monte "attracted tourists from all parts of the globe; and its name as a blessed and beloved place has been sounded in every civilized land."[106] A visitor to the hotel who prided himself on his status as a world traveler asserted, "No greater success has been achieved in combining comfort, elegance, economy and beauty in a seaside hotel than at the Hotel Del Monte in Monterey."[107]

With such a record of success, the Del Monte became the standard by which all other western resorts were measured in the last decades of the nineteenth century. Careful emulation of European watering places, great emphasis on the climatic perfection of the area, and a constant round of social activities combined to overcome the image of crudity and rawness that haunted the West. Only the promise of a "European" experience could convince most tourists to visit the region. The Del Monte, a Swiss or Gothic or Eastlake building swathed in an English park and surrounded by an Italian or French coastal scene, provided an experience that Americans craved. Resort promoters in other parts of the Far West copied the successful formula.

Denying the Landscape: The Architecture of Colorado Springs

Developers in Colorado Springs, the oldest and most socially exclusive western resort, watched the Del Monte's success. By the early 1880s, the town could no longer house the throngs of health and pleasure seekers that traveled west each season. "There is now no comfortable place for strangers to stop in the city," the local paper complained in March 1881. "Correspondents of eastern papers have advertised this fact so well that Colorado Springs seems more distinguished for the fact it has no good hotel than for anything else."[108] In an area dependent on tourists, such a situation could not continue.

Town leaders and businessmen soon convinced General Palmer and the Denver and Rio Grande Railroad of the need for a hotel. The railroad put up half the construction funds and donated a prime piece of land, assuring that Colorado Springs would have a hotel worthy of its reputation. "The building will be an elegant and artistic structure," reported the local paper. "Cultivated people accustomed to the comforts of life will be induced to remain here if they find accommodations which satisfy them. The building will be an ornament to the city and a sightly object from the railroad station."[109]

A city that had gained its reputation by developing a "Little London" in the midst of the "Switzerland of America" certainly knew where to turn for architectural inspiration. Dr. Samuel E. Solly, the English climatologist largely responsible for making General Palmer's resort a famous watering place, drew up some very English designs for the hotel. Palmer and the other investors loved the gables, turrets, and towers; and they hired a Boston architectural firm, Peabody and Stearns, to make these a reality. The hotel required two full years for construction and cost nearly twice the original estimate, but General Palmer gladly picked up the difference. He also chose its name when it occurred to him that the great expanse of the hotel lobby would be the perfect spot to display his large trophy collection. By the spring of 1883, the entire town of Colorado Springs anxiously awaited the opening of its new attraction, the Antlers.[110]

When it opened on June 1, 1883, the Antlers disappointed no one. Officially, the architects called its design Queen Anne, but the Antlers had a style all of its own. At first glance it seemed to be an odd combination of castle and Tudor town house, with the first three stories of cut stone and the upper two stories boasting delicate woodwork. One admirer of the building's castle motif wrote that "the edifice is constructed of gray lava stone, with battlements and pinnacles so artistically arranged as to give an impression of massive yet graceful architecture."[111] Another promoter focused on the upper floors, which "present many peculiar, novel, and attractive features in their architectural design."[112] Like the Del Monte, the Antlers combined as many European attributes as possible.

The interior of the hotel had been carefully decorated in the most

HARPER'S WEEKLY.
JOURNAL OF CIVILIZATION.

Vol. XXX.—No. 1561.
Copyright, 1886, by Harper & Brothers.

NEW YORK, SATURDAY, NOVEMBER 20, 1886.

TEN CENTS A COPY.
$4.00 PER YEAR, IN ADVANCE.

"THE ANTLERS," COLORADO SPRINGS.—Drawn by Charles Graham.—[See Page 747.]

Antlers Hotel

The combination of the beauties of the Rocky Mountains and the splendor of the Antlers's mix of architectural styles attracted large numbers of visitors. Its fame had spread far enough by 1886 to make it worthy of the cover of *Harper's Weekly*. (*Harper's Weekly* 30 [November 1886]. Courtesy of the Bancroft Library.)

opulent fashion. Furnished with Gothic-style walnut furniture, elaborate wall hangings, thick imported carpets, and massive chandeliers, it echoed the hodgepodge effect of the exterior. The Colorado Springs paper described the splendor of the lobby décor, which included a red Wilton carpet, oak-and-leather chairs, and blue-and-gold Turkoman draperies. The paper emphasized the English touches in the hotel's interior, such as "andirons and fenders of polished steel and wrought iron, a combination of metals very fashionable in England at the present time."[113]

Like the Hotel Del Monte, the Antlers offered guests a wide variety of services. Billiards rooms, card rooms, children's nurseries, parlors, wide piazzas, and a splendid dining room promised to keep people occupied. The management of the hotel made sure the grounds surrounding the hotel had promenades, swings, and attractive carriage drives. The hotel's central location made it a popular gathering spot for local socialites and visitors. In accordance with Colorado Springs's reputation as a health resort, the Antlers boasted central heating, electric light, Turkish baths, fire alarms, and "everything that the inventive genius and progress of the day deem necessary for a first class hotel."[114]

The undeniably first-class hotel rapidly attained an impressive reputation, competing directly with the Hotel Del Monte. Publicists for the Antlers claimed, "In the superiority of its accommodations, it is unexcelled by any hotel in Colorado, or, in fact, the entire West."[115] Its attractions included an orchestra that played daily and elaborate balls to entertain people in the evenings, just as in the grandest European watering places. In keeping with the general European theme, the management lured French chefs from New York City and Paris and served tea each afternoon in the elegant parlors. Truly, a tourist could find "no hotel between Chicago and San Francisco where the appointments are more elegant, the neatness more manifest, or the cuisine more absolutely perfect."[116]

Like the Del Monte, the success of the Antlers depended on how much it reminded American visitors of a European resort. The setting, of course, provided a European atmosphere. Promoters constantly reminded tourists that Colorado was the Switzerland of America and that Colorado Springs especially had "views which challenge comparison with the most noted Alpine prospects."[117] According to the region's boosters, the scenery around Colorado Springs offered everything that Europe could and more: "sublime scenery bordering on the weird and supernatural, quiet vales and dells far excelling those of Europe."[118]

The Antlers fit right into this scene. It made the already booming Colorado Springs region a great success by giving visiting socialites a glamorous spot to spend the winter season. Women represented by the elegant Mrs. Forrester in Willa Cather's novel of the 1880s, *A Lost Lady*, frequented the hotel each season, drinking tea and dancing to the music of the orchestra. Visiting dignitaries always stopped at the Antlers while on a tour of the West. President Arthur recuperated there after his trip to Yellowstone in 1883, where he had intended to regain his health. With its Swiss setting, gray turrets, glittering chandeliers, and exclusive clientele, the Antlers evoked images of a European resort located in the American West.

The Colorado Springs region, however, did not reach the zenith of its European grandeur until the 1890s. The rebuilding of the Antlers and the construction of the Broadmoor Casino made the European analogy complete. In 1885 a Polish count named James M. Pourtales arrived in Colorado Springs, attracted by its money-making possibilities. He had come to the United States hoping to raise enough funds to buy back the family estate in Silesia, which had been lost because of generations of bad investments. He managed to scrape up enough cash to buy a failing dairy farm on a large parcel of land just south of Colorado Springs. After five years of constant effort and equally constant failure, he concluded that dairy farming would never solve his financial problems and he formed a land-development company.[119]

Pourtales envisioned a beautiful, tree-covered city of large homes surrounding a lake, even though the land had no lake and no trees. As a way to attract investors he also included a casino, which would be a "beautiful palace of refined pleasure."[120] Pourtales went right to work. He dug a huge hole and dammed up a stream to make a lake. He then planted about four thousand trees in a fifteen-acre park surrounding the casino. Despite the fact that the lake would not hold water and the unfortunate coincidence of the Johnstown flood, Count Pourtales remained confident of his success. Proudly, he claimed that "this spot of earth no longer looked like prairie land."[121] Trees and water slowly masked the dry Colorado plateau.

The count's casino would also help to transform the prairie into some-

Broadmoor Casino, ca. 1892

The sweeping wings of the Broadmoor Casino looked particularly out of place in the barren foothills of Colorado. Its completion, however, gave Colorado Springs a distinct European flavor that both residents and tourists enjoyed. (Courtesy of the Denver Public Library, Western History Department.)

thing more appealing to visitors. Pourtales built the casino next to the Cheyenne Mountain Country Club, which offered polo, tennis, hunting, and golf to athletically inclined residents and visitors. These activities and the grand casino would ensure Colorado Springs's supremacy as a resort area. "The completion of the Casino may fairly be said to mark an epoch in the history of the city," the local paper remarked hopefully. "There is now no good reason why such people as go in large numbers every winter to Italy and Southern France should not seek the superior climate of Colorado."[122]

The new epoch began on July 1, 1891, when the Broadmoor Casino opened. Lindley Johnson, a Philadelphia architect, modeled it after a German palace. Painted a brilliant white, the building presented a stately front portal supported by four Ionic columns and was decorated with painted iron grillwork. Graceful wings with open verandas swept to both sides. Inside, elegant dining rooms, ballrooms, game and billiards rooms, and a stupendous bar greeted the throngs of visitors on that opening day. Pourtales hired an equally glamorous staff to run his establishment. An imported French chef, a splendidly uniformed Hungarian orchestra, and a maître d'hôtel from one of New York's finest clubs dazzled the opening day crowds. Delighted with the success of Pourtales's project, the Colorado springs *Weekly Gazette* boasted, "Through the enterprise of a company of our own citizens we have a casino today, as handsome, as splendidly equipped and managed as any in Europe, and surpassing anything in the United States."[123]

Promoters did not hesitate to point out the cosmopolitan wonders of Colorado Springs's newest attraction. They emphasized the variety of activities in which one could indulge while visiting the casino. Dancing, gambling, polo, fishing, swimming, rowing, and sailing numbered among the charms of the Broadmoor. Pamphlets issued by the Colorado Springs Promotional Committee and the Denver and Rio Grande boasted about its electric plant, its electric railway, its charming pavilions and ornamental gardens, and the quality of its evening concerts. Most of all, promoters noted the casino's resemblance to the grandest of European resorts. "It has commanded the admiration, not unmixed with astonishment, of all visitors, and none the less when these had perfect acquaintance with the noted resorts of the East and with the German, French and Italian spas," one writer noted.[124]

The building completed the European fantasy that General Palmer and his railroad had begun in the Colorado Rockies twenty years earlier. American tourists could travel to Colorado and stay in the English grandeur of the Antlers, sipping tea in the afternoons. They could breathe dry air and look at mountain scenery in an American Switzerland. If they grew bored with England or Switzerland, they could drive out to the Broadmoor Casino and dine on French cuisine and drink French wine. In a building modeled after a German palace, they could gamble as if on the Italian or French Riviera while listening to the strains of a Hungarian orchestra. Once again, the Del Monte's formula of combining every possible European style proved to be appealing to American tourists.

Because its promoters played on powerful American desires to find a version of Europe in the United States, even financial disaster and devastating fire did not ruin the fortunes of Colorado Springs. When the Broadmoor Casino burned down in 1897, Pourtales decided to rebuild, though his land venture had long since strayed into bankruptcy. Although visitors adored his casino, no one bought plots of land on the dry prairie surrounding it. The new casino, opened in 1898, was a slightly

Broadmoor Casino, ca. 1898

The second version of the Broadmoor Casino arose from the ashes of the first in 1898. The building was smaller, but its white paint and elaborate portico still created a vision of European splendor. (Courtesy of the Denver Public Library, Western History Department.)

smaller structure but equally elegant. A local architect, Thomas McClaren, designed smaller wings but made the columned front portico even more impressive. The building's brilliant white paint still evoked images of an Italian Riviera at the base of the Rocky Mountains.

In October of 1898, about a year after fire destroyed the first Broadmoor Casino, the Antlers burned to the ground. Railroad officials immediately assured worried citizens that the Antlers would be rebuilt even bigger and better than before. Six well-known architectural firms submitted plans for the new hotel; and Varian and Sterner, a New York firm that had designed the Greenbriar Hotel in the Virginia resort of White Sulfur Springs, won the contract. Nearly three years after the fire, the new Antlers opened its doors to an eagerly waiting public.[125]

The architects produced a conglomeration of continental styles in the new structure. The exterior of the hotel seemed to be Italian Renaissance

Antlers Hotel, ca. 1902

The second edition of the Antlers presented a new mixture of European styles, this time tending toward Italian and Spanish design rather than using the mixture of English styles demonstrated in the first. (Courtesy of the Denver Public Library, Western History Department.)

with walls of silver gray brick and a red tiled roof. "Bold projecting eaves, loggias, and other features to obtain beautiful effects of light and shades, such as are found in Spanish buildings" added detail to the façade.[126] Two large towers and sixty decorative cast-iron balconies with green-and-white-striped awnings overlooked the street. An enormous piazza covered the entire front of the hotel, and an ornamental garden stretched out from the back.[127]

The interior combined more European motifs. One of the architects of the building called the style of the hotel's lavish décor "Napoleonic Empire," indicating the geographical range of the interior design. In the lobby, he created a color scheme that included red, gold, and ivory, dark green upholstered chairs, a floor of Venetian mosaic covered with oriental rugs, and tapestries "artistically arranged about the walls." A marble fireplace on one end and an orchestra balcony on the other framed the room, and an immense Italian marble staircase became the centerpiece. Light flooding through leaded stained-glass windows created brilliant effects in the entire room. A main dining room with a Spanish motif, private dining rooms of "François le Premier," and two smoking rooms (one Japanesque and the other with Flemish décor) added to the international glamour.[128] Such excess seemed necessary to assauge American doubts about the viability of a resort in the Far West.

The combination of the Antlers Hotel and the Broadmoor Casino completed the transformation of Colorado Springs from a high, dry, western plateau into an American version of a European resort. If certain environmental facts were ignored, the setting could be compared to Switzerland; the climate resembled that of the Pyrenees or the Alps; the towns echoed Swiss villages or English country manors; and the great hotel and casino could stand comparison with any spa in Europe. Investors, builders, and promoters alike recognized the American penchant for things European, and consciously chose architectural styles wealthy Americans wanted to see and used promotional vocabulary they wanted to hear.

Buildings like the Antlers Hotel, the Broadmoor Casino, and the Hotel Del Monte helped to assure concerned Americans that the vast expanses of the American West could be tamed. Railroads, cattle, wheat, gold, surveys, and small towns represented only the beginnings of a physical victory over the western landscape. A cultural taming would be much more difficult to achieve. In a nation that defined its status by comparison to the achievements of the Old World, the landscape of the West could only be appreciated when it could be successfully compared with Europe. Descriptions like "the American Switzerland" or "the American Italy" and carefully designed resort areas that molded the landscape into European replicas comforted insecure Americans.

Developing the Tourists' West: Scenes of European Splendor

The Far West included many landscapes that challenged American concepts of beauty, but it did contain small islands of spectacular scenery that could be transformed into bastions of a culture borrowed from Europe. As the first and most splendid of the early western resorts, Colorado Springs and the Hotel Del Monte became the models for other resort areas. As the railroads made other scenically suitable, regions accessible, luxurious hotels sprang up, their owners' hoping to repeat the success of the Del Monte and Colorado Springs. Almost all of these clustered on the California coast or in the Rocky Mountains where the scenery could be compared to familiar parts of Europe.

Of the hotels built during the late nineteenth century in "the American Italy," southern California, the Hotel Del Coronado in San Diego was the most opulent. When the transcontinental railroad connected San Diego to the rest of the nation in 1885, the old town became the newest boom town in rapidly growing southern California. Predictably, promoters boasted about the wonders of the San Diego climate, employing the usual European comparisons. In 1886, the writer Theodore Van Dyke claimed San Diego "is to Southern California what Italy is to Europe, the aggregation of its highest development of all its beauties and advantages."[129]

Reading such claims, two California entrepreneurs lately transplanted from the Midwest sensed the possibilities of a barren peninsula that stretched across the bay of San Diego. Elisha S. Babcock and H. L. Story bought up more than four thousand acres of land on the Coronado Peninsula and formed the Coronado Beach Company. Just as General Palmer had planned in Colorado Springs, Babcock and Story intended to build a community of homes. Rather late in the planning, they realized that a splendid hotel would be an excellent drawing card and found some architects to design and build one.

Babcock, the driving force behind the development, hired two young architects, James and Merritt Reid, to design his hotel. Because he had promised his investors that the hotel would be open within a year, Babcock gave the Reids little time to plan. They drew up some preliminary sketches for promotional materials but never had a chance to make detailed drawings. The construction of the hotel began in March of 1887, and the architects made daily plans for the construction crew of nearly two thousand Chinese laborers who had to be trained on the job. Miraculously, only eleven months after the pouring of the foundation, Babcock opened his splendid hotel on February 19, 1888.[130]

Despite the rush job and the inexperience of the architects, the Hotel Del Coronado was an immediate success. Like the Hotel Del Monte, it offered reminders of a variety of European regions to its visitors. Its great

Hotel Del Coronado, ca. 1890

The tremendous bulk of the Hotel Del Coronado with its acres of red roofs, white walls, and glass dominated the coast near San Diego. No single term could hope to define its architectural heritage. (Courtesy of the Bancroft Library.)

white expanse had elements of various architectural styles. A pamphlet describing the hotel explained that the design "is of a mixed character, partaking largely of the Queen Anne style, and having also much that is characteristic of the Elizabethan era." Fearing insult to aficionados of other styles, the writer added, "These styles, however, the architect has cleverly modified, and had associated them with many of the excellences of other schools."[131] The San Diego newspaper told its readers that the Del Coronado "is in the classical old Norman style of architecture, and, viewed from the sea, one may imagine himself approaching one of the famous old castles in Normandy."[132] The polyglot appearance demonstrated the desperation of far western developers to mimic Europe.

The structure rose five stories, providing space for over one thousand guests in rooms surrounding a central courtyard. A separate wing housed the cavernous dining room and the eleven-thousand-square-foot ballroom. The courtyard provided a focal point for the hotel, where a guest could easily forget he or she stood on a windy peninsula in southern California. Lush plants, marble statues, and playing fountains and streams were supplemented with a large orchestra and brilliant electric lighting at night, reminiscent of the Italian Riviera with hints of tropic delights.[133]

White Drawing Room, ca. 1890

This drawing room in the Hotel Del Coronado shows the ornate and eclectic style of décor favored by late nineteenth-century tourists. The room includes objects from nearly every part of the globe. (Courtesy of the Bancroft Library.)

Hoping to please every taste, the architects designed the interior décor in a variety of styles. Advertising pamphlets described the furnishings and décor in intricate detail. "You wonder whether you are in a fairy palace or a hotel of the nineteenth century," claimed one writer.[134] Another noted that "the frescoeing *[sic]* of the ceilings and the walls is the work of a master and not surpassed by anything of the kind in the palaces of Europe."[135] Others emphasized the more exotic splendor of "the soft Persian rugs, the oriental tapestries, the antique designs of the furniture, the luxurious baths, the odor of the orange and pomegranate blossoms."[136]

Tourists responded positively to this European elegance, finding its mélange of influences inspiring rather than confusing. As in Monterey and Colorado Springs, the tourists came to San Diego because of its billing as the Italy of America. The town itself, however, did not look Italian in the least. When the railroad began delivering tourists in the late 1880s, San Diego had ramshackle buildings, dusty streets, and lounging Indians—all that American tourists found embarrassing about the Far West. Just across the bay, however, the Del Coronado offered insulation from such crudities as crumbling missions and destitute Indians. Guests could sit in the spectacular courtyard, protected from the winds that plagued Coronado, and imagine themselves on the Riviera. They could dine gazing out at an American bay of Naples. Lounging in a parlor stuffed with velvet upholstered furniture and frescoed walls, a visitor could pretend he sat in a European palace. For these reasons, the Del Coronado appealed to the tourists who could afford to stay there.

The same kind of appeal drew tourists to another hotel, this one located in the midst of the Colorado Rockies. In 1885, a wealthy mining engineer named Walter Devereaux discovered coal in Glenwood Canyon on the western slope of the Rocky Mountains. Devereaux also noticed some hot springs bubbling up on the edge of the Colorado River as it ran through the canyon. Local Indians had known about the medicinal qualities of the largest of these springs, the Yampah, for centuries. The area also presented the kind of scenic qualities that appealed to American tourists. Ernest Ingersoll, who had traveled through the canyon in 1885, predicted that "hither will come the painters, who need not go to Switzerland for snowy bergs, nor to Scotland for lochs, nor to Norway for splendid forests of pine and spruce."[137] Devereaux had discovered another bastion of Europe in the Far West.

The combination of beautiful scenery and coal convinced both the Denver and Rio Grande and the Colorado Midland railroads to build extensions into the region. When the Denver and Rio Grande reached Glenwood Springs in 1887, Devereaux began to develop his new resort in earnest. Within a year he had landscaped a large area with trees, lawns, flower beds, and paved walks and had built a five-hundred-foot-long pool. Devereaux hired a Viennese architect, Theodore von Rosenberg, to build the largest hot springs pool in the world, elegantly called the Natatorium. Von Rosenberg also built a stone bathhouse, which he promised would be "a bit of old Vienna in a Colorado setting." The three-story bathhouse included forty-two Roman baths equipped with imported tile and porcelain tubs sent from England, a lobby, and men's and women's parlors. The top floor contained a men's casino that required full formal dress.[138]

Before the Natatorium and bathhouse reached completion, Devereaux began advertising his new spa. He convinced both the Denver and Rio Grande and the Colorado Midland to print promotional tracts detailing the scenic and health attractions of the area and the opulence of the new buildings. Naturally, they emphasized the European qualities of Colorado's newest resort. "We pass the beautiful bath-house, built in medieval style, begetting dreams of the Rhine,—see the great hot springs, bubbling forth from nature's bosom, healing the sick, invigorating the well," noted one advertisement.[139] Another bragged about the efficacy of the waters in comparison to European spas. "Taken internally, as at Kissengen, Hamburg and other springs, these waters stimulate the gastric juices and intestinal secretions, promote the action of the bowels and the flow of bile and improve the circulation."[140] A Denver and Rio Grande pamphlet coined the phrase "the Kissengen of America," referring to a reknowned German spa. To add weight to its claims, the pamphlet listed the diseases the waters from the Yampah spring could cure: "blood diseases, indigestion, constipation, hemorrhoids, scrofula, salt rheum and diseases of the skin in all their various forms, nervous prostration, general debility, rheumatism, and gout."[141]

Tourists, of course, found this all very attractive. "The large red stone building set in the midst of a beautiful park on the bank of a river with the terraced lawns and the great mountain for a background . . . all go to make up a picturesque scene which at once enchants the visitor," reported an early observer.[142] An enthusiastic tourist predicted, "In a few years Glenwood Springs will doubtless be one of the most popular and attractive resorts in the Rockies, and its fame will become as world-wide as Wiesbaden."[143]

Such responses prompted Devereaux to add more European flourishes. Observing the success of Colorado Springs, in 1890 he formed the Glenwood Polo and Racing Association, which catered to the wealthy tourists who stayed in small guest houses now dotting the canyon. The association built a grandstand and a splendid clubhouse overlooking immaculate polo grounds and a race track. At the same time, Devereaux hired the New York architectural firm of Boring, Tilton, and Mellon to design a hotel to complement his already lavish development.[144]

The architects chose the Villa Medici in Rome as a model for the new hotel. They placed the huge structure on a hill overlooking the Natatorium to make it visible from miles around. Two central towers rose above a three-sided building, surrounding a central court that contained sloped terraces and a large Florentine fountain. Elaborate loggias festooned the exterior of the building, which was constructed of peach sandstone and cream-colored brick and was capped with an ornate tile roof. Devereaux's Hotel Colorado cost $850,000 and took two years to build.[145]

Hotel Colorado and Natatorium, ca. 1894

The grandly Italianate Hotel Colorado in Glenwood Springs overlooked landscaped grounds and the imposing structure of the Natatorium, which included a full casino as well as the largest hot-springs pool in the world. (Courtesy of the Denver Public Library, Western History Department.)

When the hotel opened on June 10, 1893, the company planned a gala weekend and shipped in all of Colorado's elite and a huge number of reporters. The crowd responded enthusiastically. The Denver *Times* called the hotel "a monument of architectural grace and elegance." Reporters found the interior of the hotel equally impressive with its ballroom, music room, billiards rooms, and innumerable parlors. "The furnishings are costly, artistic and complete," the paper reported. "The foot sinks ankle deep in Persian rugs and velvet carpets, wall hangings and tapestries meet the eye in effective places and heavy antique furniture adorns the dining room and corridors." The dining room received special acclaim. Its five-thousand-square-foot expanse included acres of glass and a deep pool stocked with trout, from which guests could choose their breakfast fish.[146]

The Hotel Colorado echoed the formula resort builders had developed in Colorado Springs and Monterey. As one advertising pamphlet promised, it "was the Hotel del Monte with improvements."[147] Walter Raymond, the first manager of the hotel, had run a successful tour company for wealthy easterners out of Boston and understood what attracted American tourists. He convinced the Denver and Rio Grande to include the Hotel Colorado in a huge promotional effort. The railroad flooded the nation with pamphlets, books, and posters. The European-style scenic and health attractions along with the Italian elegance of the buildings were all calculated to attract elite tourists. The elegant Natatorium, the Inhalatorium, the casino, the alpine scenery, and the "stately Italian palace, built of red sandstone and Italian brick" where one could "listen to the music of a German quartette band" played on American concerns about their culture's comparability to that of Europe.[148] Once again, the success of the hotel rested on its ability to re-create a European experience in an American setting.

In the Far West, railroads and land developers had discovered the perfect region in which to build glamorous resorts. To be successful, an American resort had to evoke images of Europe. It had to be located in an area offering scenery that could be described in European terms. Because many European resorts were famous for the healthy benefits of their climates, and because of the concern about health in the late nineteenth century, American resorts had to promise miraculous climatic cures. With their spectacular scenery, cool sea coasts, and high-altitude mountain areas, California and Colorado provided ideal natural settings.

Scenery and climate contributed only part of the attraction for a resort area. American tourists demanded architecture modeled after the most well-known European designs. Their concern about emulating Europe made opulent furnishings, elaborate landscape design, and elegant entertainment a requirement. Such attributes insulated them from the wilderness that still made up a large part of the far western landscape. Because comparison to Europe had created such a large part of the culture of nineteenth-century America, most wealthy and educated Americans could only be comfortable in surroundings where they could use familiar European analogies. Clever promoters recognized this need and carved European citadels out of the far western landscape.

Such an approach, however, faltered as the railroads opened up more and more of the Far West for tourists to inspect. Too many places had no resemblance to European scenes but still had spectacular qualities. As trains carried them across new parts of the far western landscape, Americans discovered places that offered stunning beauty, but that could not be described in the terms they had borrowed from Europe. The discovery of this variety and distinctive beauty, along with a growing sense of American self-confidence, jolted Americans out of their dependence on European scenery.

CHAPTER 5

The Far Away Nearby: Discovering the Far Western Landscape, 1885–1915

Even as tourists eagerly sought an American version of Europe in the Far West and clamored for European replicas in their hotels, the pressures of economy and curiosity pushed exploration and development beyond the confines of the transcontinental railroad line. New railroad routes opened up great tracts of land for public inspection, and well-publicized government surveys once again brought back news of strange but spectacular wonders. An explosion of information in the 1870s and 1880s, with its wealth of written description and pictorial evidence, steadily eroded the fragile framework Americans had adopted to describe the far western landscape. New enthnographic and geologic discoveries complemented changing attitudes toward the value of the wilderness. These changes, in addition to a growing national self-confidence, provided the language and tools necessary to create a distinct American aesthetic.

A New America: The Language of the Great Surveys

The process began as American scientists and explorers looked beyond the narrow band of the forty-first parallel. In the wake of the opening of the transcontinental railroad and the huge demand for public information about the lands it made available to the public, the government sponsored a series of scientific surveys. The first, headed by geologist Clarence King, began in 1867. King, though only twenty-five years of age, had already made his mark in geological circles as part of the official Survey of California and had published popular articles in leading magazines. Over the course of several years, King planned to map a swath of land one hundred miles wide along the line of the fortieth parallel from Denver to Virginia City. Although the Union and Central Pacific railroads ran close to the line of the survey, the *New York Times* called it a "wild and unknown region."[1] From 1868 until 1872, when the survey officially ended, King's exploits kept the Far West in the headlines.[2]

Though King's survey was the most scholarly, and perhaps the most thorough, the surveys of the 1870s were even more spectacular in showcasing the wonders of the Far West. In 1871, the United States Army sent Lieutenant George Montague Wheeler to explore "those portions of the United States territory lying south of the Central Pacific Railroad, embracing parts of Eastern Nevada and Arizona."[3] Aside from the rapid 1853 survey of the region in search of a possible railroad route, few whites had visited this part of the continent. In order to publicize the survey, Wheeler hired photographers Timothy O'Sullivan and William Bell and brought along reporters Frederick J. Loring from *Appleton's* and William Henry Rideing from *Harper's* to chronicle the expedition.

The photographs and articles brought back a new world to Americans, one that could not be described in European terms. Wheeler's men found much beauty in the bleakest part of the Great Basin, including Death Valley, the deserts of southern Nevada and Utah, and parts of the Sonoran desert. Trying to sum up the strange appearance of the landscape, William Rideing explained that it was both "rugged, weird, and depressing" and "beautiful, luxuriant, and inspiring."[4] By 1878 when the survey concluded, Wheeler had accurately mapped much of the Southwest, catalogued the great variety of plant and animal life, and made considerable contributions to knowledge about the native peoples of the region. More importantly, his survey took the first step in introducing Americans to the unfamiliar grandeur of the Southwest.

During the same years, the first entirely civilian expedition, funded by the Department of the Interior, examined other parts of the Far West.

Led by Dr. Ferdinand Vandiveer Hayden, the survey ranged all over the mountain west, from Montana to New Mexico. Hayden, a master at public relations, received generous funding for nearly a decade and brought back photographs, paintings, and written reports to prove the wonders of the West. His success included detailed accounts of the Yellowstone country, the southern Rockies, and the cliff dwellings of Mesa Verde—regions that held "some of the grandest, as well as the most beautiful forms of scenery in the world," as Hayden explained. He worked hard to publicize the West and to make Americans believe that "neglecting the handiwork of Nature" in the West signaled "a want of education and good taste."[5] He also wrote lavishly illustrated books and articles, handed out photographs and lithographs of western scenery to friends, family, and members of Congress, and succeeded in keeping western exploration newsworthy.

Hayden's greatest contribution may have been his expeditions to the Yellowstone in 1871 and 1872, which brought back scientific and pictorial evidence of bizarre and spectacular scenery. Rumors of a land of boiling lakes, gigantic mountains, and erupting geysers in the northern Rockies had circulated since 1807 when John Colter, a fur trader and former member of Lewis and Clark's expedition, stumbled into the area while escaping from some Indians. "Colter's Hell," however, was not explored by whites in any systematic way until 1869. The region received its first national attention from an 1870 expedition headed by Nathaniel P. Langford, former governor of Montana and agent of the Northern Pacific Railroad.

Langford brought back news of a landscape that looked like nothing anyone had seen before. Brilliantly colored hot springs, strange limestone and sulfur formations, stupendous geysers, great waterfalls, and awe-inspiring canyons dazzled these early explorers. In a series of articles in *Scribner's Magazine*, Langford attempted to describe what he had seen. Faced with the old dilemma of inadequate vocabulary, Langford explained that "the scene surpasses description. It must be seen to be felt."[6]

Some parts of the thermal regions of the Yellowstone in northeastern Wyoming could be described with architectural analogies, and Langford made the most of these. He listed the "great variety of fantastic forms," the "turrets, castles, spires, keeps, and towers" created by water, time, and chemical action.[7] Other aspects of the landscape did not lend them-

Yellowstone's Thermal Formations

This engraving from *Scribner's* exaggerated both the size and the odd shape of the thermal formations in Yellowstone. This article and the illustrations that accompanied it gave American readers their first view of the strange world that became known as Wonderland. (In Nathanael P. Langford, "The Wonders of the Yellowstone," *Scribner's Monthly* 2 [June 1871]. Courtesy of the Bancroft Library.)

selves so easily to grand comparisons. Many of the geothermal wonders, like mud pots, boiling springs, and vapor caverns, disgusted Langford's party with "the foulness of the vapors, the infernal contents, the treacherous incrustation, the noisy ebullition, the general appearance of desolation."[8] The geysers, however, represented a known quantity and could be favorably compared to those in other parts of the world. Travel writers made much of the geysers in Iceland, first popularized in the mid-nineteenth century, but Yellowstone's were undeniably more spectacular. Once again, the United States had scenic wonders that made others "dwindle into insignificance."[9]

Langford's reports created immediate national interest in Yellowstone; and Congress authorized a large civilian expedition, headed by F. V. Hayden, to explore the area in great detail. Hayden recognized the public-relations value of such a trip and managed to convince a photographer, William Henry Jackson, and a painter, Thomas Moran, to accom-

Thomas Moran, *Castle Geyser, Upper Geyser Basin* (1873)

Moran's watercolor presented Americans with a startling new world. He captured the vibrant color, unfamiliar forms, and the powerful forces of nature that made the Yellowstone region unique. (Chromolithograph in F. V. Hayden, *The Yellowstone National Park and the Mountain Regions of Portions of Idaho, Nevada, Colorado, and Utah*, 1876. Courtesy of the Bancroft Library.)

pany him without pay. Jackson scraped up a bit of his own money, while Thomas Moran got an advance from *Scribner's* and a five-hundred-dollar "gift" from Jay Cooke of the Northern Pacific Railroad. No pictures had yet been made of the thermal wonders and the mountain scenery; and, as W. H. Jackson remembered, "Dr. Hayden was determined that the first ones should be good."[10]

Upon his return, Hayden wasted no time in publicizing his trip and the territory he had explored. He published an elaborate government report, illustrated with Jackson's photographs and engravings of Moran's drawings and paintings, which he distributed to members of Congress and other important officials. He also wrote articles for popular magazines describing the fabulous wonders he had seen. He reported the existence of "one remarkable vision after another, each unique of its kind and surpassing all others in the known world."[11]

William Henry Jackson, *Castle Geyser and Still Spring* (1871)

Jackson's photograph of Castle Geyser demonstrates that Moran's paintings were hardly exaggerations. The fantastic shapes and the steaming earth seem even more otherworldly in the photograph taken of the same scene. (In U.S.G.S. Survey of the Territories, Photographs, 1871, vol. 1. Courtesy of the Bancroft Library.)

Hayden, a trained geologist, did not have to struggle for words in the same way as Langford did. He recognized immediately that European analogies had no relevance in this new world, and the language of science now served him well. He rarely used architectural terms or the rhetoric of the sublime. Instead he described the sights in precise geological terms, emphasizing evidence of the earth's creation.[12] For Hayden, the remarkable geysers and hot springs of the regions did not evoke images of Dante's inferno, but were "nothing more than the closing stages of that wonder period of volcanic action that began in Tertiary times."[13] Hayden detailed the vibrant colors created by mineral deposits and varying water temperatures at Mammoth Hot Springs with an eye for scientific accuracy rather than an ear for European metaphor. When words occasionally failed him, the stark grandeur of Jackson's photographs and the brilliant color of Moran's paintings filled the gaps.

The rich description and stunning visual evidence convinced the government to form the world's first national park—a preserve of wild land set off for the use and pleasure of the nation's people. Langford had suggested the possibility of preserving the Yellowstone landscape to influential railroad and government officials. Hayden also advocated the creation of such a park, asking "why will not Congress at once pass a law setting it apart as a great public park for all time to come?"[14] Congress, with pressure from the Northern Pacific Railroad and other speculators, responded; and, on March 1, 1872, President Grant signed the bill making Yellowstone into "a public park or pleasuring ground for the benefit and enjoyment of the people."[15]

This particular government action did not receive much attention. The remote and wild location of the new national park made it inaccessible to most tourists, and many years would pass before the Northern Pacific line reached it. Given the desire of most tourists to luxuriate in splendid hotels in settings that reminded them of Europe, Yellowstone had little attraction in the last decades of the nineteenth century.

Many Americans found the descriptions of Yellowstone uncomfortably strange. A review of Thomas Moran's huge painting, *The Grand Canyon of the Yellowstone*, bought by the Congress and hung in the rotunda of the Capitol, showed discomfort with the unique scenery. The reviewer complained about the "outlandish yellows" in the painting and accused Moran of omitting "the magic which converts crudity into splendor." Nature, he believed, surely gave the canyon walls an occasional "studio-light" or "some refinement of a pinkish dawn."[16] This reviewer, along with many other Americans, was not yet prepared for the new world offered by the far western landscape.

Yellowstone Park represented only one of the spectacular "discoveries" of the 1870s. In a series of three expeditions, Major John Wesley Powell examined the last truly unknown portion of the Far West, the canyonlands of the Colorado River. Powell's first explorations, thrilling boat trips through the rapids of the Colorado River into the heart of the Grand Canyon region, received tremendous publicity. Throughout the 1870s, Powell's survey gathered information that astonished scientists and the general public. Popular accounts of his expeditions appeared in *Scribner's*

Thomas Moran, *Grand Canyon of the Yellowstone* (1872)

Moran's tremendous painting brought the fantastic beauty of Yellowstone to American viewers. He enlarged the canyon, but he painted the unusual colors and the geological features with painstaking accuracy. (National Collection of American Art, Smithsonian Institution. Lent by the U.S. Department of the Interior, Office of the Secretary.)

Monthly, and an edited version of his government report became a classic in western adventure literature.[17]

Describing the Grand Canyon and the plateau surrounding it presented a challenge to Powell and other members of his expeditions. The sheer canyon walls, the great pinnacles of rock, and the strikingly unfamiliar colors rendered the usual descriptive terms useless. The artist William Henry Holmes put the problem succinctly when he called it "a great innovation in natural scenery."[18] Most early explorers of the canyonlands relied on the architectural analogies that had served western travelers for more than half a century. Powell, who read Longfellow, Scott, Whittier, and Coleridge aloud to his men, wrote of it as "a weird, grand region . . . a whole landscape of naked rock with giant forms carved on it, cathedral shaped buttes towering hundreds or thousands of feet."[19] Frederick Dellenbaugh, who accompanied Powell on his second expedition, saw "a thousand strange and fantastic suggestions from the dark tower against which Childe Roland with his slug horn blew defiance, to the airy structures evolved by the wonderful lamp of Aladdin."[20]

Grand Canyon of the Colorado

Overarching and pinnacled rock walls and an apocalyptic sunset romanticize this early view of the Grand Canyon. The illustration dramatized Powell's account of his daring trip through the unknown canyon. (In J. W. Powell, "The Canons of the Colorado," *Scribner's Monthly* 9 [March 1875].)

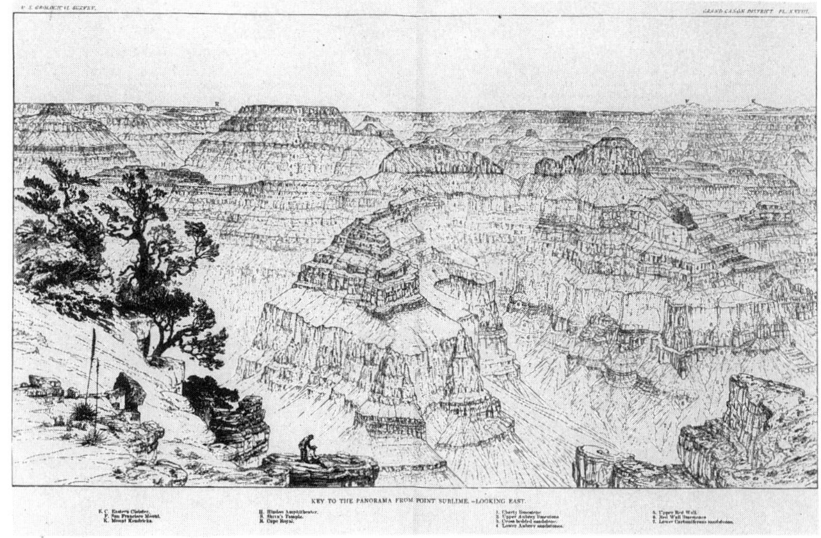

William Henry Holmes, *Panorama from Point Sublime* (1882)

William Henry Holmes's precise drawing attempted to grasp the size and splendor of the Grand Canyon. His carefully labeled and intensely accurate view portrayed the unimaginable sweep of the view from the south rim. (In Clarence E. Dutton, *Tertiary History of the Grand Canyon District*, 1882. Courtesy of the Bancroft Library.)

None of these analogies seemed entirely satisfactory. The explorers attempted to describe the colors of the region, "the vermilion gleams, and the roseate hues, blended with tints of green and gray," but often, words simply failed them.[21] "Language fails to describe the emotions engendered by the sublimity of this scene," admitted E. O. Beaman, photographer for one of the expeditions.[22] Powell himself often found the landscape "too vast, too complex, too grand for verbal description."[23]

The most successful of Powell's observers and scientists to capture the region of the Grand Canyon in words was Major Clarence E. Dutton. After years of surveying among the canyonlands and the plateaus of the Southwest, Dutton learned to describe without ornate verbiage or the crutch of Old World comparisons. Because he understood the exceptional quality of the plateau region, he recognized the need for a new vision. "The lover of nature," he explained, "whose perceptions have been trained

William Henry Holmes, *Sunset on the Kanab Desert* (1882)

Holmes's painting, though perhaps not as geologically accurate as his line drawings, captures the silence and the power of evening in the canyonlands. (In Clarence E. Dutton, *Tertiary History of the Grand Canyon District*, 1882. Courtesy of the Bancroft Library.)

in the Alps, Italy, Germany, or New England, in the Appalachians or Cordilleras, in Scotland or Colorado, would enter this strange region with a shock."[24]

Dutton described what he saw methodically, using geology, color, shape, and size. In looking at the canyon from Point Sublime, a vista that would later become familiar to tourists, Dutton approached his task in an orderly way. First, he explained, he had to "dismiss from his mind, so far as practicable, any preconceived notion" of the landscape.[25] Then, he allowed his eye to sweep panoramically across the fifty miles of visible landscape. The canyon wall, he noted, was not "sharp and flat," but rather "rambles in and out" with "angles that are acute and descend as sharp spurs like the forward edge of a plowshare."[26]

After viewing the grand sweep, Dutton moved in for a more focused look. His eyes moved vertically, describing the towering walls as "a series of many ledges and slopes, like a molded plinth, in which every stratum is disclosed as a line or a course of masonry."[27] Precisely, Dutton illuminated the geology and appearance of the spectacular scene from top to bottom. The "summit strata," he wrote, "are pale gray, with a faint yellowish cast." Then came "the cross-bedded sandstone," characterized by "a mottled surface of pale pinkish hue." Systematically, he moved through the "nearly 1,000 feet of" the "intensely brilliant red lower Aubrey sandstone" to the "purplish red" of the "Red Wall limestone from 2,000 to 3,000 feet," to the final layer of the "deep browns of lower Carboniferous."[28]

To complete his description of the complex and splendid view, Dutton depicted the changes in its appearance over the course of the day. Again, he used a careful blend of scientific terminology, color, and shape but allowed himself a more dramatic tone. In the morning, he explained, "the chasm slumbers," its recesses shadowed and covered with haze. As the day progresses, however, light slowly wakes the shapes of the canyon, and "their wilted, drooping, flattened faces expand into relief." Suddenly "colors begin to glow," and "the haze loses its opaque density."[29] At sunset, the sight reached a visual crescendo. "Broad slant beams of yellow light, shot through with glory-rifts" illuminate the depths of the canyon, revealing "kingly colors." For a fleeting moment, Dutton wrote, "the summit band is brilliant yellow, the next below is pale rose" and "the grand expanse within is a deep, luminous, resplendent red."[30] Such descriptive passages show that Dutton understood the novelty of the landscape he was attempting to envison for his readers. He hoped that an orderly movement over space and time, using ordinary words and basic scientific terms, would serve his readers better than vague analogies to European scenes or famous works of literature.

Dutton did use some familiar architectural terms, but he often chose references to the Far East to express the alien and exotic quality of the landscape. In preparing maps for the survey, Dutton had the opportunity to name many topographical features. He filled the depths of the Grand Canyon with shrines, temples, thrones, and castles lived in and sat upon by Wotan, Shiva, Vishnu, Isis, and even King Arthur. In his eccentric mixture of geological terminology, clear description similar to Mark Twain's passages on the Mississippi River, and his poetic use of Eastern and mythological analogy, Dutton represented an important step in understanding the unique scenery.

The surveys of the 1870s brought Americans more than a set of new wonders to ponder. The scientists of these surveys also introduced a different attitude toward native Americans. The new science of ethnography and the "discovery" of settled Indian cultures in the Southwest complicated white American ideas about Indians. As the members of each survey catalogued plants, animals, rock formations, and topographical features, they also kept careful records of Indian populations and made an effort to learn Indian languages and to collect artifacts and artwork. In the eyes of white nineteenth-century observers, such discoveries gave Indian peoples a history and culture that white Americans could understand.

The first highly publicized discovery of this sort occurred in 1874 when William Henry Jackson led a party of Hayden's survey on a photography mission through southwestern Colorado. Quite by accident they came upon the great cliff dwellings on the Mesa Verde. For Jackson, the sight of the tiny houses lining the walls of the great, sheer cliff "was worth everything I possessed."[31] The party took photographs and made drawings of their surprising find, while the journalist and naturalist Ernest Ingersoll, who had accompanied the expedition, quickly wrote a series of articles for the *New York Tribune* and *Harper's*. Jackson later designed and built plaster models of the ruins, which Hayden displayed as part of the Geological Survey's exhibit at the 1876 Centennial in Philadelphia. Jackson reported proudly that his display "attracted more attention than the many photographs and all the rocks and relics of Dr. Hayden's career."[32]

With the triple revelations of ancient civilizations in the Southwest, the Grand Canyon, and Yellowstone as centerpieces, the elaborate surveys of the 1870s served to awaken public interest in previously unknown or abhorred regions of the Far West. The attention given the surveys reflected the new interest in incorporating the West into national culture. As additional railroad lines stretched from east to west, increasing the sense of connection between regions, Americans looked to the West for the materials to build a national culture. The material had always been there, but now Americans were developing the cultural ability to use it.[33] The surveys, the descriptive techniques their scientists used, and the history they uncovered influenced American conceptions of the Far West in significant ways.

For the first time in several decades, Americans saw something of interest beyond the line of the transcontinental railroad and outside of the

Cliff Dwellings

The news of the discovery of cliff dwellings that had housed an ancient and sophisticated people thrilled Americans. Now they had an ancient and admirable past of their own. (In Ernest Ingersoll, *The Crest of the Continent*, 1885. Courtesy of the Bancroft Library.)

European citadels of California and Colorado. However, attempts to force these new sights into the framework so carefully developed to explain the Far West in earlier years seemed futile. The sheer novelty of these western visions required different methods of description. Simpler language, using color, shape, and geographic and geological terms, seemed more appropriate. Beauty no longer seemed to require elaborate analogy. The members of the surveys had made forays into several descriptive alternatives, which would change the way the American public responded to the far western landscape.

Grappling with the New: First Forays into the Southwest

Even though many Americans grew curious about the wonders uncovered by the surveys, the locations of most of these sights remained inaccessible to all but the hardiest travelers. In 1876 F. V. Hayden described the beauties of the canyonlands of the Southwest, but he warned such terrain would "ever be dedicated to nature," for to reach it, travelers would "be obliged to cross gorge after gorge, with nearly vertical walls, three thousand feet or more in depth."[34] Only five years after this prediction, the Atlantic and Pacific Railroad (which would later become part of the Santa Fe route) and the Southern Pacific opened a route across New Mexico and Arizona to the Pacific. In 1883, the Northern Pacific completed its line from Minneapolis to Seattle. By the beginning of the twentieth century, four separate railroads stretched from the Mississippi River to the Pacific Ocean, allowing travelers to view a much fuller range of the far western landscape. Physically, the nation had been connected, but it still required cultural unification.[35]

The presence of newly uncovered scenic splendors and the ability of railroad cars to take Americans to them created a series of challenges for speculators, promoters, and tourists. In addition to the acknowledged wonders of Yellowstone, the Grand Canyon, and the cliff dwellings, the new railroad routes opened up vast tracts of strange but often beautiful landscape. In order to attract tourists and investors, promoters had to find a way to describe these regions. Few areas could be categorized as American versions of Europe; thus, promoters, as well as writers, artists, and tourists, had to look elsewhere for descriptive methods. The efforts of the surveys had provided some clues.

Few Americans knew what to expect as the first trains rolled across the Southwest or into unknown regions of the Northwest. Many worried about the monotony of travel through the desert but felt the lack of altitude change and the dry air would be more healthful. Some travelers chose the southern routes because they "possessed the merit of keeping one largely out of the snow and frost."[36] Others had "the desire to see the strange life of a less hackneyed region" than the old Pacific Railroad route.[37] They relished the novelty of a region for which the "inevitable latest [guidebook] editions which follow the track of the steam horse were not yet in existence."[38] Some tourists spoke enthusiastically of the advantages of seeing the "ancient homes of the Cliff Dwellers" or the "weird sights of the Yellowstone."[39] No one seemed to be looking for an American Europe in these places.

The interest in seeing "less hackneyed regions" and the clear inappropriateness of European analogies along most of the new railroad lines attracted some Americans and horrified others. As each railroad line opened and as each survey published yearly reports, photographs, and articles in popular magazines, it became increasingly obvious that the far western landscape represented something other than American versions of Switzerland, Italy, or other parts of the Old World. It offered something distinctive. Americans had been informed of the strange and wonderful aspects of the West since the days of Lewis and Clark's pioneering expedition, but distance and culture had allowed them to see only the familiar. Now, in the last quarter of the nineteenth century, the calls for recognition and pride in the unfamiliar became insistent and loud. More importantly, Americans began to listen.

Many writers complained how little Americans knew about their own country. Because most travelers still chose to go to Europe, "to the majority of New Englanders, Denver is more a mystery than Paris," claimed an 1885 railroad guidebook.[40] One writer mourned that the "Americans who prefer not to be brutally ignorant of their own land multiply slowly," while another noted that for "64,980,000 of the 65,000,000 of population" most of the Far West remained a "*terra incognita*".[41] Even the increasing numbers of Americans who did travel west missed most of the wondrous landscape because they only wanted "to see America provided it is made over to conform with the accepted European model."[42]

Such complaints signaled an increasing frustration with the "accepted

European model." The difficulty, of course, was finding a new model. Artists, writers, and intellectuals of all sorts had worried over the derivative nature of American culture since the early part of the nineteenth century. Many people had heralded the landscape as a source of cultural independence; but, as we have seen, most simply used old analogies and models to interpret the new landscape.[43] The oddities of the Far West, however, had always challenged this method of interpretation. The discoveries of the 1870s and the 1880s and the accessibility of the landscape made possible by the railroads in the 1880s and the 1890s rendered the older model even less useful.

People sought alternative forms of expression and models of interpretation, demanding "Americanism" in literature, art, and in general outlook. "Regional" literature describing the various cultures of the South, the West, and the East demonstrated the growing strength and confidence of American traditions. A call for "something peculiarly indigenous to our soil and clime" filled the pages of popular journals.[44] Interest in national history generated museum and restoration projects that celebrated the heritage of the United States.[45] The parochialism that had characterized most of the nineteenth century seemed to be fading. The first great propagandist of the Southwest, Charles Lummis, wrote in 1891, "If we would cease to depend so much on other countries for our models of life and thought, we would have taken the first step toward the Americanism which should be, but is not, ours."[46]

A way to begin the process of developing Americanism was to look seriously at what the United States had to offer. Just as it had in the early nineteenth century, the landscape seemed a crucial place to start, especially the recently discovered and accessible terrain of the Far West. "We need not run to other lands to gratify our longing for the curious and wonderful," explained Charles Lummis. "The whole West is filled with wonders."[47] Some promoters claimed it was "a matter of patriotism and pride" to visit the Far West and to learn of "the variety of climate, scenery, and resources between the Missouri River and the Pacific Ocean."[48]

Railroad promoters, quite naturally, leaped at the opportunities offered by the new interest in American scenery. Happily, the Pennsylvania Railroad announced a new series of western tours that would "gratify this patriotic inclination in the most satisfactory, comfortable, and profitable manner."[49] Even though many publicity agents recognized "the American people are awakening to the realization that there is something to be seen in their own land," at first, few gave up the European analogies that had served them so well in earlier decades.

They did, however, use these analogies in a different way. Instead of claiming that the western United States replicated Europe, many writers used Europe as a reference point to claim that the far western landscape was bigger, better, and more wondrous. An early promoter for the national parks announced that "the far-famed Swiss Alps are equalled and excelled by the scenery of several of our national parks."[50] Even the Indians could be described in terms of American superiority. "The Hopis, Havasupais, Apaches, and Navajos are more picturesque than the Swiss, Irish, Serbian, or Russian peasants," claimed a guidebook to the Southwest.[51] A tourist visiting California in 1883 noted smugly that "Southern California is fairer than Italy in climate, and its peer in vegetation."[52]

Other writers edged away from these comparisons by claiming that the scenery of the Far West was so superior and so original that any comparison to Europe was a mistake. "Occasionally [the Rockies] are called the Alps of America by one of those absurd whims of literary nomenclature," noted one writer with a touch of annoyance, "just as though there were nothing distinctly original, and Nature had simply duplicated her handiwork across the seas in creating the present United States." He explained that "the precipices wear outlines of their own, the soil has its peculiar vegetation, the clouds and sky have their distinct physiognomy."[53]

Whether or not comparisons to Europe appeared in these descriptions, it had become clear to most observers that the far western landscape offered something distinct from the rest of the world. Even *Baedeker's Guide to the United States* now pointed out differences rather than similarities to Europe. "The traveller," warned the *Guide*'s author, "should take care not to hamper his vision by preconceptions as to the beauty of natural scenery based upon the physiography of the old world."[54] A Union Pacific guidebook explained that even Americans could not have "a faint conception" of "the whirling panorama of perpetual contrasts and surprises" contained in the West.[55]

The most daring writers and promoters rejected European analogies entirely. The Far West, explained one journalist, "is not Swiss, or English, or Italian. It is American."[56] Charles Dudley Warner, who had so proudly coined the phrase "Our Italy" to describe California in the 1870s, wrote in 1888 that the West "is defiantly American"[57] Such descriptions demonstrated a growing sense of pride in the curious appearance of the Far West. For these journalists, and for scientists like Clarence Dutton and artists like Thomas Moran, what made the West interesting was its difference from the Old World. Places like the Grand Canyon and Yellowstone made the United States unique. No longer searching for Europe, they now sought what was American.

Despite the proud claims of artists, writers, and promoters, the newly discovered parts of the Far West received a mixed reaction from tourists who viewed them from trains in the 1880s. Areas that had long been described as horrendous deserts or terrifying wastes could not suddenly become sites of wondrous beauty. At first, the Santa Fe, the Atlantic and Pacific, and the Southern Pacific railroads all advertised that their lines covered the narrowest strip of desert and had the least amount of alkali dust.[58]

Americans might have enjoyed the engravings of the Grand Canyon in *Scribner's* and *Harper's* or the descriptions of desert beauties by the scientists of the surveys, but they did not seem to enjoy traveling over the desert in the 1880s. Rather than writing of brilliant color and fascinating rock formations, they complained of "an arid cactus desert, dusty and repellent to the eyes and other senses."[59] Arizona might hold the glories of the canyonlands within its borders, but the portion seen by early train passengers offered nothing but "deserts, sands, cacti, mountains, desperadoes, horned toads, and rattlesnakes."[60] The cactus, symbol of the desert, became "the reptile of the vegetable world" in the eyes of one horrified tourist.[61]

Most visitors responded to the desert much as they had decades earlier while crossing Nevada and Utah on the Central Pacific. It seemed useless and unfamiliar. Even Thomas Moran, who had recognized the strange beauties of Yellowstone and the Grand Canyon, despised much of the desert. While traveling with John Wesley Powell to examine the Grand Canyon, Moran complained about less spectacular desert regions. "It is an awful country that we have been traveling over," he wrote to his wife, "and I cannot conceive how human beings can stand to live on it."[62] An 1883 tourist recorded a similar reaction when she stated, "nothing can be more desolately dreadful than the alkali plains of Arizona."[63]

For many of the earliest visitors, the developed areas of the Southwest offered little more attraction than the desert. Santa Fe, the historic trading center of the region and meeting place of Indian, Spanish, and Anglo cultures, disappointed the first train passengers. One tourist saw only "mud huts, innocent of the commonest toilet conveniences; hence the filthiness of the natives."[64] Another, more generous, observer noted that "it is old, if that is an advantage." Even so, he found little that seemed "picturesque" or that could "satisfy the artistic sense."[65] Rather than finding charm in the cultural mix of the old city, many travelers saw it as dirty and backwards from their Anglo-American perspective.

Many of the southwestern Indian tribes created a similar reaction among tourists. Despite the beginnings of new interest in Indian culture and history and the publicity surrounding the discovery of the cliff dwellings, few of the first tourists to travel through the region on the train saw anything attractive about native cultures. Because tourists rarely got off the train to look at cliff dwellings or to observe other aspects of Indian life, their view was necessarily distorted. When the train stopped at stations, visitors saw Indians "running from every direction and congregating on the platform, their object being to sell pottery and bits of stone."[66] Such performances did not impress most tourists, who found themselves "greatly disappointed in the red men."[67]

Tourists ignored other points of potential interest in the Southwest. Even though the travels of Major John Wesley Powell and other scientists and the paintings of Thomas Moran had brought the Grand Canyon into national focus, few tourists visited it before the beginning of the twentieth century. The Atlantic and Pacific and the Santa Fe line brought travelers within twenty-five miles of the Grand Canyon in 1883, but few chose to spend the three days necessary for a tour.

At first, promoters did little to encourage tourist travel in the Southwest. In the early 1880s, the railroads rarely mentioned the presence of the Grand Canyon in their advertising material. The Boston tour company of Raymond and Whitcomb, which specialized in luring easterners to the Far West, only mentioned the presence of the Grand Canyon in the descriptions of their tours in the 1880s and early 1890s. Not until almost the turn of the century did they make it an optional stop for touring parties, even though stagecoach trips had been available for nearly a decade.[68] American attitudes toward scenery had not yet changed enough for promoters to recognize and utilize the tourist potential of the Grand Canyon.

Even in the earliest years of tourist travel in the Southwest, however, a few visitors did notice the possibility of a different beauty. A journalist for *Harper's* wrote that on "general principles" he expected "such a country" to be "depressing"; but, much to his surprise, he found it "entertaining instead." He explained further that the desert "was a stimulus to the curiosity, and ends by having a real fascination."[69] Others found the dry climate especially appealing, while a few noted the wonders of desert color and plant life. These observers foreshadowed a more general change in attitude that would make the Southwest a popular tourist spot by 1900. In the early 1880s, however, the combination of American desires to find Europe and attitudes about beautiful scenery made the Southwest difficult to interpret.

Reactions to Yellowstone showed a similar pattern. Very few people visited the region until 1883, when the completion of the Northern Pacific brought tourists to Livingston, Montana, about thirty miles from the northern border of the park. Even then not many tourists actually made the trip into the park, which required five full days of stagecoaching along bumpy and dusty roads. The British writer Rudyard Kipling, visiting the park in 1888, noted in his journal after the first day's travel that "today I am in Yellowstone Park, and I wish I were dead."[70]

As in the Southwest, the strangeness of the scenery visitors found after such a grueling journey often did not meet their expectations. Those who hoped to see visions of Thomas Moran paintings over every horizon were inevitably disappointed. Architectural wonders and European vistas did exist in the park, but much of the scenery involved something new. "The revolting and unearthly appearance of these mud volcanoes," remarked one early tourist, "soon satisfied our curiosity, . . . and we pass on without much desire to look at them"[71] Another visitor, horrified by the appearance of the Upper Geyser basin, attempted to explain her reaction. "This was our first sight of any geyser basin, and this may have caused the awful desolation of it all to seem much more awful."[72]

Yellowstone would require two things before it could become a major tourist destination: new ways to interpret its sights and easier and more comfortable access. Tourists constantly struggled to find proper analogies. Some wrote that the geysers had the same force as "Vesuvius and Etna," while others noted that "Sahara's plains are soft and beautiful" compared to the desolation of the geyser basins."[73] A baffled visitor confessed in 1886 that "I could not bring myself to understand what sort of sights we saw."[74] Nearly every visitor complained about the rough travel and the lack of proper accommodations. The Raymond and Whitcomb Company did not conduct tours into Yellowstone until the 1890s, "feeling that even all its wonders would not compensate the travelers for discomforts he must inevitably encounter."[75] As in the case of the Grand Canyon, it would take more than a railroad passing by to make the region appealing to Americans.

Uncovering "American" History

If the appearance of deserts, boiling springs, and geysers did not please most tourists in the 1880s, gradually the discovery of the historical aspects of the landscape did. Americans had always made much of the natural history of their continent. Now, in the last decades of the nineteenth century, they began to find a usable human history. This history became especially important in interpreting the Southwest. Suddenly, instead of being barren, dirty, and backward, it was charming and antique.

The relatively new field of ethnography made the most important contributions to the discovery of American antiquities. After Lewis Henry Morgan's pioneering study of the Iroquois, published in 1851, native American culture held new interest for scientists. The discoveries made by the surveys of the 1870s led to the formation of the Bureau of Ethnography in 1879, directed by Major John Wesley Powell. Much of this intellectual activity focused its attention on the Indian tribes of the Far West. By the 1880s ethnologists, archaeologists, and anthropologists had combed large areas of the West, uncovering evidence of ancient and contemporary cultures that had complex societies and produced objects of great beauty. In native American culture white Americans had discovered a dignified history that they could use for their own cultural needs. This history gave whites a past linked to the American continent, rather than to distant European landscapes.[76]

By the late 1880s, the Southwest had become a land of history and culture, rather than one of hostile desert and Indians. Railroad publicity agents and other promoters quickly picked up on the desire for a historical past. "New Mexico and Arizona are unquestionably the oldest settled portion of our country," a Raymond and Whitcomb pamphlet promised tourists.[77] A railroad guidebook claimed that "before the Pilgrims landed upon the shores of New England . . . before, in fact, America was known to the world . . . the great Southwest was peopled by a race who enjoyed a high degree of civilization."[78] Another promoter went as far as to state, "This is the *old* world instead of the *new*."[79]

Strides in the science of geology also gave the Far West new attraction in the eyes of scientists, promoters, and tourists in the closing decades of the nineteenth century. The work of the great surveys of the 1870s and 1880s, eventually subsumed by the United States Geological Survey in 1879, turned the Far West into a workshop for the study of the earth's creation. As early as 1863, the famous geologist Louis Agassiz claimed in the *Atlantic Monthly* that "America, so far as her physical history is concerned, has been falsely denominated the *New World*." He explained that as a matter of scientific fact "hers was the first dry land lifted out of the waters."[80] The study of the ancient canyons and landforms of the Southwest, as well as the geothermic wonders of Yellowstone, gave the Far West even more importance in geological history.

Predictably, promoters made the most of these discoveries. "For the masterpiece of creation, you must come to Colorado," crowed the author of a guidebook to the state.[81] A journalist in *Harper's* wrote dramatically that in the West "the ruined earth itself, sprinkled with ruined dwellings of man, tells us with awful eloquence of the antiquity of the world."[82] Robert Sterling Yard, a publicist for the national parks, claimed that the "chiefest glory" of the parks was "that they are among the completest expressions of earth's history."[83] By the turn of the twentieth century, the desire and ability to locate human and geological history in the Far West had significantly altered the way Americans looked at the region. Instead of seeing Europe when they gazed at snow-covered peaks, they saw "hoary, historic mountains" and "time sentinels of history and geology."[84]

In the deserts, mountains, and canyons of the Southwest, white Americans had found a history that they could claim as their own. The combination of prehistoric cultures and geological wonders thrilled observers of all kinds. In 1892, Charles Lummis claimed that "the wonderland of the Southwest, with its strange landscapes, its noble ruins of a prehistoric past, and the astounding customs of its present aborigines" far outdid Europe in terms of interest for the tourist.[85] Another writer boasted that Arizona had a "peculiar atmosphere of extreme antiquity" because of its combination of "overwhelming chasms that have lain unchanged since the infancy of the world" and its "ruins of once populous cities."[86] As one tourist noted, upon crossing the New Mexico border he had entered "Ancient America."[87]

Tourists, infatuated with the idea of ancient history in the United States, now sought out the very Indians they had so long avoided. Guidebooks gave information about how, where, and why visitors should look for native American culture. A guidebook written for children told its readers that "the most important antiquities of the United States are the aborigines."[88] The Denver and Rio Grande Railroad advised that "to the south of Mancos station, within a day's drive, and easily accessible, are the ruins of the strange habitations of an extinct and mysterious race known as the Cliff Dwellers."[89] A pamphlet issued by the Southern Pacific Railroad pointed out that the ancient cultures of America were as intriguing as "those found in Egypt or Peru."[90]

Such enticing claims brought increasing numbers of visitors to the Southwest. The new popularity of the old town of Santa Fe, New Mexico, provides a good example of changing American reactions to the Southwest. Before the mid-1880s, tourists had described the old trading center as a collection of mud huts, lazy Mexicans, and dirty, begging Indians. Now they praised the architecture, which included "the oldest church and the oldest dwelling" in the United States. The "simplicity and evident antiquity" of the two structures pleased one visitor.[91] Another tourist described the architecture as "a happy combination of Indian Pueblo and early Spanish style."[92]

While many visitors remarked on the architectural style of the buildings or the quaint dress of the town's inhabitants, every tourist seemed most impressed with the simple fact of Santa Fe's age. "Santa Fe is the oldest town on the continent," remarked one visitor, as he happily catalogued his day's activities. "We see the ruins of the oldest house, visit the oldest church, and gaze on the oldest palace."[93] A more cynical tourist noted the ubiquity of Santa Fe's claim to great age. Not only did he get to see ancient buildings, but his tour guide "told us some of the most ancient jokes in the United States" and directed his party to a restaurant where they were "served some of the oldest chicken in the United States."[94]

The foreignness of Santa Fe also struck most visitors. Interestingly, few people made comparisons to the old towns of Europe. If they made any Old World connections, they were to Egypt, Syria, Palestine, or the Orient.[95] Most, however, saw Santa Fe as something different. One observer described it as "a strange city, and foreign, but nothing European." He went on to characterize it as "Southwestern, Indian, Mexican, adobe, and remote."[96] Another visitor could only say Santa Fe was "Un-American! Old!"[97] Despite the assumption made by this tourist that anything old was un-American, what enthralled nearly every American who came to Santa Fe were the facts of its American location and its ancientness.

Railroad agents and other publicists now made the claim that Americans had no reason to go to Europe. Earlier, even the most patriotic travelers had admitted that while the United States offered scenic wonders of incomparable grandeur, "places in this country lack the atmosphere that age alone can give." The work of ethnographers and geologists in the last decades of the nineteenth century had provided Americans with "a place not only of historic, but pre-historic interest."[98] Scientists, artists, and writers also provided new ways to describe the landscape. The direct descriptive style used by these observers of the Southwest gave Americans words for the beauty and heritage of the region.

Americans, now convinced they had scenery equal to that of the Old World in appearance and antiquity in the landscape of the Far West, looked beyond the West's similarities to Europe to examine its differences. Because they had discovered cultural and historical value in the landscape that did not depend on European standards, Americans could accept differences more confidently. In this same period at the end of the nineteenth century, Americans discovered new cultural importance in something their continent had always had—the wilderness.

The same wilderness that had terrified Americans for nearly three centuries no longer seemed to be a threat. By the end of the nineteenth century, the land mass of the United States had been explored and much of it had been settled. Even though settlers on the Great Plains and miners working the precious metal and mineral lodes of the Far West still suffered great privations from a raw environment, most Americans viewed the continent as conquered. The wilderness, no longer seen as an enemy threatening to engulf a fragile civilization, suddenly attained new status. Historians, philosophers, and politicians gave the wildness of the continent credit for providing the nation with character, strength, and inventiveness. Suddenly an object of nostalgia and pride, rather than of fear and embarrassment, the American wilderness enjoyed new popularity.[99]

The urban civilization Americans had worked so hard to create now became the enemy. The soft life of the city dweller threatened to sap the nation of its vitality. Modern society had become overcivilized. "Our electro-steam civilization has put a fresh strain upon our constitutions," warned a California journalist. "Cities, excitement, and sedentary occupations are enfeebling us."[100] Cosseted by urban comforts and spoiled by urban vice, Americans feared that future generations could not meet the challenges presented by the rapidly growing nation. Many people began to question assumptions about the gifts of modernity and technology. Perhaps progress did not necessarily mean an improvement in the quality of human life. They began to search nostalgically for the clean, simple life they believed Americans had once lived.[101]

Such nostalgia led people to look upon the city with increasing suspicion. More and more often, Americans characterized the city as a threatening wilderness filled with unfamiliar immigrants, labor unrest, dangerous criminals, and unhealthy crowds. In contrast, the great forests, plains, and deserts that still covered significant portions of the continent appeared safe and even healthful. Nearly every magazine published articles on the dangers of the city and the necessity for wilderness, reflecting the growing obsession with health in the period.[102] This attitude toward unsettled landscape gave the Far West new importance. It offered huge expanses of healthful wilderness and innumerable opportunities to escape the ravages of civilization.

Americans now wanted to learn about the wilderness and especially about the Far West. Natural history writers and evangelists, such as John Burroughs, Ernest Thompson Seton, and John Muir, numbered among the best-selling authors of the day. Tourists clamored to be outdoors. Many no longer sequestered themselves in overheated hotels and plush Pullman cars, choosing tents, horses, and their own feet instead. John Muir commented on the "delightful tendency" that people now had to seek out the wilderness. "Thousands of tired, nerve-shaken, over-civilized people are beginning to find out that . . . wilderness is a necessity," he stated happily in 1901.[103]

All kinds of promoters pointed out the advantages and importance of a trip to the Far West. Many parts of the region had long been advertised as fountains of health and youth, but more because of their lack of disease and the particularities of their climates. The great disadvantage of far western resorts had been their distance from urban centers and their lack of civilized amenities. Now, these lackings had become enormous advantages. A pamphlet issued by the Denver and Rio Grande Railroad claimed that vacations at luxurious resorts were "insipid" when compared with "the freedom and enjoyment of outdoor life in the mountains."[104]

Most promotional material focused on the healthful aspects of outdoor activity. One brochure called the Rocky Mountains "Nature's Primitive Repair Shops, where rusting frames are oiled, tightened, and set a-going."[105] The Santa Fe Railroad told its passengers that "sensible folk and unwise as well are discovering that it truly pays to change environments occasionally."[106] "Everyone needs to play," warned a promoter for the national parks. "Without parks and outdoor life all that is best in civilization will be smothered."[107]

Tourists, who had rarely ventured off resort lawns or beyond the station platform in earlier decades, responded enthusiastically to the wilderness in the years after 1880. "Never in my life," reported a satisfied traveler, "have I enjoyed anything half so much as our rough, wild life of the past few weeks." She reveled in the "delicious pure air," "the strange sights and experiences," and the "sense of utter freedom and independence."[108] Grace Thompson Seton, the wife of nature writer Ernest Thompson Seton, recorded her reactions to her first trip to the western wilderness. "The secret of it, the fascination of the wild life, was revealed to me. At last I understood why the birds sing."[109]

Grace Thompson Seton, like most other people who described their experiences with "roughing it" in the Far West in these years, commented specifically on the delights of escaping from civilization. She wrote that while under the "spell of the West," she did not care whether "there were such things as gold beads and crepe, . . . the music, arts, drama . . . civilization, in a word." Instead, she took pleasure in "being at least a healthy, if not an intelligent animal."[110] She reveled in her animal nature, something that would have horrified earlier travelers, who swaddled themselves in the trappings of civilization.

Rather than searching for citadels of European-inspired civilization, many Americans seemed to seek a return to more primitive forms of existence. Civilization had made them ill; now it seemed that only savagery could cure them, and the West contained much of the savage life that had become so important. "It seems undoubted that there is an element of savagery in our nature," claimed a railroad advertisement. It recommended further that this element was crucial to human development, for "it is the gravel of wild life in the crop of civilization that aids digestion of the whole."[111] A writer in *Lippincott's Magazine* recommended long visits to the Far West, noting that "the natural remedy for the illness or illnesses which arise from close confinement, too much excitement . . . or in other words, too much civilization, is simply to relapse into barbarism."[112]

The concept of the healthful aspects of finding one's primitive or barbaric nature led to increasing interest in native American cultures, which complemented recent ethnographic and anthropological discoveries. Not only did Indians give America a historical past, they could provide clues for healthy ways to live in the present. The interest in Indians and the lessons they could teach whites permeated American culture in the early years of the twentieth century. Articles appeared in the major journals describing the longevity and health of Indians as a result of living in the outdoors and of having to fight for their survival.[113]

In order to uphold the health of American youth, Ernest Thompson Seton developed a popular organization for American boys, which would later provide the model for the Boy Scouts. Using a mishmash of customs from various tribes, the Woodcraft Indians proposed to teach boys how to cope in the modern world by learning Indian virtues. They wore Indian clothing, received honors by getting a series of "coups," and learned Indian stories and wilderness lore.[114]

At the same time white Americans looked to native Americans for inspiration about how to survive the modern world, they also took a few cues from them about actively protecting nature. People could not rejuvenate themselves in the wilderness and lead the simple, clean life of the Indian if no wilderness existed. As early as the 1860s, a few people had advocated the protection of wildlife and of the natural landscape. In 1864 George Perkins Marsh published an influential book, *Man And Nature: or, Physical Geography as Modified by Human Action*, that demonstrated the necessity of undeveloped land for modern civilization. The 1860s and 1870s saw the formation of the Audubon Society and the American

Ornithological Union, organizations dedicated to the protection of America's birdlife. In the last decades of the century, interest in conservation and preservation of the wilderness resulted in a burst of new activity. The near destruction of the buffalo and the extinction of the passenger pigeon brought attention to the issue in the public mind. The Appalachian Mountain Club, the Boone and Crockett Club, the Sierra Club, and the Mazamas of Oregon—all sought to protect the natural environment.[115]

Ironically, the region with the most wilderness in the United States, the Far West, received the least attention in the early stages of this new movement. Americans, especially wealthy easterners who could afford vacations in the wilderness, had not yet become well enough acquainted with the scenic wonders of the West to work hard to preserve them. However, the new desire to enjoy the wilderness, combined with the discovery of ancient history in the Far West, focused more attention on it. Slowly, the effects of comfortable and convenient travel, increased publicity, and a new confidence in the unique qualities of American landscape led to a public discovery of the delights of the Far West.

New Words for New Sights: The Introduction to the Southwest

The attention given to the desert Southwest provides a good example of the process of discovery. Even though the railroads had made travel through the region possible in the early 1880s, few tourists enjoyed the trip. They viewed the desert as merely something to be endured until they reached the more familiar sights of California. Even though the great surveys had brought back wondrous information, little of it reached the public. The Southwest remained nearly unphotographed until the 1890s. With the exception of government photographers, even the Grand Canyon received little attention. William Henry Jackson made the first successful commercial series of the canyon in 1892.[116] The simultaneous "discoveries" of ancient America and of the value of wilderness gave the region new importance. These discoveries, combined with the increasing national confidence of Americans, created an atmosphere in which the unfamiliar beauties of the Southwest could be recognized.

In the last years of the nineteenth century, as historian Patricia Nelson

Limerick has put it, "nation and desert had not yet been introduced."[117] George Wharton James, a former Methodist minister defrocked because of a sensational divorce, took it upon himself to make the necessary introductions. His preaching about the wonders of the desert took the form of more than forty books, numerous articles, and countless lectures. He aimed his message at the growing numbers of tourists who now traveled west for health, recreation, and education. Once they realized the tremendous potential of James's appeal, railroad companies, land speculators, and resort developers all vied for his time.[118]

James went to great lengths to make the desert seem attractive to tourists. He had to make it safe and interesting, overcoming centuries of fear and disgust. Playing on the new pride Americans had gradually developed in the distinctive appearance of their landscape, he claimed that the desert was "strange, wonderful, and beautiful" and that it offered "things that are unknown to cities and the unobservant everywhere."[119]

James explained that the desert was not something "to be shunned, feared, dreaded," but rather a pleasant place filled with "marvels, revelations, and wonders."[120] Understanding that most tourists needed to be told exactly what these wonders were and how to look for them, James provided a kind of laundry list of desert "surprises" for the train passenger. By encouraging visitors to look for surprises rather than objects that seemed familiar, James overthrew a century of tradition in the observation of landscape. Europe no longer controlled description.

Like Clarence Dutton or Thomas Moran, James used a new method of description that relied on color, shape, geology, and analogies to ordinary objects. He pointed out the clarity of the desert air in which "everything stands out with startling vividness."[121] The strange plants of arid regions, James promised, would entertain the tourist for hours with their "weird and stately shapes" and their "profusion of color in bloom." He described the "noble" yucca plant, for example, in terms that would surely appeal to Americans. He claimed that when the plant was in bloom, "it needs little stretch of the imagination to see it as a glorious golden candlestick flaming before the hillside altar of God's majesty."[122]

The colors present in the desert landscape provided "a never-ending source of delightful surprise" for the observant traveler. James claimed the desert to be "God's color showroom" and "His divine exhibition showroom to which He freely invites all men."[123] Depicting the desert as

George Wharton James, *Flowers of the Prickly Pear*

The delicate blooms of this fierce prickly pear demonstrated the attractive side of the desert that George Wharton James urged people to seek. (In George Wharton James, *Arizona, the Wonderland*, 1917. Courtesy of the Bancroft Library.)

a place blessed, rather than forsaken by God, George Wharton James made the desert sound inviting and pleasant, not like the barren and threatening landscape of Dante's *Inferno* as so many other writers had depicted it.

If the marvelous appearance of the desert were not enough to attract visitors, the health-inducing qualities of the climate would surely do so. James called the region a "manufactory of health" because it had "the purest sunshine, purest air, purest soil." In the desert, the invalid slept "on mother Earth's bosom" and drew "life and vigor from her maternal founts."[124] With such comforting imagery, James hoped to give people a new perspective on the desert. He wanted it to become an enjoyable destination, rather than a place to avoid or to endure.

James accepted the novelty of the desert landscape, and he reveled in its eccentricities. He almost never made comparisons to other kinds of landscapes. Europe, and its aesthetic values, simply had no relevance here. For him, the southwestern desert was something uniquely American and, therefore, something in which to take great pride. It never occurred to him that its strangeness could be anything but an advantage.

A lone
palm
in
Andreas
Canyon

Desert Surprise

This drawing shows one of the "surprises" a visitor might find in the desert: a lone green palm tree in a narrow and seemingly barren desert canyon. (In George Wharton James, *The Wonders of the Colorado Desert*, 1906. Courtesy of the Bancroft Library.)

He saw it as a place that encouraged innovative thought, informing and enriching American culture.

George Wharton James's efforts, combined with increasing interest on the part of artists, scientists, and other writers, did have an effect on western travelers. Paintings by artists as diverse as Frederic Remington and Thomas Moran gave the desert new importance by depicting the unforgiving light, the fantastic landforms, the countless varieties of plant life, and the subtle shadings within the vibrant colors that appeared in desert sky, earth, plants, and creatures. By 1915, George Wharton James reported happily that the southwestern desert "is no longer the 'country that God forgot,' but the thoughtful and discerning are seeing in it 'the Garden of Allah.' "[125]

Well before the turn of the century, railroad officials and other people interested in increasing tourist travel recognized the importance of these changing attitudes toward the desert. Guidebooks began to change and lengthen their descriptions of New Mexico, Arizona, and desert portions of California. One journalist recommended the route of the Atlantic and Pacific Railway, noting that on its line a passenger would see "active civilization, much Mexican passivity, strange rock scenery and stranger vegetation, and enough Indians of all kinds to quite satisfy his curiosity."[126] While not wildly complimentary of the scenery, such a description differed greatly from earlier ones that simply recommended pulling the shade during the hours of desert travel. A few years later, a Santa Fe advertisement ranted about a desert sunset in which "fascination changes into a charming mystery impossible to comprehend."[127]

Tourists, too, became increasingly interested in the desert landscape. As soon as they no longer pulled the shades across the train windows during desert travel, they discovered "there is a great deal to be learned in the desert, and a great deal to be had from it."[128] Another observer offered a more grudging compliment, explaining that despite "all its dreariness" the desert was "not without offering subjects for the pencil."[129] Few visitors reacted to the arid scenery with the unreserved enthusiasm of George Wharton James, but most found that aspects of the desert had "a strange and beguiling beauty" once they learned to recognize and describe them.[130]

Almost every observer responded to the striking landforms erupting out of the ground in the Southwest and described them using color, shape, and geological terms. They commented on the passing parade of "wide terraces, towering mountains, tremendous chasms, burnt-out volcanoes, lava beds, painted rocks, mesas and buttes."[131] They did not entirely reject older methods of description. Many tourists enjoyed these geological wonders because they could often be compared with familiar architectural forms. In the time-, wind-, and sand-sculpted forms they could see towers, domes, temples, and even "broad imposing facades with columns, capitals, cornices, and entablatures of perfect proportion and design."[132]

The use of such analogies, however, did not represent a simple reversion to the older style of a search for Europe in America. Geology had given Americans a new vocabulary and historical framework to portray the southwestern landscape. Observers now regularly referred to the landscape as a demonstration of geological action. A feature on the land might be described as a fortress or a castle, but its observers often noted that it had been "wrought by the action of the elements" or by "some mighty convulsion of Nature."[133] Not only did tourists see domes, capitals, and towers, however; they now saw buttes, mesas, plateaus, and canyons.

None of these words had been part of general usage until the very last years of the nineteenth century. *Canyon* provides a good example. The great gashes in the earth that characterize the Southwest could hardly be described as valleys, vales, or passes. The words *chasm* and *gorge* came closer to describing the unique features but did not exactly fit. Gradually, Americans adopted the Spanish word *cañon*, which expressed the geology of the region more clearly. Finally, they anglicized it, making the word *canyon*.

In 1888, one writer felt obliged to tell his readers that "a cañon is a mighty gorge cut in the mountains by an irresistible torrent on its way to the sea."[134] Poet and essayist William Cullen Bryant, as editor of *Picturesque America*, noted that the remarkable features of the Southwest had "enriched our language with a new word, *cañon* as the Spaniards write it, or *canyon*." He explained that the word "signifies one of those chasms between perpendicular walls of rock—chasms of fearful depth and of length."[135] By 1900, George Wharton James insisted on the anglicized *canyon*, demonstrating that the word had come to stay.[136]

Words like *canyon* gave Americans a vocabulary to describe accurately what they saw in the Southwest. They could look at a spectacular geographical formation and give it a name, rather than searching for analogies from a culture that had no similar landscape. Descriptive words and geological knowledge made the Southwest more comprehensible to American travelers. As they came to understand its origins and its appearance, the region had more appeal for tourists. Instead of drawing the shades or beginning a card game, train travelers gazed eagerly at the passing scenery. Instead of describing the landscape as a terrifying and hideous waste, tourists now reported that the desert had "a fascination equal to that of the mountain or forest."[137]

Now that they actually looked at what the desert offered, tourists discovered a myriad of interesting things. The wide variety of plant life provided constant entertainment. Most tourists commented on the giant saguaro cactus and the yucca plant, calling them "a sight novel to our eyes."[138] Clearly, novelty was no longer threatening. One observer described the giant cacti as "strange and monstrous" and wondered "what do you say to a prickly red cucumber six feet long and two feet thick?"[139] The Raymond and Whitcomb Tour Company, having discovered the profitability of attracting tourists to the desert, promised its clients they would see cacti forty feet tall that resembled "a Corinthian column surmounted by candelabra."[140]

Many travelers found the delicate and often startlingly profuse flowering plants especially appealing. One tourist reported that he had successfully captured a yucca plant in bloom. "It was scarcely four feet in height," he recalled with evident delight, "yet 880 flowers and buds were actually counted upon its stem."[141] Obviously surprised, another observer discovered wild roses, pink abronia, erigerons, gilias, and poppies growing "not only along stream-banks, but in the hot sand and ashes in openings among the sage-brush."[142]

If the surprisingly rich plant life did not impress visitors, the other vibrant colors of the desert almost always did. The combination of dry, clear air, deeply hued sandstone, and spectacular cloud effects gave the Southwest a unique appearance. An 1894 guidebook promised tourists that the desert could never be dreary, "for in addition to its unaccustomed natural and human interest, it is full of vivid color."[143] No one who commented at all about the desert missed the opportunity to rave about its rich colors, different from anything they had seen before.

CHOLLA.

YUCCA.

PRICKLY PEAR.
Found growing on the Arid Lands of Arizona.

Ocatilla Plant

The cactus family no longer horrified visitors to the Southwest after 1900. These plants were now attractions tourists eagerly sought to identify. (In George Wharton James, *Arizona, the Wonderland*, 1917. Courtesy of the Bancroft Library.)

As George Wharton James noted of the desert landscape, "here is color supreme."[144] Color gave observers a way to describe what they saw accurately. Like the geologist Clarence Dutton, tourists delighted in the varied mixtures of color created by minerals in the soil and rock. One visitor was struck by the "great *buttes* girdled with yellow bands and bright vermillion patches set against the neutral tints of this weird spectral land."[145] Another tourist enjoyed the "terra-cotta hue" of the soil, contrasted with the "dark green color" of the pine forests and the "blue and purple mountains, flecked with flying cloud shadows."[146]

The desert sky seemed to evoke the most enthusiastic responses from observers. Even though many people began their description of the desert sky with disclaimers about it being "indescribable," they worked very hard to create intricately colored word pictures for their readers. Tourists who normally used quite mundane language to describe what they saw suddenly became almost poetic when faced with the desert sky. One woman who had contented herself with statistics about the size of the towns she passed, the miles of track she had crossed, and occasionally the height of a mountain or a rock saw "bars of pencilled grey spreading like rays from the horizon, or stretching wings of the softest peach color" in the early light of a desert dawn.[147] Another traveler wrote about an "indescribably grand" sunset. "Black threatening clouds roll in the West, edged with a golden yellow; a vast ocean of tossing billows is in the South, just beyond a still, silvery lake," he explained, surveying the horizon. He concluded that "such a sunset is worth a journey to New Mexico."[148]

Others spoke more specifically about the quality of the light, something that has always intrigued artists who attempt to depict the region. A Santa Fe advertising pamphlet claimed that "nowhere else can you find sky of deeper blue, sunlight more dazzling, shadows more intense, clouds more luminously white, or stars that throb with redder fire."[149] It did seem as if Americans could see more clearly in this brilliantly lit landscape. "Nothing seemed so strange as the light," remembered one visitor, "and no light which we had ever seen seemed so celestial, planting within us new eyes for old."[150]

Americans did see the desert with new eyes by the turn of the century. Its color and form had captured their attention, and geology and history had given them the confidence to describe it. The usual mode of descrip-

Enchanted Mesa

By the turn of the century, Americans enjoyed the striking shapes of the desert landscape. The landforms were now enchanting and dreamlike rather than barren and threatening. (In C. A. Higgins, *To California over the Santa Fe Trail*, 1902. Courtesy of the Bancroft Library.)

tion had changed. The search for "associations" had lessened in intensity. One place did not have to remind travelers of another to make it worth visiting. Rather than explaining what a particular view reminded them of, tourists now tried to report what it looked like. Because they had accepted the idea that the Southwest did not look like any part of Europe, and that such differences could be a point of pride, many American tourists replaced association with accuracy. Careful descriptions of geological forms, plants, and vivid color demonstrated a new vision of the desert.

Even with the innumerable descriptions of the impressive beauty and profusion of life in the desert, its reputation as a barren waste did not simply fade away. The growing appreciation of its beauties could never mask the fact that the desert was a harsh world. Few Americans would ever feel truly comfortable with the cruel beauty of the arid landscape. An early twentieth-century tourist recorded his anxieties as he approached the Arizona border. "We might be met by giant-armed cacti, Gila Monsters, alkali flats, Apaches, and chances to die a thousand deaths at poison springs and in the smoking sands," he worried.[151] The desert also covered a vast expanse, and many tourists admitted that "a small amount of desert is satisfying and our specimen had been very large."[152]

Even with such reservations about the desert, American attitudes toward southwestern scenery had changed considerably. Pride had replaced fear and revulsion.

Packaging the American Indian

Like deserts, native Americans had long been a source of disappointment for tourists. And, like deserts, Indians received new attention from tourists as a result of changing attitudes toward the Far West in the last decades of the nineteenth century. In the 1860s and 1870s, tourists had discovered that the Indians they met along the tracks of the transcontinental railroad did not resemble the Noble Savage a generation of literary tradition had taught them to expect. The combination of the violent mid-century Indian Wars and the sight of impoverished and displaced Indians begging at railroad stations replaced the noble image with one of fear and disgust.[153]

By the end of the nineteenth century, however, some Indians had once again become objects of interest and admiration. Part of this change developed out of new attitudes toward the wilderness. The turn-of-the-century celebration of the wilderness revived older romantic ideas about Indians as pure from the taints of civilization. Their skills in the woods, plains, and deserts could be used as models for civilized white Americans who wished to reinvigorate themselves in the wilderness. Perhaps more importantly, Indians had been discovered as the keepers of an ancient American culture. Especially in the Southwest, the evidence of ancient ruins and a vibrant living cultural tradition provided the far western landscape with a history, something that white Americans had craved.

In addition, observing and "appreciating" the Indians had become safe. By the 1880s, most Indians tribes had been forced to sign treaties with the United States, and many had been restricted to reservations. The Dawes Severalty Act of 1887 formally recognized the reservation system by allotting each family and tribe plots of land, ending any Indian hopes of retaining traditional ways of living. Most of the "savage" Indians who had refused to give in to white demands for land without a battle were now either dead or safely incarcerated on reservations. Now that Indians had lost the power to threaten national development, white Americans felt confident enough to take a closer look.

Indian culture, quite suddenly, became something to preserve rather than to destroy. A strain of this attitude had been present in white Americans since the beginning of the nineteenth century, as evidenced by the work of people like George Catlin and Henry Rowe Schoolcraft. In the late nineteenth century, however, this attitude became much more popular. Helen Hunt Jackson, perhaps the best-known supporter of Indians, published *A Century of Dishonor* in 1881, chronicling the mistreatment Indians had received at the hands of the United States government. The book did not fundamentally change the way Indians were treated, but it did awaken a few Americans to the misery government actions and public apathy had created.

By the last decade of the nineteenth century, Indians had become wards of the government and a "problem" for reforming philanthropists to solve. Most solutions involved forcing Indians to live like white Americans, "an entire change of these people from a savage to a civilized life."[154] In their efforts to "civilize" Indians, philanthropists, journalists, and scientists created a new, equally narrow stereotype of the reservation Indian. "Many years ago," explained a journalist, "the people of the East took their idea of the Indian from Cooper's novels and 'Hiawatha.' " Now, he wrote, "they have been taught to look upon the Indian as a 'problem' and to consider him as either a national nuisance or as a much-cheated and ill-used brother."[155]

Most tourists, however, did not abandon their romantic conception of Indians. They simply added the stereotype of the degenerate, drunken reservation Indian to their list of what the ideal Indian was not. White Americans seemed to cherish the idea of Indians living as they had for centuries, roaming free and hunting game in the forests and on the plains. They wanted them to do this, however, in such a way that it would not interfere with white settlement and exploitation of the land.

White reaction to the Apaches provides an example of the complex attitudes toward Indians that had developed late in the nineteenth century. The age celebrated a neoromantic vision of Indians who lived by the hunt, moved with the seasons, and made war with other tribes, but white Americans also required Indians to live on small reservations and to practice settled farming. A few bands of Apaches refused to accede to such demands. Even though the way these Indians chose to live was celebrated by white Americans in fiction and in art, they were characterized as "untameable," "destruction incarnate," and "noted for their cunning and cruelty."[156] In 1876, for example, the very mention of the name Geronimo terrified Americans. By 1900, however, Geronimo had become a national celebrity who appeared at expositions and state fairs. A guidebook explained that until the Apaches had been "decimated and rendered harmless," they could not form "a romantic background to a thriving Anglo-Saxon civilization."[157]

"Good" Indians, it seemed, stayed happily on their reservations, retaining only the parts of their tribal culture to give them an appealing "flavor" for white observers. "Good" Indians were those who lived by white rules but did not assimilate so much that they lost the traits that allowed white Americans to romanticize them. "Bad" Indians fell into two categories: those who refused to give in graciously to white demands and those who assimilated too much and picked up the bad habits of white culture. White Americans wanted to celebrate the Indians for their ancient culture and for their ability to live in the wilderness, but they wanted Indians to fulfill this role on white terms.[158]

The simultaneous incarceration of Indians on reservations and the discovery of their rich and ancient cultures made western Indians newly attractive to tourists. Visitors now used different language to describe the Indians they saw. Tourists no longer used as a standard the mythical Noble Savage as portrayed by Cooper and other writers. Now, they wanted to see specific tribal customs and evidence of ancient culture.[159]

Because the presence of Indians no longer threatened their lives or the development of the nation, and because they now represented history, tourists sought out Indians. A passenger on the Santa Fe line delighted in "the dusky denizens of dug outs" and reported happily that "the genuine aborigines swarm about the train, offering bits of topaz, turquoise, and small bits of pottery."[160] Another tourist, thrilled by his first view of "a real, live, fast-color red man," explained that "his powerful stature and historic ancestry made him a desirable model for an amateur photographer."[161] Another visitor wondered, "Who would not be filled with desire to look upon dwellings erected by a race whose history . . . is revealed by these structures of a forgotten age?"[162]

The desire to see evidence of ancient culture, combined with attitudes about what constituted a "good" Indian, made many of the southwestern tribes especially attractive to white Americans. Because they lived in houses; farmed; made usable rugs, baskets, and jewelry; and had a recog-

Apache Indians

By the end of the nineteenth century, the formerly terrifying Apache had become a source of interest rather than fear. This illustration from a guidebook presents a group of Indians that look peaceful enough for a museum. (In C. A. Higgins, *New Guide to the Pacific Coast, Santa Fe Route*, 1894. Courtesy of the Bancroft Library.)

Moki Hair Dressing

Tourists now wanted to learn about the tribal customs of various Indian tribes, and guidebooks devoted many pages to descriptions of social customs and domestic arrangements of southwestern Indians. (In C. A. Higgins. *To California and Back*, 1902. Courtesy of the Bancroft Library.)

nizable religion and history, tourists found these Indians understandable yet exotic enough to be appealing. Charles Lummis wrote of his astonishment at finding Indians "who dwelt in excellent houses, with comfortable furniture and clean beds, and clothing and food." Even better, he explained, they had "learned none of these things from us, but were living thus before our Saxon forefathers had found so much as the shore of New England."[163] Such settle Indians offered Americans a history they could connect to their own lives.

Many visitors commented on the rich tradition offered by the folklore and religion of the Zuni and the Hopi. A journalist for *Harper's* told his readers that the Zuni had "a vast accumulation of fables and folk-lore, and the past of the nation is given in what may be termed the Zuni bible."[164] Others noted "the comfort and beauty of the structures built by these tribes" as evidence of their advanced civilization and their strong culture. A guidebook claimed that the "antiquity" of these buildings rivaled "the storied stones of the Old World."[165]

The folklore, religion, fine arts, and architecture of the southwestern Indians demonstrated that North America did offer a rich historical tradition and one that differed a great deal from the Old World culture admired by white Americans. Significantly, in the closing years of the nineteenth century, American tourists embraced traditions and places far removed from the Old World. They had learned that native American cultures did not have to resemble European ones to have value. Just as they had with the unfamiliar beauty of the desert landscape, white Americans began to appreciate the variety of Indian cultures in the Southwest.

The measure of the new-found interest in Indians can be taken by the alacrity with which the railroads and other enterprises began advertising the presence of Indians. An 1889 edition of a guidebook entitled *Over the Range to the Golden Gate* rarely mentioned Indians, except to assure tourists that they were no longer to be feared. Later editions of the book gradually added more and more information about various Indian tribes and their customs. By 1912, the editor devoted nearly the entire southwestern section of the book to pictures of native villages, clothing, jewelry, and baskets. The text included short descriptions of tribal customs, designed to convince the tourist to get out at train stations. The Pueblo Indians, promised the guidebook, "delight to adorn themselves in gay colors, and form very interesting and picturesque subjects for the artist."[166] If not an enlightening ethnographic description, it was far more complimentary than descriptions that had appeared twenty years earlier.

By the turn of the century tourists wanted to examine Indian life firsthand. The railroads now found it advantageous to point out the locations of Indian villages and reservations and to emphasize their closeness to railroad stations. In the 1860s and 1870s, railroad publicists had assured passengers that their tracks ran nowhere near any Indian settlements. By 1904, however, the Santa Fe Railroad promised that from Albuquerque visitors could see many Indian villages, where "tourists are warmly and kindly welcomed." As a further attraction, the pamphlet added that "nowhere else can the tourist so pleasantly and quickly acquaint himself with the homelife of our brothers in red."[167] A tourist aboard a train full of conventioneers bound for California remembered with great pleasure that the stationmaster in Wallace, New Mexico, had "conceived of the idea of treating the Sir Knights to the sight of an Indian dance." He hired two hundred Indians from local tribes to surround the station and dance. He also set up a special concession stand to sell Indian wares.[168] The stationmaster's actions demonstrated that Indians, rather than being objects of fear or disgust, had become profitable tourist attractions.

The Southwest was not the only region to profit from new interest in indigenous cultures. The tourist industry in California received a big boost from visitors' desires to see evidence of Indian history, especially the quickly romanticized mission Indians. Earlier, the story of Indians who had been Christianized by Spanish missionaries had been ignored by white Americans. At best, they had denigrated this aspect of Spanish history, describing mission buildings as crude and crumbling and the life in the missions as lazy and corrupt. Americans preferred to make California into a version of Italy, which seemed more refined by the European standards against which they measured themselves. By the 1890s, however, mission architecture appeared all over California; the mission priests became saintly heroes; and tales of mission Indians fascinated visitors.

In part, the credit for the new interest in the heritage of the missions can be given to Helen Hunt Jackson. Frustrated by the lack of response to *Century of Dishonor*, her passionate account of government injustices against the Indians, she decided to write a novel that would reach a wider audience. As one result of *Century of Dishonor*, Jackson had been appointed to a commission to examine the condition of California Indians. She heard harrowing stories of Indians being forced off of mission lands as they were taken over by the government. Jackson, like other Americans, found it easy to sympathize with the mission Indians because they had been "civilized" with a familiar religion and with settled agriculture.[169]

Jackson intended her novel, *Ramona*, published in 1884, to be an indictment of the treatment the mission Indians received at the hands of greedy Americans. Instead, its readers ignored the message about the plight of the Indians and concentrated on the idyllic world of the Spanish missions and the benevolent Californio landholders.[170] Because Americans wanted to find a history that matched their landscape rather than one that simply imitated the Old World, Jackson's introduction to the world of the missions appeared exactly at the right moment. Indians and missions no longer seemed embarrassingly strange and crude to American tourists. By the 1880s they provided an indigenous history that gave the beautiful landscape meaning for a newly confident American culture.

Other promoters, George Wharton James and Charles Fletcher Lummis among them, recognized the importance the myth of the missions could have for southern California. James wrote several books on the history of the missions and the romantic landscape of California. He made the most of the moment when "the wealth and culture of the American race began to wake up to the picturesqueness and appropriateness to the landscape of these Mission buildings."[171] Charles Lummis, a writer for the *Los Angeles Times* and later editor of *Land of Sunshine*, the organ of the Los Angeles Chamber of Commerce, spread the romance of California history across the nation.

Tourists arrived in California expecting to see mission-style buildings and the unique landscape described in Jackson's enormously popular novel. Guidebooks argued over where the "true" home of the entirely fictional heroine was located. The missions, long neglected, suddenly became tourist attractions. An article in *Sunset*, the promotional arm of the Southern Pacific, described a drive along the El Camino Real as "posted with romantic legend and historic tradition" that would remain "forever California, ready in every condition of atmosphere, local color, and tradition."[172]

Hotels, rather than boasting Italianate, Gothic, or Queen Anne designs, now focused attention on the indigenous mission style. When the

Santa Barbara Mission

This view of a Santa Barbara mission evoked the mystery and romance Americans attached to the idea of the Spanish missions. Hooded priests, trickling fountains, and crumbling architecture were important attributes of the mission myth. (In Helen Hunt Jackson, *Glimpses of California and the Missions*, 1907. Courtesy of the Bancroft Library.)

Glenwood Mission Inn, ca. 1907

The Glenwood Mission Inn in Riverside, with its collection of mission bells and church crosses, its Spanish architecture, and its luxurious gardens, met all of the requirements of tourists who sought a "genuine" California experience. (Courtesy of the Bancroft Library.)

Raymond Hotel in Pasadena, a gloriously Italian Renaissance structure, burned down at the turn of the century, its Boston owners decided to rebuild it in "the old Spanish or Mission architecture," complete with "the graceful arches, the richly colored stucco, and the tiled roof."[173] A tourist reported happily in 1904 that he had stayed at the Glenwood Hotel in Riverside, which he called "California's Mission Hotel." He noted that the building "carried out the mission scheme in every detail, the furnishings being quaintly consistent with this idea."[174] Tourists now wanted to find evidence of a history and culture that came out of the California landscape, rather than attempting to graft Italian history and metaphor onto the Pacific coast. Mission architecture and the romanticized picture of mission Indians offered a pleasant myth that seemed to have roots in the American landscape.

New Eyes, New Words, Old Landscape

The interest in local color and American history even affected attitudes toward areas earlier tourists had simply despised. The trip through Utah and Nevada, universally hated by generations of travelers, received new attention from visitors by the 1890s, reflecting the confidence Americans were developing in their landscape. The language of geology provided observers with ways to read the landscape. The basin and range country of the Great Basin provided a textbook for learning the ancient history of the Far West. Where guidebooks had once recommended card games to pass the time or had been reduced to dull listings of distances, times, and town names, the books now promised train passengers they would "see many things in this region indicating a thrilling geological history."[175]

By the late 1880s, guidebooks used precise geological terms to describe the landscape, pointing out "striations" that marked "the water line of a vast, pre-historic inland sea" and "uncanny sinks, in which rivers disappear completely."[176] An 1890 edition of *Crofutt's Guide*, which in 1870 had complained about the absolute barrenness of the region, now promised "those who wish to delve into nature's mysteries can here find pleasant employment."[177] The discovery of the earth's ancient history and the development of a language to describe it interested Americans in regions like the Great Basin.

The Great American Desert had ceased to be a place of fear and loathing, which contained "no green thing that could sustain animal life" and whose "only landscape feature is dry, brown, and bare mountains."[178] Instead, it had become a "peculiar and enchanted environment," filled with "wonderfully vivid colors" revealed in "stratified buttresses and pinnacles."[179] Now that Americans had learned that the familiar palette of greens, blues, and browns did not apply to the Far West, they could appreciate the vibrant reds, yellows, and purples of the desert landscape. Nearly every tourist commented on the stunning range of color that "transformed the desert waste into such a scene that would delight an artist to reproduce."[180]

The Great Basin also offered evidence of Indian life, newly renovated in white American eyes. Twenty years earlier, tourists had found the tribes inhabiting the Nevada and Utah desert hideous and depraved, and guidebooks had rarely mentioned their presence. Now, a Raymond and Whitcomb tour pamphlet advertised that the trip across Nevada included "several Indian villages near the railway," where "Shoshone and Paiutes are frequently seen" along with the added attraction of "now and then a papoose for inspection."[181] Turn-of-the-century railroad guidebooks listed each Indian village, including information about the dress and social habits of its inhabitants. Indians and deserts, rather than being embarrassments, had become marketing advantages.

The railroads caught on very quickly to the changed interest in far western scenery and history. The Santa Fe Railroad, which ran through the heart of the newly popular Southwest, along with its hotel and restaurant subsidiary, the Fred Harvey Company, immersed itself completely in the language and imagery of the region. They devised an advertising system featuring Indian faces, artwork, and southwestern landforms on publicity materials; museums housing Indian artifacts and paintings of far western scenery; and station and hotel buildings built in Spanish and Indian styles. Archaeologists and ethnologists were given special travel rates in return for a share in their findings and the publicity the railroad got from their adventures. In 1901, the Santa Fe adopted a red cross inscribed in a white circle as its symbol, a motif that had been used by both the Indians and the Spanish for centuries.[182] Clearly, railroad publicists believed that this strategy would attract tourists, who now wanted to see evidence of American, rather than European, scenery and history.

The Santa Fe invested great sums of money on this assumption. Between 1896 and 1920 they built seventeen large hotels of regional design and an equal number of station buildings boasting the same southwestern style. As early as 1903 a proud Arizona resident wrote to the Santa Fe general passenger agent, J. J. Byrne, that his railroad had done more to "perpetuate the history" of the region by the style and names of their hotels "than all the books that have been written about it."[183]

Most of the hotels took their names from Spanish explorers and missionaries and adopted various versions of the "mission style" in their architecture. A Fred Harvey pamphlet pointed out that the station hotel at Albuquerque, the Alvarado, took its name from "a captain of artillery in Coronado's expedition" and that it looked "like a Spanish mission" with "rough, warm-gray walls and a long procession of arches, all under a red tile roof." It looked out upon the beautiful southwestern landscape with its "distant purple mountains, set against the turquoise sky."[184] The Castaneda, located at Las Vegas, New Mexico, offered visitors a building "patterned after the old California missions."[185] Southwestern history, design, and color suddenly attracted tourists to places that had once embarrassed and repelled them.

The Santa Fe and Fred Harvey also made the most of the Southwest's Indian heritage, which turn-of-the-century white Americans found increasingly fascinating. In 1902, the Fred Harvey Company formed an Indian department, designed to interest tourists in native artwork and culture. They began selling Indian crafts in many of the Santa Fe stations and built an impressive collection of artifacts to display in hotels, stations, and curio shops. A year later, the company opened its Indian building, adjacent to the Santa Fe station in Albuquerque. Here, tourists could see a room in which "a summer home of the Navajos has been cunningly wrought," where "patient Navajo squaws weave blankets" and "their men engage in fashioning showy bracelets, rings, and trinkets." Another room housed Indians from the pueblos of Acoma and Laguna making pottery and Hopis weaving baskets.[186] The idea, of course, was to encourage tourists to buy such goods. The strategy apparently worked. As one tourist reported after spending an afternoon at the Indian building, "those of us who had previously resisted the Indian bacilli here became inoculated, and we are all now hunting for blankets, baskets, and the gory scalping-knife."[187]

White Americans eagerly sought reminders of "the First Families of America"[188] and of the spectacular wilderness of the Far West, and the railroads were only too happy to provide them. Making the West attractive for tourists no longer meant making it look like Europe. Railroads, in catering to public demand, now described aspects of the Far West that seemed most distinctively American. They adopted the language of geology and ethnology to describe the peoples and places passengers would see, and they pointed out the landforms, colors, and plants that now captivated Americans.

The collaboration of the railroads with the American government in the formation of the national parks demonstrates the power of the American desire to visit and, eventually, to protect the beauties of the landscape so recently discovered. By the 1890s businessmen, intellectuals,

Santa Fe Indian Building

The fact that the Santa Fe Railroad built a museum and curio shop dedicated to southwestern Indian artifacts and crafts attested to the new interest tourists expressed in the Southwest and its native people. (In Fred Harvey, *The Great Southwest along the Santa Fe Trail*, 1919. Courtesy of the Bancroft Library.)

and reformers alike recognized the new value of the remote and once despised regions of the Far West.

As Americans grew more confident and more urban, the wilderness of the Far West grew more attractive. It could provide the atmosphere, objects, and peoples necessary to keep American culture healthy and unique. "We still have a bit of the primeval world and the spirit of the vigorous frontier," explained an enthusiast of the concept of national parks.[189] Others pointed out the scenic importance of "the great mesas of Colorado," "the painted desert," "the glaciers and snow-capped peaks of the Northwest," and the "glorious canyons of the Southwest."[190] Instead of being an embarrassment or a horror, the great sweep of the far western landscape had become the locus of pride and patriotism.

Large numbers of Americans began to demand the protection of parts of the western landscape because they saw it as a key to the development of their culture. By 1910 nearly twenty separate groups had been organized to battle for the protection of American scenery. Between 1890 and

1919 the United States government created fifteen national parks and an equal number of national monuments. Only one of these lay east of the Mississippi River, demonstrating the growing significance of the far western landscape for American culture. The protected areas included many of the great Indian ruins, parts of Grand Canyon, the distinctive formations of Zion and Bryce in southern Utah, the spectacular geothermal regions of Yellowstone, as well as the more well-known mountain landscapes of the Rockies and the Sierra Nevada. A spokesman for the Department of the Interior explained that these places had several crucial functions: "The stimulating of national patriotism, the furthering of knowledge and health; and the diverting of tourist travel to the scenic areas of the United States."[191] The Far West had evolved into a repository of American history and culture.

By the beginning of the twentieth century, most Americans who traveled west hoped to find the sources for their own culture, not a replication of Europe. A century of successful settlement gave Americans the confidence they needed to examine the more unconventional portions of the nation. Ethnology, geology, and an increasing disenchantment with urban life provided ways to interpret the unfamiliar landscape of the Far West. In turn, the new interpretation of deserts, wilderness, Indian ruins, and geological wonders required a different aesthetic framework—one that was uniquely American.

The importance and spread of the desire to find evidence of American, rather than Europe, in the Far West is evident in the railroads' response to tourist demands. They worked along with the government to develop once despised and feared regions into convenient objects of national pride. The aesthetic sense developing out of the encounter with the western landscape appeared clearly in the places railroads chose to develop, in the architectural styles they chose for buildings, and in the way they encouraged tourists to use these areas. An examination of the resorts built by the railroads between 1900 and 1920 provides the story for the last chapter.

CHAPTER 6

American Log Palaces: Far Western Resorts at the Turn of the Century, 1900–1915

By the beginning of the twentieth century, tourists' expectations for the scenery of the American Far West had changed considerably. In the West they hoped to find America, rather than Europe. They wanted to see deserts, Indians, geological wonders, and wilderness. Some Americans even went so far as to demand that the government protect such scenic and historic landscapes in the form of national parks and monuments. Regions that had formerly been considered useless or inappropriate for development because of their strange appearance now attracted both tourists and businessmen.

The railroads, always interested in attracting passengers, publicity, and profit, responded quickly to the changing demands. The railroad corporations also recognized the public-relations opportunities presented by the new attitudes toward western landscape evident in the national park idea and made the most of them. As the government created parks, railroad officials made sure that their lines carried people to the new parks and that their trains, hotels, restaurants, and shops met the needs of visitors. The efforts of the railroads, especially the Northern Pacific, the Santa Fe, and the Great Northern, made the new national parks into popular tourist destinations.

To lure American tourists into places like Yellowstone, the Grand Canyon, or Glacier National Park, the railroads and the federal government had to make such places accessible, comfortable, and attractive. In earlier years, the railroads had accomplished this task by promising a version of European scenery in the far western landscape and by building small enclaves of Europe in the form of glamorous resorts. By the first decade of the twentieth century, however, growing American confidence in the unique beauties of the Far West made this approach obsolete. Now railroad officials and speculators emphasized the special American qualities of the landscape and built resorts celebrating the very deserts, Indians, and wilderness Americans had once abhorred. An examination of the development between 1900 and 1920 of three national parks illustrates the depth of this change. In Yellowstone, Grand Canyon, and Glacier national parks, railroads made showcases of the far western landscape.

Wonderland: Yellowstone and the Northern Pacific Railroad

In the first decades of its existence, American tourists hardly considered Yellowstone National Park, created by Congress in 1872, a viable option for travel. Even though Northern Pacific Railroad officials had been among the first to suggest that the Yellowstone region be made into a protected reserve and had done much to force the park bill through Congress, the company did little to make the park accessible to tourists.[1] The park's remote location in northern Wyoming meant that it could not be reached by railroad. To make matters worse, Yellowstone had few roads passing through it, and it offered no accommodations for tourists.

Because of the panic of 1873 and the near collapse of the Northern Pacific, the fledgling transcontinental line remained stalled in the Dakota Territories. When Henry Villard took over the Northern Pacific in 1882, the railroad and the development of Yellowstone became going concerns. By this time the Department of the Interior, weary of the constant stream of applications to build within the park and frustrated by their own lack of funds for development, granted a near monopoly of concession privileges to the Northern Pacific. At the same time, the government began building a loop road that would allow visitors to travel around the park.[2]

In 1883, the railroad reached Livingston, Montana, just north of the national park and began encouraging tourist travel. To inaugurate the accessibility of Yellowstone, Rufus Hatch, a large investor in the Northern Pacific's efforts to develop the park, engineered a tremendous publicity trip for a train load of speculators and reporters. That same year President Arthur made a three-week hunting trip into Yellowstone in an effort to regain his health. These events gave the park its first national exposure as reports of the scenic wonders and the gradually improving accommodations appeared in newspapers and magazines.[3]

After a series of bankruptcies, antitrust accusations, and corporate maneuvers between 1883 and 1886, the Northern Pacific managed to consolidate its position as the sole concessionaire for Yellowstone. The Department of the Interior, in charge of the park's operation, granted the railroad long-term leases for land at the most promising tourist sights, including Mammoth Hot Springs, the Upper and Lower geyser basins, Yellowstone Lake, and the Grand Canyon of the Yellowstone.[4] Now all that remained was to build appropriate hotels and passable roads and to convince tourists the region was safe, attractive, and worth visiting.

In the 1880s and early 1890s, Yellowstone still seemed remote, uncivilized, and strange. Even though the United States Army had taken over the task of its protection from the beleaguered Department of Interior in 1886, the national park remained largely a wilderness. Few roads cut through the nearly two million acres, and these were often impassable with snow, mud, or dust. Even so, the Yellowstone Park Association, a subsidiary of the Northern Pacific Railroad, had built a few rudimentary hotels and had devised a transportation system to carry visitors to various popular spots in the park.

In spite of the primitive conditions, an increasing number of tourists stepped off the train in Gardiner, Montana, to visit Yellowstone. By the late 1880s, nearly six thousand people toured the park each summer, and that number would increase steadily.[5] What early visitors found there, however, was not always what they expected or what they had been promised.

Like most guidebooks of the 1880s, guides to the Yellowstone region occasionally tried to convince their readers that the landscape resembled Europe. They claimed that "the best of the Rhine, the Hudson . . . and the whole of Switzerland" could not compare with the glories of "the National Park on the Yellowstone."[6] A pamphlet from the Boston tour company of Raymond and Whitcomb explained that "the resemblance between Yellowstone Lake and the Swiss lakes is quite marked."[7] A tourist made a similar comparison to the English lakes, which, he noted, "without their associations, are not so fair as this."[8]

More often, however, guidebooks and tourists emphasized the singular nature of the landscape. When faced with the stunning evidence of geothermic processes or with a sight like the Grand Canyon of the Yellowstone, European analogies seemed inappropriate, just as they had in the desert Southwest. "No country in the world," claimed an early visitor, "contains half the natural curiosities or one tithe the wonderful freaks and marvelous formations of nature."[9] Another tourist reported that she rubbed her eyes every day to be sure she "was not either in a dream or in a new world."[10] A Raymond and Whitcomb publication stated grandly that "words which have served to ennoble lesser objects are weak and ineffectual in describing such a vast collection of marvels."[11] John Muir wrote that the Yellowstone did indeed "belong to some other world," one that required a "coinage of new words . . . to convey this varied and continual color, and give an intelligent conception of the commotion of waters."[12] Muir obviously recognized the importance of language in understanding the Yellowstone landscape.

By the 1890s, most visitors realized the value of the new world offered by Yellowstone and began to describe it without the crutch of European analogy. "To call our National Park the 'Switzerland of America' would be absurd," wrote the famous lecturer John L. Stoddard in 1898. He stated unequivocally that Yellowstone "is not Switzerland, it is not Iceland, it is not Norway; it is unique, and the unique cannot be compared."[13] Most observers apparently agreed with Stoddard's statement and attempted to depict what they saw in more original terms.

Some parts of Yellowstone seemed especially difficult to describe because of their novelty. The sight of the thermal regions stunned most visitors, who were "brought to a standstill, hushed and awe-stricken before phenomena wholly new."[14] "Just imagine the steam coming up from a thousand orifices, the transparent element spouting forth from a dozen cauldrons at once," wrote one astounded observer.[15] Others found the geyser basins threatening, explaining that "in these steaming cauldrons, the spouting geysers, the dark, venomous-looking mud pots, there is active hate."[16] Rarely, however, did they use the older analogies to

Dante's *Inferno* or to the biblical Hell that many of the first visitors to Yellowstone had adopted.

Unanimously, tourists reveled in the sight of the Grand Canyon of the Yellowstone. The great gash in the earth, heralded by explorers and represented in the popular 1872 painting by Thomas Moran, *The Grand Canyon of the Yellowstone*, met their expectations. Both promoters and tourists celebrated the canyon as an example of the spectacular landscape present in the American Far West and made few attempts to find European analogies.

Like the rock formations in the desert Southwest, the Grand Canyon of the Yellowstone required a distinctive kind of description. The vibrant colors of the canyon impressed most observers and provided them with a way to analyze what they saw. The English man of letters Rudyard Kipling, who visited Yellowstone in 1888, recorded his surprise when "without warning or preparation I looked into a gulf seventeen hundred feet deep." He described it vividly as a "wide welter of colour—crimson, emerald, cobalt, ochre, amber, honey splashed with port wine, snow-white, vermilion, lemon, and silver grey in wide washes."[17] A pamphlet produced by the Northern Pacific claimed that the canyon could be "compared to nothing but the most gorgeous sunset."[18] The "utter opulence of color" that looked "as though rainbows had fallen out of the sky" fascinated another observer.[19]

By the end of the nineteenth century, visitors and promoters understood the value of the exceptional appearance of the landscape and no longer felt obliged to make it look like something else. The intensive exploration of the Far West and the increased accessibility to formerly remote regions had forced Americans to accept and to appreciate the novel qualities of places like Yellowstone. By the 1880s and 1890s when the Northern Pacific reached Yellowstone, Americans no longer expected to find European vistas in the national park. They came to see fabulous thermal formations and the brilliant colors of the canyon, as well as to experience an untouched wilderness.

Now that Americans wanted to see the kind of landscape that Yellowstone offered, the Northern Pacific began to advertise and develop it in earnest. President Arthur's 1883 trip and the publicity excursions undertaken by Rufus Hatch, owner of the first hotel in the park, and by Henry Villard, president of the Northern Pacific, helped bring the park national

Yellowstone Coaches, ca. 1903

These sturdy but well-loaded coaches carried tourists around Yellowstone Park until 1915 when cars were allowed into the park, quickly replacing the slow and bumpy coaches. (Photo by F. J. Haynes; courtesy of the Montana Historical Society, Helena.)

attention. As early as 1886, a tourist noted the efforts of the railroad to publicize the park. As he rode toward Wyoming, booksellers pestered him to buy numerous pamphlets, and railroad employees "distributed a brightly colored map of the district, with a brightly illustrated description."[20]

Tourists recognized the scenic wonders in Yellowstone, but they needed to be convinced that they could see them safely and comfortably. One observer explained that in the early 1880s a tour of the park required "a ride on a rickety-rattling, jolting stage coach," which, he added, "is perfectly preposterous to those in high life who are unused to anything less than a Pullman palace-car."[21] In spite of such discomforts and the horrors of the primitive hotels built before the consolidation of the Northern Pacific's interests, tourists did begin to visit the park in the last decades of the century.

Even more significantly, the exclusive Boston tour company of Raymond and Whitcomb brought in organized tours of the park in the late 1880s. Because Raymond and Whitcomb prided themselves on the comfort and convenience they offered to their clientele, Yellowstone clearly had reached acceptable standards in its accommodations and transportation. A description of a tour of the national park assured Raymond and Whitcomb clients that "the journeys about the park may now be made easily and safely, while good hotels, in place of 'camps,' afford delightful resting places."[22]

Such commendations convinced ever larger numbers of people to visit the park. Many aspects of Yellowstone pleased tourists. Almost universally, they enjoyed the scenery. In fact, they enjoyed it too much, according to many of the park superintendents. Tourists who carved their names on trees, geothermal foundations, and in the canyon walls or who carted away bits and pieces of the landscape proved to be an insurmountable problem. "I do not believe," wrote one beleaguered superintendent, "10,000 men could prevent tourists from mutilating the beautiful formations in the Park."[23] Tourists gazed at the spouting geysers and the splendor of the canyon and happily scratched their names at the bottoms of thermal pools, and, as Rudyard Kipling observed, "returned to the hotel to put down their impressions in diaries and notebooks which they wrote up ostentatiously on the verandahs."[24]

Many visitors, however, did not express the same appreciation for the man-made portions of the landscape, no matter what Northern Pacific promotional material or Raymond and Whitcomb guidebooks told them. Somehow, the scenery did not look as good while tourists were jolted across rough, dusty roads, suffering from an aching back or from food poisoning. In 1892, one visitor remembered that his party had to ford a river twice, and "once the passengers were obliged to leave the wagon and remove a fallen tree from the way." He concluded that his trip would have been far more pleasant "if there had been less dust, fewer mosquitoes, and better roads."[25] Throughout the 1890s, bitter complaints about the quality of the roads and the hotels filled the files of the Yellowstone Park superintendents.[26]

Part of the problem was one of expectation. Tourists had no real idea of what to expect when they arrived in the park. Undoubtably, many came with a literal idea of what the word *park* meant. According to an early guidebook, many visitors looked for "beautifully aligned walks and roadways, carpet-like lawns, formal beds of flowers, and other features of the conventional city-park."[27] Instead, they found "everything in its natural condition—rude, stern and wild," including the accommodations and the roads.[28] One tourist complained about the lack of amenities in a letter to Superintendent John Pitcher. Not only did the disgruntled visitor demand improved roads and hotels, but he also suggested that "it would be a very welcome improvement to many visitors if a considerable number of seats were placed about the Hot Springs."[29] Obviously, not every American was prepared to rough it in the wilderness.

Even though the federal government and officials of the Northern Pacific Railroad recognized the potential value of the Yellowstone landscape, they were not sure how best to develop and market it. Certainly, Americans had become enamored with the idea of wilderness in the late nineteenth century, and much of Yellowstone's attraction came from its wildness. Few visitors, however, could appreciate the scenery in a truly natural state. As a compromise, the Department of the Interior granted the Northern Pacific the right to develop seven sites near popular scenic features in the park and built a loop road connecting these spots.

The Northern Pacific, in the guise of the Yellowstone Park Improvement Company, built its first hotel at Mammoth Hot Springs in 1883. The rapidly constructed hotel, a vast, cavernous structure, opened its doors to the public in 1884. Painted green with a red roof, it presented what advertisers called a "Queen Anne look" with gables and turrets of various sizes. Using the standard conventions of resort architecture, the Mammoth Hotel contained 151 rooms, a spacious and ornately decorated lobby and dining room, and a great veranda that stretched across the front of the building. Despite such outward grandeur, neither tourists nor park officials found the hotel satisfactory.[30]

Many visitors found its architecture and forced elegance rather jarring in the wilderness setting. One tourist, thrilled at being "at the threshold of the world's wonderland, surrounded by mountain peaks and hemmed in by pine mantled ridges," was stunned to find "a vision of verandas . . . of turrets, towers, and Juliet balconies."[31] Another guest of the hotel complained that its management "insisted on a brass band's tooting a good part of the time," and further that the "noise it made was execrable."[32] The poet Joaquin Miller "deplored" the fact that such a structure was "thrust out in the face of the noblest things in nature." He commented further that he did not "journey all the way to Yellowstone to see a big barn."[33] To these visitors, the Mammoth Hotel seemed a noisy and obtrusive presence in the wilderness they hoped to find.

Unpleasant music and startling design seemed like petty complaints to many of the hotel's clientele. "Chilly, dreary rooms" and "as poor excuses for meals as could be found in many a day's travel" horrified travelers who had been promised great luxury by Northern Pacific advertising.[34] One tourist warned that during crowded periods, "one is compelled to take a bed in a room with several others and may even be forced to crowd two in a bed."[35] Park administrators were well aware of the hotel's shortcomings. In his annual report of 1888, Superintendent Moses Harris wrote to his superiors at the Department of the Interior, alerting them to the shoddy nature of the hotel's construction and its inadequate rooms and public facilities. "The money it cost was badly invested," he stated bluntly, recommending that the concession lease be turned over to a more reliable organization.[36]

The Mammoth Hotel, however, looked marvelous in comparison with the accommodations offered in the rest of the park. The Northern Pacific organization built tent "hotels" at the geyser basins and the Grand Canyon, which, according to the superintendent of the park, "were not of the most desirable character." He understood that given the cold temperatures and high altitude, "tent domiciles" could "by no stretch of the imagination be made to appear comfortable."[37] John Yancey, a local entrepreneur who had been granted a lease before the Northern Pacific managed to obtain a stranglehold on park concessions, offered tourists equally unpleasant lodgings near the sights in Firehole Basin. A tourist commented with evident disgust that the beds at Yancey's "showed they were changed at least twice, once in the spring, and once in the fall of each year."[38]

Reports of such conditions alarmed park administrators who believed that the poor quality of accommodation had become a "shame and a discredit to the National Park."[39] In 1888, the superintendent's *Annual Report* summed up the progress made by the Northern Pacific's Yellowstone Park Association as "entirely inadequate to the demands of travel." He noted that the "cold and leaky buildings" of "cheap and poor construction" were the cause of "frequent and bitter complaint by patrons," who had to pay first-class rates for abysmal accommodations.[40]

With continual pressure from the Department of the Interior, conditions had improved considerably by the mid-1890s. Tourists could now enter Yellowstone Park and make a five-day loop trip. The Yellowstone Park Association and the Northern Pacific had built a series of decent, if rather nondescript, hotels at the most popular tourist attractions, including the major geyser basins, Yellowstone Lake, and the Grand Canyon of the Yellowstone. None of the hotels, however, measured up to the standards expected by wealthy tourists.[41]

In spite of these drawbacks, tourist travel increased steadily. By the late 1890s, nearly ten thousand people entered the park each year. Even with these impressive numbers, the Northern Pacific had not yet made a profit on its Yellowstone operations. Between 1898 and 1901, the railroad, tired of shoddy management and poor returns, reorganized its interests and turned over the operation of the Yellowstone Park Association to a Montana land-and-cattle speculator, Harry Child. Already the major stockholder of the Yellowstone Park Transportation Company, Child, backed by the financial power of the Northern Pacific, set out to make the park more attractive to tourists.[42]

Aware that "good roads and comfortable places of entertainment"[43] were essential to pleasing the wealthy clientele he hoped to attract, Child first turned his attention to the park's hotels. Not only did the existing structures need considerable refurbishing, but the increased numbers of people visiting the park had made the construction of a large, new hotel necessary. Both the Northern Pacific and the Department of the Interior had long been encouraging the development of a site in the Upper Geyser Basin. With the government's blessings, and a $100,000 loan from the railroad company, Child began to plan a grand hotel directly in front of the Old Faithful geyser.[44]

Child wanted to build something that would bring national attention to Yellowstone as well as profits for his coffers. He hoped to capitalize on the exceptional nature of the Yellowstone environment by constructing a hotel that would remind visitors of their surroundings rather than insulating them from the landscape. Recognizing the growing penchant among Americans for the wilderness and for indigenous forms, he knew the Queen Anne or plain clapboard designs of the other hotels in the park were old-fashioned and inappropriate. Child hoped to create a grand showpiece in the most modern style.

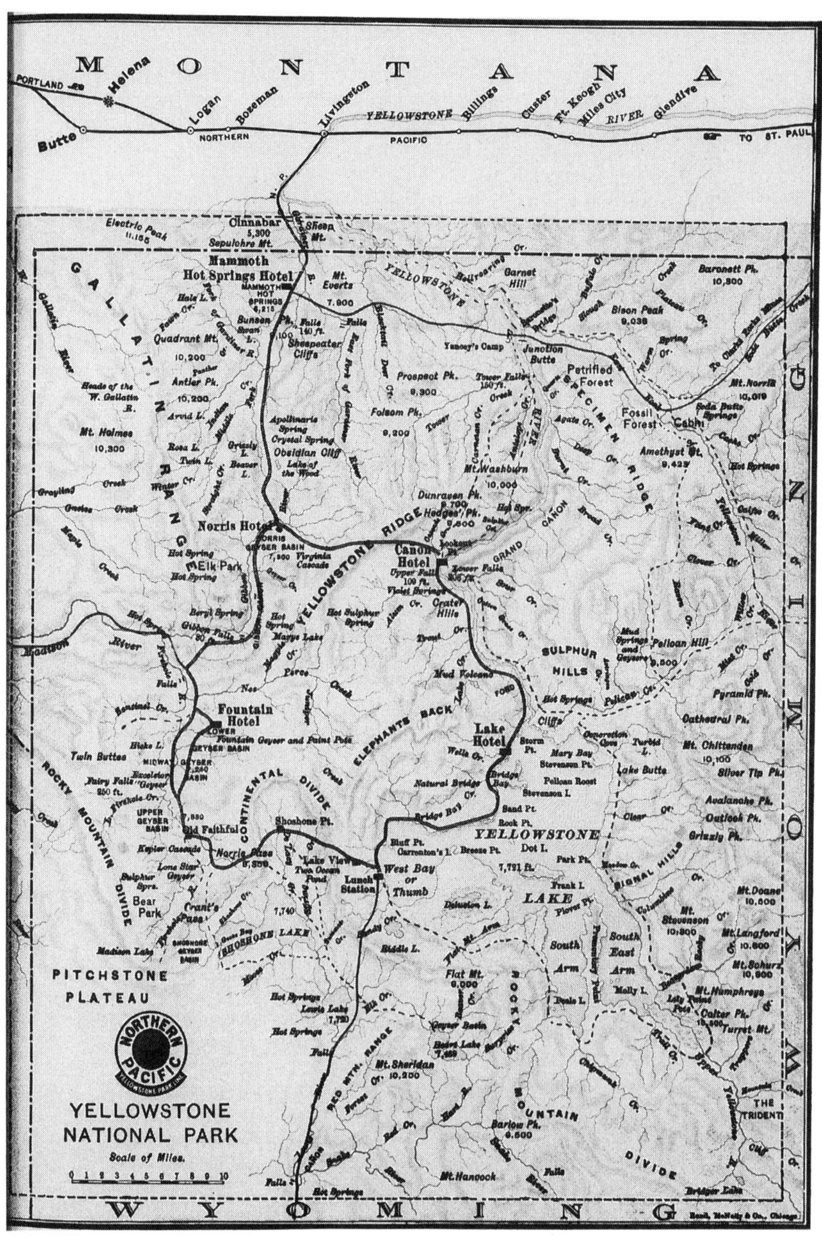

Northern Pacific Map of Yellowstone Park

The map shows the five-day loop trip that carried tourists to all of the high points of Yellowstone Park, as well as to the hotels built to accommodate demanding American tourists. (In Olin D. Wheeler, *Wonderland 1900*. Courtesy of the Bancroft Library.)

His first step was to hire architect Robert Reamer, who had worked for Harry Child and for the Northern Pacific Railroad on several other projects. Reamer, a midwesterner, had studied in Chicago where he had undoubtably been influenced by Louis Sullivan, Frank Lloyd Wright, and the Prairie School. He had met Harry Child in San Diego, where the Child family often wintered and where Reamer was designing bungalows on the Coronado Peninsula. Child, impressed with Reamer's work, got him a commission to design the Northern Pacific depot at Gardiner, Montana, the entrance station for Yellowstone. A modified log cabin, the building was constructed of stone and wood, which created a rustic effect that welcomed tourists into the Yellowstone landscape. To complement the building, Reamer also designed the Roosevelt Arch, which marked the northern border of the park. The arch, dedicated by President Theodore Roosevelt in 1902, rose up from the ground to form a rough stone structure. For its construction, Reamer used basalt stone quarried in the area, making the arch blend into the landscape.[45]

Reamer's design for the Old Faithful Inn exaggerated the rustic and natural elements of his earlier projects. Clearly, he wanted the building to appear as a natural addition to the landscape. He spent months studying the site and choosing the materials for the building, intent on making it an intimate part of the Yellowstone environment. Reamer oriented the building so that its front porch faced the steaming Upper Geyser Basin. The central attraction, Old Faithful, erupted regularly only one hundred feet from the main drive. Unpeeled logs, native stone, and cedar shingles adorned the strikingly innovative structure, built primarily in the winter of 1903–1904.[46]

The hotel that opened in the summer of 1904 was exactly the showpiece Harry Child wanted. It presented a ninety-three-foot-high main building with symmetrical wings extending to each side. The central portion of the structure boasted an enormous sloping shingled roof, broken by a double row of dormer windows and a great log port couchere and porch. The massive structure rested on a solid foundation of stone and unhewn horizonal logs.[47]

The design displayed the structural features of the building. Reamer's attention to such detail showed his interest in the Chicago School and the craft tradition popular at the turn of the century. Increasingly, American architects had begun to build "honestly," showcasing structural features,

Old Faithful Inn, Yellowstone National Park, ca. 1910

The Old Faithful Inn rose up out of the Yellowstone landscape. Made from local stone and wood, it complimented the natural scene that surrounded it. (Courtesy of the Montana Historical Society, Helena.)

rather than hiding them in plaster and ornate detail. In Old Faithful Inn, sturdy log walls and massive beams and brackets (also made of native logs) supported the weight of the great main gable, demonstrating Reamer's debt to American architectural trends.[48]

However, Reamer's design also showed great innovation. The novelties of the far western landscape clearly provided inspiration. Reamer allowed the particularities of the site to dictate the style of the building, necessitating a new architectural vocabulary. Just as the scenery had required new words, images, and analogies to describe it adequately, Reamer believed that it needed fresh architectural interpretations as well.

The Old Faithful Inn appeared as if it had been spawned by the same forces of nature that had created Yellowstone. The rough stone and the huge logs suggested a forceful and primeval permanence, while the gnarled and twisted branches used as exterior trim and porch railing demonstrated the same malevolent forces that had tortured the earth in the thermal basins. A writer in *Western Architect* magazine who viewed the building in 1904 described it as "a product of the forest, built with ax, saw, and hammer."[49] Another observer noted the strange, twisted form of the wood Reamer had chosen, commenting that "these abnormal growths are in perfect keeping with the unusual character of the this Wonderland and Old Faithful Inn harmonizes completely with its strange surroundings."[50]

Reamer exaggerated these same ideas in the interior of the building. A large front door, made of rough-sawed lumber and hung on old-fashioned cast-iron hinges, welcomed the visitor into the inn. Once inside, the huge open space of the lobby, soaring up seven full stories, awed observers expecting the enclosed space of a log cabin. A series of staircases and balconies surrounded the edges of the lobby, growing smaller and smaller until they reached a small crow's-nest perched at the top of the ceiling.[51]

To heighten the rustic effect, Reamer used native materials at every opportunity. Split logs formed the steps on the complex of staircases. The newel posts, handrails, and balcony railings were all made out of crooked and twisted branches, "with immense gumboils and other protuberances upon them."[52] Huge peeled logs supported the array of balconies and staircases. The variety and scale of the wooden interior impressed one writer as representing "the grandeur of vast forests conquered."[53]

Reamer built a stone chimney sixteen feet square as the focal point of the lobby to complement the scale of the room. Made out of local lava stone, it stretched upward nearly the full height of the building. The tremendous obelisk contained four large and four small fireplaces surrounded by large wooden armchairs, and acted as the central gathering spot for the hotel. Reamer also designed an immense cast-iron popcorn popper, which hung by the chimney, to be used as part of the evenings' entertainment.[54]

In the guest rooms in the original part of the building, Reamer used a more intimate version of the same rustic style. Low ceilings, small doors and windows, rough pine boards for walls, and simple furniture made up the décor of these rooms. A 1905 guest described her room as "a paradise of restfulness, though in a rough and rustic fashion." Another visitor remarked on the rough plank walls, "redolent with the fragrance of the mountain pine."[55]

Despite the studied primitive qualities of Old Faithful Inn's design,

Old Faithful Inn Lobby

The interior of Old Faithful Inn continued the rustic effect of the exterior. Reamer used oddly shaped peeled logs for the balconies that rose seven stories to the roof, and he insisted on solid wooden furniture to compliment his design. (Courtesy of the Montana Historical Society, Helena.)

Reamer did not simply create a gigantic log cabin. "With all this rusticity," explained one observer, "comfort, convenience and even elegance are everywhere."[56] The rooms offered private baths, hot- and cold-running water, and electric call buttons. The lobby had floors of polished hardwood, covered with the best quality oriental rugs; the windows used the heaviest leaded glass and were covered with dainty French curtains. Electric chandeliers, supplementing the light from the fireplaces, hung in the dining room over tables set with fine linen, china, and silver. A 1909 tourist commented on the novelty of "eating in a room that is the last expression of a lodge in some wilderness, where the latest French cookery tempts your appetite."[57]

Robert Reamer did not invent the blend of rustic elegance that characterized Old Faithful Inn. It developed out of new attitudes toward the

American landscape that appeared in the last years of the nineteenth century. As Americans began to look at the wilderness as friendly rather than dangerous and as rural simplicity began to look more attractive than urban complexity, they explored new forms of recreation. Rather than avoiding the American wilderness, Americans now sought ways to experience it. Architectural and decorative styles reflected these changes.

The first indication of the new architectural style evolved out of the retreats built by wealthy easterners in the Adirondack mountains of upper New York State. Beginning in the 1880s, the still wild Adirondacks became summer and weekend havens for weary urban tycoons. They built extensive "camps," which used deliberately primitive materials to camouflage considerable luxury. Because of the remote locations of the mountain camps, most architects used local materials and construction teams to build their structures.[58] The result was an Adirondack style using logs and stone as its main materials, with the major décor elements being peeled logs; unfinished boards; and solid, unadorned furniture.[59]

The same desires for simple, native styles appeared in other locales as well, especially from the increasingly influential Midwest and Far West. Urban architects like Frank Lloyd Wright, Bernard Maybeck, and Charles S. and Henry M. Greene had also begun to rebel against the overly ornate architectural styles imported from Europe. Exhibiting a growing confidence in an American aesthetic, they designed houses to suit the varieties of the American environment. Although far more elaborate than the Adirondack camps, the work of these architects demonstrated many of the same beliefs in simplicity, native materials, and the importance of the building blending into the site.

On a more popular level, a furniture maker named Gustave Stickley developed a line of furniture with the trade name of Craftsman. He garnered wide attention for his products by publishing a popular magazine called *The Craftsman*, which included plans for making his furniture as well as suggestions for house building and home décor. Emphasizing the concepts of honest handiwork and utility, Stickley adapted the ideas of the English designers and philosophers William Morris and John Ruskin to appeal to a mass American market in the first years of the twentieth century.[60]

Such changes in American taste and architecture must have inspired Robert Reamer's designs for Old Faithful Inn. His Chicago training, and his California practice where he had designed a mission-style office building and a series of vacation bungalows, had clearly influenced his ideas about materials and design. The inn's startling appearance did not evolve directly from the unique landscape of Yellowstone. Rather, it signaled the strength of an important cultural shift that blended concepts from the eastern and western parts of the United States.

Even if the style of the hotel was not entirely new, Reamer was one of the first to adapt the entirely domestic rustic style to a large, public building. Because the encounter with the far western landscape had helped Americans in the search for an aesthetic of their own, it seemed appropriate that a structure in the midst of the western wilderness should demonstrate the possibilities of native styles.

The Northern Pacific Railroad recognized that it had introduced something new into the world of resorts with the appearance of the Old Faithful Inn. The originality of the building required new promotional methods. It could not be depicted in familiar architectural terms. Rather than describing the resemblance of Old Faithful Inn to other buildings, as promoters had done with resorts of an earlier era, advertisers proudly pointed out its radical departure from traditional resort styles. "You can't call it a chalet," a 1909 brochure explained, "no Swiss ever dreamed of anything like this; nor yet a chateau, no Frenchman could think one out like it."[61] Instead, Old Faithful Inn offered something entirely different.

The word *unique* appeared ubiquitously in advertisements. According to the Northern Pacific, Old Faithful Inn was "a most unique hotel in a most unique region."[62] One pamphlet advised visitors to "enjoy a unique experience in a unique hotel in a unique land," while another commented on "this most charming, most unique, queer, fascinating place."[63] Clearly, by 1904 when Old Faithful Inn opened, unique architecture in a unique landscape had become a point of pride, rather than one of embarrassment.

Because Americans had begun to recognize the beauties present in places like Yellowstone, they wanted architecture to reflect that landscape. In the case of Old Faithful Inn, advertisers pointed out that the structure was "truly as much a product of the park as is the noble geyser from which it derives its name."[64] Because it "harmonizes perfectly with its surroundings," promised promoters, Old Faithful Inn "preserves carefully the integrity and charm of the forest."[65] The new interest in harmonizing with the landscape rather than denying its realities had clearly affected architecture.

The fact that the hotel appeared to be "a product of the wilderness which surrounds it"[66] also demonstrated the changing attitudes toward wilderness held by turn-of-the-century Americans. Even though not everyone wanted to experience the full range of "the strenuous life," many Americans yearned for a taste of the primitive. Advertisers felt enough confidence in the appeal of raw wilderness to emphasize the "rough blocks of stone" and the "unhewn logs" that made Old Faithful Inn appear to be "of a rough, rustic order," attributes that would have convinced many nineteenth-century tourists to seek lodging elsewhere.[67]

At the same time, however, promoters made sure that potential guests understood that the rustic nature of the hotel was "a finished elegant rusticity" and that there was "nothing uncouth about it."[68] The concept of a great hotel in a rustic style represented a significant departure from what most people expected in a resort, and the Northern Pacific did not want to lose clientele or profits on an architectural gamble. Their advertisements promised that "the Inn is not in the least a freaky affair" and that it offered every modern convenience.[69] Despite the fact that it was "finished in the rough" and that "one might imagine material comforts lacking," Old Faithful Inn had electric lights, steam heat, and furnishings that cost $200,000. In addition, the hotel offered its guests an orchestra and "cuisine equal to that of the best metropolitan hotels."[70] Old Faithful Inn presented the comforts of civilization packaged in a primitive container.

The combination of rustic and grand appealed to Yellowstone tourists from the moment the hotel opened. They loved the inn's novel architecture, its harmony with nature, and its elegant comforts. Like promoters, early visitors seemed unsure about how to describe Old Faithful Inn because it did not resemble any hotel they had seen before. A tourist who called the inn "the showplace of the Park" characterized it as a "log house sublimated, raised to the n'th degree."[71]

Most observers gave up attempting to label Old Faithful Inn, happy with the idea that it was simply unique, a word that appeared in most tourists' descriptions of the building. A 1904 visitor credited the building with having "a startling oddness which one learns to adore." Another described it as "a revelation of simplicity and beauty."[72] The eccentric interior delighted most observers, and they commented on the "queer forms of growth that enter into the construction of the curious, rustic interior."[73]

Such use of surrounding landscape in the building itself appealed to most of the inn's guests. One visitor noted approvingly that both the interior and the exterior of the building were "constructed in a style appropriate for its setting."[74] Others reported their "fascination" with "every detail constructed from trees in their own shape of growth," so that "even the drinking fountain is a log."[75] The writer and reformer Charles Francis Adams, Jr., visited Yellowstone in 1912 and complimented Old Faithful Inn by writing that it "looks as though it grew there."[76]

The appearance of the landscape now pleased Americans enough to incorporate it into their architecture. They no longer wanted to go into a resort to escape reminders of the American landscape; they now hoped to discover it. Old Faithful Inn provided a place where Americans could taste the wilderness and savor their landscape without giving up the comforts of urban life. Its rustic and grand style reflected the new desires of tourists who traveled west in the beginning of the twentieth century. As one tourist put it, she "wouldn't have missed seeing it for anything."[77] The Northern Pacific and its innovative architect, Robert Reamer, had discovered a style of architecture that would influence western resorts for the next several decades.

Even as Reamer designed Old Faithful Inn, his employer Harry Child had his eye on several other Yellowstone projects. One popular hotel could not ensure a pleasant impression of the park if all of the others were dismal. Because the standard tour of Yellowstone required tourists to spend at least four nights in the park, Child worked to upgrade the other hostelries. Child seemed to be worried about the appeal of the daring style of the new Old Faithful Inn and chose more standard styles for many of the other structures in the park. Hoping to please every taste, he envisioned a variety of hotels that would make Yellowstone into a renowned resort.

After approving the plans for Old Faithful Inn, Child asked Reamer to remodel the Lake Hotel on the shores of Yellowstone Lake in a more traditional style. Reamer took him at his word and made the boxy, clapboard structure into a neoclassical wonder. He built three large gables, upheld by fifty-foot columns, on the front of the hotel. To add interest to the upper levels, Reamer added a series of false balconies on the third-floor windows and decorative moldings along the roof line. He

Lake Hotel

The yellow-and-white colonial-style Lake Hotel was a startling contrast to the rustic and novel Old Faithful Inn. The design of the rather conventional Lake Hotel displayed a lack of confidence on the part of Northern Pacific officials over the bold departure represented by Old Faithful Inn. (Courtesy of the Montana Historical Society, Helena.)

painted the entire structure a warm yellow with the exception of the columns and moldings, which he kept a brilliant white.[78] If Harry Child had wanted something entirely different from Old Faithful Inn at Yellowstone Lake, he certainly got it. The Lake Hotel echoed the European styles employed by the railroads in Colorado and California twenty years earlier.

Tourists liked the Lake Hotel. Because it resembled many of the buildings built in eastern resort areas, they found it familiar and easy to describe. Visitors noted its "great Corinthian pillars," which made its entrance "not unlike the entrance to the White House"; its "spacious lobby rich in mahogany"; and its "polished floors strewn with Oriental rugs."[79] They described the Lake Hotel as pleasant, quiet, and restful and noted its resemblance to other places of resort in the East and in Europe.

Such responses must have pleased Harry Child and the Northern Pacific, who intended the Lake Hotel as a place where guests would make long stays. With its golf course, tennis courts, and classical motif, it seemed apart from the rest of Yellowstone.[80] In fact, its atmosphere of luxurious rest and repose, modeled on eastern resorts, seemed quite alien to tourists who came to the park to see natural phenomena and to experience the western wilderness.

Despite Harry Child's careful planning, however, the Lake Hotel never elicited the same enthusiasm as Old Faithful Inn, and tourists rarely made the kind of extended stays Child had hoped they would. Though they commented favorably about the hotel, tourists never raved over its harmony with the natural landscape or its ingenious design. Unlike Old Faithful Inn, the Lake Hotel did not seem to grow out of the Yellowstone environment. It became a place to spend the night between the wonders of the geyser basins and the Grand Canyon of the Yellowstone and nothing more.

If the Lake Hotel seemed out of place to twentieth-century visitors, so did the Mammoth Hot Springs Hotel. Harry Child renovated it, hoping to make it a social center for the park. Here guests could partake of "highballs and cocktails," while lounging on the wide porches in the evening. Later, the "Yellowstone Park Orchestra" played "their catchy music" as hotel guests danced in the ballroom.[81] "If you wish civilization and hotsprings mixed," explained a 1909 visitor, "you will prefer Mammoth." He liked the fact that one could dress for dinner "without being stared at" and that stock quotations were posted daily in the lobby.[82]

Most tourists, apparently, did not prefer Mammoth. Its elegant amenities impressed them as inappropriate to the park setting, rather than as social advantages. Tourists came to Mammoth Hot Springs to see the hot springs terraces with their vibrant natural colors, not to hear an orchestra or to examine the latest clothing fashions. Most visitors used the Mammoth Hotel as a starting point for their trip through the park, rarely spending more than one night. Few people commented on the hotel, except to say it offered good food and pleasant accommodations, and reserved their compliments for the novel experience of staying at Old Faithful Inn.

Harry Child's Yellowstone Park Association, granted the exclusive right to build hotels in the park, learned from its experiments with hotel styles. The overwhelmingly positive response to Old Faithful Inn and the lack of enthusiasm for the more traditional Lake and Mammoth hotels demonstrated a change in American taste. By the first decade of the twentieth century, most Americans no longer wanted to pretend the far western landscape could be molded into a European landscape. Because the unique features of the wild landscape now attracted them, tourists wanted to experience it in a direct way. They came to Yellowstone to see thermal formations, great chasms in the earth, wild animals, and a safe version of the American wilderness. Most visitors demanded a resort that highlighted this experience rather than one that denied it. Old Faithful Inn, with its rock-and-log exterior, grand rustic interior, its wide porches for viewing the geyser basins, and its rooftop searchlight that played on Old Faithful geyser and the park bears, met these new requirements admirably.

When travel through Yellowstone had increased enough to warrant the construction of another large hotel in 1910, Child and the Northern Pacific hired Robert Reamer to create another structure to reflect the growing American taste for the rustic and the wild. They chose a site on the edge of the Grand Canyon of the Yellowstone. Once again Reamer designed a building that seemed in keeping with the landscape.

A lower, more sprawling structure than Old Faithful Inn, the Canyon Hotel had the same dominant, overhanging roof but with cleaner, more modern lines. A Northern Pacific publicist noted that the hotel was "never in ornate competition with the landscape."[83] Reamer obviously sensed the futility of building anything that could compete with the grandeur of the Grand Canyon of the Yellowstone. "I built it in keeping with the place where it stands," he explained. "To be at dischord with the landscape would be almost a crime. To try and improve upon it would be an impertinence."[84] An enthusiastic tourist appreciated Reamer's efforts when he pointed out that the hotel "was colored like the walls of the canyon . . . a harmony in form and color. It was all," he concluded, "in perfect taste with the magnificent natural surroundings."[85]

Reamer also paid careful attention to the interior of the Canyon Hotel. In a huge central lounge, measuring two hundred by one hundred feet, he emphasized space and light, again echoing the central attributes of the Grand Canyon itself. Where in Old Faithful Inn the visitor felt as if he

Canyon Hotel, ca. 1915

The Canyon Hotel, built in 1913 to overlook the Grand Canyon of the Yellowstone, demonstrated that the rustic style had won out in Yellowstone. The landscape itself dictated the design of the building. (Courtesy of the Montana Historical Society, Helena.)

had stepped into a gigantic treehouse with branches stretching one hundred feet overhead, the visitor to the Canyon Hotel entered into a yawning, bright, open space that stretched out horizontally. The walls of the huge lounge, lined with picture windows, let in the light and color emanating from the canyon. Even though the motif of the interior seemed less whimsically rustic than Old Faithful Inn, it still boasted the great wooden beams, the plank walls, and severely plain furniture styles.[86] The Canyon Hotel appeared to be as much a product of the landscape as Old Faithful Inn, but it reflected the stark grandeur of the canyon site rather than the richly forested Upper Geyser Basin site.

The success of buildings like Old Faithful Inn and the Canyon Hotel became central to the Northern Pacific's efforts to get people into the park. "The hotels are now as much a matter of wonder as are the geysers," claimed one brochure.[87] Such advertisements raved about the comfort and modernity of the Yellowstone hotels; but, most importantly, they explained, "The Hotels of the Yellowstone recognize the obligation of their surroundings. They have been designed and built to meet this obligation."[88]

Recognizing an obligation to the landscape allowed the Northern Pacific to create the kind of far western resort that twentieth-century Americans wanted and expected. They demanded good roads, good food, comfortable and convenient lodging—all provided in a way that permitted them to enjoy the landscape safely but with little obvious interference. By the first decades of the twentieth century, Yellowstone and the Northern Pacific could provide just this kind of experience. "The fine roads, the splendid trout fishing, the mountain climbing, the weird character of the scenery, and the wild animals distinguish this tourist resort from any other," a 1912 advertisement claimed proudly.[89]

Americans responded to such lures in droves. By 1915, more than fifty thousand people visited the park during its short summer season, ten times the number who had come twenty years earlier.[90] These visitors reveled in the new experiences offered by Yellowstone. One tourist remembered that he could hardly restrain his delight as he stepped from the train at the Yellowstone station and "stood face to face with the strenuous life of the West."[91] Another visitor reported that from her comfortable bed in Old Faithful Inn she could "hear the geysers playing all around us," as well as "wildcats, wolves, and bears fighting."[92] An even more dramatic supporter of the park exhorted Americans to "thank God" for Yellowstone, because "there you can see a part of the Old West—your own West—as it was in the beginning, and you can travel and live in perfect comfort."[93]

By combining comfort, wilderness, and distinctively American scenery, the Northern Pacific Railroad had created "a pleasure-ground of extraordinary quality."[94] In order to tailor the resort to match changing tourist desires, company officials adopted a style of architecture for the hotels in this natural pleasure ground that enhanced the wilderness setting and made it accessible to urban visitors. The popularity of Old Faithful Inn and the Canyon Hotel signaled that Americans had grown comfortable enough with the far western landscape to want it represented in their architecture.

Elliot Hunter, Canyon Hotel Lounge (1913)

The lobby of the Canyon Hotel appeared as striking as the canyon that it overlooked. Huge windows and light-colored wood imitated the brilliant colors of the canyon itself. (Courtesy of the Montana Historical Society, Helena.)

Not only did the Northern Pacific attract increasing numbers of visitors to Yellowstone, but, best of all, after 1905 it finally made a profit on its park operations. Now that increasing numbers of Americans knew about the park and wanted to visit it, the Northern Pacific's monopoly on its accessibility and operation proved to be an enormous advantage. The corporation's owners and operators discovered that having a national park along their line was a public-relations bonanza. Other railroads, of course, noted the success of the Northern Pacific in this realm and soon moved to emulate it.

Titan of Chasms: The Grand Canyon and the Santa Fe Railroad

In the Southwest, the Santa Fe Railroad and its hotel and restaurant subsidiary, the Fred Harvey Company, had learned that playing up the scenic and historic qualities of the landscape was good for business. From almost the moment the line opened in 1881, railroad publicity agents had worked to convince the traveling public of the value of the region's desert landscape and ancient Indian heritage. Their efforts, in combination with changing American attitudes toward the Far West, had made the Southwest into a tourist destination by the 1890s.[95]

Given such a history, it seems odd that the Santa Fe and Fred Harvey did not immediately exploit the potential value of the greatest scenic attraction in the Southwest, the Grand Canyon of the Colorado. The most spectacular part of the canyon, located in northern Arizona, stretched parallel to the Santa Fe Railroad, often less than thirty miles from it. In spite of the canyon's proximity, railroad publications in the 1880s rarely mentioned its presence, even though Americans were well aware of its existence. The exploits of John Wesley Powell and other early explorers of the Colorado River had been well publicized. As early as 1882 a guide to American scenery had predicted that "soon, tourist parties will be organized to picnic on the topmost cliffs of the almost immeasurable gorges."[96] This did not happen, however, for another two decades.

Some enterprising people had sensed the value of the Grand Canyon for the tourist trade earlier. In the late 1880s, a few local residents set up stage routes from both Williams and Flagstaff, Arizona, the settlements closest to the canyon. An 1886 advertisement noted the presence of these stage routes and promised further that "a fine hotel is being built to accommodate all visitors."[97] More than ten years later, however, no hotel had appeared, and little else had been done to facilitate tourist travel.

Even so, tourists apparently wanted to see the Grand Canyon. Aware of this growing interest, the Santa Fe Railroad took over the operation of several of the stage lines in 1892. In the mid-1890s, Raymond and Whitcomb began advertising an optional three-day tour of the canyon from Flagstaff. At about the same time, a new edition of *Baedeker's Guide to the United States* included a map of the Grand Canyon region and instructions on how to reach it, though it did warn of the possible hardships of such a trip.[98]

Santa Fe publications also began pointing out the attractions of the canyon, but could not deny the difficulty and discomfort involved in seeing it. Visitors got off the train at Flagstaff and boarded huge freight wagons for the eleven-hour trip to the south rim. Once at the canyon, tourists stayed in wooden-floored tents at a permanent camp. Because the stages only ran three times a week, visitors had a day to spend looking at the scenery. For this grueling trip they paid three dollars a night for lodging, a dollar for each meal, and fifteen dollars for round-trip stage fare.[99]

In 1897, the same year the Grand Canyon was placed under the protection of the Department of Interior, a Flagstaff saloon keeper named Peter Berry built the Grandview Hotel, a two-story log structure overlooking the canyon. A few other entrepreneurs opened equally primitive hotels, hoping to cash in on the growing tourist trade. Even with such additional luxury, George Wharton James, an early promoter of the Grand Canyon, admitted it was "a trip only a fairly strong and healthful person may take."[100] A prolific publicist for the Santa Fe Railroad, Charles W. Higgins, mourned that "the world's most stupendous panorama was known principally through report" because of the unpleasant traveling conditions, "which deterred all except the most indefatigable enthusiasts."[101]

The tough visitors who did take the trip to the rim of the Grand Canyon found it an astounding sight. As Charles Dudley Warner explained, when they first peered over the rim, they "had come into a new world."[102] Now that Americans had begun to accept the idea that the landscape did not have to echo Europe's to be glorious, the world of the canyon captivated them. Almost every observer marveled at the absolute novelty of the scene, remarking that it "involved something utterly different from anything that more than 99 per cent of the inhabitants of the world have ever seen."[103] An 1893 tourist wondered "why Americans will go to Europe, where they can see nothing to equal it, before they have looked upon this marvelous spectacle in their own land?"[104]

Another visitor's remark provides the answer to this question. After an eleven-hour stage ride on a hot summer day, Gertrude Stevens recorded her feelings about the Grand Canyon. "This is a warm place," she wrote in the visitor's registry. "I fainted when I saw this awful looking cañon. I never wanted a drink so bad in my life."[105] Clearly, even if Americans recognized the scenic value of the gash in the earth's surface, a great majority of them required at least some of the amenities of civilization to appreciate it.

The Santa Fe Railroad, having carefully watched the growing tourist interest in the region, decided that a railroad line to the south rim would turn a profit. In 1901, they opened a sixty-four-mile spur from Williams to what would become Grand Canyon Village at the head of Bright Angel Trail. Now, visitors could make a six-hour round-trip excursion to the canyon in comfortable passenger cars. In expectation of the increased demand for accommodations, the railroad had purchased and renovated the Bright Angel Hotel. At the same time, they began to make bigger plans to make the south rim into a resort to attract large numbers of wealthy tourists.[106]

Almost immediately, the Santa Fe and the Fred Harvey Company began advertising the joys of travel to the Grand Canyon. In 1902, the railroad issued two extravagantly illustrated and colored brochures. One of these, written and compiled by Charles A. Higgins and entitled *The Titan of Chasms*, would be reissued almost annually for the next twenty-five years. It contained prints of Thomas Moran's paintings of the canyon and pages of description by Joaquin Miller, Charles Dudley Warner, John Muir, and John Wesley Powell—all of whom assured tourists that the canyon was an American vision not to be missed.[107]

The promotional efforts also focused on the comfort of travel on the new railroad line. "Of the three greatest wonders of the western world, the Yellowstone, the Yosemite, and the Grand Canyon," boasted a Fred Harvey pamphlet, "the latter is the most easily reached." Railroad promotional material stressed the "perfect comfort" of a trip that was "entirely feasible for every traveler every day of the year."[108] Not only could tourists reach the canyon with great ease, once they arrived they would find suitable accommodations in the charming Bright Angel Lodge. It offered clean and comfortable rooms that were "tastefully" decorated with "Navajo Indian rugs" and "old-fashioned fireplaces."[109] A 1904 tour group recalled taking their luxurious private railway car to the rim of the canyon one evening and viewing the first of its wonders "from the comfort of their beds." The following morning they took a leisurely drive along the rim, until they reached the "attractive log cabin hotel."[110] This represented the way in which Americans wanted to view their recently discovered far western landscape.

Eager to provide the means to satisfy new tourist desires, the Santa Fe and Fred Harvey began planning a resort on the rim of the Grand Canyon to attract the expanding numbers of visitors. Given the example of Yellowstone and the Northern Pacific's success with large, expensive hotels, they hoped to make the Grand Canyon into a popular destination that would increase ridership on their lines. The railroad, which had already discovered the value of playing up the southwestern landscape in its buildings with its line of regionally styled hotels, restaurants, and souvenir shops, decided to adopt this approach on a grand scale for the new hotel.

To design the hotel, Fred Harvey and the Santa Fe looked to architect Charles Whittlesley, the chief architect of the Santa Fe Railroad who had built the railroad hotel at Albuquerque as well as several station buildings. Whittlesley, who had trained in the Chicago office of Louis Sullivan, used the region's Spanish and Indian heritage to inspire his earlier buildings, recognizing the attraction such elements had for twentieth-century Americans. He had also designed several houses for wealthy businessmen in the Flagstaff area, so he knew the local landscape well. Whittlesley, like Robert Reamer, intended to create a building that fit its surroundings—no simple task for a structure that would teeter on the edge of the Grand Canyon.[111]

Whittlesley designed the hotel so that it would not interrupt the visual line of the south rim. Like Old Faithful Inn, the structure would look as if it grew there. He chose native limestone and local Douglas fir logs and shingles as his major exterior building materials for the one-hundred-room hotel. "The idea of the architect is to bring the building into harmony with the wonderful scenery of the canyon rather than to put a blot upon its beauty by the erection of a conventional structure," the Flagstaff *Coconino Sun* reported happily as the hotel's foundation rose from the ground.[112]

As the grand and rustic building took shape, a debate over the name for the hotel developed. Fred Harvey and the Santa Fe had planned to call it the Bright Angel Tavern; but a powerful local resident took issue with this name, feeling that it did not reflect the grandeur of the setting, the building, or the history of the region. Because Coronado, the Spanish explorer whose expedition discovered the canyon, and Cardeñas, the first white man actually to see the canyon, already had hotels named after them, he suggested the name El Tovar for the new structure. He explained to a series of Santa Fe officials that Don Pedro de Tobar was the first white person to hear reports about the existence of the canyon. He

El Tovar Hotel

El Tovar, completed in 1905, offered tourists luxurious accommodations in a rustic style. Built on the edge of the Grand Canyon, the wood-and-stone exterior echoed the natural surroundings of the canyon landscape. (In Santa Fe Railroad, *Titan of Chasms: The Grand Canyon of Arizona*, 1910. Courtesy of the Bancroft Library.)

suggested that because the spelling T-O-B-A-R might offend teetotaling guests, that the name Tovar, with the Spanish definite article *el* in front of it, would be appropriate. Santa Fe officials, apparently delighted with this solution, adopted the name for their showplace hotel.[113]

El Tovar opened in January of 1905. Its low profile hugged the edge of the rim with two long arms that spread out from a main building that housed the public rooms of the hotel. Its design demonstrated a split personality, as Whittlesley used many attributes of the newly popular rustic style but supported them with more traditional architectural details. The entire structure featured logs and sawed boards, stained a dark brown, along with a stone foundation. Whittlesley used his most rustic elements for the great front porch, which presented arched stone sup-

El Tovar Lobby

The lobby of El Tovar, called the Rendezvous, was intended to resemble a hunting lodge, complete with animal trophies, log walls, and rustic furniture. Other rooms in the hotel employed more refined and traditional styles. (In *El Tovar, Grand Canyon of Arizona*, 1909. Courtesy of the Bancroft Library.)

ports, a peeled-log floor and stairs, and a low overhanging roof. Because of the rustic aspects of the building's construction, Santa Fe advertising material boasted that it was "in complete harmony with the surroundings."[114]

The rest of the building, less explicitly rustic, employed a dazzling array of design elements. An elaborately carved wooden balustrade surrounded the entire roof line, and a pointed Swiss tower capped the building. Gabled windows protruded from the top floors of the guest-room wings, which sported a version of a mansard roof. Such traditional details diluted the rustic effect of the building. One observer concluded that the plan of El Tovar was "hardly so happily conceived or so well carried out as that of the Old Faithful Inn" because it had "less of the genuine atmosphere of the wild about it."[115]

The same "split personality" in the exterior design of the hotel appeared in its interior, which blended rustic with more traditionally elegant motifs. Whittlesley chose huge wooden beams and trusses, peeled logs, stone fireplaces, and rough-hewn timber to grace the largest of El Tovar's public rooms. The tremendous oak front door opened into a room called the "Rendezvous" or "Nimrod's Cabin." The room emphasized the local history of the Grand Canyon region in a most graphic style. Finished to resemble a log cabin, the large room combined "grey Navajo rugs," "the heads of deer, elk, moose, mountain sheep, and buffalo," along with "the curiously shaped and gaudily tinted jars from the Southwest pueblos."[116] The dining room employed a similar motif, minus the animal heads, with its arched, beamed ceiling, "rough board" walls, and two "capacious stone fireplaces."[117] As in Old Faithful Inn, the furnishings in these rooms were genuine arts-and-crafts style from the Stickley Brothers factory.

Fred Harvey and the Santa Fe chose entirely different settings for other public rooms, which included a solarium, a music room, and a ladies' lounge. These rooms had fully plastered walls, wallpaper, oriental carpets, French lace curtains, and velvet upholstered furniture, much like resorts from an earlier era. The guest rooms offered visitors a choice. Some were "tinted in Nile green, buff, and cream colors," with Wilton carpets imported from England. Others presented "colonial style" accommodations or "weathered oak, old mission style."[118]

Apparently, Santa Fe officials and designers did not have complete confidence in the American reception of rustic or local design elements. The Northern Pacific had chosen to build two different hotels, the Old Faithful Inn and the Lake Hotel, to make sure its accommodations suited every taste. The Santa Fe and Fred Harvey elected to combine these elements in a single hotel. El Tovar followed the rules of a rustic structure, but its architect and interior designers included enough reminders of traditional resort elegance to assure visitors of the hotel's comfort and grandeur.

The Santa Fe's gamble worked, even though El Tovar may not have been an entirely successful example of the rustic style. Advertising techniques mirrored those used by the Northern Pacific. Claims about the hotel's rustic style; its modernity and comfort; and, above all, its uniqueness filled pamphlets, books, and posters. Most described it as a "rustic building, built of boulders and pine logs on a magnificent scale." Promoters emphasized the building's suitability to the magnificent canyon setting, explaining that a "usual" hotel would never do; the unique surroundings required a unique hotel.[119]

To convince potential visitors that they would not be enduring a stay in a primitive log cabin, however, the Santa Fe also pointed out El Tovar's status as "one of the most comfortable and one of the costliest resort hotels in the Southwest."[120] Advertisers stressed the modernity of its plumbing, heating plants, and kitchens. El Tovar was "highly modern throughout" because "money has here summoned the beneficent genii who minister to our bodily comfort."[121] The combination of the structure's rustic style and its luxurious amenities, according to its operators and promoters, made it "most unique" and "unprecedented."[122]

Even though the designers made sure that El Tovar had the comforts of an eastern hotel and integrated some European elements into its design, a stay at the south rim of the Grand Canyon remained a decidedly "western" experience. As Fred Harvey and the Santa Fe built El Tovar, they also created another structure across the drive from the great hotel. Hopi House, intended as a showroom for Indian crafts and other "curios," was an amalgamation of the housing styles of several southwestern Indian tribes. Designed by Mary Elizabeth Jane Colter, Hopi House represented a serious attempt to celebrate the Indian heritage of the Southwest.

Colter, hired by the Fred Harvey Company as an architect and designer in 1902, had been largely responsible for the success and the authenticity of the Indian Building in Albuquerque, which housed showrooms for southwestern Indian art. She had made a careful study of the architecture and crafts of southwestern tribes; and the utility, simplicity, and appropriateness of their buildings impressed her deeply. When she received the commission for the Grand Canyon site, she chose the Hopi dwellings at Oraibi, Arizona, as her models. Colter insisted on using native materials and Hopi workers to construct the three-story wood, stone, and adobe building.[123]

When the building opened in January of 1905, its lower floors contained displays of Hopi baskets, Navajo jewelry, and northwestern Indian totems and masks. An exhibit of special pride of the Fred Harvey Company was the collection of ancient Navajo blankets that had just won a grand prize at the St. Louis World's Fair. Hopi Indians lived in the upper floors of the building and provided daily exhibitions of their living styles and artistry. The Fred Harvey Company also managed to hire some Navajos to build hogans on the grounds of Hopi House and to display their weaving and jewelry-making skills. Both the appearance and

Hopi House

Hopi House, built across the drive from El Tovar, reflected the interest tourists now expressed in the native tribes of the area. The primitive building housed crafts displays as well as representatives from several local tribes. (In *El Tovar: Grand Canyon of Arizona*, 1909. Courtesy of the Bancroft Library.)

the function of Hopi House underscored the importance of local Indian traditions in attracting tourists to the Southwest.[124]

Fred Harvey and the Santa Fe obviously recognized the growing interest in Indians on the part of white Americans. Not only could El Tovar guests learn about the rich artistic tradition of native Americans in the Hopi House, the hotel itself housed several galleries and salesrooms for Indian art. By this time, the sale of Indian art had become a big moneymaker for Fred Harvey and for the local tribes. Tourist demand for such goods had also altered traditional techniques and styles. Many of the Navajo, with the promise of tremendous orders from Harvey buyers, had switched from making blankets to making rugs, which white Americans seemed to find more attractive. Indian weavers also gave up natural dyes in favor of the brighter and more colorfast chemical dyes provided by white traders.[125]

In addition to the delights of blankets, rugs, and jewelry, live Indians offered even more excitement. A Santa Fe advertisement boasted that aside from the resident Hopis, members of the Navajo and Supai tribes often visited the hotel. "At times," the pamphlet claimed, "the three tribes are represented by fifty members."[126] Several times a week, the evening's entertainment featured Hopi dances in a specially built outdoor fire circle. One tourist, impressed by the "picturesque costumes" and "the beat of their tom-toms," believed the scene to be "a spectacle which will linger long in memory."[127]

The presence of Indians, the combination of rusticity and comfort offered by El Tovar, and the spectacular scenery made the Grand Canyon a desirable tourist stop in the early twentieth century. To make sure that its large investment in the region did not go unnoticed, the Santa Fe Railroad advertised aggressively. In 1907, the Flagstaff newspaper commented on a "new scheme" the railroad had adopted to "exploit the famous Grand Canyon of Arizona." At strategic sites along the railroad line, the Santa Fe erected huge billboards with a view of the canyon from the dining room of El Tovar painted on them. The painting was "so realistic," the paper reported, "that the passerby will involuntarily get a grip on something to keep from falling in."[128]

In 1915, the year of the Panama Pacific Exhibition in San Francisco, the Santa Fe came up with an even more clever advertising technique to ensure that exhibition goers used their railroad and stopped at the Grand Canyon. Railroad promoters had discovered that sophisticated twentieth-century tourists needed to be approached in new ways. They used urban entertainment devices to attract city dwellers into a carefully orchestrated wilderness. The railroad built a six-acre exhibit at the exhibition featuring a model of the Grand Canyon and of several Pueblo Indian villages. To view the elaborately wrought model, people rode along a trestle in miniature parlor cars along the "rim," made to look real with rocks and plants shipped from the canyon itself. The fifteen-minute "ride" allowed observers to "see seven of the most distinctive points of the Canyon."[129]

Apparently, such schemes worked. The numbers of people visiting the canyon increased dramatically. Soon, the tourists arriving on the Santa Fe Grand Canyon spur filled El Tovar nearly year round. In the years before the formation of the National Park Service in 1916, the Santa Fe and Fred Harvey made a number of improvements at the canyon. They updated the roads along the rim and the trails down into the canyon. Mary Colter designed and supervised the building of two structures on the rim called Hermit's Rest and the Lookout, which took the rustic motif to an extreme. A 1916 tourist marveled that the Grand Canyon had become "a resort, rather then merely a stopping place."[130]

Because the twentieth-century tourist no longer wanted simply to lounge on the veranda of a hotel, the Santa Fe began to advertise the myriad of activities possible at their growing resort. These activities emphasized the invigorating nature of wild surroundings and the delight of outdoor exercise. They ranged from "easy and gentle drives over forest roads" to "more vigorous horseback exercise" to "strenuous walks" down into "the Titan of Chasms." All such endeavors, promised promotional material, "had the power to recuperate man's exhausted energies."[131]

In order to encourage such physical activity, Fred Harvey and the Santa Fe built a series of structures that offered resting places to weary walkers, riders, and drivers. The design of these buildings demonstrated the success and popularity of the rustic style that would dominate the south rim's architecture. Mary Colter intended Hermit's Rest, built in 1914, to look as if it had been created by an untrained builder out of sticks and stones from the immediate area. The uneven stone building resembled a grotto with an opening that looked over a stunning view of the canyon. From a distance, Hermit's Rest blended into the canyon walls. Colter even designed the furnishings out of stumps and twisted bits of wood, not unlike the interior of Old Faithful Inn. The same year, the Lookout, another building designed by Colter with the same rustic effects, was built on the rim closer to El Tovar.[132]

In their design and purpose, both buildings demonstrated the new appeal the far western landscape had for tourists and the important effect it had had on resort architecture. The Santa Fe Railroad and the Fred Harvey Company had discovered the value of the unique southwestern scenery and heritage in attracting American tourists to their railroad and hotels. Architecture that borrowed from native peoples and the western landscape and that played on the growing interest in wilderness and "the strenuous life" appealed to tourists who wanted a "Western" experience.

By the turn of the century a successful western resort needed to provide this wild flavor, but with luxurious underpinnings. El Tovar, with its mixture of rustic logs, boulders, electric lights, and plush carpet-

Hermit's Rest, at Head of Hermit Trail

An Interior View, Hermit's Rest

Hermits Rest

Mary Colter's Hermits Rest took the interest in the rustic to an extreme. The building looked as if it grew out of the ground, blending into the canyon walls so that it did not disturb the grandeur of the natural scenery. (In Santa Fe Railroad, *Titan of Chasms: The Grand Canyon of Arizona*, 1915. Courtesy of the Bancroft Library.)

ing, made a good start in this direction. The presence of Mary Colter's more authentic buildings and the emphasis on outdoor activity and the natural environment made a trip to the Santa Fe's kingdom on the south rim of the Grand Canyon an even more satisfying experience. A contented visitor explained that with the Santa Fe's efforts, "the world's greatest wonder became the playground of the American people."[133]

Railroad companies had discovered that they had to change their tactics to attract twentieth-century tourists. The European citadels popular only a decade earlier no longer seemed appropriate in the distinctively American settings in which the railroads now developed resorts. As tourists learned to describe and appreciate landscapes that did not resemble European views, they began to demand accommodations that reflected and enhanced the far western scenery. Architectural styles based on American trends from the East Coast and Chicago, and blended with the unique attributes of the Far West, provided an answer to these demands. The success of Old Faithful Inn and El Tovar demonstrated the new and powerful attraction of the most "un-European" parts of the Far West.

The Call of the Wild: Glacier and the Great Northern Railroad

The influence of the novel style developed by the railroads spread over the entire West. More than fifteen hundred miles north of the Grand Canyon, the Great Northern Railroad carved another playground out of a section of the Rocky Mountains. The landscape that would become Glacier National Park lay in the northwest corner of Montana between the Canadian border and the Great Northern Railroad line. It included a mountainous region of spectacular glacially carved peaks, living glaciers, and pristine mountain lakes. Long the home of the Blackfoot Indians, the remote area also provided a habitat for grizzly bears, Bighorn sheep, elk, and mountain goats, all increasingly rare in the rest of the Rocky Mountains. Until the late 1880s, the scenic wealth of the Glacier region remained almost entirely unknown to the majority of Americans.

The Glacier area received its first important national notice when the ethnologist and naturalist George Bird Grinnell visited it in 1885. Grinnell had been asked to examine the horrendous condition of the Blackfoot Indians, recently forced onto reservations. Unable to adapt easily to agricultural life and robbed of their traditional food source by the near extinction of the buffalo, thousands of Indians had starved during the unusually harsh winter of 1883–84. Grinnell published a series of fourteen articles in *Forest and Stream* and several other influential pieces in the *Century* about his discoveries in the region. His publicity efforts did help induce the government to improve conditions on the Blackfoot reservation. His work also alerted Americans to the beauties of the region.[134]

Grinnell's articles described a place the Indians called "The Walled-In-Lakes." Stunned by the wealth of scenic beauty and wildlife, Grinnell believed he was seeing one of the last truly wild places in the West. He wrote of his contact with Blackfoot, Kootenai, and Gros Ventre Indians and of the excitement of hunting with them. In loving detail, he told of the wondrous shape of the mountains and of the presence of a multitude of rare wild animals.

What is interesting about Grinnell's description is its lack of European analogy. The Glacier region looks more like alpine Switzerland than any other part of the United States. It does have glaciers and the same sharply carved mountains. The climate, wetter and cooler than the rest of the Rockies, makes even the vegetation resemble Switzerland. Grinnell rarely made those comparisons, partly because he was a trained naturalist and had scientific words to serve him and partly because he did not look for them.

To describe Chief Mountain, one of the most striking landmarks in the area, he used geometry, botany, color, and American analogy. "Its shape," he explained, "was that of an enormous truncated cone . . . reminding me somewhat of the so-called Liberty Cap at the Mammoth Hot Springs in the National Park."[135] In another passage, he noted that the rocks making up the mountain were "all dark in color, black and dull green and dark red and purple; and these with the different hues of the foliage and the white snow, gave the mountain a most varied aspect."[136] Like Clarence Dutton, who had used similar techniques to describe the Grand Canyon, Grinnell had decided that finding a Europe in the midst of the Rockies was no longer useful.

Following Grinnell, other observers noted the potential Glacier had for attracting tourists. James Jerome Hill, who had begun building his Great Northern Railroad from Minneapolis across Montana, understood the importance such a scenic region could have for his railroad. Having watched the success of the Northern Pacific in Yellowstone and the Santa Fe in the Southwest, he understood the public-relations bonanza a popular tourist area could provide.

When the Great Northern reached the Pacific Coast in 1893, Hill began to examine the region in earnest. One of his passenger agents asked the geologist Dr. Lyman Sperry to look for evidence of living glaciers. "If any of them are of sufficient size . . . and near enough our line to be made accessible," the agent explained, "we would like to know it and bring them to the attention of travelers."[137] Similarly, Walter Raymond, a founder of the Raymond and Whitcomb Tour Company, always alert to possible attractions for tourists, wrote to the Great Northern and suggested that they build a "good road" and set of trails to make the "various glaciers, lakes, and other points of interest" accessible to the traveling public.[138]

James Hill and his son Louis recognized the need for roads and tourist accommodations, but they also understood the difficulty of such an undertaking. When George Bird Grinnell led a movement in the first years of the twentieth century to form a national park in the Glacier area, the Hills supported it wholeheartedly. Louis Hill, who replaced his father as president of the Great Northern in 1907, took special interest in the battle to create Glacier National Park. Not only would national park status publicize the Glacier region, it would also require the government to built roads and trails to make it accessible. As tourists came to examine the new park, they would increase the number of passengers on Hill's railroad and, he hoped, stay in the hotels built and operated by the Great Northern.[139]

When President Taft signed the legislation making the northwest corner of Montana into Glacier National Park in May 1910, the Great Northern Railroad began developing the tourist facilities in the park. Louis Hill took this job on himself. He recognized that his first task was to make Americans aware of the region. "It will," boasted an early advertisement, "be a leading resort of the continent when it becomes more familiar to the tourist."[140] Because the newest national park did not have the advantage of a long and well-publicized history of exploration like Yellowstone and the Grand Canyon, Hill planned an elaborate national publicity campaign.

Playing on the new American interest in wilderness, Indians, and distinctive scenery, Hill began his crusade with the "Great Northern Art Show," which toured the nation for the next several years. The show focused on large hand-tinted photographs by a Portland photographer. At the same time he hired a German artist named John Fery whose paintings of Glacier's spectacular landscape soon filled Great Northern hotels, train stations, and art shows. In 1913, a Chicago newspaper reported that people "went into ecstasy" over "Louis Hill's $50,000 art exhibit of scenes in Uncle Sam's newest playground" displayed at the United States Land Irrigation Exposition.[141]

The same year, New Yorkers crowded the New York Travel and Vacation Show, which, according to a local paper, "averaged ten thousand daily attendance." For this extravaganza, Hill had shipped in ten Blackfoot Indians who camped on the roof of a downtown hotel, creating much attention in the local press. The combination of the Indians and "the marvelous beauty presented by the scenic photographs and paintings," explained a newspaper report, "made the Glacier Park booth easily the attraction of the show."[142]

In addition to bringing Glacier Park to the attention of potential tourists, Hill also orchestrated events that brought newspaper reporters to the park. In 1912, along with the American Automobile Association, he organized an elaborate "See America First" campaign to promote American tourism. The promotional effort began with a trip for several hundred reporters from St. Paul to Glacier Park abroad a luxurious Great Northern hotel train. The train had a printing press and telegraphic service aboard and published its own daily paper, the *Glacier Park Blazer*. The highlight of the trip occurred when the train reached Glacier, and some local Blackfoot Indians initiated Louis Hill into their tribe.[143]

Hill and his creative advertising bureau used every possible medium to advertise the Great Northern effort in Glacier National Park. In 1911 he took moving pictures of the "Last Grass Dance" of the Blackfoot, which he showed at exhibitions all over the United States. The moment radio began to be important in American households in the early 1920s, he recognized its publicity potential. Now radio listeners could hear Blackfoot songs and music. Hill even managed "the world's most novel treat in radio-broadcasting" when he arranged to have a "shrill piccolo-like chorus of the whistling marmots that populate Glacier National Park" broadcast over national radio. Even better, the story of the whistling marmots appeared in 155 newspapers in 38 different states.[144]

Spread over a twenty-year period, Louis Hill's publicity stunts brought Glacier to the attention of Americans. As early as 1912, more than six thousand tourists visited the park, more than three times the number that visited Yosemite the same year.[145] From being virtually unknown in 1910, Glacier had become a popular destination. Louis Hill understood what Americans wanted to see in their national parks, and he crafted his advertising schemes for Glacier to appeal to such desires. The landscape of this portion of the Rockies offered a pristine wilderness, native American traditions, and spectacular scenery that had uniquely American attributes, as well as the added attraction of a real resemblance to Switzerland.

Hill and the Great Northern used all of these elements to make the park appealing. Many people noted the resemblance to Switzerland; but by the early twentieth century, most observers preferred to highlight difference rather than similarities. One pamphlet noted that even though the region "more nearly resembles the Swiss Alps than any other part of this country," it seemed "unique among our playground reservations."[146] "Here are the new Alps of the Western World," proclaimed a publicist for the national parks. He hastened to add, however, that the Glacier area "possessed individuality to a high degree" and that "geologically it is markedly different."[147] Apparently, most promoters had discovered that comparisons to Europe no longer sold the far western landscape; tourists wanted to see something specifically American.

Because of these changed desires, some publicists used strictly American analogies to explain Glacier's special appeal. "The wonder," explained the famous dude rancher Howard Eaton, "is this conjunction of the stupendous with the delicate, the Grand Canyon with something softer, greener, and more intimately alluring than the Berkshires."[148] According to other advertisers, its remote location and rugged topography made Glacier especially attractive. Here, boasted a newspaper clipping, "the visitor must gain the summits afoot or on horseback, without the aid of the funicular or cog railway."[149] Glacier represented a collage of American landscapes as well as a glimpse of the nation's frontier past. Its unspoiled mountain scenery would also lure Americans to take healthy physical exercise, increasingly important to twentieth-century urban tourists.

In addition to these attractions, every writer and promoter for the new park made much of its Indian heritage. Even the names given to mountains, lakes and other topographical features reflected the growing interest in Indians. Unlike sites at Yellowstone and the Grand Canyon, which had names from an array of mythological, biblical, European, and local white historical sources, most of Glacier's names, though Anglicized, came from the local Indians. Great Northern publications told visitors that Glacier had been "the home of the Blackfeet or Piegan Indians for centuries" and that "their history and legends are perpetuated in the names of many of the mountains, lakes and glaciers in the Park."[150] Names like Rising Wolf, Going-to-the-Sun, Swiftcurrent, or Two Medicine would delight "the American who from earliest boyhood has thrilled to the tales of trappers and Indians."[151]

Not only had the heritage of the Indians been preserved; but, as in the Grand Canyon, the presence of living Indians made visiting Glacier even more exciting. One writer exulted over the "picturesqueness and primitiveness" of the local Blackfoot, explaining that they were "less corrupted by contact with whites than many other tribes." He promised that these Indians would "clasp hands with the white tourists, greeting them with smiles and friendliness."[152] The Great Northern promised tourists that the Blackfoot Indians made "their summer encampments in the park and will entertain you with their legends, their songs and dances."[153] Clearly, the Indian presence in the park helped to create the unique experience that visitors expected from the far western landscape.

Advertising represented only a small portion of the Great Northern Railroad's efforts in Glacier National Park. As other railroads had learned, no amount of spectacular scenery, frontier flavor, or Indian culture would attract tourists if comfortable and attractive accommodations were not provided. The moment Louis Hill began advertising the American wonder along his railroad line, he also began building hotels. The Great Northern worked faster to develop its natural playground than any other railroad. In four years, with almost no help from the government, the company built two tremendous hotels, nine chalets, three tepee camps, and a system of roads and trails to connect them.

The first hotel opened in 1913, only three years after President Taft had created the park. Named the Glacier Park Lodge, the hotel stood immediately opposite the Great Northern depot at Midvale or Glacier Park Station on the east side of Glacier National Park. Louis Hill, never far from the railroad's operations in Glacier, came up with the general

Glacier Park Lodge Exterior, 1913

The massive structure of Glacier Park Lodge greeted tourists as they stepped off of Great Northern trains. Tremendous stone foundations and great log pillars provided interest to the rather plain rustic exterior. (Courtesy of the Montana Historical Society, Helena.)

concept for the hotel and hired a St. Paul architect, Thomas D. McMahon, to design the 172-room structure.[154] Hill and McMahon clearly wanted to create a building that would complement the Glacier landscape and that would give tourists the luxurious wilderness experience they now demanded.

Like Robert Reamer's Yellowstone hotels and Whittlesley's El Tovar, Glacier Park Lodge sported a rustic motif on a grand scale. Built largely of local materials in a deliberately unfinished style, its tremendous size and studied primitive design echoed the stunning environment that surrounded the structure. Guests stepped off of the train and walked through a forty-foot log gateway onto the hotel grounds. Here they were "met by the sound of tom-toms beaten by a group of Blackfeet Indians, robed in bright blankets."[155] Escorted by Indians or by dressed-up cowboys, the guests walked or were driven through the landscaped grounds to the front door of the hotel.

As they came up the drive, visitors saw two three-story buildings connected by a short walkway. Huge log columns supporting great gabled and overhanging roofs formed the major components of the exterior of Glacier Park Lodge. Stone chimneys and foundations punctuated the log-and-shingle exterior. Wide porches and balconies decorated with deer and elk antlers gave interest to the rather plain exterior and emphasized the wilderness motif. The wide, modified triangles of the roof line added a northern European or "Swiss Chalet" flavor to the more generalized rustic style. By 1913, the rustic style had become common enough that few visitors spent much time describing the exterior of the building, except to say it was "delightfully rustic" or that the architecture "might well be called the forestry type."[156]

Tourists and promoters devoted most of their description to the startling interior of the main building, which was, according to the Great Northern, "an unexpected treat." The main lobby, an open space nearly two hundred feet long and three stories high, resembled a giant forest. Huge Douglas firs, imported from the Pacific Northwest, upheld the great open-timbered roof in two long colonnades. The trees, each more than three feet in diameter and sixty feet high, made an impressive visual impact, as one observer put it "surely justifying the title which the Indians have bestowed—the Lodge of the Big Trees."[157] A Great Northern promotional material explained, the effect of the lobby was to "bring the outdoors indoors."[158]

The décor of the lobby also emphasized natural and historical elements present in the park. In the center of the room, an open campfire, "the only one ever built in the rotunda of a hotel," burned throughout the day.[159] Smaller stone fireplaces, rustic furniture, and animal-skin rugs decorated the floor of the lobby, while a stunning variety of animal heads and horns decked the walls. The galleries that surrounded the upper floors of the lobby offered displays of photographs and paintings of the Glacier landscape.

Local Blackfoot heritage received a great deal of attention. A series of large picture-writing panels, painted by local tribes to depict episodes in Blackfoot history, hung from the walls. The Great Northern obligingly provided a key so that tourists could "read" the pictographs. Three tepees sat in the corners of the lobby, acting as card rooms; and two huge canoes hung from the log rafters. In the evenings, "Indians in their gaily bedecked native costumes became the center of attraction to the guests," by singing and dancing in the flicker of firelight.[160]

Glacier Park Lodge Interior

The interior of Glacier Park Lodge stunned and delighted visitors. Its rows of gigantic log columns whimsically topped with capitals, combined with tepees, Blackfoot wall hangings, and animal trophies, elevated the rustic motif to a grand level. (Courtesy of the Montana Historical Society, Helena.)

Louis Hill and the Great Northern Railroad hoped to make the hotel into a kind of introduction to Glacier National Park. Its rustic design and use of Indian décor would prepare visitors for the experience they would have in seeing the wilderness the park offered. Like the new words and images developed to describe the far western landscape, the architecture of the hotel provided appropriate ways to experience Glacier. Most tourists found such reminders of the far western environment suitable and enticing. One woman commented on her delight at the "western" flavor of the hotel, remarking that "nothing could be more unfit at this entrance to a wilderness of forested mountain beauty than an eastern type of architecture."[161] Another found the design of Glacier Park Lodge "quite in keeping" with the landscape and "its Indians, cowboys, and mountains."[162]

In addition to their efforts to make Glacier Park Lodge properly rustic, the Great Northern, like the other railroads, made sure that rusticity did not go too far. They wanted it to be unique and to have authentic western flavor, but they also wanted it to attract wealthy eastern visitors, accustomed to luxurious accommodations. As was the case for hotels in Yellowstone and the Grand Canyon, advertisements boasted that Glacier Park Lodge offered "all the comforts and luxuries of the most elaborate of modern city hotels."[163] George Wharton James explained, "It would be a great error to conceive of this hotel as a mere mountain makeshift" because it "cost well over half a million dollars" to build. Guests reluctant to "rough it" in the wilderness could enjoy the heated pool, the tennis courts, the flower gardens, and dress in "shimmering silks and white shirts."[164]

Apparently fearing that the raw logs and Indian artifacts might unnerve some patrons, Louis Hill and Thomas McMahon attempted to tame and domesticate the interior a bit. Oddly carved Ionic capitals topped the great log pillars lining the lobby. Even though they were suitably rustic, the use of capitals seemed far removed from the studiously primitive conception of the building. Another strange touch, probably the work of Louis Hill, appeared in the Japanese lanterns that festooned the central part of the lobby. Hill, an enthusiast of Asian art, may also have insisted on the presence of Japanese tea carts tended by women in native costumes each afternoon. One outspoken visitor found the combination of "bear skin rugs, imitation cherry blossoms, Navajo rugs" added to the sound of "old Chief Three Bears making war-dance music" and the "shrill bleating of a pianola" all rather jarring.[165]

These additions may have been a reflection of the interest in exotic cultures and eclectic design rampant at the turn of the century. Similar to the Wilton carpets and gold-leaf trim in parts of El Tovar, they also demonstrated the split desires of tourists and the difficulty hotel builders had in dealing with them. Americans wanted to taste the wilderness and to experience and enjoy the far western environment, but they wanted to do it in luxurious style. Many tourists wanted to believe they were delving into the strenuous life without straining themselves at all. The grand, yet rustic design of Glacier Park Lodge, with its Blackfoot pictographs and Japanese lanterns, attempted to solve this problem.

The other hotel in Glacier National Park worked on the paradox of roughing it in luxury in a different way. Many Glacier, located further in the interior of the park on Lake McDermott, was completed in 1915 as the largest hotel in the park. Designed by the same architect as Glacier Park Lodge, Many Glacier presented many similarities in appearance. McMahon designed the four-story hotel in two separate buildings. Using locally harvested and milled spruce on top of a stone foundation, he created familiar rustic effects. Many Glacier, however, did not rest on the same tremendous unpeeled logs. Clapboard siding, painted a dark brown, gave the exterior a slightly more finished, yet less magnificent appearance. Because of the hotel's location on a mountain lake at the foot of a glacier, McMahon chose to emphasize Swiss details on the exterior. Yellow wooden trim and carved balconies surrounded the building, and the roof line had a series of chalet gables.[166]

The interior, however, made more of the unique aspects of Glacier National Park and downplayed the Swiss theme. The main building of Many Glacier had a spacious open lobby extending the full four stories with rustic décor based on the same concepts as Glacier Park Lodge. Though only about half the size of the lobby at Glacier Park Lodge, Many Glacier's lobby had the same great tree trunks supporting a log superstructure of balconies. These logs, however, were peeled and stood in a square without creating the stately effect of the natural colonnade present in the other hotel. Apparently, Thomas McMahon and the Great Northern want to make this hotel less grand.

Many Glacier resembled a western hunting lodge more than anything

Many Glacier Hotel

Many Glacier, the Great Northern hotel in the interior of the park, used now-familiar rustic themes. Its massive forms and wooden exterior suited the splendid surroundings and striking landforms that characterized the park's setting. (Courtesy of the Montana Historical Society, Helena.)

else. A great stone hearth stood at the very center of the lobby. Twenty-four buffalo heads protruded from the lobby's walls, and twenty-four bearskins hung from the railings of the balconies to remind visitors of the proximity of the wilderness. A 180-foot mural, painted by Blackfoot artists, covered an entire wall, giving evidence of the area's Indian heritage. The building was, as the Great Northern proudly explained, "a Glacier Park Product."[167]

The décor of Many Glacier made less of an attempt at combining the rustic and the traditionally elegant. No Ionic capitals stood atop the log supports; no flower beds surrounded tepees set up on a manicured lawn. Even though the hotel offered all the amenities of civilization with hot showers, extravagant meals, and luxurious beds, its design encouraged a more direct encounter with the wilderness. Aside from the great central lobby, Many Glacier had few public rooms devoted to reading or card playing or letter writing. The lobby offered a place where guests could gather after their day in the wilderness and exchange stories. Similarly, the Swiss details on the exterior and the lederhosen on some of the staff reminded tourists of the delights of walking in the mountains. The campfire, the animal trophies, and the Indian artifacts signaled the presence of a rugged American frontier tradition in which Americans could still take part.

Advertising emphasized the outdoor delights offered by a stay at Many Glacier. The hotel gave "the best opportunity to all to see and enjoy the mountains."[168] At this "fascinating hub of outdoor recreation, " tourists could rent horses or walk along trails built by the railroad. The more vigorous could climb a glacier or take a several-day pack trip into the interior of the park. And, lest they frighten off more sedentary visitors, the railroad promoters promised that "those who cannot walk or climb may sit on the veranda and view a long stretch of the Continental Divide."[169] After a day enjoying a version of the "strenuous life," tourists could enjoy an elaborate meal served on china and cut glass and then listen to an Indian story or see a demonstration of an Indian dance. They could then retire to comfortable rooms, feeling as if they had experienced something genuinely American. They had, as the Great Northern and other railroads had asked them to, "seen America First."

The Great Northern advertised Glacier National Park as "the wildest part of America"[170] and as a place where Americans could see their national heritage from train windows and rough it under the most comfortable conditions. The grand rustic style of Glacier Park Lodge and Many Glacier introduced visitors to the landscape and to the people it had supported. The design of the hotel used "wild" and American materials, like logs and Indian pictographs, and molded them into more traditional and even classical forms. It seemed quite proper to bring a tree into a hotel when it was topped by an Ionic capital. A campfire delighted tourists who would never consider spending a night in the open when it burned safely in the middle of a hotel lobby.

A New American Style

The Great Northern, like other western railroads, had discovered that Indians and wilderness no longer threatened Americans. In building grandly rustic hotels, which combined luxurious elements with a rough and local style, they recognized the changing expectations Americans had for their scenery and their leisure time. People no longer sought out enclaves of Europe that protected them from the unique aspects of the far western landscape. In order to attract tourists, railroads promised that their lines would take passengers through especially American regions, where people could see the wild landscape and the native heritage that had helped create a national culture. Railroads now built hotels that celebrated the American wilderness and that allowed guests to participate in it safely and comfortably.

The hotels in Yellowstone, Grand Canyon, and Glacier National Parks represent only a few of the huge number of resorts built in the Far West in the first decades of the twentieth century. Railroad corporations and private entrepreneurs recognized the importance of the growing tourist trade, as well as the lure of the western landscape. A few resort areas, especially those in Colorado and California where European-inspired designs had seemed appropriate, retained the older style. The Broadmoor, rebuilt in 1917, continues as a stunningly Italianate building, while the Stanley Hotel in Estes Park Colorado, built in 1910, houses visitors in a stately Georgian style. These buildings, however, are exceptions. Most of the glamorous hotels built in the thirty years before the depression reflected the distinctive western environment.

Resorts such as the Arizona Biltmore in Phoenix, the Bishop's Lodge in Santa Fe, and the Mission Inn in Riverside, California, demonstrate the appeal of the southwestern style evident in the architecture of Charles Whittlesley and Mary Colter. The rustic, "forestry-type" designs of Robert Reamer and Thomas McMahon became so prevalent in the architecture of the national parks that some historians have called it "parkitecture."[171] The Ahwahnee in Yosemite, the Paradise Inn in Mount Rainier National Park, and the Union Pacific complex on the north rim of the Grand Canyon all provide examples of this style. Even the venerable Hotel Del Monte did not remain immune to the new trends. Its management put in a cactus garden at the turn of the century and built a rustic day lodge along the Seventeen Mile Drive in 1908.

The construction of such hotels signaled an important change. Decades of scientific effort to uncover the mysteries of the far western landscape and the work of thousands of writers, artists, and photographers had presented the Far West's variety and beauty. By the start of the twentieth century, Americans had the language and confidence necessary to recognize the value of the landscape. For an American culture seeking an identity of its own, the Far West offered a heritage and scenery that was entirely American.

The railroads, as primary developers of the Far West, understood the significance of changed conceptions of the region. They altered their methods and facilities to meet new tourist demands. As droves of people toured the Far West to discover a national heritage, rather than a version of Europe, railroads adopted new advertising and architectural formulas. Using materials, colors, and local influences of the Far West, combined with concepts about the importance of wilderness and national heritage from the East, railroad architects created a style mirroring the new language that decades of confrontation with the western landscape had produced. Buffalo heads, Indian artifacts, and grand log palaces replaced the French chandeliers, Italian fountains, and English manor houses of earlier decades.

The railroads, only too happy to oblige their wealthy patrons, adopted an architectural style that reflected a national culture, based on new pride in the American landscape. Rather than building structures that insulated people from the strange western environment, the railroads and their architects, inspired by the West's beauties, created buildings that celebrated them. Architects took their cues from the surrounding environment, rather than pretending it did not exist. The far western landscape had received its ultimate compliment; it had been taken inside glamorous resorts and mounted proudly on the walls.

Epilogue

Western railroad companies discovered that American tourists responded with enthusiasm to the packaging of wilderness, deserts, and Indians in a luxurious yet rustic setting. With the creation of resorts built in indigenous American styles that celebrated the far western landscape, railroad promoters may have believed they had solved the problem of selling the Far West. Tourists now recognized the region as an integral part of American culture and, filled with pride about the discovery, rushed to see it for themselves. Much to the delight of the railroads, the Far West became the most popular tourist area in the United States. During World War I, for the first time more travelers came west than went to Europe. This pattern would continue after the war.[1]

After the turn of the century, national parks became the focal point of far western travel. By 1920, nearly one million people visited the parks and monuments in a single year. In the minds of these visitors, the parks represented what seemed best about the United States. The landscape offered evidence of the rich history, spectacular scenery, and invigorating wilderness that made their culture distinctive. The parks protected this cultural wellspring and made it, theoretically, available to all Americans. The railroads, however, especially in the cases of the Northern Pacific, the Santa Fe, and the Great Northern, because of their efforts in developing the parks and in building tracks and roads to take people there, had almost complete control over access to and activities within the parks.

As technology and higher standards of living made travel possible for growing numbers of Americans, the railroads lost their monopoly over the western tourist industry. The interest in western wilderness and heritage that first lured wealthy easterners onto railroads and into resorts created a boom in tourist travel that passed by the astonished railroad companies. Several important changes in American culture ended the railroad domination of the parks. Automobiles, new ideas about wilderness and leisure, and increased government intervention changed the way Americans saw and used national parks and monuments.

As the Far West became increasingly integrated into American culture, and as its distinctive landscape became recognized as a piece of cultural heritage, it took on new importance in the minds of Americans. They wanted to see it and to protect it for future generations. The battle over the development and meaning of the national parks exemplifies the significance of the Far West had taken on, both economically and culturally.

The huge expanses of the region—including great deserts, mountain scenery, and Indian villages—seemed perfectly suited to the new technology of the automobile, which allowed people to see the sights at their own pace, free from the strict timetables necessitated by train travel. Great tracts of wilderness, available only in the Far West, presented Americans with an opportunity to lead the strenuous life, so essential, in their view, to renewing health and vigor. At the same time, the national parks, grudgingly set up by nineteenth-century politicians, offered a perfect place to experiment with progressive government agencies in the twentieth century. The railroad officials' dreams of wealthy tourists who boarded palace cars and lounged at exclusive resorts in railroad-controlled parks suddenly evaporated as automobiles full of penny-pinching, middle-class visitors arrived to stay in government-built campgrounds.

When cars first began appearing in the national parks at the turn of the century, no one could have imagined the impact they would have. In the early years of "automobiling," car travel was slow, inconvenient, dangerous, and expensive, only appealing to a few rich eccentrics. The first car arrived on the south rim of the Grand Canyon in 1902 after a three-day trip from Flagstaff, a trip that took only a few hours by train. Early daredevils attempted to see Yellowstone by automobile, but with such disastrous results that park officials banned them from the park in 1902. They claimed that park roads were too primitive for the delicate machinery in cars and that the noisy vehicles frightened horses. An early visitor to Glacier predicted that it would "never be a place for the honking automobile."[2]

Such predictions proved to be premature as Americans began to buy cars in startling numbers. In 1910, less than half a million people owned cars in the United States; but by 1920, the number had increased to nearly eight million. Automobile enthusiasts lobbied hard to be allowed into the parks. Even though railroad companies objected vigorously to the idea of automobile traffic, not wanting to lose their monopoly on transportation services, the Department of the Interior soon relented to the demands of tourists. By 1912 Glacier National Park permitted auto traffic, and Yellowstone followed suit in 1915.[3]

Cars rapidly poured into the parks. To the great dismay of railroad companies, the restrictions on train travel during 1917 and 1918 caused by the military requirements of World War I increased the numbers of automobile tourists even more quickly. By 1919 more than sixty thousand people visited Yellowstone, and two-thirds of these came by private automobile. Not only did the stream of cars threaten the railroad's monopoly on transportation, it also brought in new groups of tourists who did not stay in the elaborate hostelries built by the railroads to house train travelers.

In 1919, the superintendent of Yellowstone noted that nearly 60 percent of the tourists who arrived in cars brought their own camping equipment and stayed in the free campgrounds being built by the government. "The popularity of these camps," he concluded, "fully warrants their development on a large scale."[4] Only ten thousand people stayed in the Northern Pacific's expensive hotels that year. An observant visitor saw the boarded-up edifice of the Fountain Hotel, which had been closed in 1917, as a mute symbol of the new popularity of car travel. He surmised its closure was "a result of the camp kits slung on the running boards of the endless stream of private cars on the road."[5]

Some railroads recognized the inevitability of car travel and of new classes of tourists and had attempted to adjust to them graciously. The Great Northern Railroad tried to cash in on these new travelers from the very beginning. They designed three different levels of accommodations in Glacier so that the park would attract visitors from a wide range of economic statuses. The less-expensive accommodations were also intended to attract those who wanted a more strenuous vacation, one that would bring them into closer contact with the wilderness. Such desires reflected new attitudes about leisure in the first decades of the twentieth century. By building plush hotels as well as rustic cabins, the Great Northern hoped to accommodate every kind of tourist.

In addition to the splendors of Glacier Park Lodge and Many Glacier, the railroad constructed a series of chalets to house more adventurous or economically minded tourists. The stone-and-log chalets, built in standard rustic style following the wishes of company president Louis Hill, offered visitors a bed in a dormitory and meals in a family-style dining room. A Great Northern advertisement boasted that "log-thatched ceilings, gay Indian blankets, potted pines, and huge fireplaces make these hostelries as picturesque within as they are without."[6] Tourists could either walk, ride horses, or drive between the various chalets; and promoters insisted that the chalets offered the best way to see the glories of the park.

Recognizing that the four-dollar-per-day charge for meals and lodging in the chalets might strain some budgets, the Great Northern devised another system for tourists with the most modest means. Near each of the chalets they built a series of "teepee camps." Here tourists slept on cots in wooden-floored teepees. A large central teepee offered a kitchen and dining area where people could do their own cooking. These facilities, which cost only fifty cents per night, attracted thrifty visitors as well as those who wanted a more "genuine" wilderness experience.[7]

A similar system had been created in Yellowstone National Park with the "permanent camps." Initially, Harry Child and the Northern Pacific had battled to prevent the development of such camps. Eventually, with pressure from the Department of the Interior, they capitulated and began to build a monopoly of these services as well. These camps, operated by the Northern Pacific's Yellowstone Transportation Company, as well as by several independent companies, resembled tent villages.[8]

Clusters of floored and heated sleeping tents surrounded dining halls, recreation pavilions, and assembly halls. Advertising pamphlets assured visitors that everything was "clean, informal, and pleasurable" and that "there is nothing rough or coarse."[9] Yellowstone officials claimed that "the camps both embody and interpret the freedom and spirit of the Yellowstone."[10] The establishment of the permanent camps demonstrated the growing appeal of "roughing it" and of the special pleasures offered by a trip to the Far West. These facilities attracted "that large class of visitors who, while touring the Park, desire to get away from the ceremony of convention and revel in Nature."[11] More and more people traveled west to discover American places and experiences; and the Northern Pacific, desperate to keep its hold on Yellowstone National Park and the tourists that now flooded it, tried to meet these changing demands.

The Santa Fe Railroad, however, attempted to ignore the growing numbers of automobile tourists. A flurry of letters between the park superintendent, Stephen Mather, the director of the National Park Service, and Santa Fe officials demonstrates the tensions the new automobile tourists created between the railroad and the park service. Supertintendent William Eakin called Santa Fe officials "singularly devoid of vision" because they refused to build a large autocamp behind El Tovar and their new Bright Angel Lodge.[12] A year later, campgrounds had still not been built, and the plans drawn up by Santa Fe architects were not only inadequate to the needs of park tourists but also "entirely missed the motif and spirit" of a national park campground.[13] The railroad, of course, wanted to be sure that paying customers would fill its hostelries before allowing campers into the park. The park service, however, won out; and auto campers soon filled the campgrounds at the south rim of the canyon.

In addition to the problems presented by cars and campers, the railroads faced a newly formed National Park Service that took great interest in the control and operation of the national parks. After a vigorous campaign, Stephen T. Mather succeeded in getting the National Park Service Act passed in 1916. This legislation allowed him to set up an innovative and responsive system of administering the parks, independent of the slow-moving Department of the Interior. The new government agency had a dual responsibility: "to conserve the scenery and the natural and historic objects and the wildlife" in the parks, and "to provide for the enjoyment of the same" in a way that would "leave them unimpaired for future generations."[14] This meant preventing eager developers from creating urban blight in the midst of the wilderness, while still keeping the parks accessible to visitors of all physical and financial abilities.

These goals did not always mesh with those of the railroads, which centered on turning a profit. After 1916, railroad companies were no longer free to develop the parks as they saw fit. The creation of the National Park Service placed strict limitations on what and how the railroads could build in the parks. Because of new public interest in the parks, and the perceptions about their importance to the nation, the government felt it had to regulate all aspects of park improvement.

Because the national parks encompassed some of the most characteristic aspects of the Far West, which many Americans now recognized as important for the development of a national character, this landscape had to be protected. National parks, which, according to the Department of the Interior, had the awesome power of "stimulating national patriotism" and "furthering knowledge and health,"[15] could not be left in the hands of profit-hungry corporations.

The far western landscape had been identified as a source of national culture. Its scenic marvels provided material that allowed Americans to create distinctive national symbols. Such national assets required both protection and democratization. In order to assure all Americans of the benefits of these sights, cars, tourists, and wilderness seekers of all sorts had to be encouraged, while monopolistic railroads and aristocratic resorts had to be curtailed.

Automobiles, middle-class tourists, and the new desire to experience the wilderness signaled a defeat for the railroads in their quest to control access to the far western landscape. They also confirmed the powerful new role the West played in American culture. The area represented all that seemed indigenous, vigorous, and characteristic to Americans. It offered a history that provided a kind of cultural grounding. Americans could look to the West and find splendid ancient history as well as evidence of more recent glories. It contained wilderness, the testing ground that many Americans believed was vital to their national development. Most importantly, it offered a landscape whose forms and colors had given Americans distinctive language, artistic styles, and architecture, which were crucial to the development of a national culture.

The landscape of the Far West, unfamiliar to early nineteenth-century eyes, had been difficult to describe. Only a few places in the western part of the continent could be usefully depicted in words and styles developed for Europe and the eastern portion of the United States. The work of explorers, writers, artists, and tourists demonstrated the startling variety present in the Far West, as well as the inadequacy of the language available to describe it. The immense stretches of desert and plain, the towering rock formations and the yawning chasms, the vibrant colors, the unprecedented plant and animal life, and the presence of divergent groups of native Americans made it impossible to describe or interpret the West with frameworks borrowed from Europe.

Gradually, however, Americans developed new ways to define the landscape. By the 1880s they began to see splendid landforms in mesas and canyons, brilliant colors in the rocks of the desert and mountains, beautiful flowers in the cactus and sage, and ancient natural and human history in places they had despised and avoided because of their unfamiliarity. The strange landscape became the American landscape. A new descriptive style, based on careful observation, geological discovery, and American analogy, replaced the European literary and artistic comparison and aesthetic constructs that had mired earlier attempts at description. A set of new words, images, and styles—based on American realities—gave observers, promoters, and tourists the tools and the power to recognize the value of the far western environment.

The West offered similar challenges to artists. Early attempts to depict the landscape on canvas failed because of their dependence on European painting conventions. Until American artists had the confidence to break with tradition and the ability to see the dramatic shapes, striking colors, and vast spaces of the Far West, they remained provincial and derivative. The century-long struggle to interpret the western landscape gradually provided both the confidence and vision necessary for a distinctive American style. As geologists, writers, and promoters attached new words to the landscape, artists provided fresh visual interpretations, grounded in direct observation rather than in inappropriate tradition.

By the beginning of the twentieth century, many important American artists went west, hoping to find a landscape whose exceptional qualities would force them to give up wearied conventions. The powerful impact of the far western environment produced stunning art. Artists such as Frederic Remington, Georgia O'Keeffe, Marsden Hartley, and Maynard Dixon developed particular American styles, entirely removed from nineteenth-century European concepts, out of their efforts to come to terms with the West. The clear light, bright colors, and extraordinary landforms, plants, and animals provided artists with a new vision. In a sense, the Far West, because of its strikingly different landscape, forced the creation of a unique style, one that emphasized sharp lines and vibrant color in abstract forms.

Writers and artists had a significant impact on the way Americans perceived the Far West, but nothing could replace the experience of seeing it for themselves. Tourists, like other nineteenth-century observers, did not know what to make of the great sprawl of the West when they first viewed it in the 1860s and 1870s. To make the region attractive to these wealthy visitors, railroad promoters and other speculators and had adopted a notion put forth by some of the earliest observers that the Far West could be described as a version of Europe. Because they feared Americans might find the unfamiliar landscape threatening, the railroads built small bastions of Europe in the Switzerland and the Italy of America.

Such efforts initially pleased tourists; but as they looked beyond the confines of the splendid resorts, they discovered scenery that could not be described in such terms. Instead, tourists soon discovered that the landscape required new words to describe it—words that could only be generated out of the landscape itself. Color, shape, and texture soon dominated discussions of the scenery. The new interest in these parts of the Far West, combined with a growing fascination with wilderness and the native Americans who peopled it, gave them great importance in the eyes of tourists. Eager to capitalize on these changes, the railroads developed new methods of advertising and resort building.

Because tourists wanted to sample the varied landscapes of the Far West, rather than to be protected from them, the railroads, in concert with creative architects, developed architectural styles that celebrated the western environment. They brought the shapes, colors, and smells of the landscape inside, while at the same time encouraging tourists to explore the outdoors. The architecture that grew out of the far western landscape was not limited to railroad resorts, depots, and camps. The concept of a building making the most of the unique qualities of its setting became a hallmark of twentieth-century American architecture.

The "Prairie Style" of Frank Lloyd Wright, the "Mission Style" so prevalent in southern California, the adobe architecture of the Southwest, and the distinctive Bay Area architecture of Bernard Maybeck, Willis Polk, and Julia Morgan shared these tenets. They celebrated the western scene by using its textures, shapes, and colors in their buildings. Because

Americans saw landscape as crucial to their culture, architects learned to incorporate the land into their structures. Once again, the process of confronting the idiosyncracies and unique grandeur of the Far West had forged a singularly American style.

The far western landscape presented nineteenth-century Americans with a set of unfamiliar objects, vistas, and ideas. John C. Frémont, whose reports introduced a vast number of Americans to the region in the 1840s, struggled unsuccessfully to depict the wonders he saw for his readers, dismissing the most unfamiliar areas as "hideous waste." It would take nearly half a century to observe, describe, and interpret the full range of the West's novel landscapes.

The lengthy process of evaluation required nothing less than the creation of a new vision. The process involved testing older visions, discovering their inadequacies, and replacing them with new ones. Slowly, a combination of scientific effort and growing national confidence allowed Americans to see the far western landscape for what it was: a treasure trove of symbols for a powerful national culture, one that combined ideals developed in the East with realities presented by the West. Places like the Grand Canyon, Yellowstone, and the Great Plains came to represent the vast space, independent thought, and unlimited possibility that Americans valued.

What had once been considered a region of "savages and wild beasts," of "dreary and barren wastes," and "treacherous and lonely defiles," now became the source of an independent American culture. The tourists who poured into the national parks in trains and automobiles, clamoring to experience the true Far West, attested to the new importance the West had for Americans. The far western landscape, with its deserts, mountains, plains, and its indigenous people, provided American culture with its own vocabulary, artistic styles, and symbols.

By 1920 the Far West had been fully integrated into American culture. Its unique appearance, which once had clashed with the concepts that Americans had borrowed from Europe, now described and defined their nation. The struggle to interpret the new visions presented by the far western landscape enabled Americans to create a distinctive and national culture. The long effort to resolve these conflicts forged new cultural definitions that reflected the reality and the splendor of the entire land mass of the United States.

Notes

Introduction: John Charles Frémont and the Problem of Description

1. Herman Friss, "The Image of the American West at Mid-Century (1840–1860)," in John Francis McDermott, ed., *The Frontier Re-examined* (Urbana, 1967), 50.

2. Allan Nevins, *Frémont, Pathmaker of the West*, vol. 1 (New York, 1955), 117–19; Ferol Egan, *Frémont: Explorer for a Restless Nation* (New York, 1975), 120.

3. Ibid., 272.

4. John Charles Frémont, *Report of the Exploring Expedition to the Rocky Mountains in the Year 1842 and to Oregon and North California in the Years 1843–1844* (Washington, D.C., 1845), 19.

5. Donald Jackson and Mary Lee Spence, eds., *The Expeditions of John Charles Frémont*, vol. 1 (Urbana, 1970), 186.

6. Ibid., 232.

7. Ibid., 184.

8. Jackson and Spence, *Frémont's Expeditions*, 641.

9. Ibid., 209.

10. Ibid., 250.

11. Ibid., 255.

12. Frémont, *Report*, 60.

13. Ibid., 65.

14. Jackson and Spence, *Frémont's Expeditions*, 668.

15. Ibid., 208.

16. Ibid.

17. Ibid., 517.

18. Ibid., 471.

19. Ibid., 702.

20. Ibid., 693.
21. Ibid., 686.
22. Ibid., 699.
23. I have found the following works especially influential. Earl Pomeroy, *In Search of the Golden West: The Tourist in Western America* (New York, 1957); William H. Goetzmann, *Exploration and Empire: The Explorer and the Scientist in the Winning of the American West* (New York, 1967); William H. Goetzmann and William N. Goetzman, *The West of the Imagination* (New York, 1986); John Brinkerhoff Jackson, *The Necessity for Ruins and Other Topics* (Amherst, Mass., 1980); Yi-Fu Tuan, *Topophilia: A Study of Environmental Perceptions, Attitudes, and Values* (Englewood Cliffs, N.J., 1974) and idem, *Landscapes of Fear* (Minneapolis, 1979); Donald W. Meinig, ed., *The Interpretation of Ordinary Landscapes* (New York, 1979); John R. Stilgoe, *Common Landscapes of America, 1580–1845* (New Haven, 1982); Peter Bacon Hales, *William Henry Jackson and the Transformation of American Landscape* (Philadelphia, 1988); Barbara Novak, *Nature and Culture: American Landscape and Painting, 1825–1875* (New York, 1980); and Roderick Nash, *Wilderness and the American Mind* (New Haven, 1967).

1. Looking Far West: Assessing the Possibilities of the Landscape, 1800–1850

1. Marjorie Hope Nicholson, *Mountain Gloom, Mountain Glory: The Development of the Aesthetics of the Infinite* (Ithaca, N.Y., 1959); Christopher Hussey, *The Picturesque: Studies in a Point of View* (New York, 1927); Keith Thomas, *Man and the Natural World: History of the Modern Sensibility* (New York, 1983), 254–58.
2. Anne Scott-James and Osbert Lancaster, *The Pleasure Garden* (Ipswich, England, 1977), 54–56; Jay Appleton, *The Experience of Landscape* (London, 1975), 35–36; Christopher Thacker, *A History of Gardens* (Berkeley, 1979), 181–87.
3. Elizabeth McKinsey, *Niagra Falls: Icon of the American Sublime* (Cambridge, 1985), 58–59; Barbara Maria Stafford, *Voyage into Substance: Art, Science, Nature, and the Illustrated Travel Account, 1760–1840* (Cambridge, Mass., 1984), 3.
4. Appleton, *Experience of Landscape*, 38.
5. See Allison Lockwood, *Passionate Pilgrims: The American Traveler in Great Britain, 1800–1914* (New York, 1981) and Christopher Mulvey, *Anglo-American Landscapes: A Study of Nineteenth-Century Anglo-American Travel Literature* (Cambridge, 1983).
6. "American Travelers," *Putnam's Monthly Magazine* 5 (June 1855): 564.
7. Quoted in Cushing Strout, *The American Image of the Old World* (New York, 1964), 68.
8. Nathaniel Hawthorne, *Our Old Home* (Cambridge, Mass., 1863), 113.
9. John Burroughs, "Mellow England," *Scribner's Monthly Magazine* 8 (September 1874): 563.
10. Bayard Taylor, *At Home and Abroad: A Sketch-book of Life, Scenery, and Men* (New York, 1867), 209–10.

11. Quoted in Hans Huth, *Nature and the American: Three Centuries of Changing Attitudes* (Berkeley, 1957), 38.

12. Taylor, *At Home*, 346.

13. For discussions about American attitudes toward the wilderness, see Hans Huth, *Nature and the American: Three Centuries of Changing Attitudes* (Berkeley, 1957); Roderick Nash, *Wilderness and the American Mind*, 3d ed. (New Haven, 1982); and Bernard Rosenthal, *City of Nature: Journeys to Nature in the Age of American Romanticism* (Newark, Del., 1980).

14. Edmund Burke, *A Philosophical Enquiry into the Origin of Our Ideas of the Sublime and Beautiful* (1757; reprint, Menston, England, 1979), 51; Samuel Monk, *The Sublime* (Menston, England, 1935), 147–56.

15. Thomas, *Man and the Natural World*, 264; Nicholson, *Mountain Gloom*, 341–51.

16. McKinsey, *Niagara*, 34–35. For religious aspects of the American sublime, see Barbara Novak, *Nature and Culture: American Landscape and Painting, 1825–1875* (New York, 1980), 3–17.

17. Stafford, *Voyage*, 31–183.

18. Novak, *Nature and Culture*, 59.

19. Ibid., 15.

20. McKinsey, *Niagara*, 41–85.

21. Ibid., 133–169.

22. Thomas Cole, "Essay on American Scenery," *American Monthly Magazine* 1 (January 1836): 4.

23. Ibid., 9.

24. Allan Nevins, *America through British Eyes* (New York, 1948), 79–81.

25. Henry T. Tuckerman, *America and Her Commentators, with a Critical Sketch of Travel in the United States* (New York, 1864), 219.

26. Taylor, *At Home*, 321.

27. Thomas Wentworth Higginson, "Americanism in Literature," *Atlantic Monthly* 25 (January 1870): 57.

28. In general, my account follows Roger L. Nichols and Patrick L. Halley, *Stephen Long and American Frontier Exploration* (Newark, Del., 1980) and William H. Goetzmann, *Exploration and Empire: The Explorer and the Scientist in the Winning of the American West* (New York, 1967).

29. William H. Goetzmann and William N. Goetzmann, *The West of the Imagination* (New York, 1986), 10–14.

30. Quoted in John C. Ewers, *Artists of the Old West* (Garden City, N.J., 1973), 27.

31. Edwin James, *Account of an Expedition from Pittsburgh to the Rocky Mountains, Performed in the Years 1819–1820*, in Reuben Gold Thwaites, ed., *Early Western Travels*, vol. 15 (Cleveland, 1905), 232; Ibid., 249–50.

32. Ibid., vol. 17, 147.

33. Washington Irving, *A Tour on the Prairies* (1835; reprint, Norman, Okla., 1956), 175.

34. Washington Irving, *The Rocky Mountains; or, Scenes, Incidents, and Adventures in the Far West*, vol. 1 (Philadelphia, 1837), 244.

35. Ibid., vol. 2, 133.

36. Ibid., 129.

37. Ibid., 238.

38. Ibid., vol. 1, 20.

39. Ewers, *Artists*, 43.

40. Goetzmann and Goetzmann, *West*, 18–26; William H. Truettner, *The Natural Man Observed: A Study of Catlin's Indian Gallery* (Washington, D.C., 1979), 41.

41. Ewers, *Artists*, 71; quoted in Truettner, *Natural Man*, 36–37.

42. Ibid., 39–40; Ewers, *Artists*, 72.

43. John C. Ewers, ed., *Views of a Vanishing Frontier* (Omaha, 1984), 52–84.

44. Ibid., 81–82; Goetzmann and Goetzmann, *West*, 44–54.

45. Quoted in Ron Tyler, *Alfred Jacob Miller: Artist on the Oregon Trail* (Fort Worth, 1982), 34.

46. Ewers, *Artists*, 99–101; Goetzmann and Goetzmann, *West*, 56–57.

47. Henry Nash Smith, *Virgin Land: The American West as Symbol and Myth* (Cambridge, Mass., 1950), 39.

48. For biographical details, see Thomas L. Karnes, *William Gilpin: Western Nationalist* (Austin, 1970).

49. William Gilpin, *The Central Gold Region: The Grain, Pastoral, and Gold Regions of North America* (Philadelphia, 1860), 120; Ibid., 124.

50. Ibid., 78.

51. Ibid., 70.

52. Ibid., 65.

53. Quoted in Karnes, *William Gilpin*, 228.

54. Smith, *Virgin Land*, 123–31; Richard Slotkin, *The Fatal Environment: The Myth of the Frontier in the Age of Industrialization* (New York, 1985), 38–40.

55. Annette Kolodny, *The Land Before Her: Fantasy and Experience of the American Frontiers, 1630–1860* (Chapel Hill, N.C., 1984), 96–129; Ibid., 101.

56. Quoted in Kolodny, *Land*, 114.

57. Caroline Kirkland [Mrs. Mary Clavers], *A New Home—Who'll Follow?* (New York, 1840); Dorothy Anne Dondore, *The Prairie and the Making of Middle America: Four Centuries of Description* (Cedar Rapids, Iowa, 1926), 293–95; Kolodny, *Land*, 133–36.

58. James Fenimore Cooper, *The Prairie*, in Allan Nevins, ed., *The Leatherstocking Saga* (New York, 1982), 768.

59. Slotkin, *Fatal Environment*, 99–100: Kolodny, *Land*, 231.

60. John D. Unruh, *The Plains Across: The Overland Immigrants and the Trans-Mississippi West, 1840–1860* (Urbana, 1978), 9–10; Ibid., 4–5.

61. Quoted in Karnes, *William Gilpin*, 131.

62. William H. Goetzmann, *Army Exploration in the American West, 1803–1863* (New Haven, 1959).

63. Goetzmann and Goetzmann, *West*, 38–40.

64. David J. Weber, *Richard H. Kern: Expeditionary Artist in the Far Southwest, 1848–1853* (Albuquerque, 1985), 25–37.

65. Edwin Bryant, *What I Saw in California* (New York, 1848), 22.

66. Ibid., 25.

67. Ibid., 139.

68. Ibid., 103.

69. Ibid., 104.

70. Ibid., 116.

71. Ibid., 170.

72. Francis Parkman, Jr., *The Oregon Trail*, ed. David Levin (1849; reprint, New York, 1982), 37.

73. David Levin, introduction to *The Oregon Trail* (New York, 1982).

74. Parkman, *Oregon Trail*, 47.

75. Ibid., 68.

76. Ibid., 105–6.

77. Ibid., 210.

78. Ibid., 228.

79. Unruh, *Plains Across*, 74–75; Robert A. Burchell, "The Loss of a Reputation; or, the Image of California in Britain before 1875," *California Historical Society Quarterly* 53 (Summer 1974): 122–25.

80. Bayard Taylor, *Eldorado; or, Adventures in the Path of Empire* (New York, 1850), 2.

81. Ibid., 47.

82. Ibid., 88.

83. Ibid., 65.

84. Lee Parry, "Landscape Theater in America," *Art in America* 53 (November–December 1971): 53–54.

85. Ibid., 56–57; John Francis McDermott, *The Lost Panoramas of the Mississippi* (Chicago, 1958), 9–17.

86. Quoted in Ibid., 30.

87. McDermott, *Panoramas*, 43–57.

88. Quoted in Ibid., 32–33.

89. *Democratic Free Press* (Peoria, Ill.) 2 December 1850, quoted in John Francis McDermott, "Gold Rush Movies," *California Historical Society Quarterly* 33 (March 1954): 33; Patricia Trenton and Peter H. Hassrick, *The Rocky Mountains: A Vision for Artists in the Nineteenth Century* (Norman, Okla., 1983), 102.

90. "Jones's Pantoscope of California: A Lecture by J. Wesley Jones Together with Pencil Sketches Depicting the Journey across the Plains to California," *California Historical Society Quarterly* 6 (June 1927) and (September 1927): 112; John Ross Dix, *Amusing and Thrilling Adventures of a California Artist while Daguerreotyping a Continent* (Boston, 1854), 12–13.

91. "Jones's Pantoscope," 117.

92. Ibid., 113.

93. Ibid., 128.

94. Ibid., 131.

95. Quoted in Richard Rudisill, *The Mirror Image: The Influence of the Daguerreotype in American Society* (Albuquerque, 1971), 147.

96. Dix, *Thrilling Adventures*, 45.

97. Hans Huth, "Yosemite: The Story of an Idea," *Sierra Club Bulletin* (March 1948): 64; "The Yohamite Falls, California," *Ballou's Pictorial Drawing Room Companion* 16 (May 1859): 325.

98. Thomas Starr King, *A Vacation among the Sierras: Yosemite in 1860*, ed. John A. Hussey (San Francisco, 1962), 43.

99. Ibid., 48.

100. Huth, "Yosemite," 64.

101. King, *Vacation*, 35.

102. George D. Brewerton, "A Ride with Kit Carson through the Great American Desert and the Rocky Mountains," *Harper's New Monthly Magazine* 7 (August 1853): 312.

103. Richard F. Burton, *The City of the Saints and across the Rocky Mountains to California* (London, 1861), 3.

2. Tunnel Vision: The Spectacle of the Transcontinental Railroad, 1850–1869

1. Samuel Bowles, "The Pacific Railroad—Open: How to Go, What to See," *Atlantic Monthly* 23 (April 1869): 493.

2. Edward S. Wallace, *The Great Reconnaissance: Soldiers, Artists, and Scientists on the Frontier* (Boston, 1955), 106–11; William H. Goetzmann, *Army Exploration in the American West* (New Haven, 1959), 262–65.

3. "Editors Drawer," *Harper's New Monthly Magazine* 7 (November 1853): 851.

4. Robert Taft, *Artists and Illustrators of the Old West, 1830–1900* (New York, 1953), 5.

5. U.S. Congress, Senate, *Reports of Explorations and Surveys to Ascertain the Most Practicable and Economic Route for a Railroad from the Mississippi River to the Pacific Ocean*, 33d Cong., 2d sess., Ex. Doc. 78, vol. 6, (Washington, D.C., 1855–61), 99.

6. Solomon N. Carvalho, *Incidents of Travel and Adventure in the Far West with Colonel Frémont's Last Expedition* (New York, 1858), 82.

7. U.S. Congress, *Railroad Reports*, vol. 2, 62.

8. Ibid., vol. 3, 59.

9. Stephen Fender, *Plotting the Golden West: American Literature and the Rhetoric of the California Trail* (Cambridge, 1981), 39–46.

10. Lieutenant Joseph Christmas Ives, *Report upon the Colorado River of the West*, U.S. Congress, House of Representatives, 36th Cong., 1861, Ex. Doc. 90, 52.

11. Heinrich Baldwin Mollhausen, *Diary of a Journey from the Mississippi to the*

Coasts of the Pacific with a United States Government Expedition, vol. 1, trans. Mrs. Percy Sinnett (London, 1858), 331.

12. U.S. Congress, *Railroad Reports*, vol. 2, 60.

13. U.S. Congress, *Railroad Reports*, vol. 3, 101–2.

14. Ives, *Colorado River*, 5.

15. Ibid., 57.

16. M. McDougal, "The Pacific Railroad," *North American Review* 82 (1856): 213.

17. Ibid., 214.

18. Ibid., 235–36.

19. *Dictionary of American Biography*, vol. 7, 530.

20. Horace Greeley, *An Overland Journey from New York to San Francisco in the Summer of 1859* (New York, 1860), 88.

21. Ibid., 114.

22. Ibid., 99.

23. Ibid., 205.

24. Ibid., 270–71.

25. Ibid., 111–12.

26. Ibid., 275.

27. Ibid., 280.

28. Ibid., 301.

29. Ibid., 311–12.

30. Ibid., 386.

31. Samuel Bowles, *Across the Continent: A Summer's Journey to the Rocky Mountains, the Mormons, and the Pacific States* (Springfield, Mass., 1866), 255.

32. Albert Dean Richardson, *Beyond the Mississippi* (Hartford, 1867), 331.

33. Bowles, *Across the Continent*, iii.

34. Ibid., 13.

35. Richardson, *Beyond the Mississippi*, 33.

36. Ibid., 80.

37. Bowles, *Across the Continent*, 18.

38. Ibid., 32.

39. Ibid., 81.

40. Richardson, *Beyond the Mississippi*, 343.

41. Bowles, *Across the Continent*, 131.

42. Richardson, *Beyond the Mississippi*, 368.

43. Frank Luther Mott, *A History of American Magazines*, vol. 2 (Cambridge, Mass., 1938), 391–94.

44. Bayard Taylor, "Travel in the United States," *Atlantic Monthly* 19 (April 1867): 482–83.

45. Fitzhugh Ludlow, *The Heart of the Continent: A Record of Travel across the Plains and in Oregon* (New York, 1870), 130.

46. Ibid., 45.

47. Ibid., 205.

48. Ibid., 289.

49. Bayard Taylor, *Colorado: A Summer Trip* (New York, 1867), 161.

50. Ibid., 35.

51. William Hepworth Dixon, *New America* (Philadelphia, 1867), 108.

52. J. Ross Browne, "A Tour through Arizona," *Harper's New Monthly Magazine* 29 (October 1864): 553.

53. J. Ross Browne, "A Trip to Bodie Bluff and the Dead Sea of the West," *Harper's New Monthly Magazine* 31 (September 1865): 416.

54. Browne, "A Tour through Arizona," 568.

55. Fitzhugh Ludlow, "Among the Mormons," *Atlantic Monthly* 13 (April 1864): 482.

56. Ludlow, *Heart of the Continent*, 265.

57. Ibid., 76.

58. Taylor, *Colorado*, 23–24.

59. Robert V. Hine, *The American West: An Interpretive History* (Boston, 1973), 194–201.

60. Ludlow, *Heart of the Continent*, 195.

61. Taylor, *Colorado*, 102.

62. Bowles, *Across the Continent*, 70.

63. "The Tribes of the Thirty-fifth Parallel," *Harper's New Monthly Magazine* 17 (September 1858): 452.

64. Richardson, *Beyond the Mississippi*, 512.

65. Demas Barnes, *From the Atlantic to the Pacific, Overland* (New York, 1866), 67.

66. Gordon Hendricks, *Albert Bierstadt: Painter of the American West* (New York, 1974), 25–30; 51–58.

67. Albert Bierstadt, "Letter," *Crayon Magazine* (September 1859): 287.

68. Ibid.

69. William H. Goetzmann and William N. Goetzmann, *The West of the Imagination* (New York, 1986), 154–55; Hendricks, *Albert Bierstadt*, 149–50.

70. Henry Tuckerman quoted in Patricia Trenton and Peter N. Hassrick, *The Rocky Mountains: A Vision for Artists in the Nineteenth Century* (Norman, Okla. 1983) 139.

71. Hendricks, *Albert Bierstadt*, 155–158; Trenton and Hassrick, *Rocky Mountains*, 116.

72. Bowles, *Across the Continent*, iv.

73. Richardson, *Beyond the Mississippi*, 409.

74. George Alfred Lawrence, *Silverland* (London, 1873), 147.

75. Robert Taft, *Photography and the American Scene: A Social History, 1839–1889* (New York, 1938), 260–63; Solomon N. Carvalho, *Incidents of Travel and Adventure in the Far West with Col. Frémont's Last Expedition* (New York, 1858).

76. Peter Bacon Hales, *Silver Cities: The Photography of American Urbanization* (Philadelphia, 1984), 34–36; *Catalogue of Daguerreotype Panoramic Views in California, by R. H. Vance* (New York, 1851).

77. *Photographic Art Journal* 2 (October 1851): 252.

78. Peter E. Palmquist, *Carleton E. Watkins: Photographer of the American West* (Albuquerque, 1983), 18–19.

79. Ibid., 19; Oliver Wendell Holmes, "Doings of the Sunbeam," *Atlantic Monthly* 12 (July 1863): 8.

80. Palmquist, *Carleton E. Watkins*, 25–26; Josiah Dwight Whitney, *The Yosemite Book: A Description of the Yosemite and the Adjacent Region of the Sierra Nevada and of the Big Trees of California* (New York, 1868), 9.

81. Whitney, *Yosemite Book*, pl. 8 and 10.

82. William Culp Darrah, *Stereo Views: A History of Stereographs in America and Their Collection* (Gettysburg, Pa., 1964), 7–8.

83. William Culp Darrah, *The World of Stereographs* (Gettysburg, Pa., 1977), 20–23; quoted in Edward W. Earle, ed., *Points of View: The Stereograph in America—A Cultural History* (Rochester, N.Y., 1981), 12.

84. Oliver Wendell Holmes, "The Stereoscope and the Stereograph," *Atlantic Monthly* 3 (June 1859): 744.

85. Oliver Wendell Holmes, "Sun Painting and Sun Sculpture with a Stereoscopic Trip across the Continent," *Atlantic Monthly* 8 (July 1861): 16.

86. Darrah, *World of Stereographs*, 24–25; Palmquist, *Carleton E. Watkins*, 26.

87. Hales, *Silver Cities*, 14–16; Susan Sontag, *On Photography* (New York, 1973), 171–73.

88. Hales, *Silver Cities*.

89. Peter E. Palmquist, *Lawrence and Houseworth / Thomas Houseworth and Company: A Unique View of the West, 1860–1886* (Columbus, Ohio, 1980) 10–12; 21–23; Thomas Houseworth and Company, *Catalogue of Photographic Views of Scenery on the Pacific Coast for the Stereoscope, Portfolio, and Mammoth Size for Framing* (San Francisco, 1870), iii.

90. Lawrence and Houseworth, *Gems of California Scenery* (San Francisco, 1865); Houseworth, *Catalogue of Photographic Views*.

91. Naef and Wood, *Era of Exploration*, 44–48.

92. A. A. Hart Stereographs, *Scenes in the Sierra Nevada Mountains for the Stereoscope*, Bancroft Library, nos. 255 and 56.

93. Ibid., no. 109.

94. Alfred A. Hart, *The Traveler's Own Book: A Panorama of Overland Travel from Chicago to San Francisco* (Chicago, 1870), 25.

95. A. A. Hart Stereographs, nos. 317–56.

96. C. R. Savage, "A Photographic Tour of Nearly Nine Thousand Miles," *Philadelphia Photographer* 4 (September 1867): 288.

97. Naef and Wood, *Era of Exploration*, 201–2.

98. Ferdinand V. Hayden, *Sun Pictures of Rocky Mountain Scenery* (New York, 1870), pl. 12.

99. Ibid., pl. 11

100. Darrah, *World of Stereographs*, 14; Naef and Wood, *Era of Exploration*, 73; Hayden, *Sun Pictures*, vii–viii.

101. Dee Brown, *Hear That Lonesome Whistle Blow* (New York, 1977), 67–68.

102. Silas Seymour, *Incidents of a Trip through the Great Platte Valley to the Rocky Mountains and Laramie Plains in the Fall of 1866* (New York, 1867), 73.

103. Ibid., 89.

104. Ibid., 103.

105. Taft, *Photography and the American Scene*, 276–77; Naef and Wood, *Era of Exploration*, 43.

106. Seymour, *Incidents*, 103.

107. Ibid., 107.

108. Wesley S. Griswold, *A Work of Giants: Building the First Transcontinental Railroad* (New York, 1962), 202–3; Brown, *Hear That Whistle Blow*, 98–99.

109. Sacramento *Daily Union*, 9 December 1867, 3.

110. Ibid.

111. Ibid.

112. Ibid.

113. J. Ross Browne, "The Reese River Country," *Harper's New Monthly Magazine* 33 (June 1866): 26.

114. C. H. Webb, "A California Caravansary," *Harper's New Monthly Magazine* 34 (April 1867): 603.

115. Review of Samuel Bowles's *Our New West*, in "Editor's Book Table," *Harper's New Monthly Magazine* 39 (September 1869): 611.

116. John H. Beadle, *The Undeveloped West; or, Five Years in the Territories* (Philadelphia, 1873), 142.

117. Ibid., 79.

118. Bowles, *Our New West*, 131.

119. Margaret I. Carrington, *Ocean to Ocean: Pacific Railroad and Adjoining Territories* (Philadelphia, 1869), 12–13.

120. Beadle, *Undeveloped West*, 108.

121. Bowles, *Our New West*, 225.

122. Hilda Rosenblatt, "For Three Weeks," *Overland Monthly* 3 (December 1869): 553.

123. Samuel Bowles, *The Switzerland of America: A Summer Vacation in the Parks and Mountains of Colorado* (Springfield, Mass. 1869), 28.

124. Beadle, *Undeveloped West*, 87.

125. Rosenblatt, "For Three Weeks," 554.

126. Samuel Bowles, *The Pacific Railroad—Open: How to Go What to See* (Boston, 1869), 5–6.

127. Samuel Bowles, "The Pacific Railroad—Open" *Atlantic Monthly* 23 (April 1859): 496.

3. Passage to an American Europe: The Tourist Experience on the Transcontinental Railroad, 1869–1880

1. George A. Crofutt, *Crofutt's New Overland Tourist and Pacific Coast Guide* (Omaha, 1880), 252; John Erastus Lester, *The Atlantic to the Pacific: What to See and How to See It* (London, 1873), 224–25.

2. Lester, *Atlantic to Pacific*, 178–79; Lanson Boyer, *From the Orient to the Occident: or, L. Boyer's Trip across the Rocky Mountains* (New York, 1878), 120.

3. Henry T. Williams, *The Pacific Tourist: Williams's Illustrated Transcontinental Guide of Travel from the Atlantic to the Pacific Ocean* (New York, 1876), 294–96.

4. Samuel Williams, "Some Americans Who Travel," *Overland Monthly* 2 (May 1869): 418.

5. John H. Tice, *Over the Plains and on the Mountains: or, Kansas and Colorado Agriculturally, Mineralogically, and Aesthetically Described* (St. Louis, 1872), 188.

6. William D. Pattison, "Westward by Rail with Professor Sedgwick: A Lantern Journey of 1873," *Historical Society of Southern California Quarterly* 42 (December 1960): 337–40.

7. S. J. Sedgwick, *Announcement of Professor S. J. Sedgwick's Illustrated Course of Lectures and Catalogue of Stereoscopic Views of Scenery*, 4th ed. (New York, 1879).

8. Ibid.

9. Ibid.

10. Ibid.

11. Richard Reinhardt, *Out West on the Overland Trail: Across the Continent Excursion with Leslie's Magazine in 1877 and the Overland Trip in 1967* (Palo Alto, Calif., 1967), 58.

12. Thomas Nelson, *The Union Pacific Railroad: A Trip across the North American Continent from Omaha to Ogden* (New York, 1871), 22.

13. Samuel Clemens [Mark Twain], *Roughing It* (1872; paperback ed., New York, 1980), 29.

14. Ibid., 49.

15. Ibid., 65.

16. Ibid., 85–86.

17. Ibid., 88.

18. Ibid., 91.

19. Ibid., 115.

20. Patricia Nelson Limerick, *Desert Passages: Encounters with the American Deserts* (Albuquerque, 1985), 64.

21. Clemens, *Roughing It*, 115.

22. Ibid., 119.

23. Ibid., 114.

24. Lucius Beebe, *Mansions on Rail: The Folklore of the Private Railway Car* (Berkeley, 1959), 19; quoted in W. F. Rae, *Westward by Rail: The New Route to the East* (London, 1870), 29.

25. Robert E. Strahorn, *To the Rockies and Beyond: A Summer on the Union Pacific Railroad and Its Branches* (Omaha, 1878), 4.

26. J. G. Pangborn, *The Rocky Mountain Tourist: The Tour from the Banks of the Mississippi to the Base of the Rockies* (Topeka, Kans., 1877), 25.

27. Williams, *Pacific Tourist*, 29.

28. Charles Nordhoff, *California: For Health, Pleasure, and Residence* (New York, 1872), 23.

29. Charles Nordhoff, "California: How to Go There and What to See by the Way," *Harper's New Monthly Magazine* 44 (May 1872): 871; Williams, *Pacific Tourist*, 8–9.

30. Ralph Waldo Emerson, *Journals*, 7 February 1843, quoted in Wolfgang Schivelbusch, *The Railway Journey: Trains and Travel in the Nineteenth Century* (New York, 1977), 57.

31. Schivelbusch, *Railway Journey*, 65–66; see also Geoffrey Hindley, *Tourists, Travellers, and Pilgrims* (London, 1983), 198–205.

32. Quoted in Hindley, *Tourists*, 205.

33. Schivelbusch, *Railway Journey*, 41–47; see also Stephen Kern, *The Culture of Time and Space* (Cambridge, Mass., 1983), 10–64.

34. Mary Duffus Hardy, *Through Cities and Prairie Lands: Sketches of an American Tour* (London, 1881), 127–28.

35. George A. Crofutt, *Crofutt's Trans-Continental Tourist's Guide* (New York, 1871), 90–91.

36. Robert Harris, "The Pacific Railroad—Unopen," *Overland Monthly* 3 (September 1869): 244.

37. Crofutt, *Crofutt's New Overland and Pacific Coast Guide*, 5.

38. John H. Beadle, *The Undeveloped West; or, Five Years in the Territories* (Philadelphia, 1873), 249.

39. Crofutt, *Crofutt's Transcontinental Guide*, title page.

40. Henry T. Morford, *Morford's Short Trip Guide to America* (London, 1872), 3.

41. Crofutt, *Crofutt's New Overland and Pacific Coast Guide*, 5.

42. Lester, *Atlantic to Pacific*, 228.

43. Beadle, *Undeveloped West*, 248.

44. Thomas Nelson and Sons, *Nelson's Pictorial Guidebooks for Tourists: Great Salt Lake City and Utah Territory* (New York, 187[4]), 3.

45. Bill Dadd, *Great Transcontinental Railroad Guide* (Chicago, 1869), 18.

46. Nordhoff, "California: How to Go There," 875.

47. Thomas Nelson, *The Union Pacific Railroad: A Trip Across the Continent From Omaha to Ogden* (New York, 1870) 15.

48. Nelson, *Union Pacific: Omaha to Ogden, 1871*, 20.

49. Williams, *Pacific Tourist*, 57.

50. Nelson, *Nelson's Pictorial: Salt Lake City*, 4.

51. Williams, *Pacific Tourist*, 46.

52. Nelson, *Union Pacific: Omaha to Ogden, 1871*, 21.

53. *Appleton's Handbook of American Travel: Western Tour* (New York, 1871), 99.

54. Dadd, *Transcontinental Railroad Guide*, 73.

55. Lester, *Atlantic to Pacific*, 36.

56. Morford, *Short Trip Guide*, 58.

57. *Appleton's Handbook*, 244.

58. Dadd, *Transcontinental Railroad Guide*, 114.

59. Ibid., 144.

60. Crofutt, *Crofutt's Transcontinental Guide*, 144.

61. Ibid., 118–19.

62. Dadd, *Transcontinental Railroad Guide*, 185.

63. Thomas Nelson, *The Central Pacific Railroad: A Trip Across the North American Continent from Ogden to San Francisco* (New York, 1870), 21.

64. Ibid., 22.

65. Nordhoff, *California*, 31.

66. Nelson, *Central Pacific*, 22.

67. Grace Greenwood, *Life in New Lands: Notes of Travel* (New York, 1873), 28.

68. *From Ocean to Ocean: A Diary of Three Months Travel* (London, 1871), 53–54.

69. William Henry Rideing, *Scenery of the Pacific Railway and Colorado* (New York, 1878), 8.

70. Alexander Rivington and W. A. Harris, *Reminiscences of America in 1869* (London, 1870), 234.

71. Tice, *Over the Plains*, 257.

72. Beadle, *Undeveloped West*, 437.

73. Benjamin F. Taylor, *Between the Gates* (Chicago, 1878), 33.

74. William Lilly, *A Trip to San Francisco* (n.p., 1871), 4.

75. *Harper's Weekly Magazine* 11 (December 1867): 797.

76. Hans Huth, *Nature and the American: Three Centuries of Changing Attitudes* (Berkeley, 1957), 162–63.

77. Leslie, *California*, 46.

78. J. W. Boddam-Whetham, *Western Wanderings: A Record of Travel in the Evening Land* (London, 1874), 67.

79. Rae, *Westward by Rail*, 91.

80. W. E. Webb, *Buffalo Land: An Authentic Narrative of the Adventures and Misadventures of a Late Scientific and Sporting Party upon the Great Plains of the West* (Cincinnati, 1872), 118.

81. Tice, *Over the Plains*, 83.

82. Helen Hunt [H.H.], "A New Anvil Chorus," *Scribner's Monthly* 15 (January 1878): 387.

83. Lilly, *A Trip*, 6–7.

84. William Wilson Ross, *Ten Thousand Miles by Land and Sea* (Toronto, 1876), 49.

85. Rae, *Westward by Rail*, 89.
86. William Minturn, *Travels West* (London, 1877), 111.
87. Rivington and Harris, *Reminiscences*, 242.
88. Taylor, *Between the Gates*, 42; Williams, *Pacific Tourist*, 101; Rideing, *Scenery of the Pacific Railway*, 41.
89. Rideing, *Scenery of the Pacific Railway*, 43; Boyer, *From the Orient*, 51.
90. Rae, *Westward by Rail*, 95–96.
91. Rideing, *Scenery of the Pacific Railway*, 45–46.
92. Smiles, *Travels*, 256.
93. Greenwood, *New Life*, 185.
94. Rae, *Westward by Rail*, 226.
95. Ben C. Truman, *Tourists Illustrated Guide to the Celebrated Summer and Winter Resorts of California* (San Francisco, 1883), 78.
96. Lilly, *A Trip*, 12.
97. Leslie, *California*, 109.
98. Minturn, *Travels West*, 226.
99. Greenwood, *New Life*, 188.
100. Henry Hussey Vivian, *Notes of a Tour in America* (London, 1878), 126.
101. *From Ocean*, 40; Taylor, *Between the Gates*, 65.
102. Minturn, *Travels West*, 159.
103. William L. Cole, *California: Its Scenery, Climate, Productions, and Inhabitants, Notes of an Overland Trip to the Pacific Coast* (New York, 1872), 19–20.
104. Montague Davenport, *Under the Gridiron: A Summer in the United States and the Far West* (London, 1876), 74.
105. F. Trench Townshend, *Ten Thousand Miles of Travel, Sport, and Adventure* (London, 1869), 152.
106. Minturn, *Travels West*, 159.
107. William H. Rideing, "The Wheeler Survey in Nevada," *Harper's New Monthly Magazine* 55 (June 1877): 66.
108. Greenwood, *New Life*, 175.
109. Rideing, *Scenery of the Pacific Railway*, 62.
110. Townshend, *Ten Thousand Miles*, 211.
111. Rae, *Westward By Rail*, 194.
112. Leslie, *California*, 205.
113. Taylor, *Between the Gates*, 52.
114. George Alfred Lawrence, *Silverland* (London, 1873), 95.
115. Rideing, *Scenery of the Pacific Railway*, 6.
116. Helen Hunt [H.H.], *Bits of Travel at Home* (Boston, 1878), 9.
117. Boddam-Whetham, *Western Wanderings*, 53.
118. Lawrence, *Silverland*, 95.
119. Williams, *Pacific Tourist*, 182.
120. *From Ocean*, 68.
121. Samuel Bowles, *Our New West* (Hartford, Conn., 1869), 158.
122. George W. Pine, *Beyond the West* (Utica, N.Y., 1870), 263.

123. Colonel George Edward Nichols, "The Indian: What We Should Do with Him," *Harper's New Monthly Magazine* 40 (April 1870): 732.

124. A. B. Elliott, *Traveller's Handbook across the Continent* (Troy, N.Y., 1870), 29.

125. Samuel Manning, *American Pictures Drawn with Pencil and Pen* (London, 1876), 66.

126. Leslie, *California*, 71.

127. Greenwood, *New Life*, 138.

128. William Robertson, *Our American Tour: Being a Run of Ten Thousand Miles from the Atlantic to the Pacific in the Autumn of 1869* (Edinburgh, 1871), 79.

129. Lawrence, *Silverland*, 48.

130. Hunt, *Bits of Travel*, 17.

131. Nordhoff, *California*, 42–43.

132. Tice, *Over the Plains*, 188.

133. Truman, *Tourist's Illustrated Guide*, 77.

134. Bayard Taylor, *At Home and Abroad: A Sketch-Book of Life, Scenery, and Men* (New York, 1867), 194.

135. Tice, *Over the Plains*, 189.

136. Taylor, *At Home*, 200.

137. Manning, *American Pictures*, 31.

4. European Citadels: The Early Far Western Resorts, 1870–1900

1. Marshall Sprague, *Newport in the Rockies: The Life and Times of Colorado Springs*, rev. ed. (Athens, Ohio, 1980), 17–20.

2. Ibid., 29–30; Nancy E. Loe, *Life in the Altitudes: An Illustrated History of Colorado Springs* (Woodland Hills, Calif., 1983), 20–27.

3. John W. Reps, *Cities of the American West: A History of Frontier Urban Planning* (Princeton, 1979), 583–89.

4. Bruce Haley, *The Healthy Body and Victorian Culture* (Cambridge, Mass., 1978), 13–25.

5. Samuel A. Fisk, M.D., "Colorado as a Winter Sanitarium," *Popular Science Monthly* 28 (March 1886): 668; Bushrod W. James, *American Resorts with Notes upon Their Climates* (Philadelphia, 1889), 158.

6. George F. Drinka, *The Birth of Neurosis: Myth, Malady, and the Victorians* (New York, 1984), 184–93; George Miller Beard, *American Nervousness: Its Causes and Consequences* (New York, 1881), 6.

7. Anita Clair Fellman and Michael Fellman, *Making Sense of Self: Medical Advice Literature in Late Nineteenth-Century America* (Philadelphia, 1981), 43–46; Fisk, "Colorado," 669.

8. James, *American Resorts*, 21.

9. *Prospectus of the Fountain Colony of Colorado Located at Colorado Springs, Colorado* (n.p., 1871).

10. Sprague, *Newport,* 71–72; Billy M. Jones, *Health Seekers in the Southwest, 1817–1900* (Norman, Okla., 1967), 155–56.

11. Edwin S. Solly, M.D., *The Health Resorts of Colorado Springs and Manitou* (Colorado Springs, 1883), 112–35.

12. Denver and Rio Grande Railroad, *Rhymes of the Rockies* (Chicago, 1887), 12.

13. Thomas C. Parrish, *Colorado Springs: Its Climate, Scenery, and Society* (Colorado Springs, 1889), 9.

14. Sprague, *Newport,* 73–75.

15. Rose Georgina Kingsley, *South by West; or, Winter in the Rocky Mountains and Spring in Mexico* (London, 1874), 149.

16. Loe, *Life in the Altitudes,* 42; Colorado Springs *Daily Gazette,* March 1877, April 1877, March 1878.

17. Manly Dayton Ormes and Eleanor R. Ormes, *The Book of Colorado Springs* (Colorado Springs, 1933), 39–40.

18. Ernest Ingersoll, *The Crest of the Continent* (Chicago, 1883), 286.

19. Quoted in Julia F. Lipsey, *Travelers First Class in Colorado, 1868–1907* (Colorado Springs, 1957), 13.

20. Emily Faithful, *Three Visits to America* (New York, 1884), 146.

21. Mrs. Simeon J. Dunbar, *Colorado Springs and Manitou* (Colorado Springs, 1883), 29: *A Bouquet from the Garden of the Gods* (Chicago, 1884), 9.

22. Ibid., 9.

23. Samuel Bowles, *The Switzerland of America: A Summer Vacation in the Parks and Mountains of Colorado* (Springfield, Mass., 1869), 95.

24. Richard Baxter Townshend, *A Tenderfoot in Colorado* (1903; reprint, Norman, Okla., 1968), 67; Denver and Rio Grande Railroad, *Around the Circle: One Thousand Miles through the Rocky Mountains* (Chicago, 1892), 7.

25. Denver and Rio Grande Railroad, *The Heart of the Continent* (Chicago, 1882), 28–29.

26. Ibid., 2.

27. Eliza Greatorex, *Summer Etchings in Colorado* (New York, 1873), 35–36.

28. Ingersoll, *Crest,* 33.

29. Bowles, *Switzerland,* 47; Union Pacific Railroad, *From Summerland to the American Alps* (Omaha, 1894), 39; Earl of Dunraven, *The Great Divide: Travels in the Upper Yellowstone in the Summer of 1874* (London, 1876), 2.

30. *The Story of Manitou* (Cincinnati, 1886), 56; Rand, McNally and Company, *Guide to Colorado, New Mexico, and Arizona* (Chicago, 1880), 13.

31. J. G. Pangborn, *The Rocky Mountain Tourist: The Tour from the Banks of the Missouri to the Base of the Rockies* (Topeka, 1877), 9.

32. Ingersoll, *Crest,* 13.

33. *Among the Mountains: A Guide Book to Colorado Springs and the Scenery in the Neighborhood* (Colorado Springs, 1873), 108–9.

34. Businessmen of Colorado Springs, *Colorado Springs—Manitou Springs* (n.p., n.d.); George Rex Buckman, *Colorado Springs: Colorado at the Foot of Pike's Peak* (Colorado Springs, 1892), 15.

35. Denver and Rio Grande Railroad, *Panoramic Views along the Line of the Denver and Rio Grande* (Chicago, 1893).

36. Ingersoll, *Crest*, 193.

37. Union Pacific System, *Sights and Scenes in Colorado for Tourists* (Omaha, 1894), 27.

38. George A. Crofutt, *Crofutt's Grip-Sack Guide of Colorado* (Omaha, 1881), 165.

39. Ingersoll, *Crest*, 164.

40. Denver and Rio Grande Railroad, *Across the Continent by the Scenic Route: Colorado, Utah, and New Mexico via the Denver and Rio Grande Railway* (Chicago, n.d.), 6.

41. Quoted in James Fullerton Muirhead, *The Land of Contrasts: A Briton's View of His American Kin* (Boston, 1898), 212.

42. Quoted in Loe, *Life in the Altitudes*, 22.

43. Isabella L. Bird, *A Lady's Life in the Rocky Mountains* (London, 1879), 177–78.

44. Kingsley, *South by West*, 149.

45. Amanda M. Ellis, *The Colorado Springs Story* (Colorado Springs, 1954), 17; *Manitou: Its Springs and a Brief Description of Its Many Points of Interest* (Denver, 1902); Greatorex, *Summer Etchings*, 31–32; Hattie Horner, *Not at Home* (New York, 1889), 124.

46. *Manitou: Its Springs.*

47. Loe, *Life in the Altitudes*, 30; "Denver Illustrated," *The Grand Army Magazine* 1 (July 1883): 457.

48. Emma Abbott Gage, *Western Wanderings and Summer Saunterings Through Picturesque Colorado* (Baltimore, 1900), 100.

49. Ingersoll, *Crest*, 264.

50. Sprague, *Newport*, 226–27; *The Antlers, Colorado Springs, Colorado* (Denver, n.d.).

51. Ellis, *Colorado Springs*, 31; Frederick J. Sterner, "The New Antlers Hotel," *Mountain Sunshine* 2 (Winter 1901): 4.

52. Sprague, *Newport*, 100–101.

53. Caroline H. Dall, *My First Holiday; or, Letters Home* (Boston, 1881), 51.

54. Lorin Blodget, *Climatology of the United States* (Philadelphia, 1857), 193–205; Kevin Starr, *Inventing the Dream: California through the Progressive Era* (New York, 1985), 54–55; John E. Baur, *The Health Seekers of Southern California, 1870–1900* (San Marino, 1959), 3–5.

55. Newton H. Chittenden, *The Watering Places, Health and Pleasure Resorts of the Pacific Coast* (Santa Barbara, 1881), 8.

56. R. W. C. Farnsworth, *A Southern California Paradise* (Pasadena, 1883), 97.

57. Quoted in *Coronado Beach, California: A Unique Corner of the Earth* (Oakland, 1890), 6.

58. E. M. Johnstone, *By Semi-Tropic Seas: Santa Barbara and Surroundings* (Buffalo, N.Y., 1888).

59. F. Weber Benton, *Zig-Zag Sketches of Semi-Tropic California* (Los Angeles, 1886), 3.

60. S. L. Welch, *Southern California: A Semi-Tropic Paradise* (Los Angeles, 1886), 146.

61. J. St. John, *The Californian Tourist's Guidebook* (San Francisco, 1886), 99.

62. John S. Hittell, *Bancroft's Pacific Coast Guide Book* (San Francisco, 1882), 72.

63. Farnsworth, *Paradise*, 97.

64. John Hoyt Williams, *A Great and Shining Road: The Epic Story of the Transcontinental Railroad* (New York, 1988), 144; John Debo Galloway, *The First Transcontinental Railway: Union Pacific, Central Pacific* (New York, 1950), 90.

65. William C. Morrow, *Souvenir of the Hotel Del Monte, Monterey, California* (n.p., 1890), 7; Oscar Lewis, *The Big Four: The Story of Huntington, Stanford, Hopkins, and Crocker, and of the Building of the Central Pacific* (New York, 1938), 121.

66. San Francisco *Newsletter*, 12 June 1880, 15.

67. Glen S. Dumke, *The Boom of the Eighties in Southern California* (San Marino, 1944), 34; Gary F. Kurutz, *Benjamin C. Truman: California Booster and Bon Vivant* (San Francisco, 1984), 57–60; Starr, *Inventing the Dream*, 44–45.

68. See, for example, Ben C. Truman, *From the Crescent City to the Golden Gate via the Sunset Route of the Southern Pacific* (New York, 1886); idem, *Tourists' Illustrated Guide to the Celebrated Summer and Winter Resorts of California* (San Francisco, 1883); idem, *Homes and Happiness in the Golden State of California* (San Francisco, 1885).

69. *Monterey, the Most Charming Resort*, 1.

70. Truman, *Summer and Winter Resorts*, 136–38.

71. *Monterey, the Most Charming Resort*, 9; Morrow, *Souvenir*, 23.

72. *History of Monterey County*, 124; Truman, *Summer and Winter Resorts*, 133; *Monterey, the Most Charming Resort*, 2.

73. N. C. Carnall, *California Guide for Tourists and Settlers* (San Francisco, 1889), 33.

74. *History of Monterey County*, 126.

75. Lewis, *Big Four*, 121; *Pennsylvania Tours to the Golden Gate* (Philadelphia, 1890), 77.

76. Walter Raymond and I. A. Whitcomb, *Raymond's Vacation Excursions: A Winter in California, 1889–1890* (Boston, 1888), 39; Truman, *Summer and Winter Resorts*, 144.

77. Harold Kirker, *California's Architectural Frontier: Style and Tradition in the Nineteenth Century* (San Marino, 1960), 110.

78. Morrow, *Souvenir*, 7; H. M. S. Lothrop, *The Golden West as Seen by the Ridgeway Club* (Boston, 1886), 378.

79. *Truman, Summer and Winter Resorts*, 144.

80. Lothrop, *Golden West*, 378.

81. San Francisco *Newsletter*, 12 June 1880.

82. *Monterey California: The Most Charming Winter Resort in the World* (San Francisco, 1881), 7; Morrow, *Souvenir*, 13; Dall, *My First Holiday*, 320; Randalla Reinstedt, *Incredible Ghosts of Old Monterey's Hotel Del Monte* (Carmel, 1980), 13.

83. Morrow, *Souvenir*, 13; Edward E. Eitel, *Picturesque Del Monte* (San Francisco, 1888), 2–3.

84. John A. Gutteridge, *Rocky Mountains to the Golden Gate: A Tourist's Guide* (Denver, 1890), 61; "A Sojourn At Monterey," *The Great Divide* 9 (May 1893): 60; Morrow, *Souvenir*, 9.

85. George Wharton James, *The Hotel Men's Mutual Benefit Association in California* (Pasadena, 1896), 283; *Monterey, the Most Charming Resort*, 8.

86. Dall, *My First Holiday*, 320; Clifford Paynter Allen, *From Geyser to Cañon with Mary* (Philadelphia, 1904); James, *Hotel Men*, 293.

87. *Monterey, the Most Charming Resort*, 13.

88. Ibid., 11.

89. Truman, *Summer and Winter Resorts*, 149.

90. William Henry Bishop, "Southern California," *Harper's New Monthly Magazine* 65 (October 1882): 728.

91. Morrow, *Souvenir*, 23.

92. James, *Hotel Men*, 303.

93. Morrow, *Souvenir*, 16.

94. Rose Pender, *A Lady's Experiences in the Wild West in 1883* (reprint, Lincoln, Nebr., 1978), 44.

95. *History of Monterey County*, 23.

96. Monterey County Chamber of Commerce, *A Souvenir of the Hotel Del Monte* (n.p., 1889), 23.

97. *History of Monterey County*, 125; *Hotel Del Monte* (San Francisco, 1898), 6; Morrow, *Souvenir*, 11.

98. Pacific Bank, *Handbook of California* (San Francisco, 1888), 152; Hittell, *Bancroft's Pacific Coast*, 5; Truman, *Summer and Winter*, 152.

99. Dall, *My First Holiday*, 3, 196, 333–34.

100. Mrs. J. A. I. Washburn, *To the Pacific and Back* (New York, 1887), 49.

101. F. Dale Pawle, *A Flying Visit to the American Continent* (London, 1896), 87.

102. Muirhead, *Land of Contrasts*, 264.

103. Kirker, *California*, 118–23.

104. Jeffrey Limerick, Nancy Ferguson, and Richard Oliver, *America's Grand Resort Hotels* (New York, 1979), 104; Walter Raymond and I. A. Whitcomb, *A Winter in California: Nine Grand Trips* (Boston, 1888), 51.

105. E. H. Harrison, *Monterey County Illustrated* (San Francisco, 1888), 12; Morrow, *Souvenir*, 13; Eitel, *Picturesque Del Monte*, 2; James, *Hotel Men*, 284.

106. Pacific Bank, *Handbook*, 46.

107. Charles Augustus Stoddard, *Beyond the Rockies: A Spring Journey in California* (New York, 1894), 145.

108. *Colorado Springs Weekly Gazette*, 19 March 1881.

109. *Colorado Springs Daily Gazette*, 19 April 1881; Ibid., 17 May 1881; Leland

Feitz, *The Antlers: A Quick History of Colorado Springs' Historic Hotel* (Denver, 1977), 1; *Colorado Springs Daily Gazette*, 17 May 1881.

110. Sprague, *Newport*, 101; Edwards Roberts, *Colorado Springs and Manitou* (Chicago, n.d.), 19–20.

111. Feitz, *Antlers*, 2.

112. *Leading Industries of the West: Scenic and Sanitary Colorado* (Chicago, 1883), 68.

113. *Colorado Springs Weekly Gazette*, 9 June 1883.

114. Sprague, *Newport*, 101–2; Loe, *Life in the Altitudes*, 53; *Leading Industries*, 68.

115. Buckman, *Colorado Springs*, 23.

116. *The Antlers*, 12; "Denver Illustrated," 456.

117. Santa Fe Railroad, *Colorado, the Santa Fe Route* (Chicago, 1894), 5.

118. Union Pacific Railroad, *A Description of the Western Resorts for Health and Pleasure Reached via the Union Pacific System* (Chicago, 1890), 6.

119. Sprague, *Newport*, 116–22.

120. James Pourtales, *Lessons Learned from Experience*, trans. M. W. Jackson (Colorado Springs, 1955), 86–93; Ibid., 83.

121. Ibid., 86.

122. *Colorado Springs Weekly Gazette*, 4 July 1891.

123. Helen M. Geiger, *The Broadmoor Story* (n.p., 1968), 17; *Colorado Springs Weekly Gazette*, 4 July 1891.

124. Denver and Rio Grande Railroad, *Sight Places and Resorts in the Rockies* (Denver, 1899), 19; W. H. Simpson, *A Colorado Summer* (Chicago, 1896), 11–12; Buckman, *Colorado Springs*, 11.

125. Limerick, *Great Resorts*, 151–52; Feitz, *Antlers*, 5.

126. Frederick J. Sterner, "The New Antlers Hotel," *Mountain Sunshine: Colorado Springs and the Pikes Peak Region* 2 (Winter 1901): 3.

127. Varian and Sterner, blueprints of the Antlers Hotel, 1899, 5.

128. Sterner, "New Antlers," 4–6.

129. Theodore S. Van Dyke, *County of San Diego, the Italy of Southern California* (San Diego, 1886), 69.

130. Reps, *Cities of the American West*, 278–80; Marcie Buckley and Stephen S. Oakford, *Official Illustrated History: Hotel Del Coronado* (San Diego, 1979), 22; Limerick, *Great Resorts*, 111; Thomas J. Morrow and William Sullivan, *Hotel Del Coronado* (Coronado, Calif., 1984), 23.

131. *Hotel Del Coronado, San Diego County* (Oakland, Calif., 1890), 6.

132. *San Diego Union*, 14 August 1887.

133. Raymond and Whitcomb, *Winter in California*, 56; *Hotel Del Coronado*, 8; Coronado Beach Company, *Coronado Beach, Hotel Del Coronado* (Chicago, 1888), 10.

134. Coronado Beach Company, *Coronado Beach, 1887*, (Chicago, 1887), 11.

135. Coronado Beach Company, *Hotel Del Coronado* (Chicago, 1889), 10.

136. Coronado Beach Company, *Coronado Beach, 1887*, 11.

137. Lena M. Uruquhart, *Glenwood Springs: Spa in the Mountains* (Boulder, Colo., 1970), 38–39; Ingersoll, *Crest*, 229.

138. Uruquhart, *Glenwood Springs*, 77; Colorado Midland Railway, *Glenwood Springs: A Sanitarium* (Chicago, 1888), 12.

139. *The Colorado: The Kissingen of America* (Boston, 1895).

140. *Hotel Colorado: The Great Health Resort of America*, (n.p., 1900), 7.

141. Colorado Midland, *From Plains to Peaks*, 65–66.

142. Horace A. Bird, *History of a Line: Colorado Midland Railway* (Denver, 1889), 76.

143. Gutteridge, *Rocky Mountains*, 45.

144. Caroline Bancroft, *Glenwood's Early Glamour* (Boulder, Colo., 1958), 14.

145. Uruquhart, *Glenwood Springs*, 97; *The Great Resorts of America* (Portland, Maine, 1893), 11.

146. *Denver Times*, 10 June, 1893, 1.

147. *Colorado: The Kissingen of America.*

148. Uruquhart, *Glenwood Springs*, 101; Henry M. Lyman, M.D., *Glenwood Springs, Colorado* (n.p., 1894), 6.

5. The Far Away Nearby: Discovering the Far Western Landscape, 1885–1915

1. *New York Times*, 8 May 1867, 8.

2. William H. Goetzmann, *Exploration and Empire: The Explorer and the Scientist in the Winning of the American West* (New York, 1967), 430–58; "American Glaciers," *Scribner's Monthly* 2 (April 1871): 687.

3. United States Army, Engineer Department, *Report upon United States Geographical Surveys West of the One Hundredth Meridian*, vol. 1, (Washington, D.C., 1889), 15–16.

4. William H. Rideing, "A Trail in the Far Southwest," *Harper's New Monthly Magazine* 53 (June 1876): 15.

5. Ferdinand Vandiveer Hayden, *Sun Pictures of the Rocky Mountain Scenery* (New York, 1870), 4–5.

6. Nathaniel P. Langford, "The Wonders of the Yellowstone," *Scribner's Monthly* 2 (May 1871): 12.

7. Nathaniel P. Langford, "The Ascent of Mount Hayden: A New Chapter of Western Discovery," *Scribner's Monthly* 6 (June 1873): 133.

8. Langford, "Wonders of Yellowstone," 11.

9. Ibid.

10. Carol Clark, *Thomas Moran: Watercolors of the American West* (Fort Worth, 1980), 15; William Henry Jackson, *Time Exposure: The Autobiography of William Henry Jackson* (New York, 1940), 196.

11. Ferdinand Vandiveer Hayden, "The Wonders of the West: More about the Yellowstone," *Scribner's Monthly* 3 (February 1872): 396.

12. U.S. Department of the Interior, United States Geological Survey of the Territories, *Descriptive Catalogue of the Photographs of the United States Geological*

Survey of the Territories for the Years 1869 to 1875, 2d ed., (Washington, D.C., 1875), 28–30.

13. United States Geological Survey, *Annual Report, F. V. Hayden, Geologist in Charge*, vol. 5 (Washington, D.C., 1867–78), 81.

14. Hayden, "Wonders of the West," 396.

15. U.S. Congress, *Statutes at Large*, vol. 17, 32.

16. "The Yellowstone Landscape at Washington," *Nation* 15 (September 1872): 158.

17. Goetzmann, *Exploration and Empire*, 551–53; Wallace Stegner, *Beyond the One Hundredth Meridian: John Wesley Powell and the Opening of the American West* (Boston, 1954), 147–52.

18. Quoted in Stegner, *Beyond the One Hundredth Meridian*, 92–93.

19. Frederick S. Dellenbaugh, *A Canyon Voyage* (New York, 1908), 27–28; John Wesley Powell, "The Cañons of the Colorado," *Scribner's Monthly* 9 (January 1875): 396.

20. Dellenbaugh, *Canyon Voyage*, 220.

21. Powell, "Cañons of the Colorado," 301.

22. E. O. Beaman, "The Cañon of the Colorado," *Appleton's Journal* 11 (May 1874): 591.

23. John Wesley Powell, *Cañons of the Colorado* (1895; reprint, New York, 1961), 329.

24. In this reading of Dutton, I am indebted to Stegner, *Beyond the One Hundredth Meridian*, 164–72; Clarence E. Dutton, *Tertiary History of the Grand Canyon District* (Washington, D.C., 1882), 141.

25. Dutton, *Tertiary History*, 142.

26. Ibid., 145.

27. Ibid.

28. Ibid., 151.

29. Ibid., 154.

30. Ibid., 155.

31. Jackson, *Time Exposure*, 232; United States Geological Survey, *Annual Report*, vol. 8, 369.

32. Goetzmann, *Exploration and Empire*, 524–26; Rick Dingus, *The Photographic Artifacts of Timothy O'Sullivan* (Albuquerque, 1982), 44; Jackson, *Time Exposure*, 243.

33. For discussions of the significance of the West in the cultural shift at the end of the nineteenth century, see Alan Trachtenberg, *The Incorporation of America: Culture and Society in the Gilded Age* (New York, 1982), 11–37; and Robert H. Wiebe, *The Search for Order, 1877–1929* (New York, 1967), 11–12. See also Peter Bacon Hales, *William Henry Jackson and the Transformation of American Landscape* (Philadelphia, 1988), 80–82.

34. Ferdinand Vandiveer Hayden, *The Yellowstone National Park and the Mountain Regions of Portions of Idaho, Nevada, Colorado, and Utah* (Boston, 1876), 45.

35. For varying views on the process of cultural integration in the last decades

of the nineteenth century, see, for example, Trachtenberg, *Incorporation of America*, esp. 11–69; and Wiebe, *Search for Order.*

36. Samuel Storey, *To the Golden Land: Sketches of a Trip to Southern California* (London, 1889), 93.

37. Almon Gunnison, *Rambles Overland: A Trip across the Continent* (Boston, 1884), 181.

38. T. S. Hudson, *A Scamper through America; or, Fifteen Thousand Miles of Ocean and Continent in Sixty Days* (London, 1882), 186.

39. Sylvester Baxter, "The Father of the Pueblos," *Harper's New Monthly Magazine* 65 (June 1882): 73.

40. Union Pacific Railroad, *The New West Illustrated* (Denver, 1885), 2.

41. Charles F. Lummis, "Three Weeks in Wonderland," *Land of Sunshine* 9 (August 1898): 111; George Wharton James, *The Hotel Men's Mutual Benefit Association in California* (Pasadena, 1896), 71.

42. Irwin S. Cobb, *Roughing It Deluxe* (New York, 1913), 121.

43. Larzer Ziff, *Literary Democracy: The Declaration of Cultural Independence in America* (New York, 1981), 297–302.

44. Herbert Bashford, "Western Writers and Creative Literature," *Sunset* 9 (June 1902): 145.

45. Trachtenberg, *Incorporation of America*, 144–45; T. J. Jackson Lears, *No Place of Grace: Anti-Modernism and the Transformation of American Culture, 1880–1920* (New York, 1981), 68–75.

46. Charles F. Lummis, *Some Strange Corners of Our Country: The Wonderland of the Southwest* (New York, 1892), 2.

47. Lummis, *Some Strange Corners*, 270.

48. Union Pacific Railroad Company, *A Description of the Western Resorts for Health and Pleasure Reached via the Union Pacific System* (Chicago, 1891), 8.

49. *Pennsylvania Tours to the Golden Gate* (Philadelphia, 1890), 3.

50. Robert Sterling Yard, *Glimpses of Our National Parks* (Washington, D.C., 1916), 3.

51. George Wharton James, *Our American Wonderlands* (Chicago, 1915), ix–xxv.

52. Gunnison, *Rambles Overland*, 242.

53. William Cullen Bryant, ed., *Picturesque America*, vol. 4 (London, 1894), 196.

54. Karl Baedeker [James F. Muirhead], *The United States with an Excursion into Mexico*, 3d ed. (Leipzig, 1904), lxxvi.

55. Denver and Rio Grande Railroad, *The Heart of the Continent* (Chicago, 1882), 3.

56. Dallas Lore Sharp, *The Better Country* (Cambridge, Mass., 1928), 178.

57. Charles Dudley Warner, "Studies of the Great West: A Far and Fair Country," *Harper's New Monthly Magazine* 76 (March 1888): 558.

58. S. L. Welch, *Southern California: A Semi-Tropic Paradise* (Los Angeles, 1886), 86; Walter Raymond and I. A. Whitcomb, *Raymond's Vacation Excursions: Three Winter Trips* (Boston, 1885).

59. Thomas P. McElrath, *A Press Club Outing* (New York, 1893), 105.

60. Agnes Crane, "The New Southern Road to Colorado and California," *Leisure Hour* (London) 32 (1883): 405.

61. Mary E. Blake, *On the Wing: Rambling Notes of a Trip to the Pacific* (Boston, 1883), 83.

62. Thomas Moran to Mary Moran, 17 July 1873, in Amy O. Bassford and Fritiof Fryxell, *Home-Thoughts from Afar: Letters of Thomas Moran to Mary Nimmo Moran* (East Hampton, N.Y., 1967), 33.

63. Blake, *On the Wing*, 82.

64. John A. Spalding, *From New England to the Pacific* (Hartford, 1884), 43.

65. Gunnison, *Rambles Overland*, 186.

66. [Zitella], *Fifty-nine of '86: Letters Written to the Lebanon Courier during the Summer of 1886* (Lebanon, Pa., 1886), 17.

67. Rose Pender, *A Lady's Experiences in the Wild West in 1883* (Lincoln, Nebr., 1978), 17–18.

68. Walter Raymond and I. A. Whitcomb, *Three Grand Trips* (Boston 1885); idem, *A Business Men's Excursion to California* (Boston, 1893); idem, *Raymond's Vacation Excursions: A Winter in California, 1889–1890* (Boston, 1888).

69. William Henry Bishop, "Across Arizona," *Harper's New Monthly Magazine* 66 (March 1883): 489.

70. Rudyard Kipling, *From Sea to Sea: Letters of Travel* (New York, 1899), 67.

71. Edwin J. Stanley, *Rambles in Wonderland; or, Up the Yellowstone* (New York, 1880), 88.

72. M. L. A., "Yellowstone Journal," 16 July 1890, Manuscript, Yellowstone National Park Library.

73. Stanley, *Rambles in Wonderland*, 156; Gunnison, *Rambles Overland*, 36.

74. J. J. Aubertin, *A Flight with Distances* (London, 1888), 85.

75. Walter Raymond and I. A. Whitcomb, *Five Grand Trips to the Yellowstone National Park* (Boston, 1890), 4.

76. Lee Clark Mitchell, *Witnesses to a Vanishing Wilderness: The Nineteenth-Century Response* (Princeton, 1981), 217–20.

77. Walter Raymond and I. A. Whitcomb, *Raymond's Vacation Excursions: California, the Pacific Northwest, and Alaska* (Boston, 1893), 26.

78. Welch, *Southern California*, 88.

79. William Makepiece Thayer, *Marvels of the New West* (Norwich, Conn., 1888), 143.

80. Louis Agassiz, "America, the Old World" *Atlantic Monthly* 11 (March 1863): 373.

81. Colorado Promotion and Publicity Committee, *Colorado: Its Hotels and Resorts* (n.p., 1904), 3.

82. Baxter, "Father of the Pueblos," 73.

83. Robert Sterling Yard, *The Book of the National Parks* (New York, 1919), 3.

84. Edmund F. Erk, *A Merry Crusade to the Golden Gate* (Pittsburgh, 1906), 18.

85. Charles F. Lummis, *A Tramp across the Continent* (New York, 1892), 142.

86. C. A. Higgins, *To California over the Santa Fe Trail* (Chicago, 1902).

87. Hezekiah Butterworth, *Zigzag Journeys in the Western States of America* (London, 188[?]), 301.

88. *Half Hours in the Wide West over Mountains, Rivers, and Prairies* (Birmingham, England, 1884), 139.

89. Denver and Rio Grande Railroad, *Around the Circle: One Thousand Miles through the Rocky Mountains* (Chicago, 1892), 19.

90. Welch, "Southern California," 88.

91. Clifton Johnson, *Highways and Byways of the Rocky Mountains* (New York, 1910), 115.

92. Vernon McGill, *Diary of a Motor Journey from Chicago to Los Angeles* (Los Angeles, 1922), 55.

93. E. B. Everitt, *Tour of the St. Elmo's from the Nutmeg State to the Golden Gate, 1883* (Meriden, Conn., 1883), 109.

94. Oliver Ayer Roberts, *The California Pilgrimage of the Boston Commandery of Knights Templars* (Boston, 1884), 95; Charles S. Gleed, *From River to Sea: A Tourists' and Miners Guide* (Chicago, 1882), 95.

95. McGill, *Diary of a Motor Journey*, 57–58.

96. Sharp, *Better Country*, 141–42.

97. *Our Country West: Youth's Companion Series* (Boston, 1900), 183.

98. David M. Steele, *Going Abroad Overland* (New York, 1917), 23–24.

99. See Trachtenberg, *Incorporation of America*, 15–17 for the cultural significance of the Turner thesis. See also Roderick Nash, *Wilderness and the American Mind* (New Haven, 1967); Lee Clark Mitchell, *Witnesses to a Vanishing America* (Princeton, N.J., 1981); and G. Edward White, *The Eastern Establishment and the Western Experience: The West of Frederic Remington, Theodore Roosevelt, and Owen Wister* (New Haven, 1968) for the role of the Far West in the development of national ideology.

100. R. W. C. Farnsworth, *A Southern California Paradise* (Pasadena, 1883), 93; Larzer Ziff, *The American 1890s: The Life and Times of a Lost Generation* (New York, 1966), 209–27.

101. Stephen Kern, *The Culture of Time and Space, 1880–1918* (Cambridge, Mass., 1983), 65–69; T. J. Jackson Lears, *No Place of Grace: Antimodernism and the Transformation of American Culture, 1880–1920* (New York, 1981), 27–38.

102. See, for example, Cyrus Edson, "Do We Live Too Fast?" *North American Review* 154 (February 1892): 281–86; T. B. Aldrich, "Insomnia," *Century* 45 (November 1892): 28; Edwin Lassiter Bynner, "Diary of a Nervous Invalid," *Atlantic Monthly* 71 (January 1893): 33–46; William James, "The Gospel of Relaxation," *Scribner's Monthly* 25 (April 1899): 499–507. For the impact of magazines on American culture in general, see Ziff, *American 1890s*, 120–30.

103. John Muir, *Our National Parks* (Boston, 1901), 1.

104. Denver and Rio Grande System, *Camping in the Rockies and Vacation Estimates* (Denver, 1908), 3.

105. James Steele, *Colorado via the Burlington Route* (Chicago, 1900), 51.

106. W. H. Simpson, *A Colorado Summer* (Chicago, 1900), 3.

107. Enos Mills, *Your National Parks* (Boston, 1917), 379.

108. Pender, *A Lady's Experiences*, 123.

109. Grace Gallatin Seton-Thompson, *A Woman Tenderfoot* (London, 1901), 79.

110. Ibid., 21.

111. Olin D. Wheeler, *Wonderland 1903: Descriptive of the Country Contiguous to the Northern Pacific Railroad* (St. Paul, 1903), 37–38.

112. Alfred Terry Bacon, "Ranch Cure," *Lippincott's Magazine* 28 (July 1881): 91.

113. See, for example, "With Gun and Palette among the Redskins," *Outing* 25 (February 1895): 355–63; or Charles Dudley Warner, "The Winter of Our Content," *Harper's New Monthly Magazine* 82 (December 1890): 39–57.

114. H. Allen Anderson, *The Chief: Ernest Thompson Seton and the Changing West* (College Station, Tex., 1986), 138–48.

115. Arthur A. Ekirch, Jr., *Man and Nature in America* (Lincoln, Nebr., 1973), 70–80; Mitchell, *Witnesses*, 57; John F. Reiger, *American Sportsmen and the Origins of Conservation* (New York, 1975), 63–69.

116. Weston J. Naef and James N. Wood, *Era of Exploration: The Rise of Landscape Photography in the American West, 1860–1885* (Buffalo, N.Y., 1975), 75–76.

117. Limerick, *Desert Passages*, 118.

118. Ibid., 113–16.

119. George Wharton James, *The Wonders of the Colorado Desert* (Boston, 1906), xxvii.

120. Ibid., xxvi–xxvii.

121. Ibid., 33.

122. George Wharton James, *Arizona, the Wonderland* (Boston, 1917), 170, 179.

123. James, *Colorado Desert*, 39, 144.

124. Ibid., xxxix.

125. James, *Our American Wonderlands*, 172.

126. John Muir, ed., *Picturesque California and the Region West of the Rocky Mountains from Alaska to Mexico*, vol. 7 (San Francisco, 1888), 332.

127. Fred Harvey, *The Great Southwest along the Santa Fe Trail* (Kansas City, 1923).

128. H. N. Rust, "On the Mojave Desert," *Land of Sunshine* 10 (February 1899): 125.

129. Bryant, *Picturesque America*, vi.

130. Carl E. Schmidt, *A Western Trip* (Detroit, n.d.), 79.

131. Charles A. Higgins, *A New Guide to the Pacific Coast, Santa Fe Route* (Chicago, 1894), 110.

132. E. M. Johnstone, *West by South: Half South* (Buffalo, N.Y., 1890), 32.

133. Thayer, *Marvels of the New West*, 5; Bryant, *Picturesque America*, vi.

134. Thayer, *Marvels of the New West*, 5.

135. Bryant, *Picturesque America*, v–vi.
136. George Wharton James, *In and around the Grand Canyon* (Boston, 1900), x.
137. Erk, *Merry Crusade*, 280.
138. Stanley Wood, *Over the Range to the Golden Gate* (Chicago, 1912), 167–68.
139. Montgomery Schuyler, *Westward the Course of Empire: Out West and Back East on the First Trip of the "Los Angeles Limited"* (New York, 1906), 46.
140. Raymond and Whitcomb, *A Business Men's Excursion.*
141. [Zitella], *Fifty-nine of '86*, 19.
142. Muir, *Picturesque California*, vol. 1, 31.
143. Higgins, *New Guide*, 70.
144. James, *Our American Wonderlands*, 173.
145. Gunnison, *Rambles Overland*, 23.
146. Olive Rand, *A Vacation Excursion: From Massachusetts Bay to Puget Sound* (Manchester, N.H., 1884), 57.
147. Gulielma Crosfield, *Two Sunny Winters in California* (London, 1904), 144.
148. Everitt, *Tour of St. Elmo's*, 108.
149. Higgins, *To California*, 19.
150. Sharp, *Better Country*, 150.
151. Ibid., 180.
152. Charles Augustus Stoddard, *Beyond the Rockies: A Spring Journey in California* (New York, 1894), 44.
153. See my chapt. 3 and Robert F. Berkhofer, Jr., *The White Man's Indian: Images of the American Indian from Columbus to the Present* (New York, 1978), 21–30.
154. Helen Hunt Jackson, *A Century of Dishonor* (Boston, 1881), 2.
155. E. Davis, *Elsie's Trip in the Rocky Mountains* (New York, 1888), 152.
156. Higgins, *New Guide*, 110; Fred Harvey Company, *The Great Southwest along the Santa Fe Trail* (Kansas City, 1921).
157. C. A. Higgins, *To California over the Santa Fe Trail* (Chicago, 1914), 30.
158. In Berkhofer, *White Man's Indian*, the author uses these same categories of "good" and "bad" but defines them differently.
159. See Robert A. Trennert, "Fair, Expositions, and the Changing Image of Southwestern Indians, 1876–1904," *New Mexico Historical Review* 62 (April 1987): 127–50 for the new attitude of Americans toward Indians as evidenced by their new presence in the great expositions of the late nineteenth and early twentieth centuries.
160. Everitt, *Tour of St. Elmo's*, 112.
161. Erk, *Merry Crusade*, 59.
162. Denver and Rio Grande Railroad, *Sight Places and Resorts in the Rockies* (Denver, 1899), 33.
163. Lummis, *Tramp across the Continent*, 93.
164. Baxter, "Father of the Pueblos," 75–76.
165. *Our Country*, 172; Baxter, "Father of the Pueblos," 72.
166. Wood, *Over the Range*, 115–22.

167. Fred Harvey Company, *The Alvarado: A New Hotel at Albuquerque, New Mexico* (Kansas City, 1904).

168. Roberts, *California Pilgrimage*, 103.

169. Antoinette May, *Helen Hunt Jackson: A Lonely Voice of Conscience* (San Francisco, 1987), 70–89.

170. Kevin Starr, *Inventing the Dream: California through the Progressive Era* (New York, 1985), 58–59; James D. Hart, *American Images of Spanish California* (Berkeley, 1960), 31–33.

171. George Wharton James, *Through Ramona's Country* (Boston, 1909), 307.

172. *Sunset* 1 (October 1898): 87.

173. *The Raymond* (Los Angeles, 1901).

174. Erk, *Merry Crusade*, 242.

175. Wood, *Over the Range*, 127.

176. Ibid., 128; *Our Country*, 155.

177. George A. Crofutt, *Crofutt's Overland Tours, Number Two* (Chicago, 1890), 93.

178. *Appleton's General Guide to the United States and Canada* (New York, 1879), 359.

179. Erk, *Merry Crusade*, 133.

180. [Zitella], *Fifty-nine of '86*, 55.

181. Raymond and Whitcomb, *Winter in California*..

182. James David Henderson, *Meals By Fred Harvey: A Pheomenon of the American West* (Fort Worth, 1969), 28–29; Patricia J. Broder, *The American West: The Modern Vision* (Boston, 1984), 21; Merle Armitage, *Operations, Santa Fe* (New York, 1948), 118–19.

183. Henderson, *Meals*, 24–26; Letter from Michael J. Riordan to J. J. Byrne, 18 September 1903, Blanche Riordan Chambers Collection, Northern Arizona Pioneers Historical Society Collection, box 3.

184. Fred Harvey Company, *Alvarado.*

185. Higgins, *To California*, 28.

186. Fred Harvey Company, *Alvarado.*

187. *On the New Santa Fe Trail: The Record of a Journey to the Land of Sunshine by Six and a Half Tenderfeet* (New York, 1903), 9.

188. Santa Fe Railroad, *Grand Canyon of Arizona Replica* (n.p., 1915).

189. Mills, *Your National Parks*, x–xi.

190. U.S. Department of the Interior, *Report of the General Superintendent and Landscape Engineer of the National Parks* (Washington, D.C., 1915), 6.

191. Alfred Runte, *National Parks: The American Experience* (Lincoln, Nebr., 1979), 82; U.S. Department of the Interior, *Report of the General Superintendent*, 6.

6. American Log Palaces: Far Western Resorts at the Turn of the Century, 1900–1915

1. The story of Yellowstone's creation and the forces behind it are told in Richard A. Bartlett, *Nature's Yellowstone* (Albuquerque, 1974); and Aubrey L.

Haines, *The Yellowstone Story: A History of Our First National Park*, 2 vols. (Yellowstone Library and Museum Association, 1977).

2. Richard A. Bartlett, *Yellowstone: A Wilderness Besieged* (Tucson, 1985), 121–24; Haines, *Yellowstone Story*, vol. 1, 179.

3. Bartlett, *Wilderness Besieged*, 44–48.

4. A. Berle Clemensen, *Historic Structure Report: Old Faithful Inn, Yellowstone National Park, Wyoming* (Denver, 1982), 2–3; Bartlett, *Wilderness Besieged*, 144–52.

5. U.S. Department of the Interior, *Report of the Superintendent of Yellowstone National Park to the Secretary of the Interior* (Washington, D.C., 1889), 3.

6. Alice Wellington Rollins, "The Three Tetons," *Harper's New Monthly Magazine* 74 (May 1887): 869.

7. Walter Raymond and I. A. Whitcomb, *Five Grand Trips to the Yellowstone National Park* (Boston, 1890), 46.

8. Almon Gunnison, *Rambles Overland: A Trip across the Continent* (Boston, 1884), 51.

9. Edwin J. Stanley, *Rambles in Wonderland; or, Up the Yellowstone* (New York, 1880), 62.

10. Northern Pacific Railroad, *Alice's Adventures in the New Wonderland* (Chicago, 1885).

11. Raymond and Whitcomb, *Yellowstone*, 3.

12. John Muir, *Our National Parks* (Boston, 1901), 49; John Muir, ed., *Picturesque California and the Region West of the Rocky Mountains from Alaska to Mexico*, vol. 8 (San Francisco, 1888), 421.

13. John L. Stoddard, *John L. Stoddard's Lectures*, vol. 10 (Chicago, 1898), 209.

14. Muir, *Our National Parks*, 41.

15. Stanley, *Rambles in Wonderland*, 98.

16. Gunnison, *Rambles Overland*, 37.

17. Rudyard Kipling, *From Sea to Sea: Letters of Travel* (New York, 1899), 102.

18. Northern Pacific, *Alice's Adventures*.

19. William Makepeace Thayer, *Marvels of the New West* (Norwich, Conn., 1888), 67.

20. J. J. Aubertin, *A Flight with Distances: The States* (London, 1888), 84–85.

21. Stanley, *Rambles in Wonderland*, 154.

22. Raymond and Whitcomb, *Yellowstone*, 24–28; idem, *A Winter in California: Nine Grand Trips* (Boston, 1888), 153.

23. U.S. Department of the Interior, *Report of the Superintendent of the Yellowstone National Park to the Secretary of the Interior* (Washington, D.C., 1890), 8.

24. Kipling, *From Sea to Sea*, 94.

25. Charles J. Gillis, *Another Summer: The Yellowstone Park and Alaska* (New York, 1893), 25.

26. Yellowstone National Park Archives, Yellowstone Park Library, Microfilm Collection, reel nos. 6 and 7.

27. Hiram Martin Chittenden, *The Yellowstone National Park* (Cincinnati, 1911), 246.

28. Northern Pacific, *Alice's Adventures.*

29. Yellowstone National Park Archives, reel no. 3, letter from Henry T. Blake to Superintendent John Pitcher, 10 August 1901.

30. Rodd L. Wheaton, "Rustic Connotations: Furnishing National Park Hostelries," *Nineteenth Century* 8 (Winter 1982): 119; Haines, *Yellowstone Story*, vol. 1, 272.

31. Charles Warren Stoddard, "In Wonderland," *Ave Maria* (Notre Dame, Ind.) 47 (August 1898): 203.

32. Carter H. Harrison, *A Summer's Outing and the Old Man's Story* (Chicago, 1891), 80.

33. Joaquin Miller, quoted in Muir, *Picturesque California*, vol. 7, 428.

34. Carl E. Schmidt, *A Western Trip* (Detroit, 1901), 12.

35. Harrison, *Summer's Outing*, 62.

36. U.S. Department of the Interior, *Report of the Superintendent of the Yellowstone National Park to the Secretary of the Interior* (Washington, D.C., 1888), 8–9.

37. Wayne Replogle, "History of Yellowstone National Park Concessions," 1976, Yellowstone National Park Library; *Superintendent's Report* (1887), 7.

38. Schmidt, *Western Trip*, 59.

39. *Superintendent's Report* (1888), 11.

40. Ibid.

41. Replogle, "Concessions."

42. U.S. Department of the Interior, Superintendents of the Yellowstone National Park, *Annual Reports, 1895–1904* (Washington, D.C., 1895–1904); Haines, *Yellowstone Story*, vol. 2, 42–50.

43. Yellowstone Archives, reel no. 3, James Abbot, special agent, "Report on Profitability," 6 November 1901.

44. Clemensen, *Historic Structure Report*, 4–8.

45. David Leavengood, "A Sense of Shelter: Robert C. Reamer," *Pacific Historical Review* (November 1985): 496–97, 509.

46. Jeffrey Limerick, Nancy Ferguson, and Richard Oliver, *America's Grand Resort Hotels* (New York, 1979), 133.

47. William C. Tweed, Laura E. Soulliere, and Henry G. Law, *National Park Service Rustic Architecture, 1916–1942* (Denver, 1977), 5; Wheaton, "Rustic Connotations," 119.

48. Gwendolyn Wright, *Building the Dream: A Social History of Housing in America* (Cambridge, Mass., 1981), 103–6; Clemensen, *Historic Structure Report*, 11.

49. Quoted in Limerick, *Resort Hotels*, 133.

50. Northern Pacific Railway, *Through Wonderland: Yellowstone National Park* (Chicago, 1910), 19.

51. Clemensen, *Historic Structure Report*, 47; Northern Pacific Railway, *Through Wonderland: Yellowstone Park* (Chicago, 1907), 19.

52. Reau Campbell, *Campbell's New Revised Complete Guide and Descriptive Book of the Yellowstone Park* (Chicago, 1907), 156; Clifford Paynter Allen, *From Geyser to Cañon with Mary* (Philadelphia, 1904), 39.

53. Jack E. Haynes, *Haynes' Official Guide: Yellowstone National Park* (St. Paul, 1915), 69.

54. Northern Pacific, *Through Wonderland*, 1910, 19; Clemensen, *Historic Structure Report*, 71; Union Pacific Railroad, *Yellowstone Park, 1909* (Omaha, 1909).

55. Mrs. E. H. Johnson, quoted in Wheaton, "Rustic Connotations," 120; Thomas D. Murphy, *Three Wonderlands of the American West* (Boston, 1912), 11.

56. Murphy, *Three Wonderlands*, 11.

57. Haynes, *Official Guide*, 70; Frederick Dumont Smith, *Book of a Hundred Bears* (Chicago, 1909), 127.

58. Harvey H. Kaiser, *Great Camps of the Adirondacks* (Boston, 1982), 11–12.

59. Ibid., 64.

60. Edgar DeN. Mayhew and Minor Myers, Jr., *A Documentary History of American Interiors from the Colonial Period to 1915* (New York, 1980), 313–14; Marcus Whiffen and Frederick Koeper, *American Architecture, 1607–1976* (Cambridge, Mass., 1981), 300–316.

61. Campbell, *Campbell's Guide*, 156.

62. Northern Pacific Railway, *Land of Geysers: Yellowstone National Park* (St. Paul, 1915), 41.

63. Northern Pacific Railway, *Through Yellowstone National Park* (Chicago, 1910), 21; Campbell, *Campbell's Guide*, 156.

64. Olin D. Wheeler, *Wonderland* (St. Paul, 1906), 14.

65. Yellowstone Park Hotel Company, *Yellowstone Park Hotels* (n.p., 1920), 3.

66. Murphy, *Three American Wonderlands*, 10.

67. Haynes, *Official Guide*, 69; Northern Pacific Railroad, *Seeing Yellowstone Park through the Gardiner Gateway* (n.p., 1912), 25.

68. Chicago, Burlington, and Quincy Railroad, *Yellowstone National Park* (Chicago, 1913), 4.

69. Northern Pacific, *Through Wonderland*, 19.

70. *Yellowstone Park: How to Get There and Cost of Tours* (Chicago, 1905); Union Pacific System, *Yellowstone National Park* (Chicago, 1916), 16; Northern Pacific Railway, *Yellowstone National Park, 1904* (Chicago, 1904), 9.

71. Smith, *Hundred Bears*, 126.

72. Edmund F. Erk, *A Merry Crusade to the Golden Gate* (Pittsburgh, 1906), 93; Allen, *From Geyser to Cañon*, 38.

73. Edward F. Colburn, *Where Gush the Geysers* (n.p., 1913), 32.

74. Dwight L. Elmendorf, "Yellowstone National Park," *The Mentor* 3 (May 1915): 7.

75. Erk, *Merry Crusade*, 94; Colburn, *Geysers*, 32.

76. Quoted in Bartlett, *Wilderness Besieged*, 183.

77. Anna Mylius, photo album of 1914 railroad trip, July 14, 1914, Montana Historical Society Photo Collection.

78. Barbara H. Dittl and Joanne Mallmann, "Plain to Fancy: The Lake Hotel, 1889–1929," *Montana* 34 (Spring 1984): 38.

79. Murphy, *Three American Wonderlands*, 24; Erk, *Merry Crusade*, 104.

80. Yellowstone Park Transportation Company, *Yellowstone Park* (n.p., 1905); Northern Pacific, *Land of Geysers*, 42.

81. Yellowstone Park Transportation Company, *Yellowstone;* Allen, *From Geyser to Cañon*, 25–26.

82. Smith, *Hundred Bears*, 208–9.

83. Leavengood, "Sense of Shelter," 505–6; John Henry Raftery, *A Miracle in Hotel Building: Being the Story of the New Canyon Hotel in Yellowstone Park* (Helena, Mont., 1912), 7; Northern Pacific Railway, *Yellowstone Park* (St. Paul, 1915).

84. Quoted in Raftery, *Miracle*, 8.

85. Elbert and Alice Hubbard, *A Little Journey to the Yellowstone* (n.p., 1915), 22–23.

86. Murphy, *Three American Wonderlands*, 16; Northern Pacific, *Yellowstone Park, 1915*, 32; Raftery, *Miracle*, 11.

87. Wheeler, *Wonderland*, 11.

88. Yellowstone Park Hotel Company, *Hotels*, 5.

89. Northern Pacific, *Seeing Yellowstone*, 6.

90. *Superintendent's Reports* (1895, 1915).

91. Erk, *Merry Crusade*, 63.

92. Anna Mylius, photo album of 1914 railroad trip, July 19, 1914, Montana Historical Society Photo Collection.

93. Emerson Hough, *Yellowstone National Park* (n.p., 1922).

94. Robert Sterling Yard, *The Book of the National Parks* (New York, 1919), 207.

95. Ibid., 367–73.

96. *Our Native Land; or, Glances at American Scenery and Places* (New York, 1882), 30.

97. S. L. Welch, *Southern California: A Semi-Tropic Paradise* (Los Angeles, 1886), 87.

98. Walter Raymond and I. A. Whitcomb, *Raymond's Vacation Excursions: Five Winter Trips, 1898–1899* (Boston, 1898), 25; Karl Baedeker, *The United States with an Excursion into Mexico*, 2d ed. (Leipzig, 1899).

99. Flagstaff *Coconino Sun*, 19 May 1892, 26 May 1892, and 19 June 1892; C. A. Higgins, *Grand Canyon of the Colorado River, Arizona* (Chicago, 1897), 6–9.

100. J. Donald Hughes, *In the House of Stone and Light: A Human History of the Grand Canyon* (Grand Canyon Natural History Association, 1978), 54; C. Gregory Crampton, *Land of Living Rock: The Grand Canyon and the High Plateaus—Arizona, Utah, Nevada* (Layton, Utah, 1985), 197–99; George Wharton James, *The Hotel Men's Mutual Benefit Association in California* (Pasadena, 1896), 178.

101. Higgins, *Grand Canyon*, 6.

102. Charles Dudley Warner, "The Heart of the Desert" (1890), in Paul Schullery, ed., *Early Impressions of the Grand Canyon* (Boulder, 1981), 41.

103. James Cox, *My Native Land* (St. Louis, 1895), 331.

104. Mattison W. Chase, quoted in G. K. Woods, *Personal Impressions of the Grand Canyon of the Colorado River Near Flagstaff Arizona as Seen through Nearly Two*

Thousand Eyes, and Written in the Private Visitor's Book of the World Famous Guide, Captain John Hance (San Francisco, 1899), 73.

105. Gertrude B. Stevens, quoted in Woods, *Personal Impressions*, 50.

106. C. A. Higgins, *To California over the Santa Fe Trail* (Chicago, 1902), 80–81; Crampton, *Land of Living Rock*, 199.

107. Santa Fe Railroad, *Titan of Chasms: The Grand Canyon of Arizona* (Chicago, 1902); Santa Fe Railroad, *Grand Canyon.*

108. Henry G. Peabody, *Glimpses of the Grand Canyon of Arizona* (Kansas City, 1902), 1; Santa Fe Railroad, *Titan of Chasms*, 28.

109. Santa Fe Railroad, *The Grand Canyon of Arizona* (Chicago, 1902), 119.

110. Erk, *Merry Crusade*, 257–61.

111. Virginia L. Grattan, *Mary Colter: Builder upon the Red Earth* (Flagstaff, 1980), 7–8.

112. Hughes, *In the House of Stone and Light*, 68–69; Limerick, *America's Grand Resort Hotels*, 127; Flagstaff *Coconino Sun*, 24 May 1902.

113. Blanche Riordan Chambers Collection, Northern Arizona University Library, box 3, M. J. Riordan to W. G. Barnwell, Santa Fe, 30 September 1903; ibid., M. J. Riordan to A. G. Wells, Santa Fe, 25 October 1903.

114. Grand Canyon Railroad, blueprints of the Grand Canyon Hotel, Charles Whittlesley Architect, 1903; Santa Fe Railroad, *Titan of Chasms: The Grand Canyon of Arizona* (Chicago, 1909), 28.

115. Grand Canyon Railroad, blueprints of the Grand Canyon Hotel; Murphy, *Three American Wonderlands*, 129.

116. Grand Canyon Railroad, blueprints of the Grand Canyon Hotel; Santa Fe Railroad, *Titan of Chasms* (1909), 28; quoted in James D. Henderson, *Meals by Fred Harvey: A Phenomenon of the American West* (Fort Worth, 1969), 30.

117. Santa Fe Railroad, *Titan of Chasms* (1909), 28; Murphy, *Three American Wonderlands*, 130.

118. National Register of Historic Places Inventory, nomination form for the El Tovar Hotel; Santa Fe Railroad, *El Tovar, Grand Canyon of Arizona* (n.p., 1909), 15.

119. United States Railroad Administration, *Grand Canyon National Park, Arizona.* (Chicago, 1919), 18; Erk, *Merry Crusade*, 274; Santa Fe Railroad, *Titan of Chasms* (1909), 27.

120. Santa Fe Railroad, *Titan of Chasms* (1909), 27.

121. Santa Fe Railroad, *El Tovar*, 10.

122. Santa Fe Railroad, *Titan of Chasms* (1909), 27; U.S. Railroad Administration, *Grand Canyon*, 18.

123. Grattan, *Mary Colter*, 1–14; Hughes, *House of Stone and Light*, 70.

124. Grattan, *Mary Colter*, 14–18; Santa Fe Railroad, *Titan of Chasms* (1909), 29.

125. Frank McNitt, *The Indian Traders* (Norman, Okla., 1962), 208–11.

126. Santa Fe Railroad, *Titan of Chasms* (1909), 29.

127. *Brooklyn Daily Eagle, The Grand Canyon Dedication Tour* (New York, 1920), 3.

128. Flagstaff *Coconino Sun*, 17 October 1907.

129. Santa Fe Railroad, *Grand Canyon of Arizona Replica* (n.p., 1915).

130. Grattan, *Mary Colter*, 32, 37, 84–86; David M. Steele, *Going Abroad Overland* (New York, 1917), 39.

131. Fred Harvey, *Trails, Drives, and Saddle Horses* (n.p., 1911), 12; Santa Fe Railroad, *Grand Canyon Outings* (Chicago, 1915), 2.

132. Grattan, *Mary Colter*, 26–30; Hughes, *House of Stone and Light*, 70.

133. *Brooklyn Daily Eagle*, *Dedication Tour*, 3.

134. C. W. Buchholtz, *Man in Glacier* (Glacier Natural History Association, 1976), 30; James W. Sheire, *Glacier National Park: Historic Resource Study* (Eastern Service Center, National Park Service, 1970), 107.

135. George Bird Grinnell, "To the Walled-In Lakes," *Forest and Stream* 25 (December 1885): 382.

136. Ibid. (February 1886): 42.

137. F. I. Whitney, Great Northern Passenger Agent to Dr. Lyman Sperry, 1894, quoted in Buchholtz, *Man in Glacier*, 38.

138. Quoted in Buchholtz, *Man in Glacier*, 39.

139. Alan S. Newell, David Walter, and James R. McDonald, *Historic Resources Study, Glacier National Park and Historic Structures Survey* (National Park Service, 1980), 5–6; Buchholtz, *Man in Glacier*, 30.

140. Great Northern Railway, *The Great Northern Country: Being the Chronicles of the Happy Travellers Club* (St. Paul, 1900), 118.

141. Newell, *Historic Resources*, 81–82; *Iron Horse West: Bicentennial Project of the Burlington Northern, Inc.* (Minneapolis, 1976), 46–49; Great Northern Railway Company, Publicity Department Scrapbooks, 1884–1970, Minnesota Historical Society, Microfilm Collection, reel no. 6.

142. Great Northern Publicity, reel no. 6.

143. Des Moines *Capital*, 30 September 1912, in Great Northern Publicity, reel no. 6.

144. Great Northern Publicity, reel no. 6.

145. U.S. Department of the Interior, *Report of the Superintendent of Glacier National Park to the Secretary of the Interior, 1912* (Washington, D.C., 1912); Seattle *Post-Intelligencer*, 20 April 1913, in Great Northern Publicity, reel no. 6.

146. Henry Ottridge Reik, *A Tour of America's National Parks* (New York, 1920), 138.

147. Steele, *Going Abroad*, 93.

148. Walter Pritchard Eaton, "The Park of the Many Glaciers," *Harper's* 135 (June 1917): 8.

149. New York *Press*, 2 August 1914, in Great Northern Publicity, reel no. 6.

150. Great Northern Railway, *Short Jaunts for Little Money, Glacier National Park* (n.p., 1913), 2.

151. Eaton, "Many Glaciers," 3.

152. James, *Hotel Men*, 217.

153. Great Northern Railroad, *The Call of the Mountains* (n.p., 1928), 7.

154. Sheire, *Glacier National Park*, 196–97; Limerick, *America's Grand Resort Hotels*, 139.

155. Thomas D. Murphy, *Seven Wonderlands of the American West* (Boston, 1925), 254; Steele, *Going Abroad*, 94.

156. Lulie Nettleton, *With the Mountaineers in Glacier National Park* (St. Paul, 1915); Mary Roberts Rinehart, *The Call of the Mountains: Vacations in Glacier National Park* (Chicago, 1927), 10.

157. Limerick, *America's Grand Resort Hotels*, 143; Murphy, *Seven Wonderlands*, 254.

158. Great Northern Railroad, *Glacier National Park* (n.p., 1915).

159. Seattle *Post-Intelligencer*, 20 April 1913.

160. Sheire, *Glacier National Park*, 198; Murphy, *Seven Wonderlands*, 256; Seattle *Post-Intelligencer*, 20 April 1913.

161. Agnes C. Laut, *Enchanted Trails of Glacier Park* (New York, 1926), 18.

162. Nettleton, *With the Mountaineers.*

163. Reik, *A Tour*, 140.

164. James, *Hotel Men*, 215; Kansas City *Post*, n.d.; and Seattle *Post-Intelligencer*, 20 April 1913, in Great Northern Publicity, reel no. 6.

165. Sheire, *Glacier National Park*, 199–200; Steele, *Going Abroad*, 94–95.

166. National Register of Historic Places Inventory, nomination form for Many Glacier Hotel, Glacier National Park Library.

167. Sheire, *Glacier National Park*, 198–99; National Register, Many Glacier; Great Northern Railroad, *Glacier.*

168. Morton J. Elrod, *Elrod's Guide and Book of Information of Glacier National Park* (Missoula, Mont., 1924), 81.

169. Great Northern Railway, *The Call of the Mountains* (n.p., 1926), 22; Elrod, *Elrod's Guide*, 81.

170. Mary Roberts Rinehart, "Through Glacier Park with Howard Eaton," *Colliers* 57 (April 1916): 11.

171. See Tweed, Soulliere, and Law, *National Park Service Rustic Architecture*, i–ii.

Epilogue

1. John A. Jakle, *The Tourist: Travel in Twentieth-Century North America* (Lincoln, Nebr., 1985), 225–26.

2. John B. Rae, *The Road and Car in American Life* (Cambridge, Mass., 1971), 48–50; Richard A. Bartlett, *Yellowstone: A Wilderness Besieged* (Tucson, 1985), 82–86; Tom Dillon, *Over the Trails of Glacier National Park* (St. Paul, 1912), 6.

3. Rae, *Road and Car*, 50; John Ise, *Our National Park Policy: A Critical History* (Baltimore, 1961), 202–03.

4. *Annual Report, Yellowstone National Park, 1919* (Washington, D.C., 1919), 21.

5. Ibid., 21–23; Wayne Replogle, "History of Yellowstone National Park Concessions," 1976, Yellowstone National Park Library.

6. Henry Ottridge Reik, *A Tour of America's National Parks* (New York, 1920), 140; Mary Roberts Rinehart, *Through Glacier Park: Seeing America First with Howard Eaton* (Boston, 1916), 72–73; James W. Sheire, *Glacier National Park: Historic Resource Study* (National Park Service, Eastern Service Center, 1970), 196; Great Northern Railroad, *Glacier National Park* (n.p., 1915).

7. Reik, *Tour*, 141; Rinehart, *Through Glacier Park*, 73; Great Northern Railway, *Short Jaunts for Little Money: Glacier National Park* (n.p., 1913), 12–13; Great Northern Railroad, *Glacier National Park, Walking Tours* (St. Paul, 1916).

8. *The Cody Road into Yellowstone Park* (Chicago, 1913), 6; Yellowstone Park Camps, *In Your Own Automobile, 1922 Season* (n.p., 1922).

9. Ibid.

10. Bartlett, *Yellowstone*, 187–88.

11. Wylie Permanent Camping Company, *Yellowstone National Park* (n.p., 1913).

12. Eakin to Mather, 4 February 1926, Grand Canyon National Park files, no. C58, Grand Canyon National Park Library.

13. Eakin to Mather, 15 February 1927, Grand Canyon National Park Files, nos. C58 and 5, Grand Canyon National Park Library.

14. United States, *Statutes At Large*, vol. 39, (Washington, D.C., 1916), 535.

15. U.S. Department of the Interior, *Report of the General Superintendent and Landscape Engineer of the National Parks* (Washington, D.C., 1915), 6.

Index